T0314286

Planning guide for conference and communication environments

Conference. Excellence

Guido Englich
Burkhard Remmers

Planning guide for conference and communication environments

Conference. Excellence

Edited by Wilkhahn

Birkhäuser
Basel · Boston · Berlin

Editor's foreword

Wilkhahn
Wilkening + Hahne GmbH+Co. KG
Fritz-Hahne-Straße 8
D 31848 Bad Münder
Germany
www.wilkhahn.com

Twenty years ago, we started a systematic dialogue with the design of communication and conference environments. We regarded the rapid spread and establishment of new communication technologies that shorten information channels and transmission times considerably as indicators that changes in the working environment would be fast-paced.

Our theory is that this highly technology-driven specialization in working life raises the need for consensus and cooperation within companies. Accordingly, places for encounter, info-exchange, learning, processing and decision-making together will be some of the central planning and furniture specifying tasks in future.

Yet for Wilkhahn, influenced by the methods of modernity as taught by Bauhaus and the Ulm Academy of Design, this cannot mean developing just any new tables and chairs. We are more interested in what really happens when people meet in order to use this as the basis for developing the right solution. We are thus concerned with a field that is still exciting and fascinating today, in which there is an interplay of psychological, organizational, technical and spatial conditions as hardly anywhere else in the office world. In the course of extensive surveys we have examined the places where people seek communication, how frequently they do so and why they spend time there, how they behave, what they speak about and what methods and didactic tools are used to support dialogues.

We developed an initial system for *classic, variable and dynamic conferences* on this basis. For the latter in particular, there had not been any coherent furnishing concept that met the demands on function, operation and enduring design before. We therefore concentrated on developing a furniture range that focused on promoting creativity, innovation and participation: the Confair range, launched as early as 1994, became the world-first, coherently designed and functionally precisely coordinated furniture range for participation-oriented workshops and team-work. A range, especially with the Confair folding table, that became a model of excellence for a new generation of furnishing and, although often copied, has continued to set an unrivalled standard until today.

But we also learned how important it is for architects, customers and users to have pre-knowledge about the complex interrelations between people, space, technology and processes within the context of communication environments. We therefore decided to publish the know-how we had compiled: the "Interior and specifiers' handbook for communication areas" came out nearly ten years ago and soon became a much-used reference work.

The last ten years have seen extremely fast-paced developments. What was a vision at the time has now become reality: the dynamics of globalization, the spread of the internet to virtually all areas of work and life, and new kinds of media have not only even further increased the importance of face-to-face communi-cation but also the scope for support with digital technologies. In 1999, we therefore founded an interdisciplinary research and development consortium for future working environments for the purpose of developing innovative solutions. The same year marked the world premiere of prototypes of tables, chairs and walls with integrated, touch-sensitive displays.

Collaboration in a European research project and widespread practical experience in recent years have enabled us to enlarge upon this basic knowledge, to perfect furnishing ranges even more and to add new solutions. Moreover, foresee, our subsidiary company, designs and develops groundbreaking media integration systems for conference and teamwork environments.

This new "Planning guide for conference and communication environments" condenses experience and knowledge from 20 years of research, development and practice into a unique hand-book. We would like to thank the two authors, Professor Guido Englich and Burkhard Remmers, for mastering this demanding task impressively.

This planning guide is intended as an aid to planning, specifying and using future-oriented, sustainable and in many ways better office working environments. We hope you will find it interesting and fascinating, and wish you plenty of inspiration, ideas of your own and above all much success in practical everyday use.

Bad Münder, January 2008

Dr. Jochen Hahne
Managing Director

Holger Jahnke
Director

Title
Planning guide for conference
and communication environments

Concept and copy
Guido Englich
Burkhard Remmers

Design
Englich + Partner, Berlin

Project management
scherrer · agentur für gestaltung und produktion,
Hanover

Translation
Susan Pfenninger, Altusried

Text set in
Frutiger 45, 46, 65

Paper
Cover printed on white, glossy, wood free TCF
(totally chlorine free and acid free), 135 g/sqm

Pages printed on Arctic the Silk, white, wood free,
semi-matt coated art paper, 130 g/sqm, (25% elementally
chlorine free and acid free, 75% totally chlorine free
and acid free), FSC certified

Printed by
Metzgerdruck, Obrigheim

Bound by
Buchwerk, Darmstadt

Library of Congress Control Number: 2007943314

Bibliographic information published by the German National
Library: The German National Library lists this publication in
the Deutsche Nationalbibliografie; detailed bibliographic data
are available on the Internet at http://dnb.d-nb.de.

This book is also available in the original German
language edition (ISBN 978-3-7643-8682-5) and in a French
language edition (ISBN 978-3-7643-8759-4) from Birkhäuser.
It has been published in Spanish (ISBN 978-3-00-021958-0)
by Wilkhahn.

© 2008 Wilkhahn · Wilkening + Hahne GmbH+Co. KG
31848 Bad Münder, Germany

We have taken pains to locate all copyright holders. In case
we were not successful in individual cases, copyright claims
should be addressed to the publishers.

Birkhäuser Verlag AG
Basel · Boston · Berlin
P.O. Box 133, CH-4010 Basel, Switzerland
Part of Springer Science+Business Media

Printed in Germany

ISBN 978-3-7643-8758-7

9 8 7 6 5 4 3 2 1

www.birkhauser.ch

Planning guide for conference and communication environments
Conference. Excellence

Contents

Planning guide for conference and communication environmentsy
Conference. Excellence

Contents

Foreword

by Prof. Dr. Gunter Henn

It is a familiar thought that the interiors which we design, construct and use do not only influence us at a given moment by creating a certain atmosphere or guiding us, but that they have a lasting effect, that architecture and interiors shape us: examining other cultures and past eras continuously relates to their buildings too, and no form of daily or artistic work can convey such an immediate impression of what it meant at these times to belong to certain peoples and parts of the globe as architecture does. From the cultural science point of view, it is understood not only as the expression of an attitude to life, a kind of religiousness, a view of the world and a form of government, but also as a means of mastering and designing life.

Architecture is not any kind of aesthetic ingredient but its influence is much more than merely a symbolic one. Psychology has thus explained the fact that it is the sensuous, spatio-physical and situative perception of architecture that influences us more deeply and also predictably. But why do we perceive architecture in the way we do? It seems paradoxical that we learn this perception somewhere else, outside the realms of architecture, and then apply it to architecture: architecture is a main feature of our environment. We can presume that architecture occupies a place at which we acquire our basic impressions, at which we gain experience both about others and about ourselves, and where we are shaped.

Perhaps the most important findings in neurology in recent decades point to high plasticity of the brain to a degree that had not been suspected so far: brain and body are not only formed in close interplay during prenatal and childhood development phases, but certain areas of the brain remain receptive to physiological changes with advanced age too. This is where our experiences are shaped, that means images evolves that to a great extent determine how we experience our world, how we are able to act and who we are. According to findings in the field of neurology and life sciences, there is growing evidence that the generation of world views and their significance can also be described physiologically, and not merely humanistically. The way in which feeling, thinking, intelligence and knowledge are embodied are thus becoming more and more conceivable.

As cultural accomplishments, the design of a building and its interior concept therefore evolve from a desire which, due to using craft skills, is able to achieve and realize certain intentions and images. On the one hand, our environment is thus equipped with an abundance of gestures, possibly even conflicting ones and, on the other hand, with sparing and powerful gestures that we search for and find in it or avoid. The process of accommodating, that means the physical correspondence that we then experience is not static: everyone contributes something personally to such a relationship by means of individual goals, wishes and actions and thus creates new inner pictures in the medium term. This takes place within the innovative and coherent "choreographies" which allow a dynamic and communicative furnishing concept and present us with a challenge, and also within the correspondence relationships in which we engage, not only with regard to the gestures of the quality of a building, but also in terms of its dimensions and materials too.

The findings of neurological research thus suggest that architectural spaces should be comprehended as the extension of such images, similar to technology having developed over millennia as the extension of the mechanical functions of our body. A similar interconnection also becomes apparent: we shape our environment according to pictures we can imagine; but this always contains the possibility of using these environmental "extensions of images" to influence positively what we imagine in the future, what we are able to feel and think. Current discussion about "architecture of the brain" thus moves away from a metaphorical context and the idea of a functional analogy. It enters into real interplay in which "architecture for the brain" can be researched which is itself based on neurological principles. The gestural effect of architecture is thus geared to scope for movement in the broadest sense; it unfolds in varying degrees and has a challenging yet not compelling character. The design of our world, our society and of ourselves by means of architecture and interiors evolves in spaces for potential which we should think of as spaces for movement.

But what architectural gestures correspond to the needs of a conference, a symposium, a workshop, a school, a room for work or study in terms of the thinking, learning and knowledge processes involved? In a nutshell: how do excellent communication environments evolve? This book provides detailed and significant answers to these questions.

Communication environments evolve out of architectural spaces; they do not exist a priori but are generated by social behaviour and largely by face-to-face communication. For companies, spatial implementation of communication-relevant places and spatial structures is one of the key tasks involved in future-oriented architectural planning.

Prof. Dr. Gunter Henn

From stone-age palaver to modern conferences

How space planning reflects internal structures

The history of conferences is as old as the history of mankind. The ability to communicate via language, to discuss and to pass on acquired knowledge is regarded as the real engine of human evolution. Even stone-age tribes of hunter-gatherers organized themselves, divided up tasks and work, had meetings, followed rituals and profited from the counsel of elders and the wise. The carefully guarded fire was the centre of a community which regulated the field of tension between the individual and the group by means of rigid hierarchies and structures. Whenever people lecture on the "nomad principle" in non-territorial office concepts today, this comparison is not conclusive as nomads did not constantly travel but moved from one pasture land to the other to settle there, if only briefly. It is therefore not surprising that all concepts for a community that are developed without due consideration to instinctively territorial orientation on the part of people encounter great resistance or even fail. As a space only takes on any importance by becoming a frame of reference of social interface, social organizations in turn require correspondingly allocated spaces.

And since the time people started to settle in one place, the development of human societies towards increasing division of labour led to locations for mutual communication being differentiated according to specific contents. On the one hand, the Greek Polis and the Roman Res Publica had different meeting

places for matters of jurisdiction, the senate and public assemblies, and on the other hand, they had various temple complexes for religious rituals.

It was the Christian Middle Ages, with the unity of church and state, which centralized the location for political and religious communication. Market squares with their town halls and churches still form the geographical centre of community life.

From time immemorial, forms of communication have played a vital role in space planning, not only on such a large scale, but in smaller dimensions too. Medieval monastery architecture is a model example of how space was allocated. The relationship between the individual and the community, personal reflection, informal communication and ritual coexistence is mirrored in the architectural division into individual cells, cloisters, the refectory and the chapel. Their positioning within the building complex is the result of careful consideration and is tailored to their intended purpose in terms of design and dimensions. Whilst in the refectory, ritual rules of the game, even extending to bans on speaking and compulsory silence, reflected an existing order and tradition, cloisters were places for informal talks. Physical movement, leaving a localized position, also served to encourage mental agility and new ideas, thus making monasteries places for gaining knowledge and scientific progress. Umberto Eco's famous book "The Name of the Rose" shows to what extent the interests of the church – focused on power politics, but quite worldly too –

to keep knowledge as "knowledge for the sake of domination" within their own walls was reflected in the spatial structures of the monastery. In spite of being a close community, there was however some space for the individual: "it may be small, but it's mine" was the principle of the cells in which individuals were at least given a minimum degree of privacy.

Even the architecture of the smallest family communities, family homes, is primarily oriented towards the basic needs for privacy and community. For thousands of years communication within the family has generally taken place during meals at a central, communal table. Dining together as the expression of strong communal bonds can therefore be found in nearly all religions – for example, in the metaphor of the Last Supper. What used to be called the "front room", the real living room, is however usually presided over by the head of the family and serves more the purpose of receiving and entertaining guests. Smaller rooms cater for the private sphere of individual members of the family or for groups.

The obvious conclusion that people, as creatures who think and behave in instinctively territorial terms, have hardly changed with regard to their fundamental needs and patterns of behaviour for thousands of years, is underpinned by anthropological theses; they assume that it takes 600 generations until cultural socialization and learnt behaviour become hereditary, instinctive behaviour.

Until today it has always been important to have areas with the paradigms of privacy (concentration) and communal activities (communication), in the working environment, too. It is important to differentiate between two central communication goals of which we are often not aware as they are apparently entrenched in the instinctive behaviour of a tribal community: ritualized forms of communication geared to projecting an internal structure and thus of demonstrating the safeguarding of the community and identity both internally and externally, and informal kinds of communication that question the status quo tendentially subversively and are a far cry from any formal communication channels and thus responsible for change and development. Translated into contemporary marketing terminology, this could mean forms of communication that focus on strengthening corporate identity and branding in order to distinguish themselves from rival "tribal communities", and forms of communication that are intended to strengthen innovation performance, change management and flexibility. Both forms are manifested in different environments which, due to their specific character, focus on supporting relevant communication goals. As there is permanent but often unconscious interplay between people and environments, people shape environments, and in turn people's behaviour is influenced by the environments they have shaped. Consequently, all planning and specifying measures for office and administration buildings should be put to the test with a view to developing building structures that are as human and thus productive as possible.

**Evolution through communication:
globalization and economic dynamics**

The greatest advances in the history of mankind seem to be inextricably linked to progress in scope for information and communication. If knowledge as "knowledge for the sake of domination" had been reserved for the privileged classes only before the invention of mechanical printing (1455); that was the turning point when education and learning became accessible to more social classes. The number of carriers of information and knowledge thus exploded, and "knowledge for the sake of dominating", which the greater majority used for keeping a small minority under control, started to lose the basis of its existence. Without this development, both the Reformation and the period of the Enlightenment would have been unthinkable. In the Modern Age, mass media have provided general accessibility and thus democratization of knowledge, a development that started with the invention of printing. That is why at the end of the year in 1999 the overwhelming majority of leading scientists throughout the world from quite different fields declared the "inventor" of mechanical printing, Johannes Gutenberg, the most important personality in the past millennium: "The Man of the Millennium".

Today with television, (mobile) telephones and the worldwide web we are in the midst of the age of communication. The fact that the quantity of information and knowledge is growing exponentially is the cause of the momentum of development in social and economic systems.

As the primary purpose for which buildings and their interiors are used is changing they have to be designed differently. Design is required that focuses on relevant tasks, users and teams and allows coordinated interplay and use of new kinds of information and communication technology with efficient space and architectural realities and corresponding equipment – such as furniture, air conditioning, lighting, acoustics.

Dr. Dr. Norbert Streitz

Globalization and specialization are both the consequences and drivers of worldwide information and data networking and of physical mobility, which has increased by leaps and bounds. Long-haul holidays have become available to the masses, and the horizon of a "day trip" nowadays can take in half the globe. The earth is becoming a global village.

Within companies, too, communication is the true driving force behind development and innovation. According to recent studies, more than 80% of all innovative and creative thinking results from personal conversation. Correspondingly, the time spent on interactive, personal communication, i.e. on conferences in the broadest sense of the word, has multiplied in the last 20 years. Top managers already spend more than 90% of their working time in communicative meetings and not at their desks.

No form of electronic communication can attain the intensity and the spectrum of the perception levels of personal conversation. Direct eye contact, body language with gestures and facial play, even smell and aura complement the spoken word with its content and intonation to form a complex message and interaction.

In addition to the content factor, this communication process always embraces emotions and moods in the psycho-social context too. That is the major strength of personal communication, as perfectly functioning communication levels reveal the state of

tension between the individual and group identity. In turn, it also spells risks and obstacles: misinterpretations, misunderstandings or deceit always arise where there is a lack of common previous knowledge, or there has been a conscious breach of the rules of the game. And latent squabbling about the "pecking order" in a tribe overrides and very often prevents factual communication goals. The more participants an organizational unit has, the more important "function carriers" representing the relevant internal structures become and the more "political" dimensions of communication forms come into play. Critical investigations of behavioural motives in large organizations work on the assumption that the majority of energy on management levels focuses on the realization of personal career ambitions in internal relations – and not on the outside world, for example, on customers.

Forms of communication for this mix of allegedly factual discussion and unexpressed manifestations of role plays have hardly changed over the millennia: proverbial palaver today still provides a suitable way of defining group identities and rankings in modern "tribes" as they are also reflected within companies. That is one of the reasons why many managers often regard conferences as an utter waste of time – and yet do not miss a single one.

In a market determined by globalization and specialization it is after all not only profiling one's image, predictability and clear recognizability that determine competitiveness, but also innovative strength, adaptability and speed. That is why the most important success potential of companies is to be found in optimized planning and implementation of conferences and meetings.

One the greatest challenges is to use the spatial and technical equipment of communication environments to combine the varying dimensions of buildings, which should primarily serve the cause of cooperation, in one coherent, holistic concept: individual and group work, the local and the global context, the real and the digital world.

Life-long learning: from an information society to a "learning organization"

Face-to-face communication in particular is not easy, but requires highly sophisticated multimedia support. Today, managers therefore need media skills, that means the feeling for the right media mix in the office. Management is communication design, and the office is a laboratory of new communication media.

Prof. Dr. Norbert Bolz

"Where is the knowledge we have lost in information?"
This question posed by T. S. Eliot pinpoints the downside of an information society: knowledge and skills require much more than mere information – on the contrary, knowledge and performance capability are at risk of drowning in a flood of data if one "cannot see the wood for the trees". It is only the transformation of information into knowledge and skills – as the real learning process – that leads to the desired degree of behavioural competence.

It was not long ago that many prophets proclaimed that interactive "face-to-face communication" would die out in the wake of electronic media. Conference, or rather communication environments, in which people meet who have something to say (to one another) were no longer planned to be integrated in the scenarios of future working environments. However, the development in recent years has shown the opposite. It is not in spite of the rapid development of technical information and communication systems, but just because of it, that the need for discussions, strategic consensus-building, training programmes, presentations, workshops or informal meetings has soared.

The momentum of development processes and the related, simultaneous increase in the complexity of interrelationships have drastically reduced the half-life of what has long been regarded as given knowledge. To claim at the end of an apprenticeship that "I have finished my training" has become an anachronism when seen in this context. In the process of education and acquiring skills, transmitting reproducible material – whereby syllabuses have no chance of keeping pace with reality anyway – has become less important than developing application skills in process-oriented methodology: for example, in order to recognize new interconnections, associations and possibilities, to transfer them to a company situation and implement them as quickly as possible.

Efficient selection of information, the structuring, evaluation and networking of specialized knowledge gleaned from the flood of data – which is threatening to become unmanageable – are the most important development tasks of modern enterprises. The essence of knowledge management, which entails the new profession of a knowledge manager, means ensuring that the right information is available at the right place, at the right time and for the right people in order to transform face-to-face processes into behavioural skills.

Structural change and new work environments: from an office factory to a centre of communication and cooperation

As long as basic conditions were relatively constant, traditional forms of work and organization influenced by Taylorism had functioned perfectly. The office with its "file-based and operations-oriented character" was defined in terms of separating living and working. The traditional world of the office was thus stable and reliable but for this very reason also inflexible and hostile to innovation. Today however, forms of work and organization have to adapt to rapidly changing market conditions. Cross-departmental project and communication and intensive teamwork are gaining an increasing foothold as "new forms of work". Development processes that used to be dealt with one after another by various departments are now initiated by interdisciplinary groups and carried out as a synchronous process.

In teams there is a continual exchange of information among members to agree on further procedures. This means that time and costly blind alleys can be avoided or at least considerably reduced. Organizational processes are dealt with in self-dependent, partly autonomous group work and continually optimized by the specialist knowledge of team members, without an "omniscient" superior dictating every individual step – a task which would totally overtax such a person in any case.

Responsibility and decision competence are moving continuously closer to the point of work. This in turn leads to increasing demands on acquiring skills and further training of all those involved, and especially demands made on executives: responsibility is shown in competent delegation of the same. What is required is no longer specialized knowledge alone, but also social and communication skills to realize what people are talking about: the structural change to a "learning organization".

New forms of work and organization require new office concepts. In the same way in which companies adapt to changed environmental and general conditions, office structures have to change as well. The link between office solutions and corporate success is becoming increasingly apparent.

Prof. Dr. Stephan Zinser

Work is future-oriented if it considers the quantity and cycle of material and energy input and also the consequences for urban space as a whole, as well as the preservation of the natural habitat.

The European charter for solar energy
in architecture and urban planning

Sustainable architecture for office buildings: balance between economic requirements, social focus and environmental responsibility

Global warming is having an increasing effect on the design of office buildings throughout the world. In the USA and Canada, for example, the green building rating system called LEED (Leadership in Energy and Environmental Design) has become established as a new standard for evaluating buildings; in Australia it is the green star rating system of GECA (Good Environmental Choice Australia) which is also connected with various ecological standards in other countries. As a reaction to environmental change, people throughout the world assign increasing importance to the ecological compatibility of architecture. In the countries mentioned, real competition has emerged among investors and architects to create optimally environmentally friendly buildings which are awarded a corresponding number of "stars". These evaluations cover the entire building with regard to materials, production, building management and possibly waste disposal. Proximity to public transport forms part of the assessment. Furniture and equipment are also assessed according to formal criteria and the score is added to the overall assessment. The focus is on production in this case and also on waste disposal and recycling possibilities as furniture does not generally have any direct, negative environmental impact during use. For the period of use, it must only be proven that the materials used do not emit any pollutants.

Although such viewpoints might be useful, they are however inadequate if the utility quality and service life of buildings and their interiors are not understood as environmentally relevant criteria too. The more enduring and better the utility quality, the higher the return on investment, both economically and ecologically. In other words: poor utility quality and short service life of buildings or interiors are per se environmentally unfriendly because they are simply superfluous – however environmentally friendly they might be during production and disposal. Time-stable design up-to-date – ideally adaptable – functionality and lasting quality are prerequisites for longevity that pay both economic and ecological rewards.

In conference and communication environments in particular, economic and ecological synergies can be achieved today that also include social aspects, for example, by means of space concepts that allow highly concentrated applications due to their versatility and flexibility and at the same time are easier to adapt to the concrete needs of user groups.

The same applies to the integration of innovative media technologies to combine teams at distributed locations within a shared, virtual communication and cooperation environment. If just a fraction of business travel can be saved in this way, such investments will pay off within a short time, and environmentally critical air traffic will also be reduced, as well as physical and family stress caused by frequent and generally unproductive travelling and flying times. A third aspect should not be omitted: high utility value and design quality have direct positive effects on the working climate and people's attitude towards life.

It is now indisputable that motivation, identification, loyalty and cooperation are inextricably linked with the quality of interior design. As personnel costs multiply with the number of participants in conference and communication environments, it is in this case particularly worthwhile to invest in promoting these "soft" human factors. That is not only beneficial to the whole of the company but to the individual as well.

In this planning guide, an approach is adopted that consistently focuses on people, and includes both economic and ecological aspects. This corresponds to the worldwide trend of regarding people in the knowledge society increasingly as the most important growth resource and, at the same time, as the greatest bottleneck – and it reflects the experience and knowledge that no corporate or organizational model can be successful in the long run which negates social human needs.

Buildings are social facts which express themselves in the form of space. They are therefore an expression of both social and cultural circumstances, and also a behavioural framework for social developments. Architectural spaces may be judged by the appearance of the interior. Architectural spaces may however also be judged according to what social spaces they allow to develop, or in other words, what new reality they permit.

Prof. Dr. Gunter Henn

Basic theses for planning conference and communication environments

On the basis of the various perspectives presented in considerations so far, relevant theses and conclusions for planning conference and communication environments may be derived:

In spite of the virtualization of business processes, the office building remains the central frame of reference for companies and organizations. But the meaning it conveys is changing: from an "office factory" à la Taylor to a "communication and cooperation centre" in the knowledge society. To reflect internal structures and social relations in a differentiated way is therefore becoming one of the central tasks in planning future-proof office working environments.

In spite of progress in civilization and technology, we have until today been dominated by the basic needs for privacy and community, to which certain space must be allocated. In terms of the working environment, this means areas for concentration and communication. While individual work could possibly take place decentrally with the aid of electronic media and at different places, for example, in a hotel or the home office, socialization, and the creation of identity and further development in the community have to have a firm location.

Conference rooms mirror corporate identity which in turn is influenced by leadership culture.

For thousands of years, classic conferences have reflected the hierarchies and rituals which have served as a means of orientation for the members of the "tribe". The importance of such places has not decreased, but in fact increased: the greater the pressure to change, the more important predictability becomes. These environments, with their accompanying rules of communication are therefore indispensable symbols of identity and reassurance within a community. In companies this task has always been reflected in the traditional type of conference.

The location and specifying of communication interiors determine the innovation potential of companies.

Information and communication are the driving force behind innovation. In addition to the identity-creating importance of conferences, an informal conversation is one of the major sources of creativity and new ideas. The more info-exchange there is, the greater the probability of creating a new link. The intensity and complexity of face-to-face meetings cannot be achieved with ingenious media technology, but can be supported by the same. Office buildings should therefore have the express aim of promoting and structuring encounters, communication and cooperation among staff in a focused way, including the integration of media technology coordinated to differentiated communication processes.

The goal of a "learning organization" promotes qualified communication and media competence – integrated into daily work.

In spite of the almost unlimited availability of information, much-cited structural change seems to be having problems taking off. The gap between theory and practical realization can only be closed or at least narrowed if continuous enhancement processes are implemented in organizational structures. In this way, human resources are the most important corporate potential to be developed and utilized effectively.

The better coordinated various design concepts in an overall concept are to basic human needs and social interplay, the higher productivity will be.

A person as an individual, embedded in the group, which in turn is part of an organization, is the focal point of four design perspectives of future working environments:

• of the design of tasks, contents and cognitive processes;
• of the information perspective with state-of-the art information and communication technology;
• of the social perspective with its forms of work and organization;
• of the architectural perspective which embraces structures, interiors and facility management.

The relations between people, space, media, organization and process are inextricably linked and subject to permanent interplay. The most efficient form therefore involves holistically coordinated concepts, such as process-oriented learning methods which are in turn influenced by the human "tribe" mentality. The success of group and project work is based on the community feeling of a manageable team, with a defined "location" for its social interface, on quasi "automatically" developed social skills, and on learning from one another and learning together with one another in a process of communication with appropriate methods and technical support.

The concept of a "cooperative" building reflects the interrelations between real and virtual space, the individual and the group and between the local and global context.

The dynamics of economic and technological basic conditions and, linked to this, increasing complexity, require a corporate image to be profiled and sharpened on the one hand and organization to be flexible and adaptable on the other hand. Both are directly linked to the quality of communication and cooperation within organizations which is influenced by interiors. A "cooperative" building requires human interplay by providing various interaction environments tuned to specific forms of communication and cooperation. The integration of innovative information and communication technologies into space and furnishing concepts thus acquires a central focus: the real environment itself becomes an interface for supporting team processes.

No planning without prior analysis!

Planning and design of conference and communication environments are therefore a key issue. For whether conferences are an unnecessary waste of time or effective work depends to a large extent on whether the right kind of room or space is selected, whether the conference method is coordinated with aims and objectives, whether the furniture provides the right set of tools for the purpose and whether appropriate media are available. That is why any application-oriented planning and specifying of interiors should be preceded by a thorough analysis: Who will be talking to whom? How often? About what? Why? And what conference aids will be required?

It is only the answers to these questions that will provide the requirements for planning and specifying communication environments.

Specific environments for meeting, conference, seminar and workshop applications

Why? **Communication goals**	How? **Forms of organization**	**Forms of interaction/Media**
To exchange information, motivate, inform, report, analyze, evaluate, decide	**Meeting and consultation**	Conversation and discussion, without or with media support
To inform, report, analyze, evaluate, refine, decide, delegate	**Formal meeting and conference**	Lecture, discussion, presentation, topic definition, with low to high level of media support depending on number of participants
To learn, teach, motivate, coach	**Training and seminar**	Lecture, presentation, discussion, group work, exercise, vocal testing, media support essential depending on method
To exchange information, collect ideas, bond the team, analyze, evaluate, develop	**Workshop and dynamic conference**	Moderation, brainstorming, discussion, group work, presentation, always with analogue visualization tools; digital media support too for lecture and presentation
To inform, to exchange information, analyze, evaluate, delegate	**Presentation and videoconference**	Talks, lecture, presentation, always with media support
To inform, report, exchange information, motivate, refine, decide	**Assembly**	Lecture, presentation … with media support depending on number of participants and contents
To inform, learn, exchange information, familiarize	**Conference, symposium and congress**	Lecture, presentation, panel discussion … with media support if large number of participants

Conversational technique	Participants	Utilization	Furnishing effect	Specifiers' options	Page
	How many?	How often?		Where?	
confidentially informal to confidentially formal	2–6	frequently	prestigious, group-oriented	**Meeting room in customer service area**	264
	6–10	frequently	functional, group-oriented	**Meeting rooms**	34, 36
	8	occasionally	prestigious, neutral	**Conference room in reception area**	282
	8–12	frequently	prestigious, neutral	**Conference rooms**	42, 44, 66
	10	frequently	prestigious, neutral	**Meeting room with videoconference furniture & equipment**	52
	8–12	frequently	uncomplicated & functional, neutral	**Multi-purpose room, mobile furniture**	104
	10	occasionally	prestigious, neutral	**Interactive command centre**	142
confidentially formal	12–16	frequently	prestigious, group-oriented	**Conference rooms, partitionable conference room/environment**	42, 66
	12–18	frequently	functional, neutral	**Multimedia conference workshop, seminar rooms**	78, 94, 102
	16–24	occasionally	prestigious, group-oriented	**Conference room, variable furniture**	68
	20–24	frequently	prestigious, neutral	**Partitionable conference rooms**	66, 72
	18–32	occasionally	functional, neutral	**Seminar rooms/multi-purpose rooms, conference workshop**	94, 102, 134
	32–45	occasionally	prestigious, neutral	**Conference halls, multimedia conference room/environment**	54, 72
semi-publicly formal	12–30	frequently	functional, neutral	**Seminar and multi-purpose rooms, conference workshop**	94, 102, 110, 134
	12	frequently	functional, neutral	**Seminar room with sophisticated media technology**	116
	15–18	frequently	prestigious, group-oriented	**Dynamic multimedia conference workshop**	78
	up to 20	frequently	functional, group-oriented	**Conference room in combi-office**	244
	10–18	occasionally	prestigious, neutral	**Conference room, interactive command centre**	46, 142
	up to 27	occasionally	prestigious, neutral	**Multimedia conference room, variable, partitionable**	72
	8–12	rarely	functional, group-oriented	**Conference area in group office or project office**	250, 254
	12–20	rarely	functional, neutral	**Info-café in customer service area**	270
semi-publicly formal and informal, depending on method	12–16	frequently	functional, neutral	**Conference workshop**	134
	18	frequently	prestigious, neutral	**Dynamic multimedia conference workshop**	78
	10	occasionally	prestigious, neutral	**Interactive command centre**	142
	8–12	occasionally	functional, group-oriented	**Conference area in combi-office, group office or project office**	244, 250
confidential to semi-publicly formal	9	frequently	prestigious, neutral	**Presentation rooms and videoconference rooms**	48, 50
	10	occasionally	prestigious, neutral	**Meeting room with video**	52
	up to 10	occasionally	prestigious, group-oriented	**Multimedia conference workshop, interactive command centre**	78, 142
public to semi-publicly formal	45	rarely	prestigious, neutral	**Conference hall**	56
	up to 100	occasionally	functional, neutral	**Conference centre, company restaurant as assembly room**	156, 154
	70	frequently	functional, neutral	**Lecture hall**	170
	94	frequently	prestigious, neutral	**Plenary assembly hall, auditorium**	168
public to semi-publicly formal	up to 100	frequently	functional, neutral	**Conference centre**	156
	94	frequently	prestigious, neutral	**Plenary assembly hall, auditorium**	168
	70	frequently	functional, neutral	**Lecture hall**	170
	36	rarely	prestigious, neutral	**Multimedia conference room, variable, partitionable**	123

Integrated areas
for communication
and cooperation

Why? Communication goals	How? Forms of organization	Forms of interaction/Media
To exchange information, motivate, inform, report, analyze, evaluate, decide	**Meeting and consultation**	Conversation, discussion, presentation without or with media support
To bond the team, self-organize, analyze, evaluate, refine	**Group work**	Communication integrated into work-flow, regular refining of individual work status; media support at the workplace, during meetings and presentations
To exchange information, collect ideas, bond the team, analyze, evaluate, develop, change	**Project work**	Moderation, brainstorming, discussion, presentation; media support at the workplace, during meetings and presentations; moderation with analogue visualization techniques
To motivate, inform, develop, decide	**Workshop**	Lecture, presentation, discussion; media support depending on contents and methods
To inform, convince, refine, evaluate, decide	**Presentation**	Lecture, presentation … always with multimedia technology
To inform, report, exchange information, motivate, bond the team	**Jour fixe**	Lecture, presentation, meeting with media support depending on number of participants and contents

Conversational technique	How many? Participants	How often? Utilization	Furnishing effect	Where? Specifiers' options	Page
confidentially informal to confidentially formal	2–4	frequently	prestigious, group-oriented	Consultation workplaces in showrooms / customer service areas	264
	2–6	frequently	functional, personal character	Conference offices	222–230
	8–10	occasionally	functional, group-oriented	Conference room close to workplace	286
	8–12	frequently	functional, group-oriented	Open communication zone in combi-office	244
	6–10	frequently	functional, group-oriented	Conference area in group office and project office	252
	10	rarely	prestigious, group-oriented	Interactive command centre	142
confidentially informal	6–12	frequently	functional, group-oriented	Group office or project office	250, 254
	8–12	frequently	functional, group-oriented	Communication zone/conference area in combi-office	243
	8–10	occasionally	functional, neutral	Conference room close to workplace	286
confidentially informal to confidentially formal	6–10	frequently	functional, group-oriented	Group office or project office	250
	8–12	frequently	functional, group-oriented	Conference room in combi-office	243
	4–6	frequently	functional, group-oriented	Conference offices	226, 230
	12–18	occasionally	prestigious, group-oriented	Dynamic multimedia conference workshop	78
	10	rarely	prestigious, group-oriented	Interactive command centre	142
confidential to semi-publicly formal	12–18	occasionally	functional, group-oriented	Conference area in a combi-office, group / project office	244, 250, 254
	8–12	occasionally	functional, group-oriented	Open communication zone in combi-office	244
	10	rarely	functional, neutral	Communication hubs in office environment	286
	12	rarely	functional, neutral	Conference room close to workplace	286
confidential to semi-publicly formal	6–10	frequently	functional, group-oriented	Conference area in group / project office	250
	8–16	frequently	functional, group-oriented	Communication zone in combi-office	246
	8–20	occasionally	functional, group-oriented	Conference room in combi-office	244
	8–10	occasionally	functional, neutral	Conference room close to workplace	286
	8–16	occasionally	functional, neutral	Communication hubs in office environment	286
	12-16	occasionally	functional, neutral	Info-café in customer service hall	270
confidentially informal to semi-publicly formal	4–6	regularly	functional, personal character	Conference offices	220–230
	6–20	regularly	functional, group-oriented	Conference area in combi-office, group / project office	244, 250, 254
	8–16	regularly	functional, group-oriented	Open communication zone in combi-office	244
	8–16	occasionally	functional, neutral	Communication hubs in office environment	286
	up to 100	rarely	functional, neutral	Company restaurant as assembly room	154

Chance encounters

Why? **Communication goals**	How? **Forms of organization**	**Forms of interaction/Media**
To exchange information, motivate, inform, report, analyze, evaluate, decide	**Conversation and info-exchange**	Conversation, discussion, presentation without or with media support
To research, compare, inform, collect ideas	**Information**	Individual interaction with integrated, analogue or digital media
To consult and inform, build up trust, analyze, compare, evaluate, decide	**Contact and sales**	Conversation, presentation … Visualization with analogue media (printed documents, exhibits) or with digital media (internet, configurators, etc.)
To exchange information, bond the team, inform, motivate	**Breaks and relaxation**	Conversation
To exchange information, familiarize, bond the team, motivate	**Celebrations**	Conversation, lecture, presentation, event performance, dining, dancing … with media support depending on the nature and occasion of the event

Conversational technique	How many? Participants	How often? Utilization	Furnishing effect	Where? Specifiers' options	Page
confidentially informal to semi-public informal	2–4	frequently	prestigious, neutral	Lounge and foyer in seminar area	284
	2–4	frequently	functional, group-oriented	Open communication zones in combi-office	246
	2–4	frequently	functional, group-oriented	Communication hubs in office environment	286
	2–4	frequently	functional, neutral	Info-café in customer service hall	270
	2–4	frequently	prestigious, neutral	Lounge in showrooms	272
	2–4	occasionally	prestigious, neutral	Reception foyer	282
	2–6	frequently	functional, neutral	Company cafeteria and restaurant	152
				Meeting points and places with info-terminals in ...	
confidentially informal to semi-public informal	2–3	frequently	functional, neutral	... Company cafeteria and restaurant	152
	2–3	frequently	functional, group-oriented	... Communication zone in combi-office	246
	2–3	frequently	prestigious, neutral	... At high tables in customer service hall	266
	2–3	frequently	functional, neutral	... Info-café in customer service hall	270
	2–3	frequently	prestigious, neutral	... Reception foyer	282
	2–3	frequently	prestigious, neutral	... Lounge and foyer in seminar area	284
	2–3	frequently	functional, group-oriented	... Communication hubs in office environment	286
	2–6	frequently	functional, neutral	Reading corner in office environment	286
	2–6	frequently	functional, group-oriented	Open communication zone in combi-office	246
confidentially informal to semi-publicly formal	2–4	frequently	prestigious, neutral	Consultation workplaces	268, 272
	2–6	frequently	prestigious, neutral	Lounge areas	266, 273
	2–6	frequently	prestigious, neutral	Info-café, bar, cafeteria	270, 272, 286, 152
	2–24	frequently	prestigious, neutral	Foyer area	282, 284
	up to 100	occasionally	functional, neutral	Conference and congress centre	158
confidential to semi-public informal	4–12	frequently	functional, group-oriented	Bar and lounge in office environment	286
	2–14	frequently	functional, group-oriented	Communication zone in combi-office	246
	2–8	frequently	functional, group-oriented	Communication hub in project office and group office	249
	20–50	occasionally	prestigious, neutral	Lounge and foyer in seminar area	284
	up to 100	frequently	functional, neutral	Company cafeteria and restaurant	152
	up to 20	occasionally	functional, neutral	Info-café in customer service hall	270
	up to 36	occasionally	prestigious, neutral	Lounge and bar in showroom	272
confidentially informal to semi-publicly formal	up to 24	occasionally	functional, neutral	Stand-up bar in office environment	286
	22–28	rarely	functional, neutral	Multi-purpose rooms with mobile or flexible furniture	106, 112
	up to 100	occasionally	functional, neutral	Company cafeteria and restaurant	154
	72	frequently	functional, neutral	Conference and congress centre	160
	94	occasionally	prestigious, neutral	Plenary assembly hall, auditorium	168

Classic conference and meeting environments

▶ Classic conference environments represent an opportunity for further development of predictive gatherings. The aims and objectives are first and foremost to safeguard identity and to create a feeling of togetherness: this is where hierarchies and procedures are reflected without which a community cannot exist. Chairmanship, seating order and methods follow strict rules and rituals largely unconsciously. Conferences with a classic character therefore have a high symbolic meaning: they are the criterion for the credibility of corporate culture. The correct balance between predictability, security and strategic further development requires prestigious and future-oriented interior arrangements that with the aid of state-of-the-art multimedia technology will bring together global locations and intensify co-worker relationships. Conference interiors are increasingly becoming a window to the world.

Classic conference environments
between prestige and functionality

**First we shape our buildings
and afterwards our buildings shape us.**
Winston Churchill

**The mirror of a community
and the basis of corporate identity**

Since time immemorial, particular value has always been assigned to the furnishing and design of classic conference environments. It is not surprising that it is in such conference rooms that the dignitaries of the corporate world meet to exchange information and to confer, to reach and take decisions. Originating in stone-age tribal palaver, classic forms of conferences are a mirror of in-company ranking, of rituals and the culture of a company or institution. For cabinet meetings, weekly mail discussions, management group sessions, departmental meetings, assessment conferences or meetings of the advisory board – what they all have in common is their fixed, regular nature and that they reflect the ranking within a community.

Conference rooms for top management or the advisory board are therefore regarded as a sanctum, as the centre of power with high symbolic significance within an organization. The focus is frequently on safeguarding and securing the status quo, albeit unconsciously, and not, for example, on change and re-orientation: that is why many floors comprising conference facilities often feature various depictions of those people and events that have had a formative influence on the respective community. From this point of view, conference rooms are a fundamental part of corporate identity. Vice versa, it may be concluded that if it is important to continue to develop or modify the positioning and culture of a community, then the organizational form and spatial arrangement of these portentous gatherings contain key potential to make change visible and comprehensible both internally and externally. For this is the area that arouses most general attention within the company and among external interest groups.

The organizational form:
formal, calculable and mediating

The chairman and leader of such conferences is generally the person extending the invitation and holding the highest position of all conference participants. He or she decides on the agenda and the respective participants, assigns tasks such as taking the minutes, is responsible for an orderly procedure, establishes the time frame and presides over events. If there is a fixed seating order it will invariably reflect current personnel constellations and groups and thus the power structure within a particular system of leadership. The "place" at the conference table thus stands as a placeholder for the allocated significance within a social ranking. As the rules of the game are frequently informal, such a seating order provides participants with necessary transparency and calculability.

Conferences with a traditional, classic character are therefore not losing in importance in spite of methods that sometimes appear anachronistic. On the contrary: the faster structures in the working world change, the more important rituals and points of orientation become that promise continuity and security. Besides, the rise in the number of meetings and discussions means that the decision-making pressure on management levels can hardly be mastered by lone fighters, but increasingly requires the psychological, social and specialist backup provided by team decisions. Beyond this, the increasing complexity and the resultant conflict of goals within management are changing the role and style of the chairperson. In addition to the function of finding, making and announcing decisions, this person is assuming more and more the role of a mediating host.

When complaints are made with regard to tiring and inefficient meetings and conferences, this only goes to show that method-specific discipline, didactic tools and the functionality of furniture and equipment have not been considered adequately. How often are participants put on the spot because they do not have required information at their fingertips? How great is the frustration about "wasting time" when information is missing or participants receive reports too late or ones that are incomplete and with subjective contents – and where it would be so much easier to prepare and agree on such information online during the meeting for everyone to see?

And last but not least, how substantial savings potential in terms of process costs might be if it were possible to arrange these gatherings of the most "costly" representatives of a company more effectively and efficiently? Clearly formulated goals and objectives, a binding agenda with sufficient advance notice and predetermined times, as well as the integration of multimedia technology linked up to a data network help to demonstrate interconnections and decision-making parameters in a manner that is more graphic, interesting and motivating.

The focal point of interior arrangements: the table

In line with the symbolic significance of conferences, designated rooms are generally in a rather exposed part of the building. The furnishings range from prestigious to luxurious and tailor-made for the usual number of participants and the occasion. Traditionally, the chairperson is seated centre-stage and the seating order is fixed accordingly. The form and finish of the tables are thus central elements of interior design. They define the degree of interaction of the participants as well as the respective management culture. Elongated table configurations, for example, emphasize hierarchical significance: in the case of seating along both sides, the chairperson always sits at the head of the table or in the middle if there is a platform layout. A "round table" contrasts with this arrangement as it does not visually have a special seat that defines leadership and thus facilitates changes in position in the literal sense too.

In the planning and design stage, special care should be paid to achieving a balance between communicating prestige and functionality. The key planning and specifying parameters are the well-being of the individual, a communication-promoting arrangement of ergonomic seating, natural integration of state-of-the-art conference technology and communication of prestige both internally and externally. It is not infrequently the case that the ambience of conference interiors tends to convey a feeling of ivory-tower orientation taking a step backwards as the design relates nostalgically to a long past era. If the specific "spirit" of the company is supposed to be representative, interior design should be tuned less to an individual interpretation of taste and more to the communal image of the company, its identity and culture.

From a conference room to a dynamic multimedia conference

Basic furniture and equipment in conference rooms

Frequent conferences and meetings have long since become an integral part of everyday life in all corporate areas. According to a European online survey in 2007, 48 per cent of office staff participate in a meeting at least once a week. Adequate, anti-glare daylight and a room and table large enough in size to accommodate the number of participants, as well as comfortable, ergonomically shaped seats form part of the vital basics of conference interiors. Translucent glass elements, for example, create transparency and make it visible to the outside that the room is occupied, without forsaking the need for privacy. Alternatively, electronic displays may be used to provide information on whether a room is occupied or not. Room reservation systems that are accessible via the internet facilitate planning, facility management and if required also cost allocation for the utilization of conference and meeting rooms and spaces.

Integration of media technology

It is absolutely necessary to have a floor port underneath the table providing the possibility for power supply, internet access (network access too, depending on the internal security level) and electronic A/V equipment, for example, in conjunction with a permanently installed digital projector or a large-format monitor. This is also advisable if no modern conference technology is planned at the beginning as subsequent additions to technology pre-installed during the building stage are relatively costly. In virtually all meetings and conferences which involve presentations, participants today tend to have their own laptops, that means their "workplace" moves with them. It is therefore very important to have suitable cable management integrated into the table, including easy access to connection points. Various, individually

configurable techni-modules may be integrated into the table to provide retractable connectivity modules ("plug-and-play"). Table portals are another alternative: they allow access to connectivity modules that are located in cable boxes and cable channels underneath the table top. These have the advantage that network adapters, battery charging devices for mobile phones and surplus cables do not lie around on the table but may be stored conveniently underneath the table so that one has virtually the whole table surface at one's disposal. Last but not least, in particularly high-quality and prestigious areas, electronically retractable monitors – if necessary complete with a keyboard – may be integrated into table surfaces direct. In conference interiors with technically complex equipment, the entire room control technology, including lighting and air conditioning, darkening the room and media technology may be operated very easily – for example, via a touch panel. If a computer display is already integrated into the table, it may also serve to operate the above functions.

Planning a table configuration: static or variable?

If the size and shape of a room or space are not variable it is advisable to specify a permanently installed table that is perfectly coordinated with the interior in terms of form and size. Round, oval or elliptical forms allow greater flexibility with regard to the number of participants, and they facilitate interaction. In the case of larger rooms, which may be divided up into smaller units using partitions as the need arises, it is however necessary to use variable or mobile table systems. Innovative cable management systems and connectivity systems now also allow such conference configurations to be equipped with state-of-the-art multimedia technology without restricting versatility and without increasing changeover time and costs.

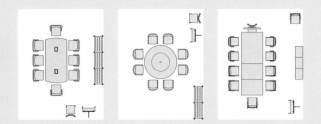

**At a glance: planning & specifying examples.
From meeting environments to a workshop
for a dynamic multimedia conference**

*Meeting rooms
for 8–10 persons,
page 34–37*

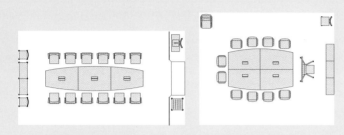
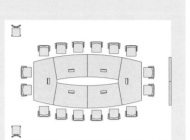
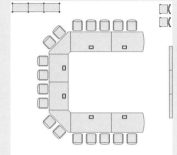

*Classic conference rooms
with integration of media technology for 10–22 persons,
page 42–47*

*Environments for presentations
and videoconferencing,
page 48–53*

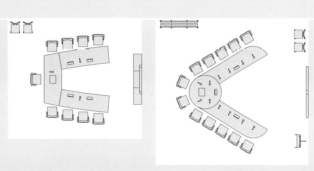

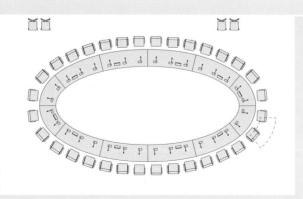

*Conference room with elliptical
table configuration or U-shaped
table configuration and platform,
page 54–57*

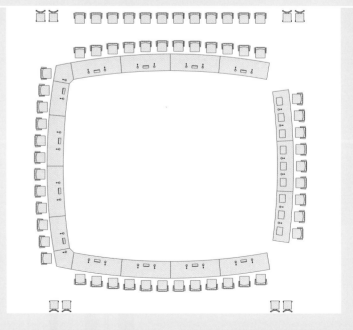

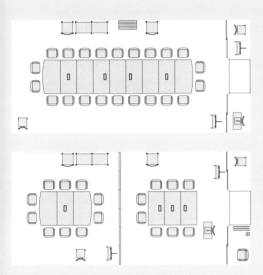

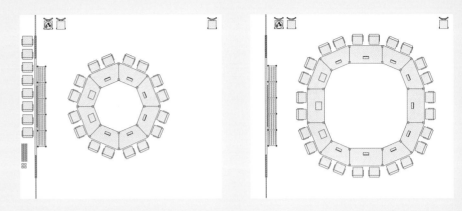

*Conference room with variable table configuration
and integrated media technology for 16 and 24 persons,
page 68*

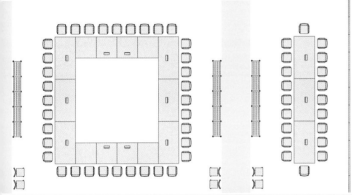

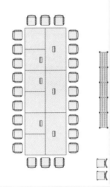

*Partitionable conference room with integrated media
technology modules and variable furniture for 22 persons,
page 66*

*Partitionable multimedia conference
room with static and mobile furniture
for 36 persons,
page 72–75*

*Dynamic multimedia conference workshop
with mobile furniture,
page 78–81*

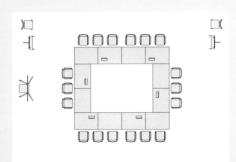

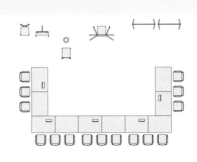

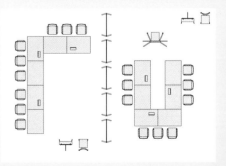

33

Conference room for 8 persons

Meeting rooms are often intended to accommodate small groups of six to eight. Groups of such a size allow most efficient cooperation as experience shows that there is the highest chance of everyone participating in such a setting. Groups of such strength tend to encourage the kind of communication behaviour that has been acquired during informal socialization. A coherent design language can be achieved if a pool of cantilever models, swivel chairs or four-legged conference versions from the same product family are available as is also used at the company's office desks. Office swivel chairs have ergonomic benefits and support facility management by using only one type of chair for workplaces and conference setups. This might, however, have a negative effect on the orderly visual pattern that is desired if chairs with different seat heights, swivel chairs turned in all directions and 3-D armrests adjusted this way and that only create a chaotic impression. Careful planning is therefore necessary.

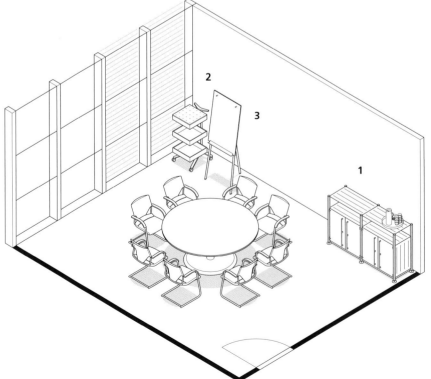

A rectangular table form defines the place of the highest-ranking person present at one end of the table. A slightly rounded table edge will serve to moderate this effect – and perhaps even provide a place for an additional participant if required.

The "round table" is regarded as a metaphor in order to communicate on an equal level and to achieve a balance of interests. Such an option provides the highest degree of interaction as well as maximum variability in terms of the number of participants.

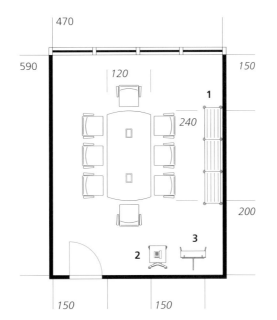

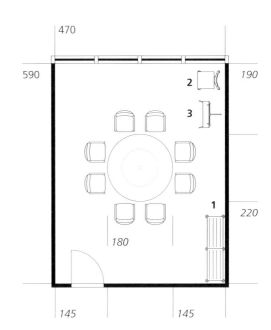

1   Sideboard for catering materials and incidentals
2   Server for telephones, desk pads and pens
3   Flipchart for documentation of group discussions
    and as visual support for elaborating on topics

Meetings may be called ad hoc or planned a long time in advance. They are held by working groups and departments on all hierarchical levels and throughout all corporate areas. They may be attended solely by company staff or also include external visitors. If meeting areas are located too far away, this will serve to inhibit communication. Such areas should therefore be located as close as possible to the workplaces of those departments and employees who use them regularly. If they are integrated into an office floor, space geometry and permanent interior features (walls, doors, flooring, lighting) will generally be defined by the modular properties and dimensions of the façade of the building.

The usual number of participants in meetings provides a relevant parameter for the size and furnishing of such areas. A small group will feel lost and uncomfortable at a large table configuration, and vice versa, a crowded room, poor air quality, insufficient work surface and not enough distance between workplaces will impair the quality of such meetings.

For an informal circle with six to eight participants, a single table with chairs along all sides will be sufficient. The depth of the table should not be less than 120 cm to provide those on both sides of the table with enough space. Round tables allow a variable number of participants and ensure equal-status seating, as well as maximum scope for human interaction. If a basic rectangular shape is rounded along the short edges, the number of participants may be extended to accommodate ten without it becoming too crowded – provided the table construction affords sufficient legroom on all sides.

No room should be without a flipchart, as a simple and spontaneously usable means of visual support. It is also useful to have an additional sideboard with drawers for paper and pens, as well as storage space for flipchart pads and company-relevant documents which should be on standby for visitors. If a meeting room is also used as a common room for lunch breaks in the department, such a sideboard could also accommodate tableware, etc.

Meeting room
for 8–10 persons

▶ If the number of participants varies very frequently and greatly, meeting rooms may alternatively be furnished with a permanently linked table configuration comprising adjoining single tables. Table clips that are simply slotted in and also serve as cable management on the table leg ensure that tables are firmly linked. A meeting room can permit many different applications if tables with suitable geometry are selected.

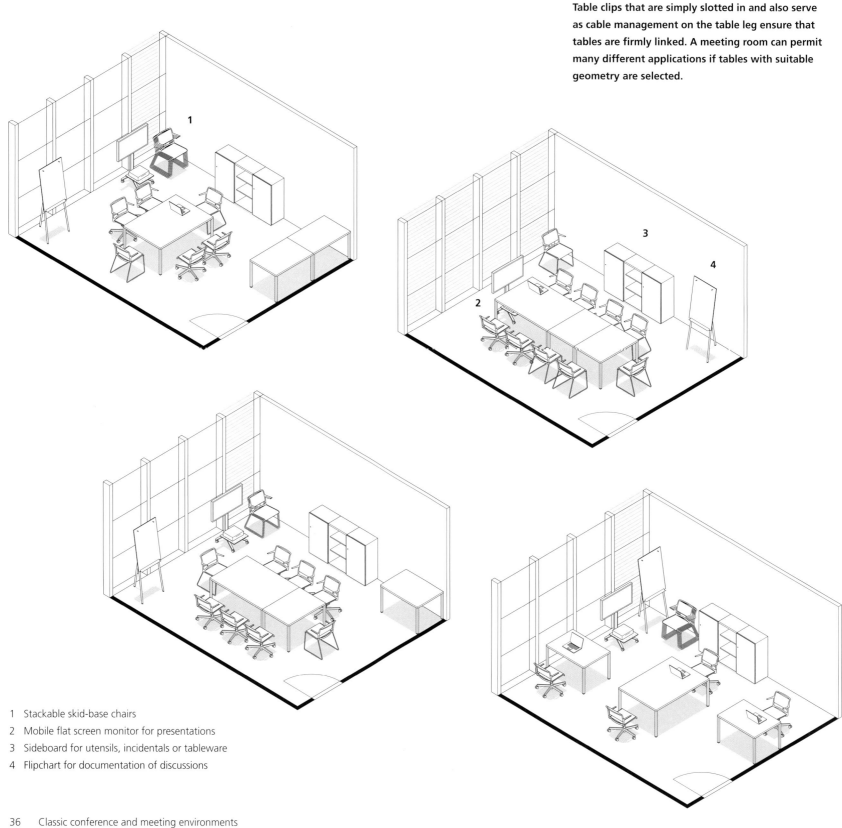

1 Stackable skid-base chairs
2 Mobile flat screen monitor for presentations
3 Sideboard for utensils, incidentals or tableware
4 Flipchart for documentation of discussions

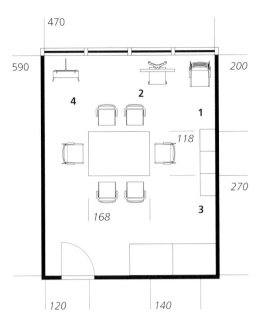

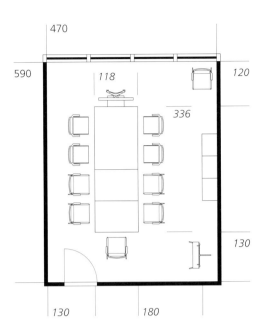

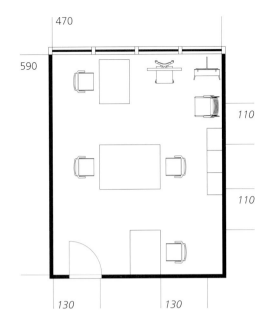

Scale 1:100 / dimensions in cm
(1 cm = 0.39 inches)
Area 30 sqm

In the example, smaller tables, exactly half the size of the larger versions but with the same proportions, have been used as "back-up" that can be added as required to extend the conference arrangement. Otherwise, they are placed along the wall and serve as storage space. Participants can do any reconfiguring required themselves quite spontaneously without any tools or facility management capacities.

The uniqueness of such tables is that the room may temporarily even be used as an overflow space for up to four workplaces. That is important for dynamic organizations in particular, for example, if members of the field force are at the office from time to time and need a workplace there – without the latter being of a permanent nature. If such scenarios are intended, corresponding power and data connections should be planned, either via a floor port or a supplementary channel. Flexible storage nets, suspended

from the underframe of the table top, offer an alternative to cable outlets or permanently integrated table leg systems. They provide storage space not only for network adapters, surplus cables or small technical devices, but if required, also for all other documents relevant to a meeting so that table surfaces may be cleared for a quick snack in between without any additional storage space being necessary.

The design of the four-legged tables has been reduced to one basic classic form to maximize application scope. The table arrangement only assumes its specific character as a table for meetings, routine work or eating when it is used in a particular context for documents, utensils, etc. The same applies to storage cabinets that should team with table surface finishes and heights in terms of material and dimensions to allow them to be integrated ad hoc for a wide variety of applications.

In line with the variable use of a meeting room/area, it is also advisable to include a mobile A/V display. This may either be used at the table configuration or rolled away and kept on standby.

The seating in this scenario should comprise a combination of stackable skid-base chairs and mobile and height-adjustable office swivel chairs; due to the limited amount of time spent in this room, complicated costly mechanical features and complex adjustment options have been omitted in favour of the aesthetic aspect. Should the meeting room be required as an office, the compactly stackable skid-base chairs may be stored in the corner. Resilient back frames and flexible upholstery material that adjust to differing body dimensions ensure sufficient room to manoeuvre and a high degree of ergonomic comfort. If semi-transparent material is used, the result will be a light and loose appearance even in high density seating arrangements.

Seating in meeting environments

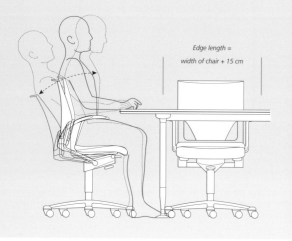

Edge length = width of chair + 15 cm

1

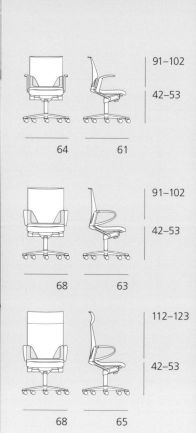

91–102
42–53
64   61

91–102
42–53
68   63

112–123
42–53
68   65

▸ **With a view to achieving coherent corporate design, chairs for furnishing various functional areas have been selected from one recognizable chair range. A complete chair family therefore comprises swivel chairs (with and without arms) and cantilever versions, optionally also four-legged visitor chairs or skid-base chairs. Virtually all functional areas can be furnished with these models: ranging from an office workplace, meeting and conference environments to seminar and training areas. The question as to what type of chair should be selected depends to a large extent on the average duration of meetings and on the required variability of the number of seats, as well as the corresponding number of chairs that have to be kept on standby. The longer the meetings, the more important exercise potential for long term seated comfort becomes.**

Swivel chairs

They are used primarily at the workplace and should feature automatic adjustment of the seat and back tilt for healthy, ergonomic sitting. Also in conferences where participants wrestle for decisions and occasionally meet for more than two hours or longer without a break, it is advisable to consider healthy sitting and to support mental alertness by means of relieving unnecessary physical strain. In addition to automatic synchro-adjustment mechanisms, it is useful to have highly resilient seat shells or back frames with stretch material that automatically adjust to differing body dimensions. They are not only more graceful than bulky padding but also provide a high degree of ventilation. Semi-transparent material enhances the impression of a light and airy furnishing arrangement.

For meeting areas where prestige is important, swivel chairs in a particularly high-quality version with wide seats and perhaps high backrests may be selected. On request, they may also be fitted with glides instead of castors. Memory return columns ensure that the chair will be correctly aligned with the table edge when the user stands up. High-grade textiles or leather are suitable as upholstery in such an environment.

Materials and surface finishes

For effective body temperature stabilization and to avoid electrostatic charge, upholstery material comprising pure wool or a blend of wool and cotton is highly suitable. Semi-transparent, air-permeable fabrics that automatically adjust to body temperatures are ideal. Materials such as die-cast aluminium (for examples, for star-bases and mechanical parts) or polypropylene (for armrests or seat shells) reduce weight and comply with requirements in terms of precision, longevity and environmentally compatible recycling.

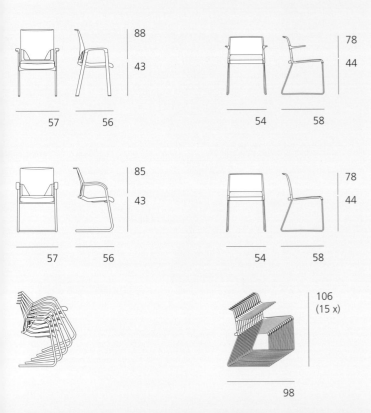

Four-legged visitor chairs

Four-legged visitor chairs are used in meeting or seminar environments. If additional chairs are to be stored compactly and kept on standby, it is useful if they are stackable. Due to the static construction of the chairs it is advisable for users to take a break and change their sitting position after at least an hour.

Materials and surface finishes
The frames of four-legged visitor chairs may be constructed from any material that can bear static stress: e.g. aluminium profile, steel tube, wood or even high performance plastic – and from combinations of various materials, which should however be separable to facilitate both repair and material-compatible and environmentally compatible recycling. The choice depends very much on the specific interior design and corporate culture. Industrially manufactured materials with a corresponding surface finish generally have a higher degree of precision and durability. Wood on the other hand is a renewable raw material that develops patina through use.

Cantilever chairs

These chairs are used as visitor chars at the workplace as well as for conference, seminar and training applications. With simple engineering, they allow comfortable, dynamic sitting due to a resilient frame. This enables the user to sit at the table for up to 90 minutes, depending on the comfort of the upholstery. If necessary, such cantilever chairs should also be available as a stackable version.

Materials and surface finishes
The frames of the cantilever chairs comprise steel tube with a powder coated, matt or bright chromium-plated finish to match the table frames. For stackable chairs, a bright chromium-plated finish should always be selected as such frames are subject to wear and tear and chrome has the most durable finish.

In prestigious areas too, chromium plating has traditionally always been regarded as the most suitable surface finish. By reflecting light, chromium-plated frames appear much more graceful and still look new even after many years of intensive use.

Skid-base chairs

They permit very graceful and light chair structures; in informal meeting areas requiring spontaneous changes in seating order they are an interesting alternative to four-legged conference chairs or cantilever models. As a stackable version they are particularly suitable for seminar areas, public area seating – e.g. for lectures – or for multifunctional areas. In a nutshell: they are a good choice for all areas of application in which frequent reconfiguration, easy handling and extremely compact stacking of standby chairs are the order of the day. Seat and back frames with flexible material ensure sufficient seated comfort for about 75 minutes.

Materials and surface finishes
Skid-base chairs comprise bright chromium-plated round steel rod that supports the front seat frame and integrates with the back rest frame at the rear to form a stable structure. If the seat and back frames are covered in flexible high performance plastic, a high degree of seated comfort combines with excellent rear ventilation and low weight. And with seat frames also functioning as a chassis, combined with a correspondingly light and graceful structure, such chairs may be stacked very compactly – and no pressure marks are left on the upholstery even after frequent stacking processes.

Single tables in meeting environments

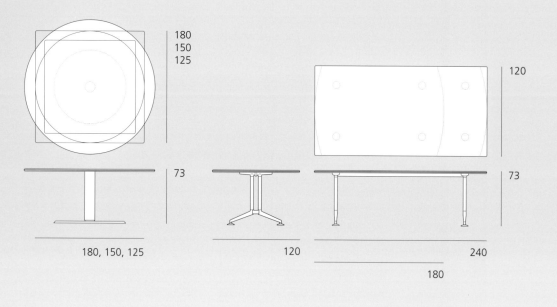

180
150
125

73

180, 150, 125

120

73

120

240

180

1

Single tables

For applications in meeting and conference areas, single tables should be at least 120 cm deep to allow those sitting opposite sufficient space for their papers. Round tables are particularly communicative. A diameter of up to 180 cm is possible as a construction with a central pedestal. A heavy duty disc base in steel provides stability. As a general rule: the more rounded the form, the higher the potential degree of human interaction and the more variable the number of seats; the more elongated the table, the more exposed the places at either end of the tables. If the short edges are rounded, a rectangular table can also support the feeling of being in a communicative circle.

A centrally positioned frame with underframes or crossbeams aligned longitudinally provides legroom all around without table legs or underframes being in the way. Besides,

such a table also looks light enough in smaller rooms so as not to dominate the interior. Alternatively, archetypal four-legged tables may be used. In the latter case, very slender underframe constructions should be given preference that do not restrict legroom. As irregularities in floor height even occur in modern buildings too, height-adjustable glides should be standard for conference tables.

If there is a possibility of grouping several tables, it is advisable to choose orthogonal table forms with straight edges. Table-to-table connectors then provide the configuration with necessary stability.

Materials and surface finishes
The foot sections in aluminium are either polished or bright chromium-plated, the uprights are optionally powder coated, anodized or bright chromium-plated. As hardwearing

impact protection, a flexible profile is integrated into the laminated wood table edge (a pleasant tactile feature). This makes the table top appear more graceful in the process. Four-legged frames should ideally have a concealed underframe in steel tube profile and straight table edges to keep visible joints to a minimum on adjoining tables. Legs flush with the table edge should be in stainless steel or similarly robust materials.

Table top finishes
Surface finishes in laminated wood, linoleum or veneer match the general colour scheme of the interior. For four-legged tables, through-dyed MDF panel with protecting lacquer offers a fresh and modern alternative to conventional table finishes.

Storage space
in meeting environments

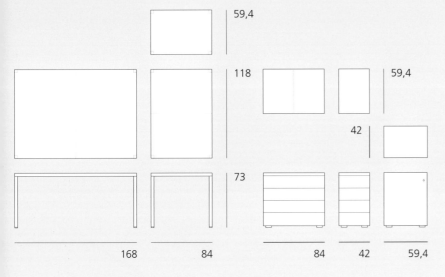

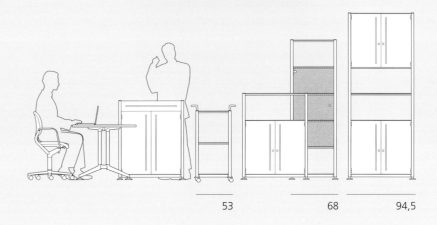

Storage space

Storage space in meeting areas may be provided by using sideboards with doors, optionally sliding, with compartments and shelves in suitable height to accommodate binders, as well as drawers, which are optimally from the same product range as the storage units used at office workplaces. If a higher degree of prestige is required, it is advisable to select surface finishes to match table finishes to achieve a coherent overall appearance. High-quality modular furniture systems offer the possibility of coordinating storage solutions individually, for example, by integrating glass display compartments which may be equipped with lights if required. To create a uniform storage surface, it is advisable to specify a decor top. To level out floor irregularities, height-adjustable glides are as indispensable for such storage units as for tables.

In the case of intended multifunctional use, for example, to include a workplace, casually grouped elements are an excellent choice which may be utilized as required as highly functional storage units. In addition to height-adjustable glides, castors may also be used; if the latter are chosen, some misalignment may have to be tolerated when modules are grouped, or elements may have to be positioned slightly apart.

Materials and surface finishes
Modular furniture requires precise, technical materials that can bear static stress such as aluminium for vertical profiles or steel for shelves allowing horizontally variable positioning. Vertical profiles with power supply permit low voltage lighting for display compartments. Teamed with table frames, the profiles are optionally bright chromium-plated or matt anodized. The fronts of the doors and drawers should match the table top finish in veneer, or perhaps have a neutral appearance, for example, in the colour silver. A coherent overall appearance may be intensified by matching the decor top as a horizontal surface with the table tops in terms of surface finish and lipping.

Casual storage elements, positioned either as a sideboard or free-standing, should have a monolithic appearance and look coherent in terms of surface finish and materials from all sides.

Specifiers' option:
cantilever chair from the Sito range at a table from the 635 range (1);
sideboard from the Conrack range (2); stackable skid-base chairs
from the Aline range at a table from the DinA range (3)

Conference room for 12 persons

▶ A conference room with a classic character for at least twelve persons is usually intended for a particular hierarchical level for regular meetings with the same participants. Such rooms are often located in an exposed part of the premises with ample daylight and an excellent view. In line with the ranking of the users and to underline the importance of the occasion, it is not only functional quality that plays a role but also prestige. Special wall coverings and flooring, fully controllable, accentuated lighting and built-in modules for media technology or storage space serve to underline the specific interior design which quite consciously differs from that of general office design. Whether an ambience is elegant or technically modern depends on the respective corporate image. Such specifications may be realized by means of the choice of colour, materials and surface finishes so that individual furniture units and architecture have a coherent appearance.

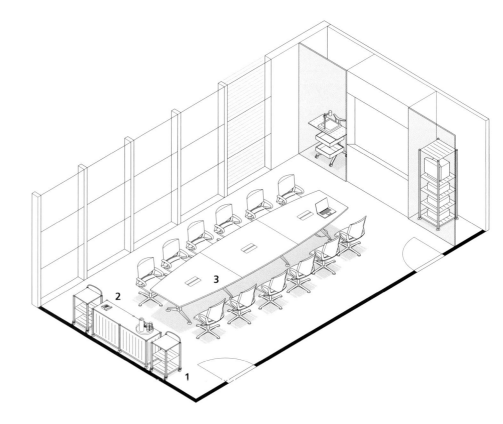

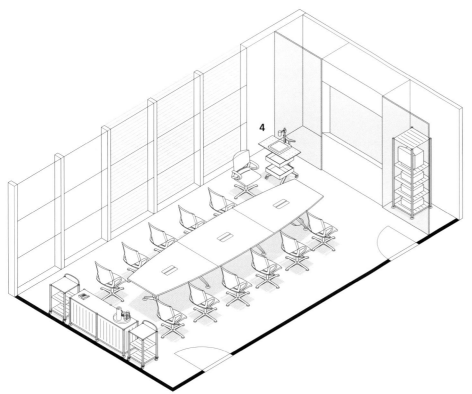

Integrated portals incorporating power & data presentation within, allow laptops to be connected with ease from every seat position. If each connection point has a "show-me function", it will be possible to connect to the shared display of the media wall.

For a presentation with overhead projection, the server with the document camera is simply moved over to the table. Due to the generous width of the shelf, there is plenty of room next to the space occupied by the visualizer for presentation documents.

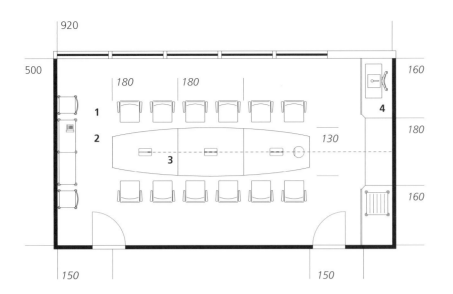

1 Catering trolley to match sideboard
2 Sideboard for catering materials, incidentals and telephone
3 Table portals with techni-stations for connecting portable computers
4 Server with video visualizer

To support decision-making processes, digital media are increasingly being used in classic conference environments too. Such media improve imaginative power by combining words and images. It should be borne in mind that even the most light-intensive projection equipment cannot compensate for direct sunlight falling onto the projection surface. Adequate anti-glare protection should therefore not be neglected. Planning and specifying should strive to combine functional necessities with the objective of achieving a coherent furnishing solution that is not dominated by technology. To this end, an excellent interior design solution would be to integrate a media wall spanning the entire length of the room that can accommodate technical equipment "behind the scenes", i.e. on the other side of the wall: for rear projection onto the central display surface, a media shelf unit with room control technology and additional, mobile units such as a document camera.

As an alternative to rear projection, a digital projector permanently mounted on the ceiling may be used for projecting onto the wall. This is an ideal solution if the room is not sufficiently deep to accommodate a media wall. However, in this case a much more light-intense digital projector has to be used to achieve the same quality – producing a correspondingly higher level of noise and heat. Yet another disadvantage is that the speaker cannot stand in front of the projection device as he or she would be dazzled by the light; also parts of the image would be reflected and a shadow would be cast upon them. What is decisive for the size of the projection area (ratio 4:3) is the maximum viewing distance. In the case of high-contrast projection with high light intensity it should amount to at least six times the width of the projection area, which in turn is defined by the height of the room. The lower edge of the projection area should be at least 120 cm from the floor to allow all participants an unimpeded view.

The rule of thumb for calculating these values: Height of the room minus 120 cm = projection height. Projection height divided by three and multiplied by four = projection width. Projection width multiplied by six = maximum viewing distance.

The media wall can be completely closed off from the room by means of sliding panels. Additionally, a second, optional level of panels allows a whiteboard or a pinboard to be moved to a central position in front of the projection area. The sliding panels should team well with all other surface finishes in terms of material and colour.

Media technology should include a server with a tripod-mounted video camera that transmits signals to the projection area. Handling is as simple as for overhead projection, yet much more versatile with regard to the objects projected. All kinds of printed matter and small, three-dimensional objects act as subject matter. A further advantage is that the visualizer does need to be placed in definite position vis-à-vis the projection or monitor area. It may be positioned where there is power supply and a connection to the digital projector.

Compared with a straight table configuration, a classic boat shape has the advantage that participants sitting along the spacious, curved edges of the table have better eye contact. If the 510 cm table in the example is supported by four centrally positioned frames, participants will have plenty of legroom.

The swivel conference chairs have been selected in view of the flexible application scope of the room in question. In a conventional type of meeting, participants sit facing one another, while they focus more on the media wall during presentations. A sideboard provides necessary storage space for documents and catering materials, and matching mobile servers facilitate serving at the table.

Conference room for 12–16 persons

▶ **In classic conference environments, visually stimulating geometries are often preferred in contrast to a conventional, rectangular shape. These can provide a counterpoint to the planning grid of the building, or present a highly creative impression of the planned or perceived activities within the space as viewed by an observer. The participants of the meeting can furthermore enjoy an experience where a highly appointed furniture specification has been considered for their tasks at hand.**

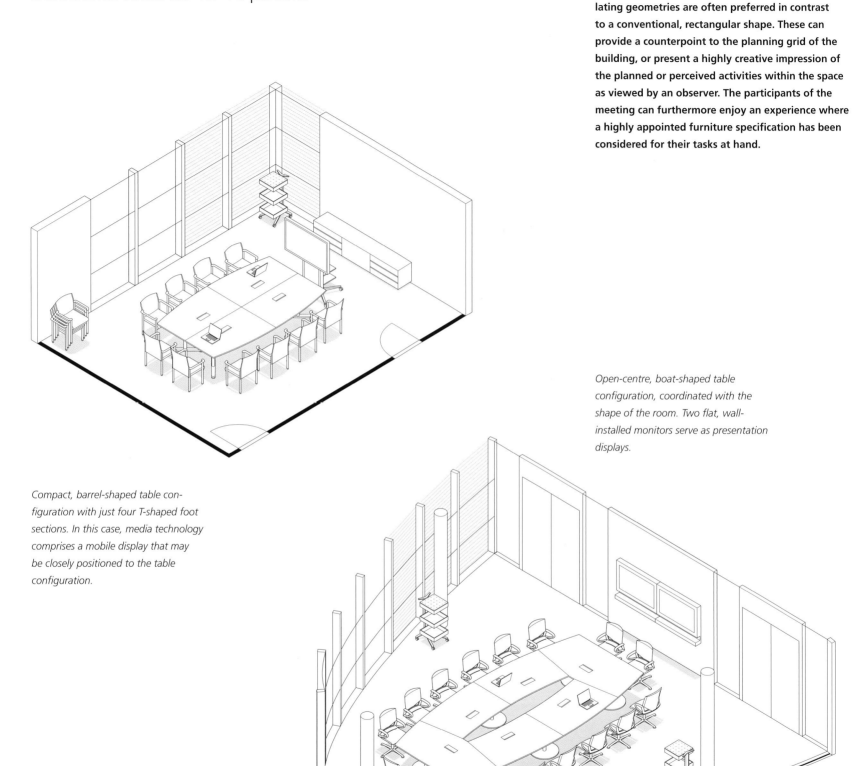

Open-centre, boat-shaped table configuration, coordinated with the shape of the room. Two flat, wall-installed monitors serve as presentation displays.

Compact, barrel-shaped table configuration with just four T-shaped foot sections. In this case, media technology comprises a mobile display that may be closely positioned to the table configuration.

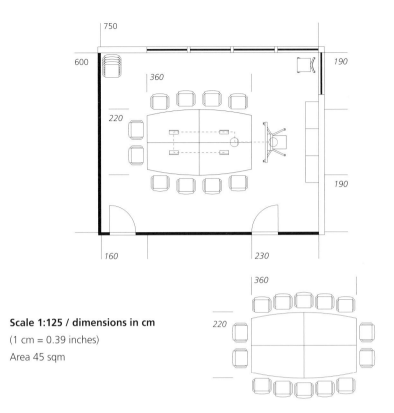

Scale 1:125 / dimensions in cm
(1 cm = 0.39 inches)
Area 45 sqm

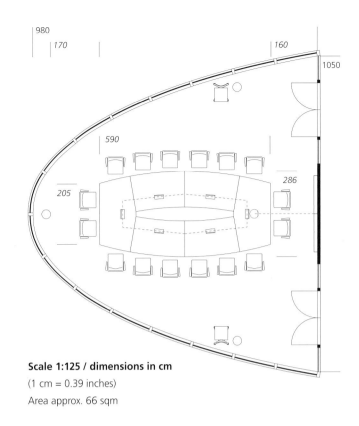

Scale 1:125 / dimensions in cm
(1 cm = 0.39 inches)
Area approx. 66 sqm

With a view to promoting human interaction, it is useful to select elliptical, barrel-shaped or boat-shaped configurations. The examples show a solid, barrel-shaped configuration, 360 cm long and 180 to 220 cm deep, that requires four T-shaped foot sections only, as well as a boat-shaped table configuration, 590 cm wide, and 205 to 286 cm deep, with six T-shaped foot sections. Specially developed, retractable cable channels, adapted to the specific length of the linking angles, to accommodate both separate cable channels and strain anchors, and user-friendly attachment of connectivity modules facilitate the perfect integration media technology required which, depending on what is envisaged, can easily result in extensive cable clutter.

The articulating linking functionality of the table legs with cantilever beams that span up to three metres permits maximum table surface with a minimum number of table legs. This provides ample legroom for all users and facilitates floor cleaning – and the long, curved edges of the table as well as the spacious shorter edges permit a high degree of flexibility in terms of the number of places. Such a permanent, static table configuration has yet another advantage: as the table configuration is centre-stage it retains its defined position and thus serves to preserve a sense of structure.

The relatively compact form of the table in the left-hand example permits, in terms of media technology, a 50 inch plasma display to be used for visual presentation purposes if it can be mobile and moved up to the table to guarantee a viewing distance not exceeding four metres. When not required, the mobile display may be simply parked in a corner. If larger viewing distances are possible, wall-installed, interlinked flat screens may be used to provide the required enlargement of the projection area.

For conference environments, swivel chairs with arms or classic, four-legged chairs are an excellent choice. For variable seating arrangements, a stackable version allows space-saving standby storage of spare chairs. Coordination of table and chair frames, as well as veneered table tops, and possibly also of the wooden armrests of chairs and the fronts and décor tops of sideboards will give the room an elegant, prestigious appearance.

Conference room for 18–22 persons

▸ Static, U-shaped table configurations are ideal for environments where participants should have eye contact and where conference media equipment should also be used if required. Such a configuration may be transformed into a solid arrangement by adding a matching mobile folding table in conference scenarios that do not need any media technology. When using open-centred configurations it is advisable to specify modesty panels to provide a degree of privacy – and at the same time to conceal cable channels and connectivity modules underneath the tables. If seats are placed along one side of the configuration only, table depths of 90-105 cm are sufficient. In the example, table top segments, underframes and table legs form modules that define the number and position of places at the table.

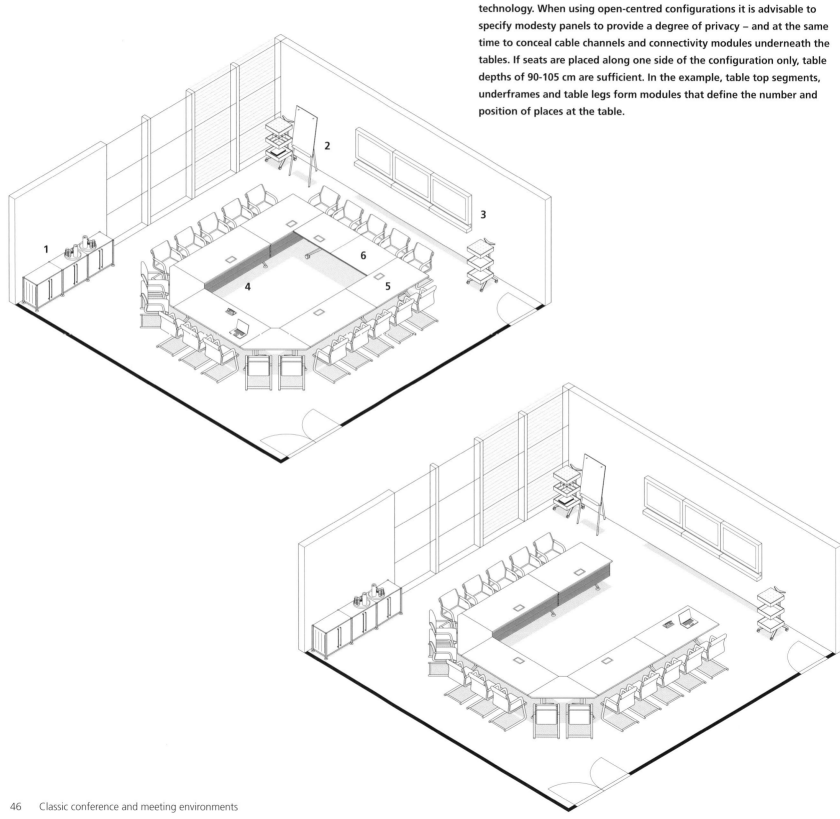

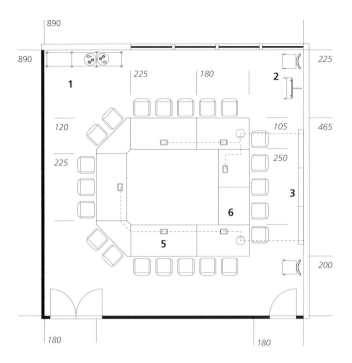

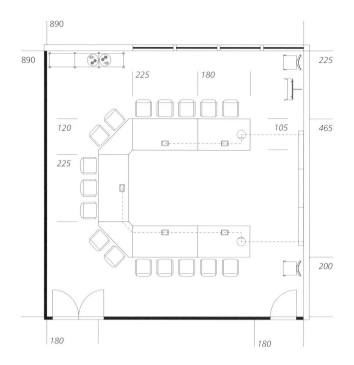

1 Sideboard for catering materials, tableware and incidentals
2 Server for writing pads and pens or catering materials
3 Wall-installed flat screens
4 Modesty panels for privacy
5 Techni-stations, flush-mounted in table tops,
  for connecting portable computers
6 Mobile folding table with integrated techni-station
  and cable management

Scale 1:125 / dimensions in cm
(1 cm = 0.39 inches)
Area 75 sqm

Technical progress in the development of (affordable) flat screens has resulted in virtually every meeting and conference room being equipped with one – providing the viewing distance is not too long in proportion to the diagonals of the screen. If several flat screens are grouped and networked accordingly, various data may be presented in parallel. This makes it easier for participants to make spontaneous comparisons or contribute additional input if a website is also open or if a call is established to a discussion partner by means of videoconferencing. If media technology is to be used for more than showing prepared presentations, i.e. it should also aim at providing support to allow shared editing of results, interactive editing facilities should also be specified. These would comprise touch-sensitive, high-resolution displays and networking with connectivity modules integrated into table tops.

Spacious, optionally stackable cantilever chairs have been used as conference seating in the example. If the upper edge of the backrests is straight they will create an optical extension of the contours of the table edge for a calm appearance.

A sideboard and a mobile server for catering materials and writing utensils form a perfect addition to the conference interior. If no interactive presentation techniques are available for all participants to use, a flipchart is an absolute must. In conferences it is essential to have the possibility for spontaneous, visual presentation of interrelated items – providing participants' input is really appreciated. If all surface finishes and frame materials are coordinated according to the desired interior theme, the result will be a coherent furnishing solution.

Conference room for presentations and videoconferencing

Scale 1:100 / dimensions in cm

(1 cm = 0.39 inches)

Area 48 sqm

1 Server for writing pads and pens or catering materials

2 Wall-installed flat screens with a camera and loudspeakers

3 Techni-stations, flush-mounted in table tops, for connecting portable computers

4 Retractable computer, flush-mounted in the table top, as the meeting convenor's workplace

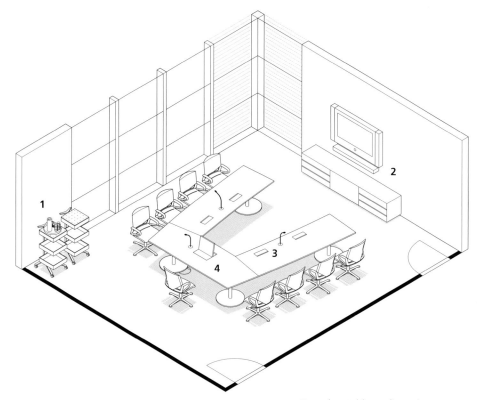

Horseshoe table configuration, facing the flat screen and providing nine to eleven places for presentation and videoconferencing applications

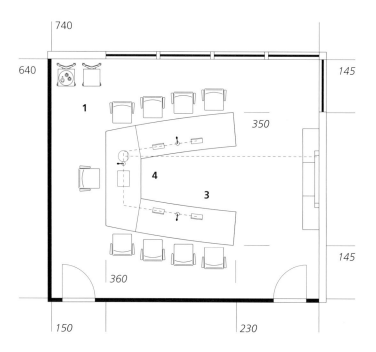

▸ Technical development has now reached a level that is both high and comparatively reasonably priced: high data transmission rates allow virtually synchronous transmission of images and sound, to a large extent jerk-free. For a videoconference, two conference rooms at different sites are each equipped with a display, a sound system and at least one integrated camera. Depending on room dimensions and the number of participants, the display will either be in the form of a large-format screen (min. 50 inch diagonals), front or rear projection. If the (wide angle) camera is positioned in the centre of the projection area (on a screen this is usually positioned in the centre at the upper edge of the projection area), image recording and image presentation will be along one visual axis so that participants have virtual eye contact.

The use of state-of-the-art multimedia technology in a conference environment now goes without saying for many companies. As well as being able to present digital or analogue data, this will tend to upgrade the significance of videoconferencing. In the wake of globalization, working at geographically distributed locations has become an integral part of everyday working life. Consensus beyond national borders and time zones is often necessary – for example, with a branch office, suppliers or customers. Establishing a call to one's discussion partners in a videoconference helps to build up confidence. Information communicated via images in addition by word and sound creates a higher level of calculability and hence security than, for example, a telephone conference. Besides, documents and objects may be shown so that both parties know exactly what is being discussed. This serves to increase the efficiency of the shared process of agreement and specific arrangements.

The number of participants in videoconferences in which interaction should involve all those at different conference sits, is by nature limited to eight to ten persons per room.

If frequent use is made of videoconferencing and presentations, it is advisable to specify a static, permanently installed table configuration that faces the display. In the illustrated specifiers' options on page 44, such a configuration comprises a horseshoe setup with angled side elements. Including a slight radius promotes interaction with one's immediate neighbour. The camera is integrated into the wall-mounted display. Such cameras generally cover a distortion-free angle of 60–90°. The maximum width of the table configuration is defined by the display diagonals, the angle of the camera and the distance from the two ends of the horseshoe configuration to the display surface. The angled position of the side sections of the configuration guarantees an unimpeded view of the display from every place, and vice versa the integrated camera can focus on any individual face. As an alternative to permanently installed camera systems, mobile versions are also available. The latter have swivel and tilt functions and automatically focus on a specific source of sound, i.e. on the person speaking at the moment.

A microphone that can pick up the sound from any direction is an adequate system for up to ten participants. Loudspeakers for output are generally integrated adjacent to the display to reproduce image and sound in the most natural and direct manner.

In the illustrated specifiers' option, the horseshoe table configuration has four disc base supports only that are linked underneath the table top by beams spanning up to three metres. Positionable table top bearers are arranged in such a manner to allow all technical equipment to be integrated into the frame and the retractable cable channels adapted to the specific length of the beams. Particularly in a conference environment equipped with high-end media technology, such equipment should be integrated as inconspicuously as possible and invisibly. To this end, four veneered table portals provide access to individually specifiable connectivity modules for two conference places each. Such modules may include power supply, image transmission, sound transmission, USB interface and "show-me function". This is where participants may connect their notebooks for the purpose of taking notes or to show their data on the presentation display if necessary. The volume of the cable channel provides adequate storage space for network adapters, battery chargers for mobile telephones and surplus cable. The dominant seat position of the horseshoe configuration is occupied by the convenor, and is equipped with an electrically retractable computer display. The back plate of the display is veneered to match the table top to create a uniform table surface when the display is retracted. The whole unit comprising a retractable mechanism, keyboard and display are integrated into one techni-frame which is an integral part of the table, thus ensuring that the weight load is supported by the table frame and not by the table top. All the functions of the large-format wall display are operated via a keyboard or a touch-sensitive display from this position: videoconferencing, presentations, DVD films, websites, etc. The entire room technology, including lighting, darkening the room, temperature and sound system can be also controlled from this workplace via an additional programmed menu.

Chairs with a memory return mechanism are recommended as a seating solution to ensure that chairs are correctly aligned with the table edge when users stand up. To complement technically high-end technology, the table configuration and seating should have a prestigious appeal: chromium-plated finishes, elegant veneers and upholstery in high-grade fabric or leather.

Videoconferences

▸ **Rooms used solely for videoconferencing purposes and ones that are networked with other similarly equipped environments at different sites may be furnished in such a way as to create the illusion of being in one single room. The more convincing this is, the more intensive human interaction and cooperation will be. As in a television studio, technical equipment for sound, camera, image and lighting is specified according to table size and format for optimal results.**

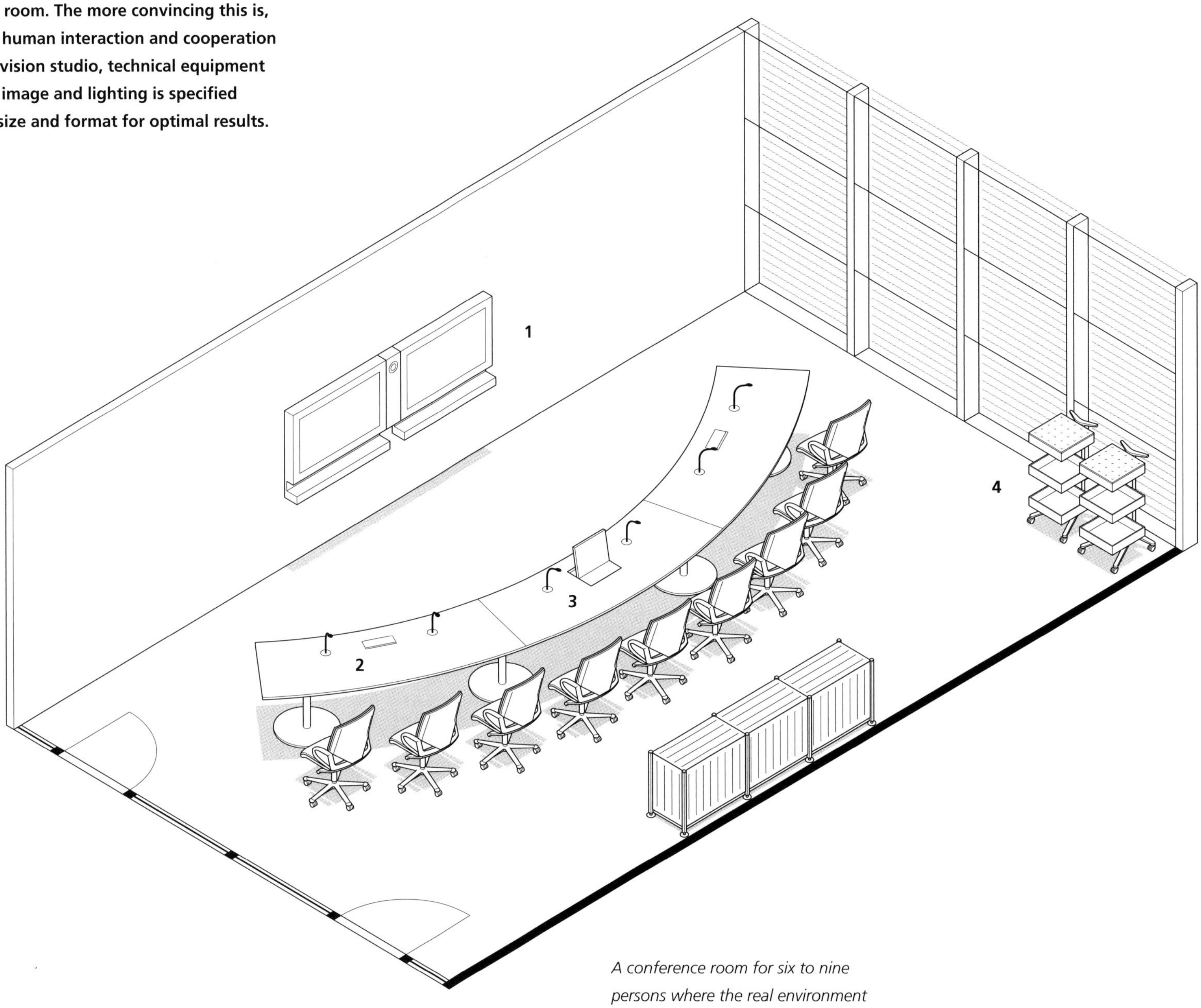

1

2

3

4

A conference room for six to nine persons where the real environment and the site that is connected for the transmission create the impression of sitting at one communal table configuration.

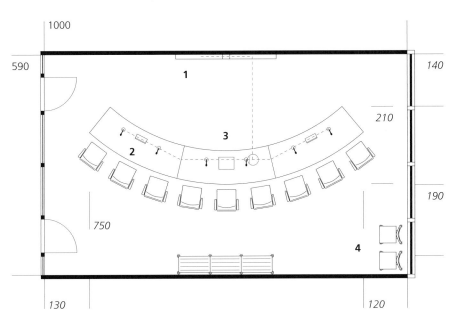

1000

590

140

210

190

750

130

120

1 Wall-mounted flat screen with a camera and loudspeakers
2 Techni-stations, flush-mounted in table tops, for connecting
   portable computers
3 Retractable computer, flush-mounted in the table top,
   as videoconference convenor's workplace
4 Server for writing utensils and pens or for catering materials

Globalization has frequently resulted in larger companies having locations spread throughout the world and thus to a rapid increase in business travel where highly paid managers in particular are not only exposed to physical strain but also to unproductive and often enough, incalculable waiting times – not to mention financial expenditure, such as for travelling, and negative ecological impact due to air traffic. Many of these personal meetings serve the exclusive purpose of reaching agreement on discussed issues. That is the reason why a growing number of companies set up professionally equipped videoconferencing facilities that are designed to merge the real environment with

the virtual part of the room connected via the transmission to form the impression of a shared workplace. Even if this saves only 20 per cent of travelling expenses, such a videoconferencing room soon pays off for companies with a high travel budget – after all, travelling expenses and time multiply with every participant.

The image projection area should if possible correspond to the width of the curved table segment which is rendered virtually in the form of a complete circle including participants from all sites. The projection area (ideally as large-format rear projection) is therefore integrated into the longest side of the room in contrast to "normal" conference environments. High-end sound technology and cameras switched in parallel are precisely coordinated with the size and form of the table configuration and the number of participants. The colour scheme of the walls forming the background is particularly important: as cameras adjust to the light values, muted, preferably darker colours are necessary so that faces are light and easily recognizable. New loudspeaker technologies avoid acoustic feedback and may be integrated completely invisibly into walls.

The table configuration comprises an elliptical table segment with a distance to the wall that is aligned with the camera angle so that it not only adjoins with the segment at the connected site. Frame constructions with just a few recessed table legs provide ample legroom and a variable number of places to avoid creating the impression of "unoccupied" places if there are varying numbers of participants. For the seating solution, the same criteria apply as described on page 45.

Variable videoconference

▸ If a conference room is used temporarily for presentations and videoconferences, but usually for meetings without media technology support, a flexible table configuration should be specified. On the one hand, it forms a solid conference table layout and on the other hand it may be changed for videoconferencing in such a way as to allow participants to have eye contact, but also to see the wall display and in turn to be focused on by the transmitting camera.

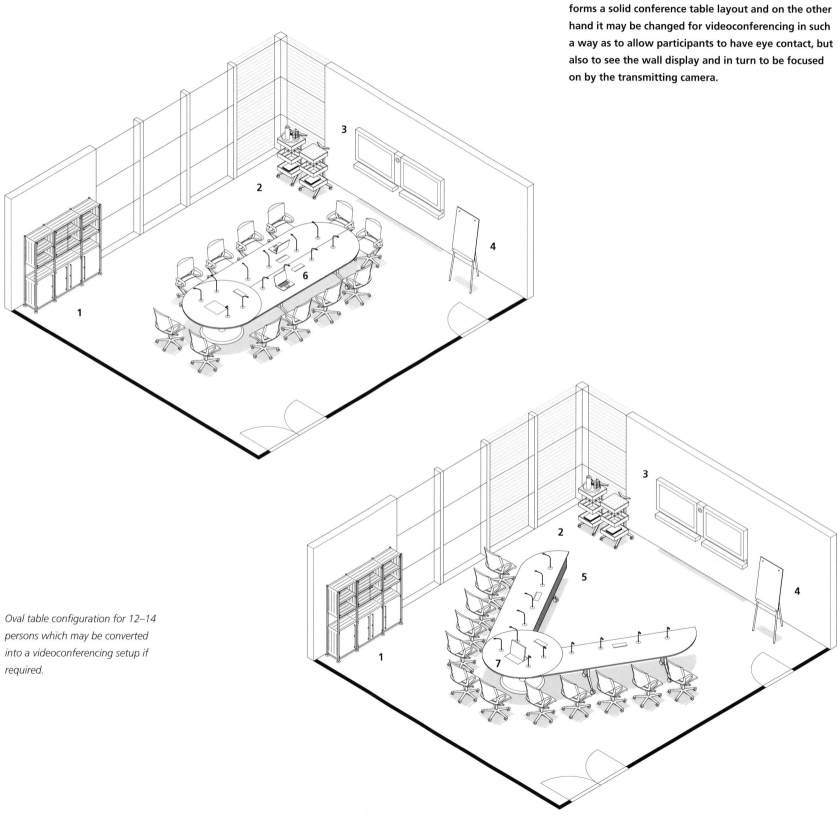

Oval table configuration for 12–14 persons which may be converted into a videoconferencing setup if required.

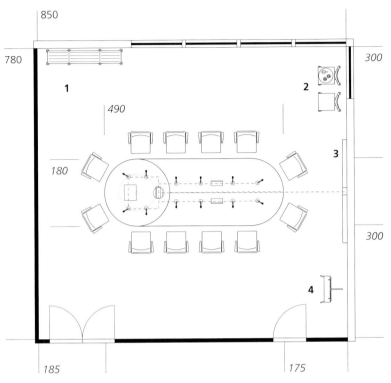

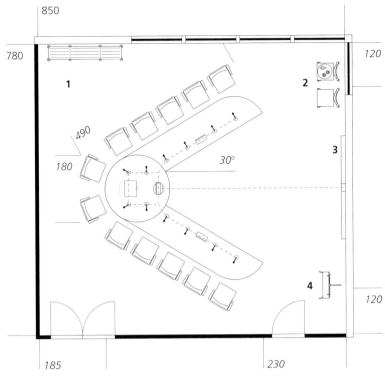

1 Sideboard for catering materials, tableware and incidentals
2 Server for writing utensils and pens or for catering materials
3 Wall-mounted flat screens
4 Flipchart for documentation of group discussions and as visual
   support for elaborating on topics
5 Modesty panels for privacy
6 Techni-stations, flush-mounted in table tops, for connecting
   portable computers
7 Retractable computer, flush-mounted in the table top,
   as videoconference convenor's workplace

In the illustrated specifiers' option, the top end of the table configuration comprises a round table with a bow-shaped guiding
rail mounted on the underside. The linked side flanks of the table
have castor wheels and, as articulating structures, they may be
opened up to face the V-shaped presentation surface. Depending
on requirements, all technical functions described in the previous
chapter may be integrated into the table configuration in this case
too. Cables are channelled in such a way as to follow the movements of the two table flanks. The round table is available with
a central pedestal base. If a master workplace with integrated display is to be specified, a construction with three table legs joined
by means of an underframe is advisable to provide the required
module depth and stability.

For surface finishes and versions the same general recommendations apply as for conference environments. Conference chairs
with swivel castors facilitate the changeover from a conventional
meeting setup to videoconferencing and back. With a view to
creating a calm overall appearance, height adjustability as well as
adjustable armrests should not be specified as described above.

Conference room for 32 persons

▸ The larger the conference room and the higher the number of participants, the more formal the conference setup becomes in order to ensure an efficient procedure. After all, spontaneous interaction with more than 20 participants is hardly possible. However, with a view to creating the feeling of equality amongst participants in spite of an unavoidably hierarchical procedure, circular tables are recommended that are coordinated with the geometry of the room. If the room is more than 12 metres long it will be necessary to specify microphone and loudspeaker systems so that even inexperienced speakers may be heard by all present. If visual media are used, the room should be high enough to ensure the required size of the projection area.

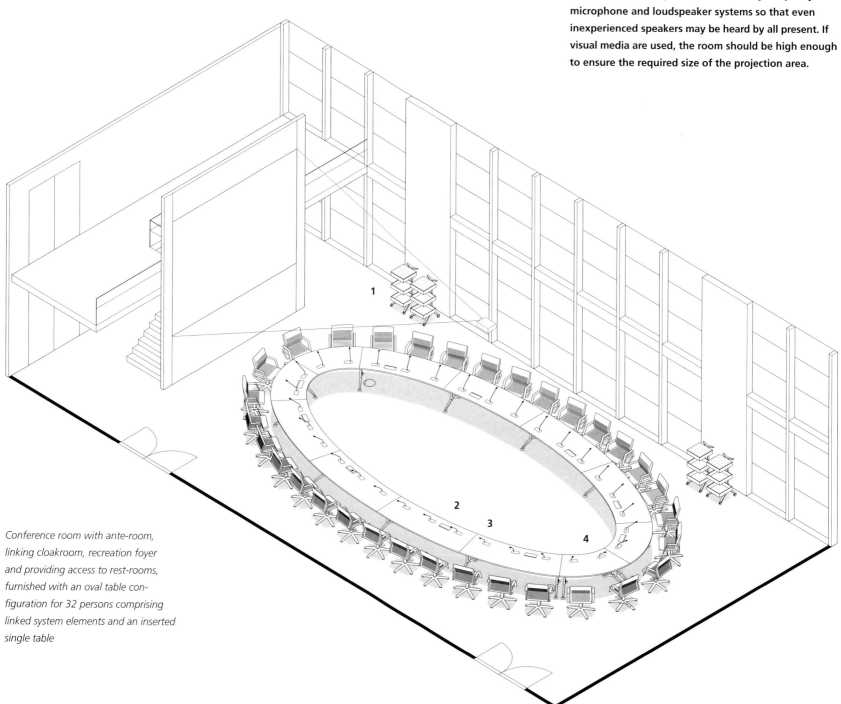

Conference room with ante-room, linking cloakroom, recreation foyer and providing access to rest-rooms, furnished with an oval table configuration for 32 persons comprising linked system elements and an inserted single table

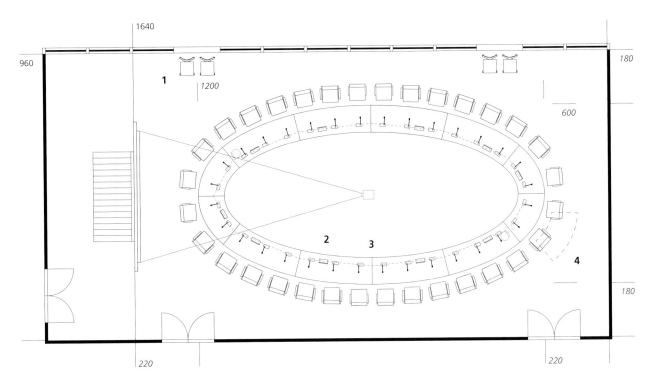

1 Server for catering materials
2 Techni-stations, flush-mounted
  in table tops, for connecting
  portable computers
3 Integrated microphone system
4 Mobile single table as removable
  segment, providing access
  to centre of table configuration

Conferences with large numbers of participants require clear structures and patterns to ensure smooth and efficient running. There are often requests to speak and lists of speakers are drawn up accordingly. It is very useful to have microphones that are activated by pressing a button so that frequent informal discussions on the side do not impair the attention of the plenary gathering. Oval to circular table forms convey a feeling of equality at all places around the table and make it easier to communicate with one's immediate neighbour. In the illustrated example, table top segments and frame structures form units which in turn define the seating order with either two or three places per segment.

Optionally it should be possible to retrofit modesty panels if a degree of privacy is required in spite of the aesthetic and almost floating appearance of the table configuration due to its open structure. Whether or not modesty panels are required depends to a large extent on how well participants know one another and on the respective corporate culture.

Besides, a point of access to the interior of solid configuration should be included so that the floor may be cleaned there without any extra effort. Using a precision-finished, dimensionally accurate table system that has linking elements, and single tables with the same aesthetic elegance on standby, a single table element may be removed from the otherwise permanently linked configuration like a "slice of cake".

In addition to microphones, techni-stations are also integrated into the table tops, providing connectivity for personal notebooks and other electronic devices.

The seating solution comprises prestigious swivel chairs with a high degree of seated comfort and ergonomic automatic synchro-adjustment that make long discussions and meetings at least physically bearable. Chairs with a restoring spring ensure that chairs are correctly aligned with the table edge when users stand up.

Conference room for 45 persons
with a table configuration and a platform

▸ In conferences with a high number of participants the table layout is frequently divided up into an auditorium and a platform. The seating order at the tables on the platform reflects the hierarchical structure of the members of the platform. A digital projector permanently mounted on the ceiling or a rear projector is used to project onto the area behind the platform. Those seated on the platform can follow presentations thus projected via screens integrated into their tables. If the number of participants exceeds the number of seats at tables, additional participants may take their seats in the second row as "backbenchers".

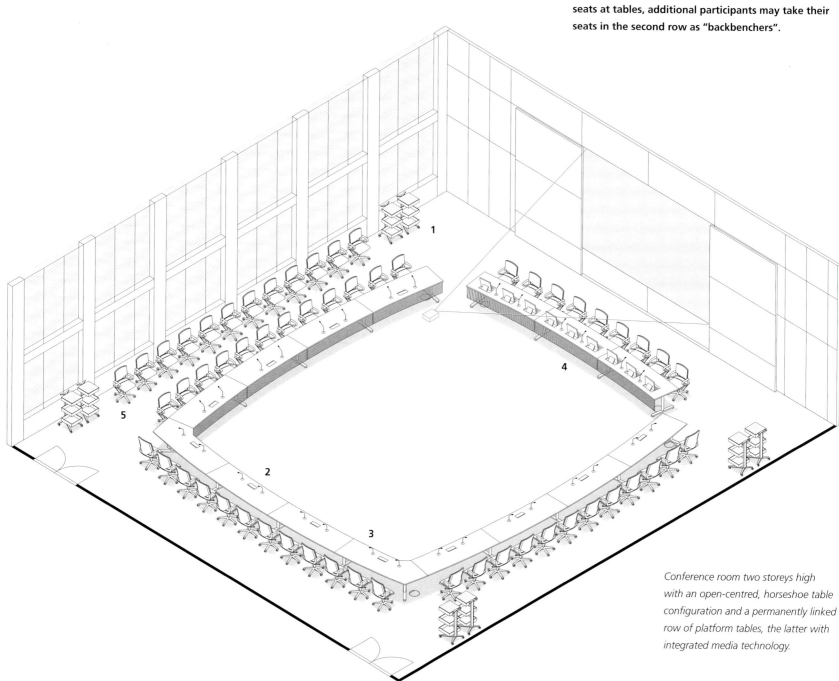

Conference room two storeys high with an open-centred, horseshoe table configuration and a permanently linked row of platform tables, the latter with integrated media technology.

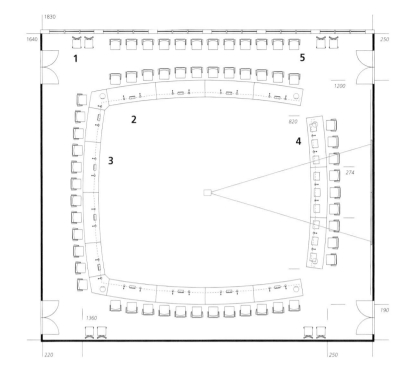

1   Server for conference material or for catering materials

2   Techni-stations, flush-mounted in table tops,
    for connecting portable computers

3   Integrated microphone system

4   Retractable flat screen display integrated into the tops
    of tables on the platform

5   Seats for assistants or interpreters

If a structure is required that is unequivocally hierarchical, for example, to emphasize the seats of board members, then a conference table configuration is divided into a platform and an auditorium. The seating order at the podium table positions the highest ranking person in the middle, while seats to the right and the left are occupied in order of descending authority. Participants in the auditorium are addressed by the speaker on the platform. If a presentation (either front or rear projection, depending on specific space requirements) is shown on the projection area behind the platform, flat screen displays integrated into the platform table may be opened up electrically to enable those on the platform to follow the presentation without having to turn round.

The seating order in the auditorium is generally laid down according to membership of sub-groups. If conference delegates are accompanied by assistants or if the auditorium comprises both board members with voting rights and general delegates, then the latter will usually sit in the second row behind the seats at tables. The same applies if interpreters are needed and no separate booths are available.

A static table configuration, customized to the radii of the horseshoe, is recommended. The radial form breaks up the strictness of the hierarchical arrangement somewhat and improves scope for interaction. Central frame structures with large spans provide generous legroom and permit chairs to be spaced as required. Besides, they facilitate floor cleaning.

Table portals with connectivity modules coherently integrated into the table tops allow state-of-the-art presentation and sound equipment, without the aesthetic appearance being dominated by technology. Depending on frame finishes, table edge finishes and veneer variations, a table system that is otherwise more "neutrally" prestigious can create a different spatial impression, ranging from conventionally dignified to highly modern.

Matching swivel chairs should be chosen that are clearly ergonomically suitable for long sessions: the more spacious the seat and back cushions, the more compact and traditional the spatial impression; the more graceful the contours, the more open and lighter the overall appearance. In this example, swivel chairs with backrests with flexible material and star bases on castors have been used to provide a dynamic quality that is both aesthetic and functional.

Table configurations
in the conference room

90

105, 120

73

90, 105, 120

180 + 75, 150, 225 +180

90° 45°

90° 45°

75, 150, 225

110, 120, 135

90, 105, 120

180 90, 105, 120

210
150

240

225

▸ Furnishing concepts for classic meeting and conference environments are frequently required to be coordinated with a specific corporate image – with a view to communicating a corresponding degree of prestige. Table configurations that meet these demands offer a host of table formats with varying, perfectly coordinated frame geometry that permit even standardized elements to be used to plan table forms to suit any specifications in terms of space and the number of participants to be accommodated. If the formats on offer are complemented by a wide selection of high-quality surface finishes and coating options, unmistakable furnishing solutions may be created.

Specifiers' option:
table configuration from the Logon range
with a chair from the Modus range

Conference table configurations

The forms of conference table configurations do not only consider basic floor space but also the type of communication preferred and the desired degree of interaction amongst participants. Standardized components may be used to create a large number of configurations: ranging from free-standing tables and elongated, linearly linked arrangements with either parallel edges or slightly boat-shaped to U-shaped configurations or open-centred layouts.

Modesty panels, which are easily inserted underneath the table tops, should be specified for U-shaped and open-centred configurations. In addition to providing a degree of privacy, they also serve as concealed cable management – for example, for microphones, headphones, plug-and-play connections, connectivity modules or integrated displays.

Frame constructions with a recessed underframe and uprights or with a central pedestal base and beams ensure generous legroom all round – at the ends of the table too.

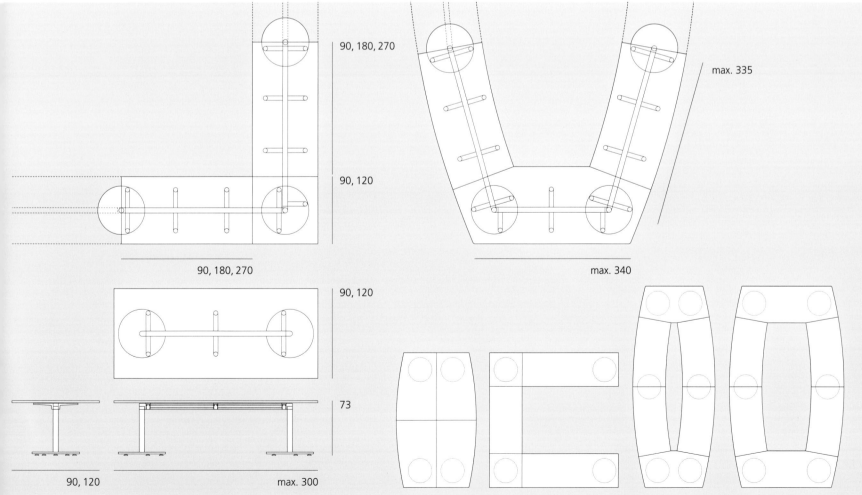

Customized conference table configurations

In spite of the wide scope afforded by series production, the construction should also allow special dimensions and formats. The ideal solution is provided by modular frame structures with individually definable beam lengths and table top bearers that are freely positionable in the beams. As the pedestal legs act as an articulating structure, linking angles may be varied to provide a supporting structure for virtually any table form and configuration. If table top segments are not tied to a certain frame structure but are freely positionable, it is advisable not only to specify the absolutely necessary feature of glides that may be adjusted to level out floor irregularities, but also to include a unique adjustment and leveller device on the table top bearers to fine-tune dimensional tolerance. This facilitates assembly and permits the entire frame structure including cable channels, power supply and integrated technical equipment to be installed before positioning and fixing table tops.

Materials and surface finishes
For table systems with smaller modules, in which table top segments and frame structures form a definite whole, foot sections and table top bearers are in die-cast aluminium, and uprights and recessed underframes are in extruded aluminium profile. Surface finishes are bright chromium-plated, polished or powder coated to match the frame concept, uprights may also optionally be clear anodized. Chromium plating for foot sections provides the hardest and most insensitive finish and such structures look lighter and more graceful as the surface is highly light reflecting.

For wider table spans, circular pedestal columns in steel tube are used, optionally with either a T-shaped base in die-cast aluminium or with a disc base in steel. Chromium-plated and coated finishes permit great versatility in terms of coordination in such a context too. It should however be considered that such reflections on large surfaces, such as a disc base in stainless steel with a high-lustre polished finish, may also divert too much attention to the area underneath the table. In this case, brushed or coated finishes would be a better option. Besides a host of standardized solutions, such table ranges with beams of varying length that may be linked with the pedestal column to form a an articulating structure permit high flexibility for specifying configurations in terms of form and format.

Different types of edging to merge with an existing design theme should be available for such table configurations: straight, double bullnose or finely chamfered edge profiles combine with table top finishes to create widely differing ambiences. For segmented table configurations, lipping in tactile laminated wood with integral impact protection in black rubber profile is a variation that is both practical and graceful. Table finishes should be in veneer, linoleum or laminated wood to match the colour scheme, materials and degree of wear and tear required by the relevant interior.

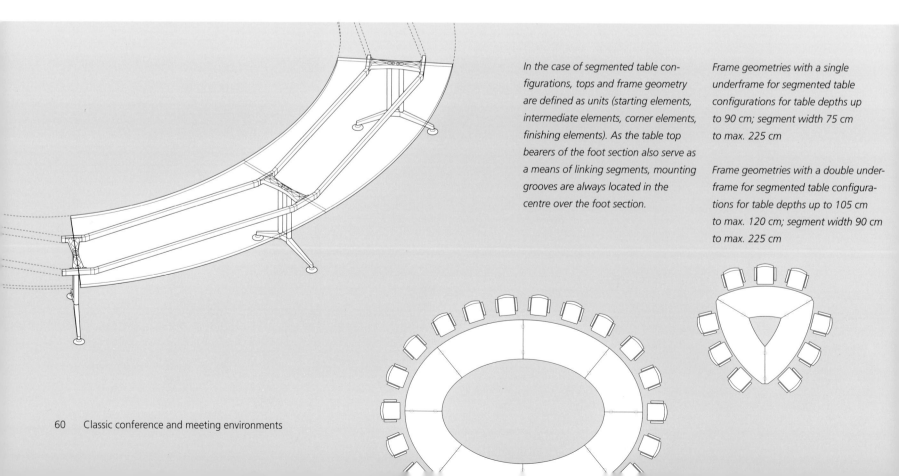

In the case of segmented table configurations, tops and frame geometry are defined as units (starting elements, intermediate elements, corner elements, finishing elements). As the table top bearers of the foot section also serve as a means of linking segments, mounting grooves are always located in the centre over the foot section.

Frame geometries with a single underframe for segmented table configurations for table depths up to 90 cm; segment width 75 cm to max. 225 cm

Frame geometries with a double underframe for segmented table configurations for table depths up to 105 cm to max. 120 cm; segment width 90 cm to max. 225 cm

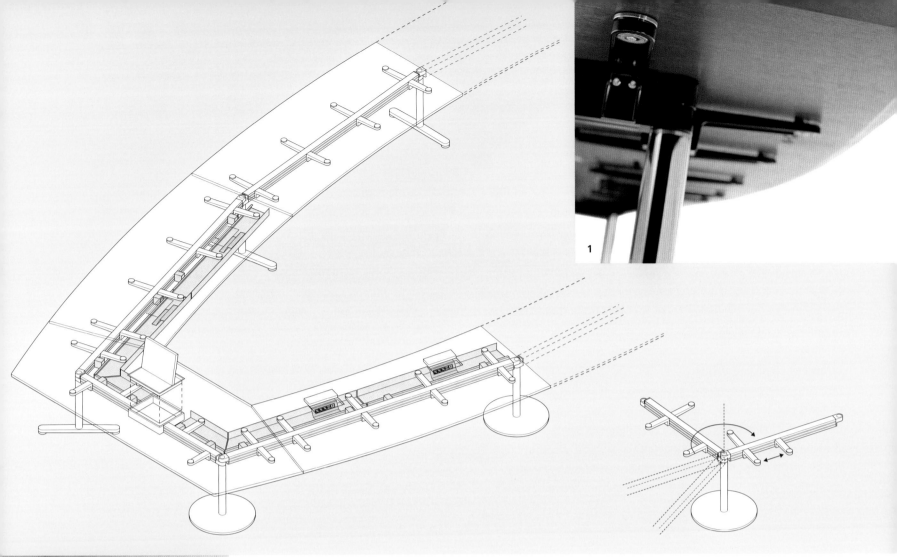

In the case of beam-structure table systems permitting flexibility in terms of form and format, the frame comprises pedestal legs that are connected via central beams with mounting grooves, to form an articulating structure. As the table top bearers slide into the mounting grooves they may be positioned or added to as required to configure a frame to suit virtually any table top geometry.

Table top segments are linked to a large extent independently of the position of the pedestal base. The only point that must be considered is that the table top should not project over the point of attachment on the pedestal support more than 45 cm.

For frame geometries infinitely articulating within a range of 90° to 180° via beams, for scalable table depths of 90 cm to 120 cm and intervals between pedestal bases of 70 cm to 300 cm.

Specifiers' option:
table configuration from the Travis range (1);
table configuration from the Logon range
with chairs from the Modus Conference range (2)

Chairs in conference environments

Conference chairs with a solid wood frame or a combination of aluminium, steel and moulded plywood are an ideal solution for conference environments where the natural appearance of wood with a perfectly crafted finish should contribute to interior design. In the USA, Asia and Australia, overall eco-balances are drawn up for buildings that also assess furniture and equipment. In addition to non-composite materials, easy repair and recyclability, the use of renewable raw materials for frames, seat and back bearers, upholstery material and covers can be an added bonus.

In view of strenuous meetings involving lengthy wrestling for decisions, not only aesthetic quality is important but also seated comfort and the ergonomic design of conference chairs. Thick upholstery may look comfortable at first glance but it frequently does not provide the necessary degree of support. Flexibility of the backrest and support in the lumbar region are absolutely vital. If conference environment involves frequent changeover between presentations and discussions, an ideal solution would be to select swivel chairs or even light conference chairs that can be moved easily to a new position to re-establish eye contact with other participants. Even in classic conference environments, swivel chairs on castors are now being used more and more. However, with a view to creating a calm appearance, chairs with height-adjustable armrests should not be specified as armrests may be damaged easily if they are caught under the edge of the table. Height-adjustable chairs are generally not necessary either as participants in conferences do not sit in one fixed position in contrast to computer work – after all a conference thrives on human interplay with correspondingly frequent changes in posture.

When selecting upholstery materials and covers, the length of intended periods of sitting should also be considered. Leather is still regarded as a symbol of highly prestigious organizations; it is extremely hardwearing and over the years it acquires a characteristic patina through traces of use, and serves to underline corporate tradition. Leather is however only air-permeable to a limited extent and depending on body heat and ambient temperature, it may be either cold or warm. Nowadays high performance fabrics are available with a suede-like appearance that have all the advantages of air-permeable materials in terms of sitting climate. Upholstery materials should also be perspiration-absorbent and air permeable. A layer of fleece between the cushion and the cover prevents wear and tear and can optimize the sitting experience. As covers are subject to faster wear and tear in terms of colour, pattern and durability than other functional parts of a chair they should always be exchangeable. This will allow any chair to look like new after exchanging the cover, should it be required, and at relatively low cost. Not only does it save money but it is also kind to the environment.

It is important to select armrests that act as a support for the user to stand up. In any case, armrest pads with a pleasant, tactile quality should be specified. Metal armrests may look aesthetic but due to the inherent conductivity of the material they are unpleasant without armrest pads. Wood, high-quality, textured plastic pads or options with fabric or leather covering are suitable material and finish variations depending on the materials and design concept used.

Depending on the specific corporate culture and design concept, conference rooms are either furnished to relate to the interiors of offices and meeting areas or may also be treated as completely independent units that are intentionally different. In the first case, it is advisable to select chair families to achieve a coherent design language in spite of their being differentiated in terms of features and appearance. In the second case, seating may be selected independently and used as an iconic design statement.

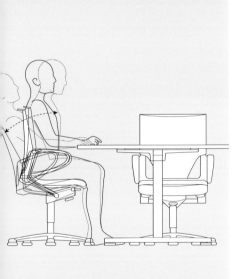

Specifiers' option:
swivel chairs from the Modus Conference range (1);
swivel chairs from the FS range (2)

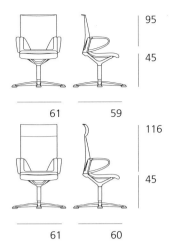

		95
		45
61	59	
		116
		45
61	60	

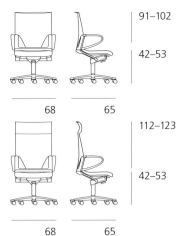

		91–102
		42–53
68	65	
		112–123
		42–53
68	65	

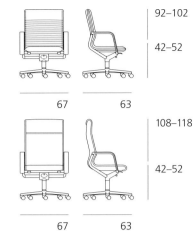

		92–102
		42–52
67	63	
		108–118
		42–52
67	63	

Swivel chairs

These chairs have the advantage of promoting changes in posture and facilitating changes in viewing direction. A four-star base is permissible if glides are specified. Swivel castors however require a five-star base. The symmetry of a four-star base has a calmer appearance allowing it to be aligned parallel to table edges. Optionally, swivel chairs may be fitted with a restoring spring which causes them to align automatically when the user stands up. If a non-dynamic sitting posture is required during conferences, a non-swivel seat bearer may be used. In the latter case, the backrest should adjust flexibly to varying body dimensions, and a pelvic support should ensure an upright sitting position. Even if firm, ergonomically designed upholstery is selected, a user should not sit on a chair without a break for more than 90 minutes.

For longer periods of sitting, it is advisable to select swivel chairs with automatic synchro-adjustment that promote change in posture and, due to optimal adjustment of the seat/backrest angle, avoid permanent, one-sided strain whilst stimulating metabolism. The seat mechanism is coordinated synchronously with the user's body when leaning backwards and creates neither pressure on thighs nor the feeling of slipping off the chair. The counter pressure of the backrest should be easily adjustable to compensate for extreme variations in body weight and height of users. Locking mechanisms generally prevent crucially necessary changes in posture, and when users stand up the result is generally a chaotic overall appearance. Without a locking mechanism, backrests automatically return to their original position. In addition to ergonomic quality, aesthetics are important in this respect too. The more slender and inconspicuous a mechanism, the less likely it is that the impression of an array of sitting machines will be created.

Materials and surface finishes
The frames and mechanisms of swivel chairs should be manufactured from precision-finished and dimensionally stable materials to ensure longevity and value preservation. In contrast to steel, aluminium is much lighter and can be either powder coated or bright chromium-plated, or also be left untreated and polished. From an ecological point of view, aluminium is also recommended for durable products as the material cycle is easy to set up, in addition to saving on the quantity of material: this material can be recycled without any quality loss whereby considerable energy can be saved compared to virgin production.

There are various, possible solutions for the seat and back: a frame construction with stretch material creates a very graceful ambience. The fabric has resilient properties for adapting to differing body dimensions and may be semi-transparent – e.g. in climatic zones where permanent ventilation is important. Slim cushions with triple-sewn seams convey a soft feel, luxurious character. Optionally, covers with stitched fluting may be used.

Air-permeable foam, sewn-in fleece and high-quality upholstery materials – natural or high performance – promote a pleasant and healthy sitting climate.

Chairs in conference rooms

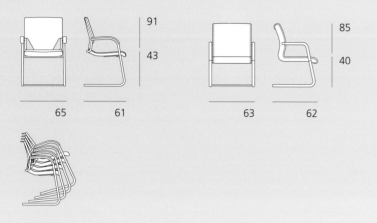

91
43

65   61

85
40

63   62

1

Cantilever chairs

Cantilever chairs are also an interesting option for a classic conference environment if they are marked by high-quality design and spacious dimensions. Due to their flexible construction, they provide a high degree of seated comfort with relatively low material dimensions. With a frame to match the table, these models give any conference environment a distinctive touch. The straight lines of the horizontal upper edge of the backrest emphasize a calm appearance by repeating the horizontals of the table edges and the ceiling.

As for swivel chairs, various seat and back constructions are available: fork-shaped, backrests with resilient material, a fully upholstered seat bearer and backrest bearer, which comprise moulded laminated wood in the illustrated specifiers' option, or – to meet very high demands – steel tube frames manufactured using traditional craft techniques, with elasticated netting embedded in foam. The same applies to the upholstered version whereby the choice is between a resilient, semi-transparent material (with frame construction) and classic upholstery with side facings.

Materials and surface finishes
Frames comprise steel tube, optionally coated, bright chromium-plated or also matt chromium-plated (to match polished surface finishes). The cross section of the steel tube may be made even more slender if structural stress is reduced by means of additional bracing. Depending on the flooring, different types of glides should be specified: glides with an additional felt insert should be used on wooden floors; soft plastic glides are required for hard floors and carpets needs either hard glides or no glides at all. With regard to upholstery materials and covers, the same applies as for swivel chairs.

2

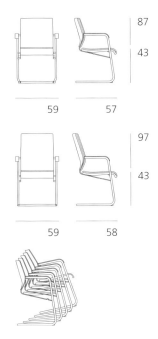

87
43
59   57

97
43
59   58

83
44
64   59

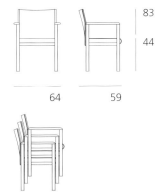

Four-legged conference chairs

With these archetypal chairs with a four-leg frame, seated comfort is not due to a mechanically dynamic and resilient frame, but to the flexibility of the backrest and the upholstery. As this flexibility is limited, depending on the degree of comfort they afford, four-legged chairs should only be used for sitting periods not exceeding 75 minutes. Participants should then take a break, stand up and move.

To facilitate changes in posture and moving chairs away from the table or back to the table or turning them round, attention should be paid to selecting lightweight models, particularly with armrests that are easy to grasp. Moreover, the static load stress is also a key criterion for choosing material. Four-legged chairs can therefore be made from solid or moulded wood (plywood), aluminium and steel constructions. With a view to reducing weight, if steel is to be specified it should be restricted to useful components such as seat bearers.

Four-legged chairs should be stackable if they are to be kept on standby for variable seating layouts. The underside of the seat platform should however be sufficiently smooth to ensure that no pressure marks are left by the stacking process.

Skid-base chairs

Due to the frame structure forming a stable structural grid, these chairs may be produced with substantially lower material cross sections, giving them an extremely graceful appearance. This impression is enhanced optically by a backrest covered in transparent material. If a curved, veneered plywood shell with an applied seat cushion is used as a seat bearer that also extends to form armrests, which are optionally covered on the inside, these chairs create an informal, almost private conference ambience. Such chairs, as well as four-legged models, are therefore more suitable for smaller conference groups where there is a high degree of familiarity among participants. For larger gatherings, such a casual look would collide with the desired formal character of the conference.

Materials and surface finishes

The leg frames and seat frames of four-legged chairs may comprise solid wood, with backrests in moulded wood or aluminium profile, and have an underframe and seat bearer in steel. The frames of skid-base chairs are formed by chromium-plated steel rod. A combination of materials is particularly attractive: metal frames with seat shells in veneered plywood or armrests in laminated wood, the latter conveying a pleasant tactile quality. Wooden surfaces may be stained in various colours, for example, to match a veneered table top.

As surface protection, low-solvent, water-based lacquer applied using an open-pore technique is advisable to maintain the natural structure of the wooden surface. If technical materials such as aluminium and steel are used, the frame should be coordinated with table frame finishes: clear anodized, bright chromium-plated or coated. Solid wood chairs should have upholstered armrests to make the natural character of the wood visible. Renewable materials such as coconut rubber may be used for the seat and backrest. Otherwise, the same criteria apply here in terms of air permeability, exchangeability and sitting climate as for swivel chairs and cantilever versions.

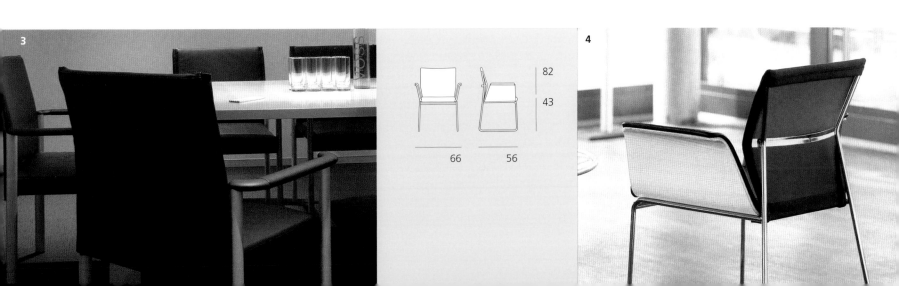

3

82
43
66   56

4

Partitionable conference room with integrated media technology for 22 persons

▸ If larger conference rooms are only needed sporadically for 20 participants or more, it is advisable from an economical point of view to equip the room with a mobile partition allowing greater application scope to achieve more efficient space utilization. A small group would also feel comfortable in the partitioned room, and two groups may even meet in parallel. This allows two small conference rooms to be saved.

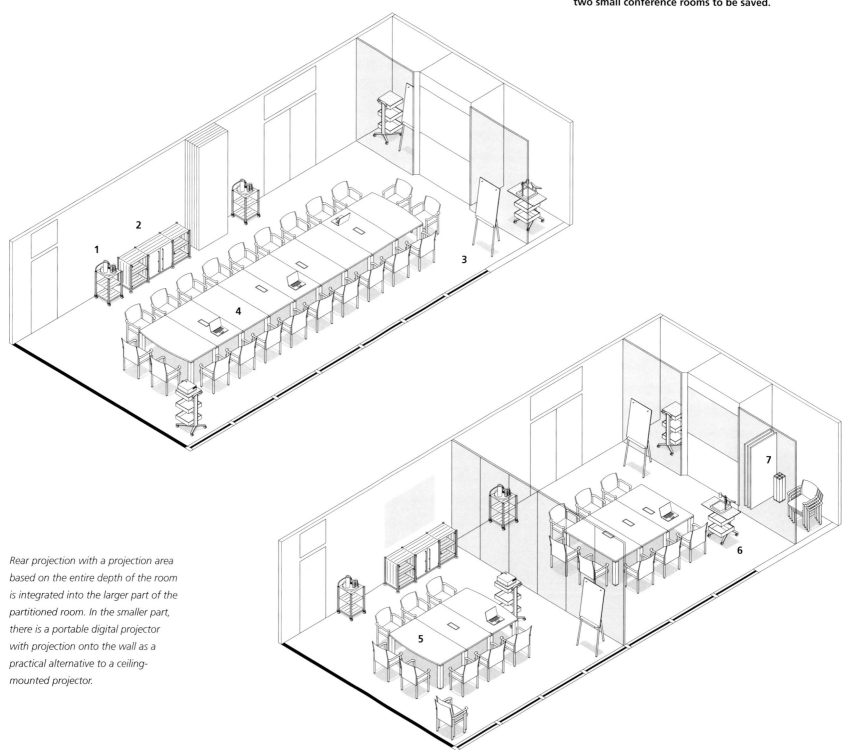

Rear projection with a projection area based on the entire depth of the room is integrated into the larger part of the partitioned room. In the smaller part, there is a portable digital projector with projection onto the wall as a practical alternative to a ceiling-mounted projector.

Scale 1:125 / dimensions in cm
(1 cm = 0.39 inches)
Area 79 sqm
Effective area 70 sqm
Store 9 sqm

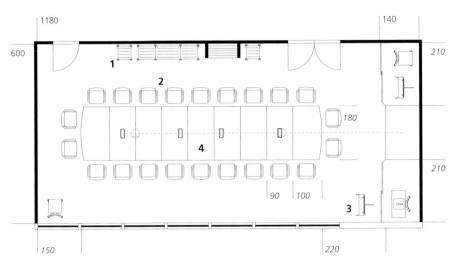

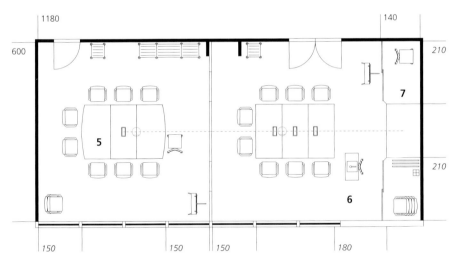

1   Catering trolley to match the sideboard
2   Sideboard for catering materials, tableware and incidentals
3   Flipchart for documentation of group discussions and as visual support
    for elaborating on topics
4   Prestigious, variable system table configuration with flush-mounted techni-station

5   Divided system table configuration after three segments have been removed
6   Server with video visualizer
7   Storage space for countless table tops, table legs and chairs after partitioning room

When planning partitionable conference rooms, the following must be considered: both halves of the room must have a separate access and lighting, and if possible also air conditioning and temperature should have separate controls. Both parts of the room should have sufficient daylight, and last but not least, the partition should have a common appearance on both sides. Conventional partitioning systems are designed to shield the rooms that are thus created in such a manner that events can easily take place in parallel, even considering acoustic aspects.

Variable application does however have certain implications with regard to furniture: instead of a tailor-made, static table configuration, such a scenario requires a table system that is firmly linked while remaining variable. For this purpose, it is advantageous to select a table construction where the choice is not between extension leaves and single tables. This facilitates storage, and when reconfiguration is necessary only some of the table surfaces have to be removed or changed around for partitioning as any table leg can be connected to any table top according to one principle. Nowadays, variable conference tables can be fitted with connectivity modules for any media technology necessary and any electronic devices that may be required at the individual workplace. Cabling between tables may be connected in series by means of permanently installed cable channels, accessible via table portals in table tops, by means of integrated connectivity modules and using simple, plug-in cable connections. Either part of the partitioned room would only need one floor port to supply the respective table configuration. For a perfect synthesis of variable space utilization and state-of-the-art conference technology.

Stackable conference chairs are coordinated with the respective application in terms of form and function. On the one hand, they are prestigious and spacious, and on the other hand, chairs that are not required at a particular time may be stored compactly.

The remaining space in the media wall is not only used to accommodate technical equipment and a video rear projection system, but also serves as a storeroom for table tops and legs not in use, as well as for spare conference chairs. Flipcharts and a materials server, a server with a visualizer, as well as a sideboard with matching catering servers complete the interior of a partitionable conference room.

Conference room with variable table configuration for 16 and 24 persons

Prestigious, octagonal table configuration with integrated techni-stations for two workplaces each and with two electrically retractable flat displays at those workplaces that do not have an unimpeded view of the projection area. The configuration may be extended by eight places using four rectangular table tops, three of which are equipped with techni-stations and one with a flat display.

▸ **With a view to being able to increase the number of seats in prestigious conference rooms too as required, a system table solution is ideal where the variable configurability of seats is not conspicuous. The octagonal table configuration, 460 cm in diameter, with two seats per table top segment, may be extended to 650 cm in diameter to accommodate a large group of 24. The distortion-free table tops without an underframe and the square table legs positioned flush with the corners convey a high degree of stability. What is however unique is that not only the table tops but also the permanently integrated connectivity modules, linked in series, may be extended by eight workplaces without any great effort in terms of installation in no time at all.**

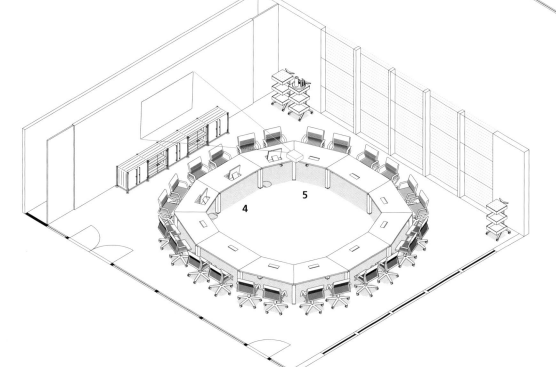

1 Storage space for conference chairs, spare table tops and legs

2 Mobile server for material and catering materials

3 Sideboard for catering materials, tableware and incidentals

4 Variable system table configuration with flush-mounted techni-stations and computer displays that are not directly facing the projection area

5 Ceiling-mounted data projector

In highly prestigious management areas, table configurations are frequently used that are intended to convey a feeling of reassuring longevity. Solid table tops, with sturdy legs and each connecting two table segments that should define places very clearly, stand for a high degree of value preservation and stability. Additionally, full connectivity for modern communication and media technology is integrated underneath the table portals that are veneered to match the table surface. The two segments with the integrated, electrically retractable displays permit participants to follow presentations in the rear room. In spite of the feeling of communicative equality conveyed by the configuration, these high-end displays clearly define their places as being reserved for conference leadership.

However, such table layouts with technically sophisticated equipment remain reconfigurable if it is easy to release table top-table leg connectors to add further extension elements, each with two legs – even if integrated conference technology may be extended correspondingly easily too.

The figure at the bottom shows an open-centred, octagonal table configuration comprising eight customized segments, each connected to the adjoining one by means of two legs. Segmented cable management channels immediately below the table surfaces with permanently installed connectivity modules serve all workplaces. It is child's play to connect adjoining segments by means of only three short plug-in cables. If the configuration is to be extended – in the example it is by adding rectangular segments on either side – just pull the plugs, unlock the legs, move

them along and add two table legs to create four free-standing "quarter segments of a circle". These are then pulled out just far enough so as to allow the extension elements (each with a cable channel segment and a display) to be positioned exactly in between. Now lock the extension elements onto the table tops, plug in the cables and the table configuration is again ready for action – now to accommodate 24 delegates and with the appearance of being permanently installed in the room.

In line with the furnishing level, high-quality conference chairs on castors have been selected as a seating solution. Table extension elements, additional table legs and extra chairs are stored neatly behind the media wall.

Scale 1:125 / dimensions in cm
(1 cm = 0.39 inches)
Area 110 sqm / Effective area 100 sqm / Store 10 sqm

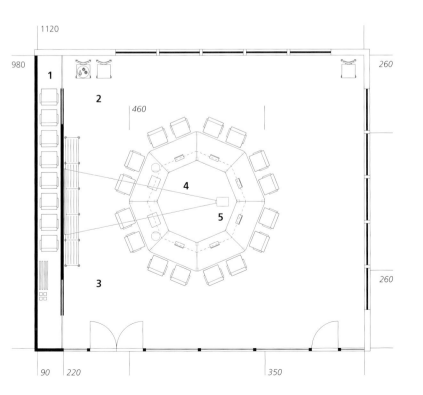

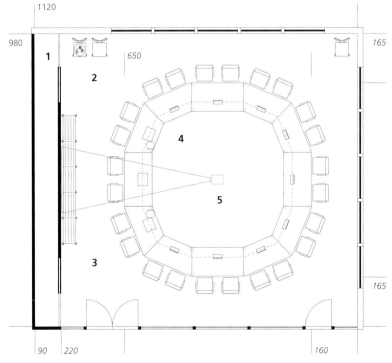

Variable table configurations

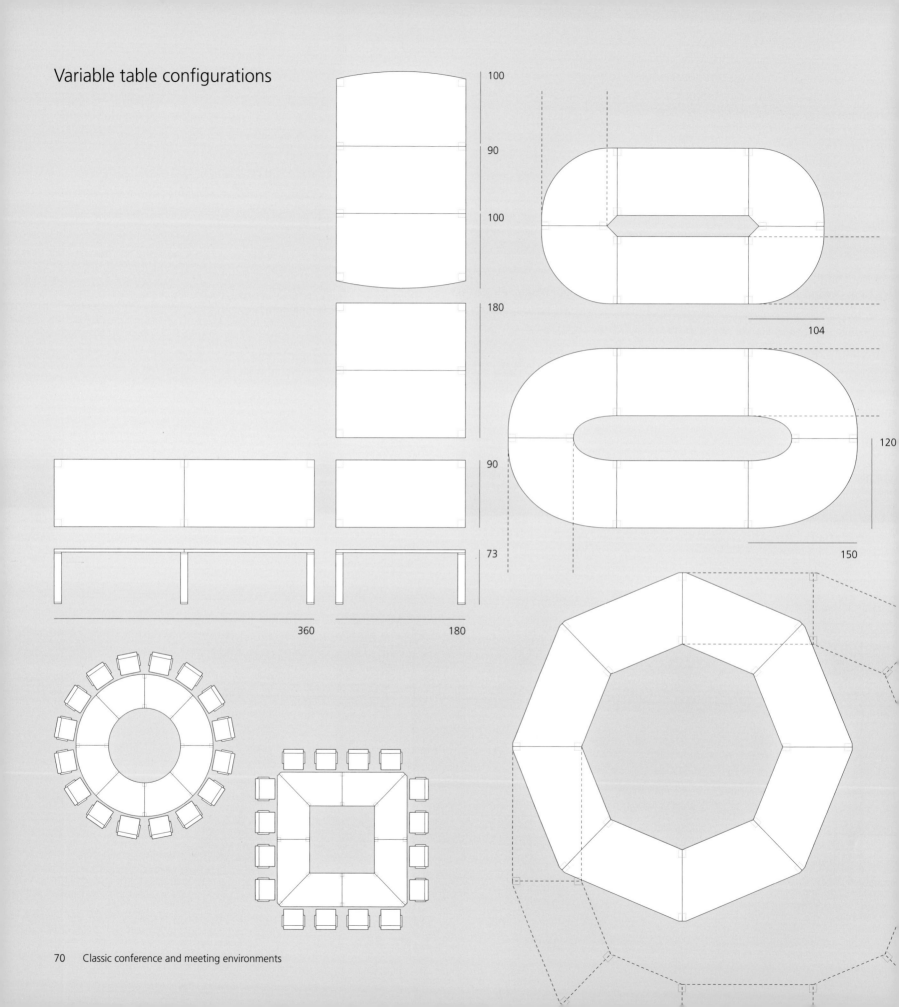

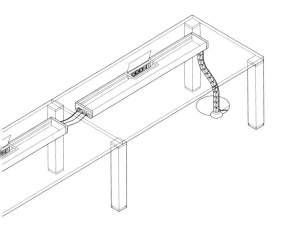

Variable table configurations

The advantage of such a system is that reconfiguration may be carried out at any time and largely without the use of tools. In a conference room that is portioned into two parts, it is advisable to position the table configuration in such a way that only one segment of the table has to be removed after dividing up the room and the greater part of the original configuration remains unchanged. In order to meet such requirements, the variability of the system should be based on an intelligent principle of connecting table legs and table surfaces.

If the table configuration is to be equipped with power supply for the integration of modern communication and media technology, corresponding table tops should be fitted with flat cable channels in light yet stable extruded aluminium profile that include permanently installed connectivity modules that are retained immediately underneath the table portals (with a hinged 180° opening mechanism). Cable channels have a side cover with integral plug-in facilities for short connecting cables. Such technology allows up to 40 delegate places to be connected modularly and in series without any quality loss in image output.

Materials and surface finishes
Distortion-free material comprising light sandwich panel or laminboard is required for table tops for the linking tables as described above. Suitable materials include linoleum or veneer, whereby the veneer leaves must be laid by the slip-match method onto the table top.

The table legs in square, extremely stable aluminium profile are clear anodized, or coated in the colour silver or black.

Specifiers' option:
table configuration from the Palette range
and chair from the Versal range

Table tops and legs may, for example, be connected by means of bayonet lock. At one end of the table such a lock accepts all four pins of a table leg. When linking table tops, the table leg is however moved along so that two of these pins are locked into the bayonet mechanism on the first table and the other two pins in the mechanism on the adjoining table top.

With this linking principle, all table tops should be sufficiently bend-resistant to make additional underframes – which would only restrict legroom – superfluous. Adjustable glides to level out floor irregularities are necessary for aligning larger table configurations.

The scope for tailoring design concepts may be extended even further by combining the locking mechanism with other forms of table legs.

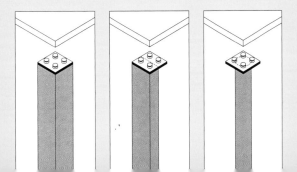

Variable multimedia conference room for 36 persons …

As hardly any conference is held today without using multimedia technology and as space is a considerable cost factor both in terms of building and maintenance, it is economically efficient to plan multimedia conference rooms allowing variable partitioning. What seemed virtually impossible years ago is now child's play: fast partitioning and variable configuration of tables to accept technically sophisticated equipment. This has become possible due to combining statically the linked table elements of a configuration with suitable mobile and folding table units, each equipped with connectivity modules for data, power and audio, optionally also for network connections. Such modules should be modular and connectable in series.

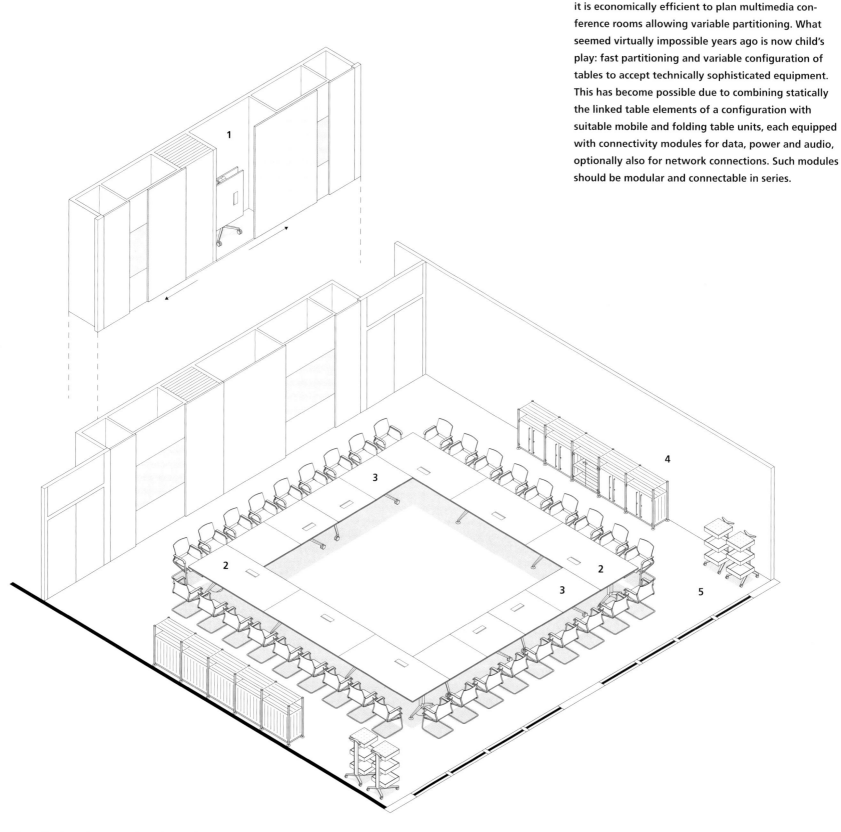

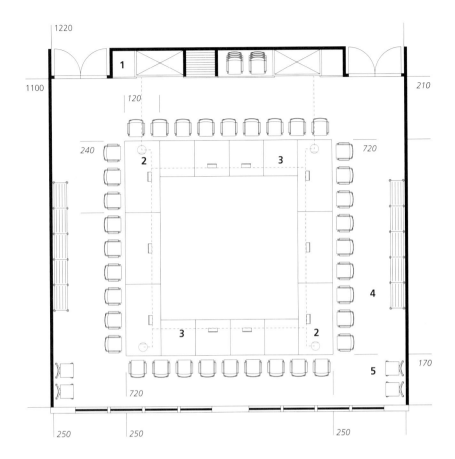

1 Technical equipment room with two rear
   projection screens, a store for spare furniture
   and storage space for the partition – lockable
   with sliding panels

2 Permanently installed table configuration ...

3 ... mobile folding tables, each with
   flush-mounted techni-stations

4 Sideboard

5 Mobile server for catering materials
   and incidentals

In the past, table configurations with technically sophisticated equipment made variability of space and table configurations impossible: installation effort that was necessary for any change in table configurations was so high that it resulted in conference rooms of varying size with permanently linked tables being reserved for specific numbers of participants rather than variable concepts being implemented. Using innovative connectivity modules and corresponding cables, it is now possible to connect up to 40 user workplaces in series with simple plug-in connections. If this technology is combined with variable table ranges, in which the required technical equipment is permanently installed, rooms and table configurations may be divided up quite easily.

Combinations of statically linked table configurations with mobile, folding tables, both with coordinated design, mark a solution that is highly variable and economical in terms of maintenance costs. Cable channels with connectivity modules are integrated into the folding tables in a way that does not impair the folding function of the table. Just three cables and corresponding plugs, which are inserted into the side covers of the cable channels, are required to link folding tables together and with static table elements.

… and partitioned for 20 and for 24 persons

Scale 1:125 / dimensions in cm
(1 cm = 0.39 inches)
Area after partitioning
72 sqm + 62 sqm

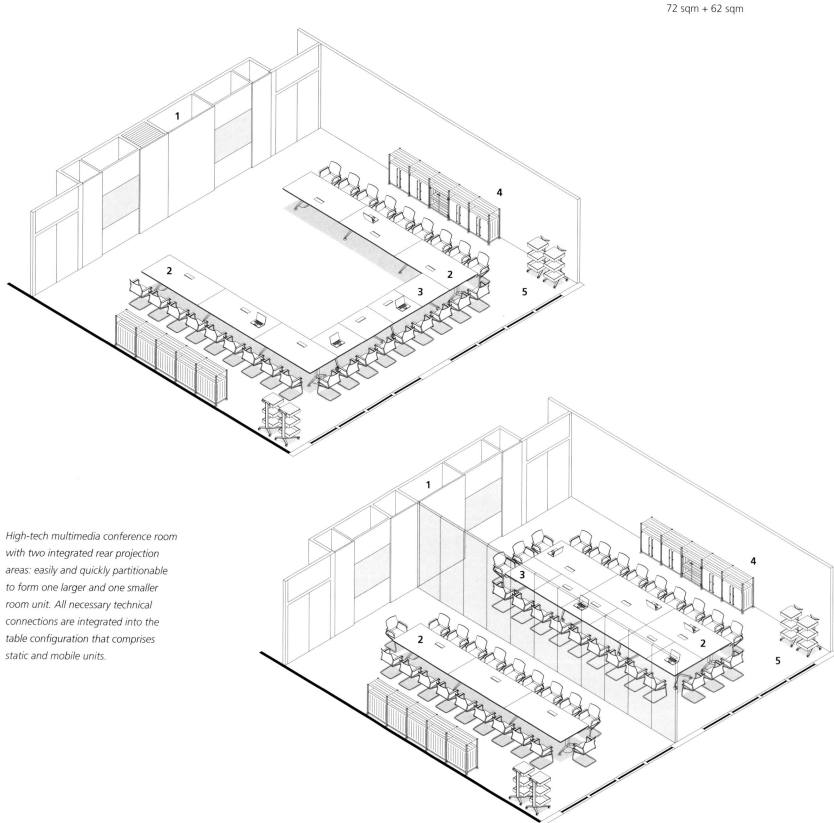

High-tech multimedia conference room with two integrated rear projection areas: easily and quickly partitionable to form one larger and one smaller room unit. All necessary technical connections are integrated into the table configuration that comprises static and mobile units.

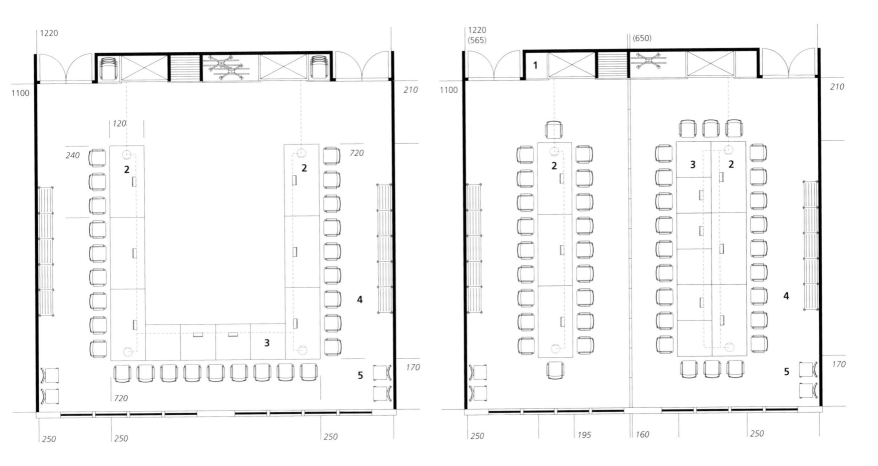

1 Technical equipment room with two rear projection
   screens, store for extra furniture and storage space
   for the partition – lockable with sliding panels
2 Permanently installed table configuration …
3 … mobile folding tables,
   each with flush-mounted techni-stations
4 Sideboard
5 Mobile server for catering materials and incidentals

Extra costs compared with static table configurations with conventional cabling pay off quickly when such solutions are chosen: rooms may be adapted to meet the requirements of conference delegates in no time at all by just one person, and no specialized IT capacities are required for operating them. In addition, a partitionable room can be more efficiently utilized by saving on extra rooms with corresponding technology. Last but not least, just one floor port with sockets is necessary per section of the room, a benefit which makes such solutions even more attractive, particularly in existing building structures.

In order to avoid damage to table edges caused by frequent reconfiguration of tables, it is advisable to specify edging with integrated rubber profile.

In the illustrated specifiers' option, 36 and 27 delegate places are available for the plenary conference and for the presentation setup – 20 and 24 places if used as partitioned rooms. It is therefore useful to select stackable cantilever chairs so that extra chairs and folding tables may be stored compactly in the storage space of the media wall.

Partitionable conference room with static and mobile furniture

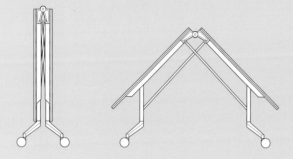

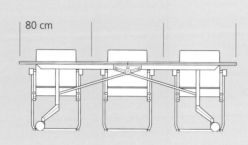

80 cm

1

For combining static table configurations and mobile, folding tables it is ideal to choose table ranges that have the same characteristic frame and table top design. It is particularly important to coordinate table top formats in terms of dimensions to allow a host of combinations. An edge length of 80 cm per person on the long sides should be specified and a table depth of 120 cm for seating on both sides. Tables with centrally positioned frames that are sufficiently recessed are recommended to provide as much legroom as possible and also to use the shorter sides of the table as full workplaces.

If all connectivity modules are accessible underneath a table portal, the positioning of the latter, which is asymmetrical due to the specific frame of folding tables, also allows seating on both sides. Table portals are in slender brushed profile, coated or veneered to match the table surface.

Integrated technical equipment should be retained in flat cable channels, if possible retractable in extruded aluminium profile coated in the same colour as the table frame, to facilitate the setting up of table configurations, to reduce weight and achieve a coherent, aesthetic appearance. If the connectivity modules, which are permanently installed and cable-linked to the lateral table-to-table connections, are positioned at a slight inclination this will guarantee convenient opertion of the modules and of the optionally integrated "show-me function".

The permanently linked segments of the table configuration must be fitted with levelling adjustable glides. The folding tables must have lockable "wheels" that are also swivel along a vertical axis, with a diameter that is sufficient for them to be moved easily from one room to another and to overcome small barriers such as low thresholds of doors or lifts too. To facilitate handling by one person only, the spring resistance of the folding mechanism must be perfectly coordinated to allow tables to be folded up and unfolded with ease.

Materials and surface finishes
For a combination comprising permanently installed table configurations and mobile, folding tables it is necessary to use materials for frames and table tops which are highly dimensionally stable. Die-cast aluminium for foot sections and table top bearers, as well as vertical uprights and horizontal underframes in aluminium profile combine reductions in weight and high stability (e.g. by constructing wide spans derived from aircraft engineering principles) with precise quality in terms of design features. Polished, bright chromium-plated or coated surface finishes offer a wide spectrum for coordination with the specific utilization and interior design concept. The same applies to table top finishes where the choice is between hardwearing coating, linoleum or veneers in various colours and staining. Impact-resilient profile integrated into the table edging prevents damage to the folding tables during transport and while configuring tables.

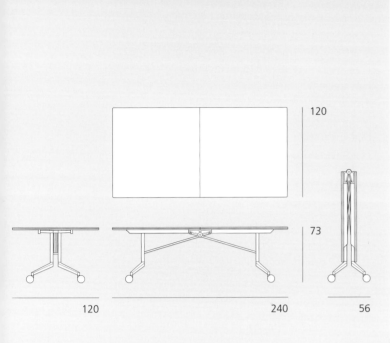

120

73

120   240   56

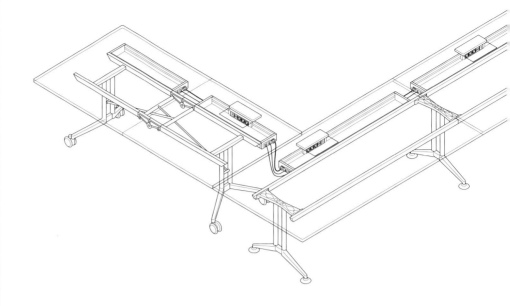

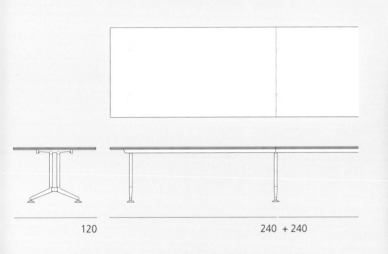

120   240 + 240

Specifiers' option:
folding table (1,2) and chairs (2) from the Confair range

2

Dynamic multimedia
conference workshop

▸ For smaller conference groups with a maximum of 22 participants who work together intensively, the concept of dynamic multimedia conference is an ideal solution. If mobile, folding table units allowing high-tech equipment are used exclusively, as well as a mobile, interactive projection display, participants may configure "their" furnishing layout themselves to meet personal requirements: configured in rows for presentations, in a U-form for presentations with a high degree of discussion and interaction or as a solid table configuration for meetings where visual presentation via a projector is only used sporadically.

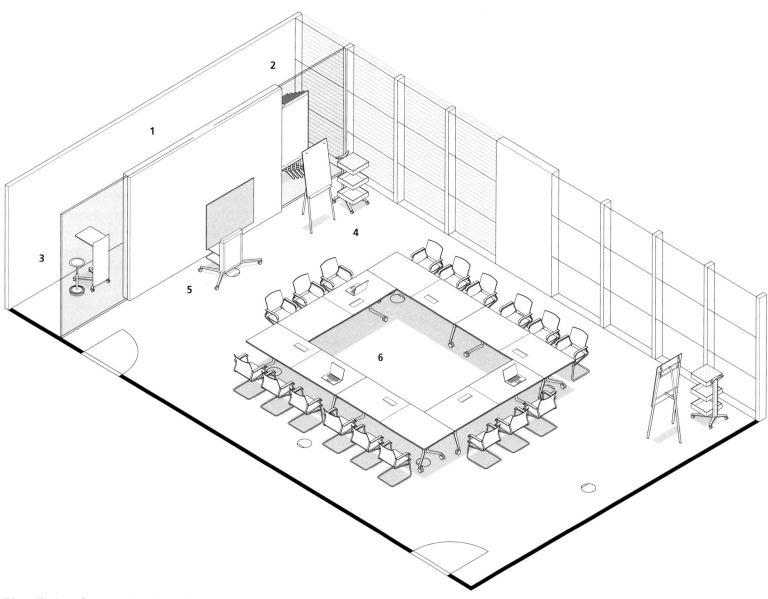

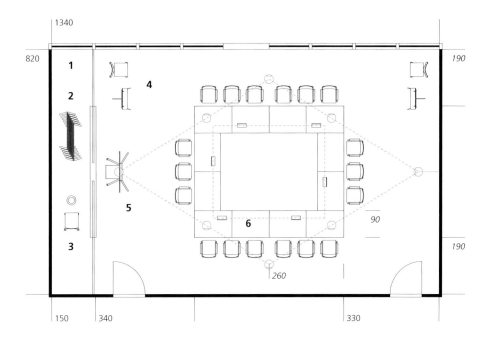

1   Store

2   Pinboards

3   Lectern with integrated network
    and power connection

4   Flipchart and server for material for hosted sessions

5   Mobile display – optionally with interactive image area

6   Mobile folding tables with integrated techni-stations

Parallel to dynamic organizational developments, meetings involving mixed groups with varying numbers of participants are also on the increase and require access to a digital information environment by means of multimedia technology. Dynamic conference interiors are a more favourable alternative in terms of maintenance compared with the cost of having rooms of various sizes each with their own table configuration and sophisticated media technology or of having to partition rooms via facility management to make them variable and reconfigure them.

For this purpose, a medium-size conference room is planned, suitable for multifunctional use and thus allowing many different scenarios. The interior is equipped with a mobile rear projection display and mobile, folding tables, each with full cabling and necessary connectivity modules. Floor ports positioned to permit a host of scenarios serve to connect the table configuration with the rear projection display. The tables required for such a setting are linked by means

of integrated table-to-table connectors either linearly, cornerwise or along the short edges, and are connected via plug-in cables and in series. With just 3 plug-in connections, power supply, data signals, USB interface and audio can be channelled to one table and then from table to table.

The connectivity modules, permanently installed underneath table surfaces, are easy to operate via flush-mounted table portals. There should be sufficient space for storing surplus cables and network adaptors for notebooks as well as battery charging devices for mobile telephones to ensure that table surfaces are as clear as possible from technical appliances and cables – apart from notebooks. If a "show-me-function" is integrated into the connectivity module, every participant can connect his or her notebook to the shared rear projection display at the push of a button.

Dynamic multimedia conference workshop

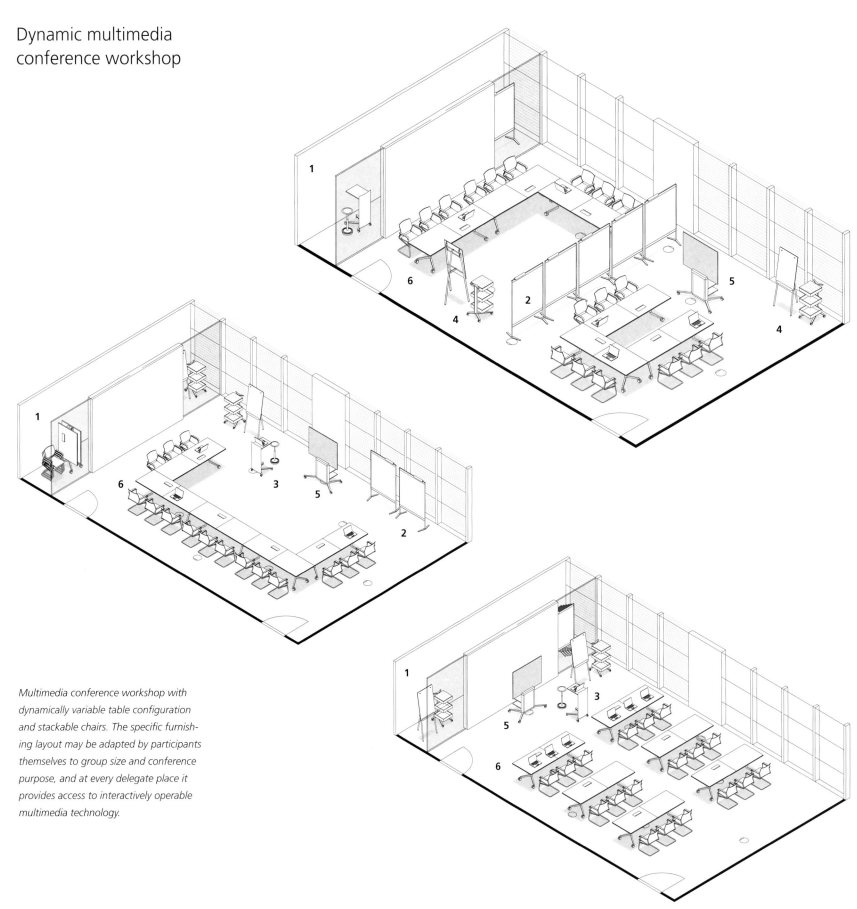

Multimedia conference workshop with dynamically variable table configuration and stackable chairs. The specific furnishing layout may be adapted by participants themselves to group size and conference purpose, and at every delegate place it provides access to interactively operable multimedia technology.

1 Store

2 Pinboards

3 Lectern with integrated network
and power connection

4 Flipchart and server for material for hosted sessions

5 Mobile display – optionally with interactive image area

6 Mobile folding tables with integrated techni-stations

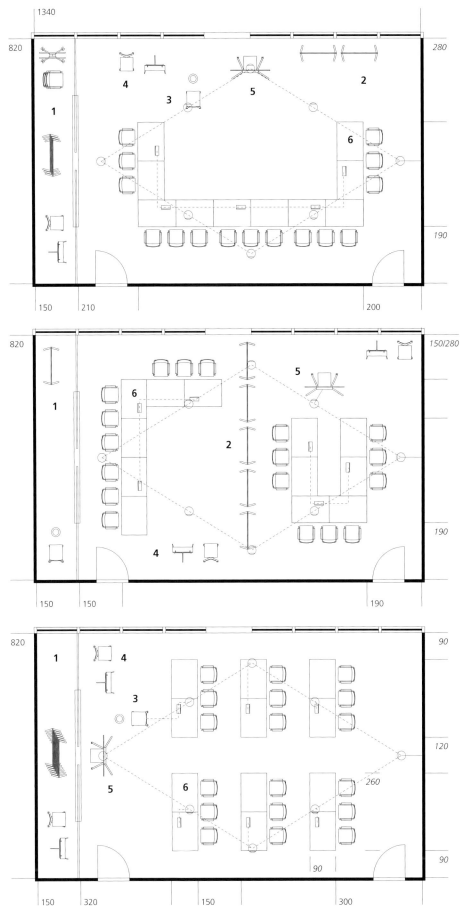

The fact that the rear projection display is mobile means that it may be moved around easily to support varying group sizes and table configurations. In contrast to front projection, it has the advantage that a presentation may be held directly in front of the display. If the projection area itself is interactive, text may be emphasized or handwritten amendments and comments may be entered into the projected document direct using a finger or a pen.

As in the previous example, it is advisable to specify tables with an integral, impact-resilient edge profile, as well as stackable cantilever chairs. If tables and chairs feature a high level of aesthetic design, elements not required at a particular time may be stored not only compactly but also visibly in the room itself.

Specifying high-quality and technically sophisticated furniture and equipment allows such a setting to be used for more formal conferences as well as for conference environments that focus on the active participation and interplay of as many members of the group as possible.

Media technology in the conference room,
Solutions ranging from integrated to variable

However, using media technology in variably and dynamically used environments primarily means providing the desired degree of flexibility in terms of positioning projection equipment and table configurations, with the possibility to network the two. This may be achieved most efficiently by going through various utilization scenarios with their corresponding setups using the floor plan of the interior in question. As just one input cable is required per table configuration, very few floor ports or wall connections are needed in general for such scenarios. This serves to reduce investment in laying cables in the floor and facilitates application in old buildings. Another advantage is that if modifi cations have to be made to cable and transmission technology these may be carried out much more easily if connectivity modules are located in tables themselves rather than in the floor.

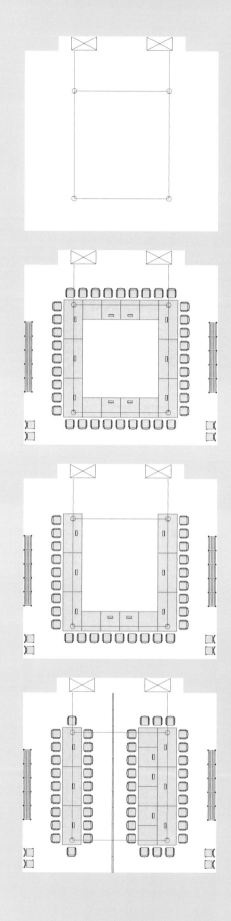

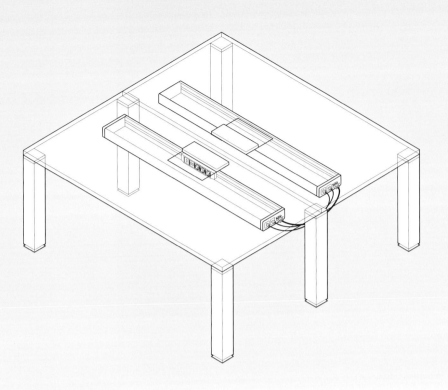

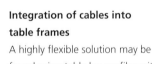

Integration of cables into table frames

A highly flexible solution may be found using table leg profiles with a sufficiently large cross section, not only to provide space for concealed cable channelling but also for a specifiable, integrated connectivity module. If table legs are not permanently joined to table tops but are removable, they may be positioned close to a floor port.

See also page 71 for variable table systems with intelligent locking mechanisms for connecting table tops and legs.

Cable connections

One central aspect is simple, intuitively comprehensible (even for the non-experienced) and graspable handling of cable connections to allow users to alter and connect up table configurations themselves. Plug-in cables should therefore be so clearly defined as to exclude cables being plugged in the wrong way from the very start.

The same applies to the operation of media technology: touch-sensitive or pen-operated displays promote interaction and can generally be used without any prior instruction and training.

Plug-and-play

The exact specifying of techni-stations integrated into tables depends on individual requirements. Input for power, data, audio and USB connections requires only three cables and provides full connectivity for operating a networked projecting device via a notebook on the table – including interactive functionality for presentations on the projection display direct.

Using the "show-me function", integrated into techni-stations, every user who is connected via a notebook may connect his or her workplace to the projection device at the push of a button. If required and if agreed on with the in-house computer department, a connection to the company's own network may be established using an additional cable and a corresponding connectivity module.

Mobile media for visual presentation
in conference and meeting environments

▸ **For visual presentations in variable conference environments, mobile projection and screen units are suitable where the display may be adapted to a given seating order and table configuration depending on the specific application and size of the group. The mobility of such devices also allows flexible use in different conference environments.**

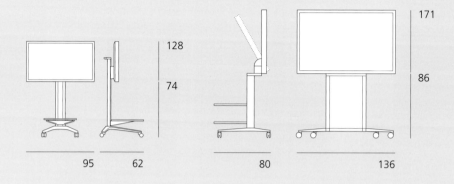

Mobile flat screens

These screens comprise a base frame with swivel castors and an integrated display module. In line with a high-quality interior, the frame structure should be coordinated with the material and surface finishes of the table configurations, single tables and chairs. A display with screen diagonals of at least 50 inches will allow text and numbers to be legible up to a distance of six metres, providing the font size recommended for presentations has been observed.

A special touch-sensitive overlay, which calculates the position of a finger or pen, is used for interaction with presentations on the screen. It even allows amendments, text to be emphasized by "hand" or to add comments and drawings. This overlay is comparable with a transparent film that is laid over an existing document and then written on. These modifications are stored via the screenshot function and are immediately available in digital form – to document decisions, for filing in a network or sending to participants as by email.

It should however be remembered that virtually all large-format screens now have a 16:9 aspect ratio while most PCs and notebooks – which are used to create data – have 4:3. Data, images and graphics that have not been converted to the former ratio will be distorted accordingly.

A second, decisive point is the quality of screen resolution. Lower priced plasma displays are used primarily for moving image renderings for TV and video applications due to their fast reaction times. For presentations or also interactive editing of digital data they are less suitable due to their limited resolution. In conference environments it is therefore advisable to use LCD displays. High-quality LCD screens can nowadays to a large extent compensate for the advantages of plasma screens in terms of high contrast ratio and fast image formation.

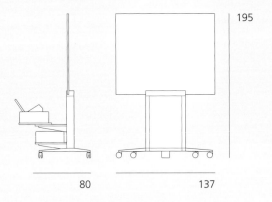

195

80   137

Mobile rear projection

Mobile rear projection devices are an aesthetically high-calibre and function-ally attractive alternative to display screens. Instead of an enclosed-frame technical device, a transparent, 70 inch glass panel with holographic function-ality is mounted on a mobile base frame. On the rear of the frame, there is a pull-out shelf to accommodate a special digital projector with a tilted mirror for projecting image data onto the glass panel from the rear.

The advantage of such a solution may be found not only in a larger projection area, permitting a viewing distance of up to eight metres, but also in the graceful transparency of the glass panel which merges perfectly with a high-quality ambience. This presen-tation module may also be fitted with functions to allow interactive control and entries by pen or finger onto the projection area direct.

Specifiers' option:
InterWall from the ConAction range

Training and seminar

▸ Knowledge as the result of transmitting information into new forms of competence requires regular further training and development of skills in all areas within a company. Providing training programmes and seminars is therefore a task of paramount importance for future-oriented corporate development and should be an integral part of daily corporate life. The key function of seminar environments is to provide optimal support for learning processes. As such interiors are used for different groups with varying numbers of participants and learning modules with different methods of instruction, the layout of tables and chairs should be easily reconfigurable in order to make seminar interiors as adaptable as possible to changing applications. This does not improve merely the learning effect: investments in intelligent equipment that may be reconfigured for fast and simple changeovers will rapidly reward through savings in office services personnel costs.

Environments for a "learning organization"

In a globalized information and learning society, the skills and competence of employees in organizations form the most important asset that a company has. In view of demographic changes in many industrialized countries, competition for the best "brains" is well under way. Discussions about the quality of education at schools and institutes of higher learning also underline the fact that today companies themselves are required more and more to provide their staff with ongoing training to communicate new skills and areas of competence. The rapid development in information and communication technologies and the dynamic change in the working world and competitive situation that it involves have made "lifelong learning" one of the key tasks of strategic corporate development.

Corporate education embraces many different fields and methods. The accelerative innovation of information systems with increasingly shorter product cycles requires administration and production to "stay on the ball" in order to remain competitive. The ongoing need for improving skills applies to both management levels and to clerical staff or skilled production staff. Digital learning platforms, so-called E-learning that even includes a "virtual university", provide many channels for accessing information for educational purposes irrespective of time or space. This may serve to replicate the mutual process of acquiring knowledge and skills in a real classroom atmosphere but it cannot replace it. For it is primarily human interplay that activates all one's senses for transporting information into new professional skills and abilities.

Interior design therefore has to address many different needs: varying numbers of participants, groups of users from all hierarchical levels, changing methods of learning and integration of state-of-the-art media technology require the highest degree of flexibility in terms of room dimensions, furnishing layouts and technical equipment. At the same time, a professional design quality is called for that can meet user requirements ranging from lower level employees up to top management.

How many places of learning today convey a questionable educational ideal of the past where learning was inherently linked to deprivation? How many congress centres in hotels that are otherwise super modern, prestigious and comfortable ignore even the most minimal requirements of promoting learning by means of ergonomic seating, the utilization quality of tables and professional presentation equipment – not to mention the design quality? In view of the cost involved per seminar and per participant in a training programme or a conference, the quality of the functionality and design of many seminar interiors verges on the grotesque. Economizing in such places only serves to impair learning progress and creates unnecessary barriers if it is necessary to train employees in the acquisition of new skills. Besides, poorly equipped and designed seminar environments increase adverse effects as periods of non-use combined with complex reconfiguration costs may far exceed acquisition costs within a short time.

Forms of organization: planned, differentiated, prepared

With regards to the number of participants and contents, seminars, training programmes, conferences and congresses are usually budgeted, planned and organized long term, generally coordinated by the human resources department if they pursue a policy of company-specific personnel development. These may take the form of in-house seminars and training programmes, or be held in external training centres and congress hotels. The choice of venue depends on the size of the company and in the case of large companies on the occupancy rate of the company's own training locations, but also on the contents of such courses and the nature of the groups of employees involved. Regular courses with a fixed time frame and schedule should logically be held in-house to reduce travelling times and to provide a familiar environment.

However, for cross-departmental, one to two-day seminars change of location to an external training centre may be beneficial. Different surroundings, spatial distance to the daily routine and spending breaks and leisure time together make it easier to concentrate on contents and serves to strengthen social relationships among participants in the process. Conveniently situated conference and seminar centres are an efficient alternative for small companies with geographically distributed business units where there is no space for in-house seminar facilities. Procedures regarding room reservation, organization and payment via the internet serve to aid efficient seminar planning without having to keep in-house capacity on standby.

Locations and contents of courses may differ, and participants too: they may all come from one company, or staff from various companies or even branches may attend a conference on related topics that is initiated and organized by a company offering professional training programmes. The same applies to all these scenarios: the better and more intelligently organization and facilities are prepared, the more positive the effect of this basic framework on learning progress is – and the more cost-efficiently these facilities may be used due to versatile scope for applications.

In the case of longer seminar and conferences it is essential to include breaks which give participants time to stand up and move around. If possible, this should also involve a change in environment. Ninety minutes without a break should not be exceeded as this inevitably results in considerable loss of concentration. Fresh air, daylight, refreshments and small snacks support regeneration phases. But it should not be forgotten that real learning in the sense of processing information takes place primarily during informal discussions outside the official programme.

The methods: learning with all one's senses

Different methods of approach are used in seminars due to specific learning and teaching requirements. These range from lectures followed by plenary discussions, to presentations, task-focused work and exercises where participants work on their own or in teams. Depending on the training programme, tests accompanied by a certificate are often used to determine whether the knowledge and skills thus acquired have really been understand and retained.

What all these methods have in common is that they need some kind of media support to relate to as many senses as possible and thus to increase learning capability. Flipcharts may be used to document spontaneous ideas, and digital projectors should be as much a standard feature nowadays as internet access to knowledge data bases.

Many people take their "workplace" along with them to seminars in the form of an electronic notebook (laptop): either to make notes or have suitable information accessible spontaneously for contributing in the seminar. The impression should however not be created that participants do not have their mind on the matter in hand but are occupied with work not related to the seminar. This does not only annoy seminar leaders but also has a negative effect on group dynamics. As opened notebooks can quickly create barriers to human interaction, it is necessary to have coordinated and perceptive solutions that on the one hand provide power supply to seminar workplaces and possibly also permit interactive image transmission, and on the other hand do not disrupt group dynamics in any way. Training modules often employ image and sound recording to give the individual and the group the possibility of analyzing exercises so that they are comprehensible and repeatable.

Facilities and furnishing: maximum flexibility, easy maintenance, high design quality

In view of the host of requirements that should be met, multifunctional and ideally partitionable facilities should be chosen as learning venues that may be coordinated, equipped and furnished to accommodate a specific type of event, number of participants, contents, aim and suitable teaching and learning methods. A useful furnishing setup therefore adapts to the particular needs in question: if the goal is to establish a new level of information by means of lectures and talks, concourse seating would be the optimal solution as the method of communication is directed more to passive listeners. Should the emphasis be on interaction, a U-shaped configuration encouraging face-to-face communication would be much more effective. A communicative, round table is recommended for discussions and workshops with "equal-status" participants. Any tests that might be necessary would require individual workplaces that have the dual function of increasing concentration and making it easy to keep an overview.

For notes, work utensils, conference documents and refreshments, tables are required which would tend to be in the way in conferences with a more dynamic character. Such environments should therefore have furnishing that is as variable as possible and may be adapted easily and quickly to varying tasks. Easy handling, compact standby storage, tool-free assembly and durable, first-class materials do not only convey an impression of professionalism but also reduce expenditure on maintenance crews. The same applies to media technology: video screens, recorders, projection areas, monitors, pinboards, digital projectors, visualizers and flipcharts should either be firmly integrated into media walls or on standby in mobile storage units. The latter have the cost advantage of not having to keep all units on standby in one room and that subsequent additions or replacement with new technologies are easier to implement.

When selecting seating, attention should be paid to ergonomic quality as longer periods of sitting can easily become an ordeal. It is equally important to consider space-saving facility management, for example, due to stackability and effort-saving handling.

When specifying such an interior, the possibility should also be included of dividing the room by means of a partition, separate access, air conditioning, lighting, media and power installations. It is also important to have room to store elements not required at a certain time and keep them on standby. As an alternative to decentral store rooms, allocated to specific areas, the operators of large conference centres in particular use the concept of a central store to equip every event individually. Rooms are cleared out completely after every event as in the "clean-desk policy" for non-territorial workplaces. This makes it easier to keep an overview of furniture and equipment in the store and saves tedious searching. The organization team, caretaker or facility management always takes care of room reservations, preparations and reconfiguration between events.

At a glance: seminar rooms with variable and mobile interiors

Seminar room with a variable interior, integrated media technology and a partition

An ideal solution for seminar rooms with variable applications are partitionable space structures with an interior design concept that already contains everything necessary for different application scenarios: a pre-installed, fitting media wall with permanently installed rear projection integrated audio technology and a store room on the side with sliding panels to accommodate tables, chairs and technical equipment not required at a particular time. In addition, it should include an acoustically efficient, folding partition permitting optimal use of the two sections of the room, intelligently positioned floor connections to cater for any application scenario, flexible furnishing comprising a variable table system, stackable chairs, units for analogue visual presentation, as well as flipcharts, and mobile trolleys for technical equipment and transport.

Page 94–99

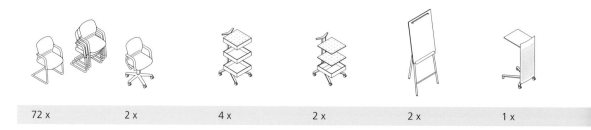

72 x   2 x   4 x   2 x   2 x   1 x

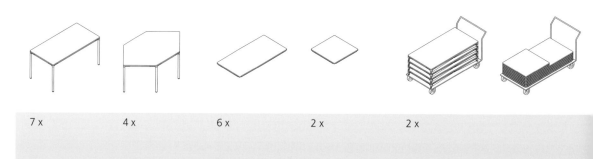

7 x   4 x   6 x   2 x   2 x

Multi-purpose room with mobile interior and a partition

Even if the size of the room does not permit a permanently installed media wall with a store room, the seminar environment may be furnished in such a way as to allow reconfiguration for various applications with little effort. In such a case, media technology would involve ceiling-mounted or mobile front projectors and projection areas that can be let down from the ceiling at the shorter ends of the room. An alternative to such a variable table system comprises single, mobile tables with a pivotable table top to allow unused tables to be stored compactly in the room without being in the way. Such tables combine maximum variability with minimum reconfiguration effort. One person only is required to prepare the room and in case of doubt, user groups can disassemble table configurations themselves, pivot table tops and change the furnishing layout as required.

Page 102–107

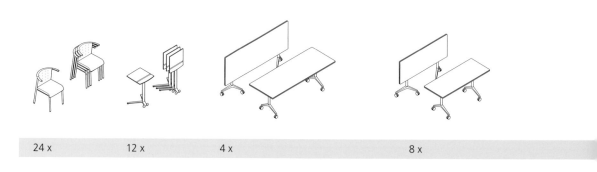

24 x   12 x   4 x   8 x

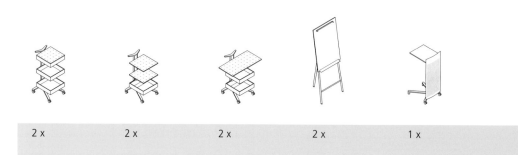

2 x   2 x   2 x   2 x   1 x

Seminar room with variable interior (page 94–99)
Area 118 sqm / Effective area 105 sqm / Store 13 sqm

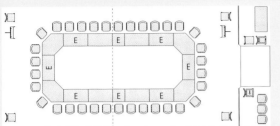

Conference configuration for 34 persons

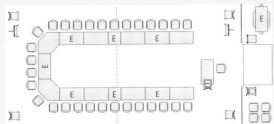

Training with scope for discussion for 30 persons

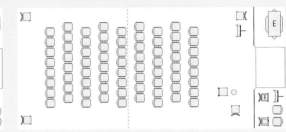

Lecture with concourse seating for 72 persons

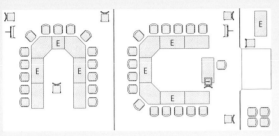

Utilization of partitioned rooms: conference for 15 persons,
training with scope for discussion for 16 persons

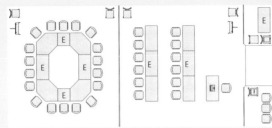

Utilization of partitioned rooms: conference
configuration for 18 persons, training for 12 persons

Multi-purpose room with mobile interior (page 102–107)
Area 100 sqm

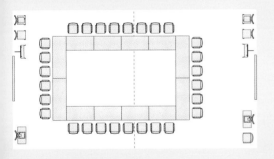

Conference configuration for 28 persons

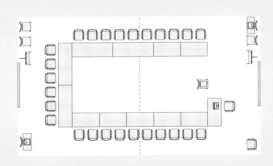

Training with scope for discussion for 26 persons

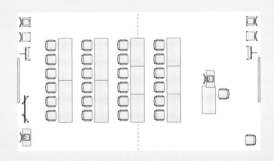

Training with tuition for 24 persons

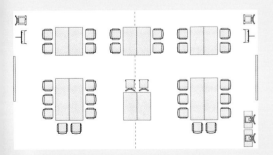

Company party for 28 persons

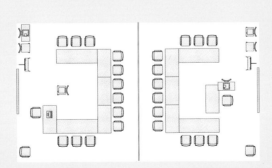

Utilization of partitioned rooms:
training in parallel for 12 persons

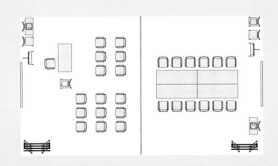

Utilization of partitioned rooms:
lecture for 15 persons, meeting for 12 persons

At a glance: seminar rooms with flexible interior and integrated media technology

Multi-purpose and seminar room with multifunctional furniture

A third alternative for variable furnishing of multi-purpose interiors and seminar environments is to use modular single tables that are therefore compact and easily transportable and movable with dimensions, design and construction allowing varying applications and configurations. Positioned in rows for training courses and linked without the use of tools, moved together for teamwork, conferences and meetings or used as a single workplace for examinations – in terms of sitting and standing height too, such tables open up an entirely new spectrum for spontaneous interaction and corresponding self-organized furnishing layouts.

Page 110–113

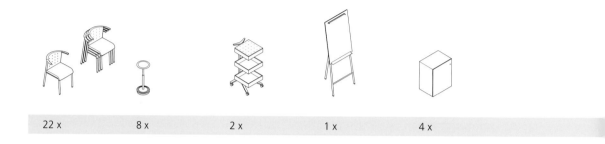

22 x	8 x	2 x	1 x	4 x

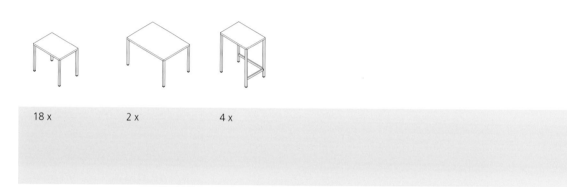

18 x	2 x	4 x

Training room with integrated, interactive media technology

Such training environments, in which work always needs digital media that is permanently integrated to support a particular method of instruction, may also be used for varying applications if they are furnished with this in mind. The combination of statically linked table configurations and partially mobile single tables, each with a permanently installed display, also permits flexible furnishing layouts to adapt to changing seminar methods – provided they have correspondingly simple cabling and connectivity technology and floor ports that are connected to shared, interactive displays.

Page 116

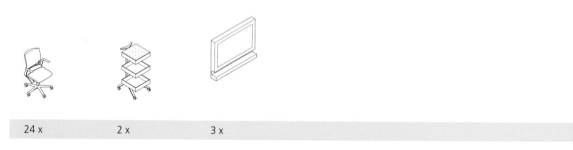

24 x	2 x	3 x

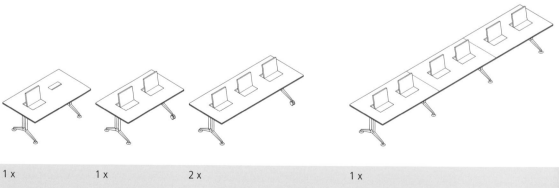

1 x	1 x	2 x	1 x

Multi-purpose room with flexible interior (page 110–113)
Area 88 sqm

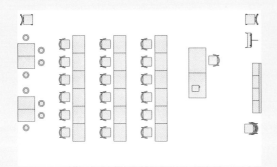

Training with single tables positioned in rows for 18 persons

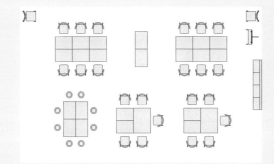

Table configuration for teamwork

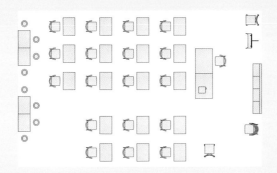

Separate configuration of single tables for examination purposes

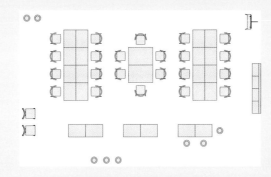

Elongated table configuration for company celebration

Integrated media training room with variable table arrangement (page 116)
Area 76 sqm

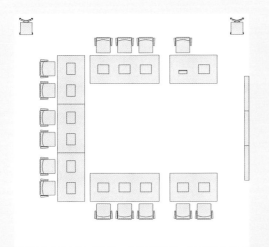

U-shaped configuration for optimal interaction among participants and at an interactive wall-mounted board

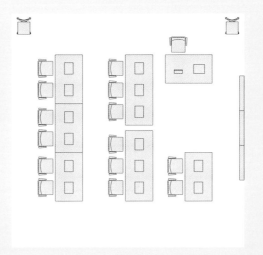

Tables configured in rows for partially mobile tables for presentations or training

Seminar room with variable interior, integrated media technology and partition

Utilization as a conference room or for training with scope for discussion

▸ For furnishing a partitionable, multifunctional seminar interior it is advisable to use an easily reconfigurable, variable table system with versatile accessories.
The principle of such a table system is based on a combination of single tables and extension elements. A host of different, modularly coordinated table top sizes and forms allows configurations not only to be adapted to space geometry but also to didactically effective seating arrangements.

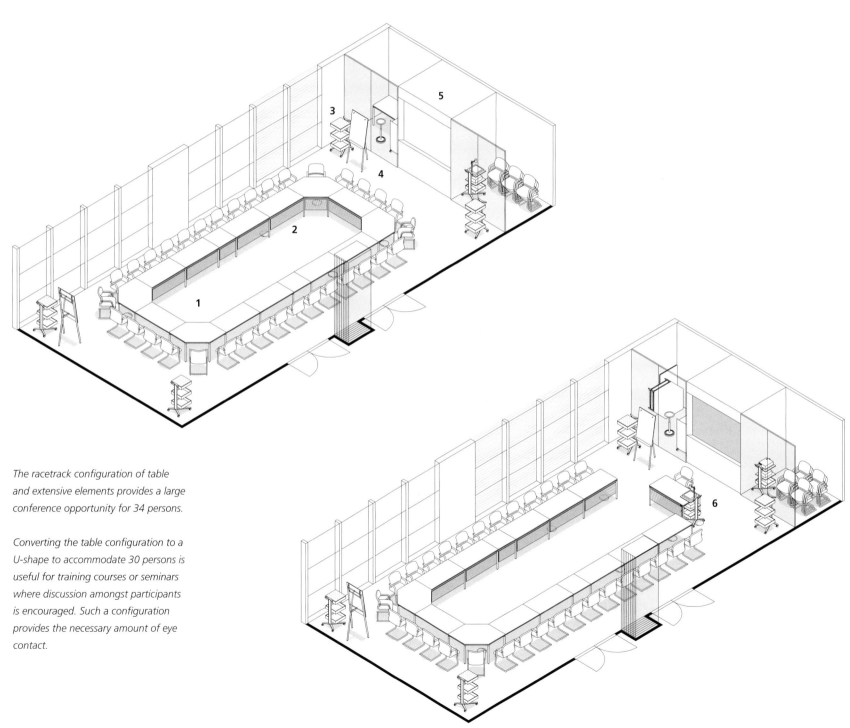

The racetrack configuration of table and extensive elements provides a large conference opportunity for 34 persons.

Converting the table configuration to a U-shape to accommodate 30 persons is useful for training courses or seminars where discussion amongst participants is encouraged. Such a configuration provides the necessary amount of eye contact.

Scale 1:100 / dimensions in cm
(1 cm = 0.39 inches)
Area 118 sqm
Effective area 105 sqm
Store 13 sqm

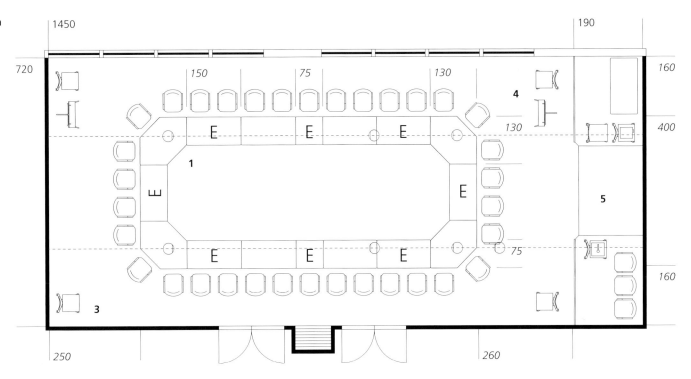

1 Racetrack table configuration comprising
   linked tables and extension elements
2 Modesty panels inserted in table underframes
3 Materials server
4 Flipchart for documentation of group discussions
   and as visual support for elaborating on topics
5 Media wall with rear projection device and storage
   space for tables, stackable chairs and servers
6 Instructor's table with mobile server at the side
   for a visualizer

If furniture is variable, a partitionable seminar room equipped with a suitable media wall and a store room may be used for many different types of events and thus ensures cost-effective space utilization. The permanently installed rear projection device only requires blinds on windows in the front section of the room and therefore will optimize alertness during a lengthy seminar. Behind the panels on the left and right there is sufficient storage space to accommodate tables, chairs, technical equipment and a transport trolley when not in use. The partitionable system allows the room to be divided into two acoustically shielded smaller rooms for parallel events.

The quality of a variable table system can be seen in its versatility: hardwearing surface finishes and edging, easy handling, simple reconfiguration as far as possible without the aid of tools, compact standby storage of stackable elements or folding mechanisms, as well as practical transport devices are the criteria for keeping the time needed for maintenance crews low and for reducing follow-up costs.

Seminar room with variable interior, integrated media technology and partition

Utilization as a lecture room

▸ **If stackable models are selected as seating for a seminar environment, surplus chairs may be kept compactly on standby in the store room for varying applications. As concourse seating is useful for "table-free" events – such as lectures – it is advisable to select models that may be firmly linked.**

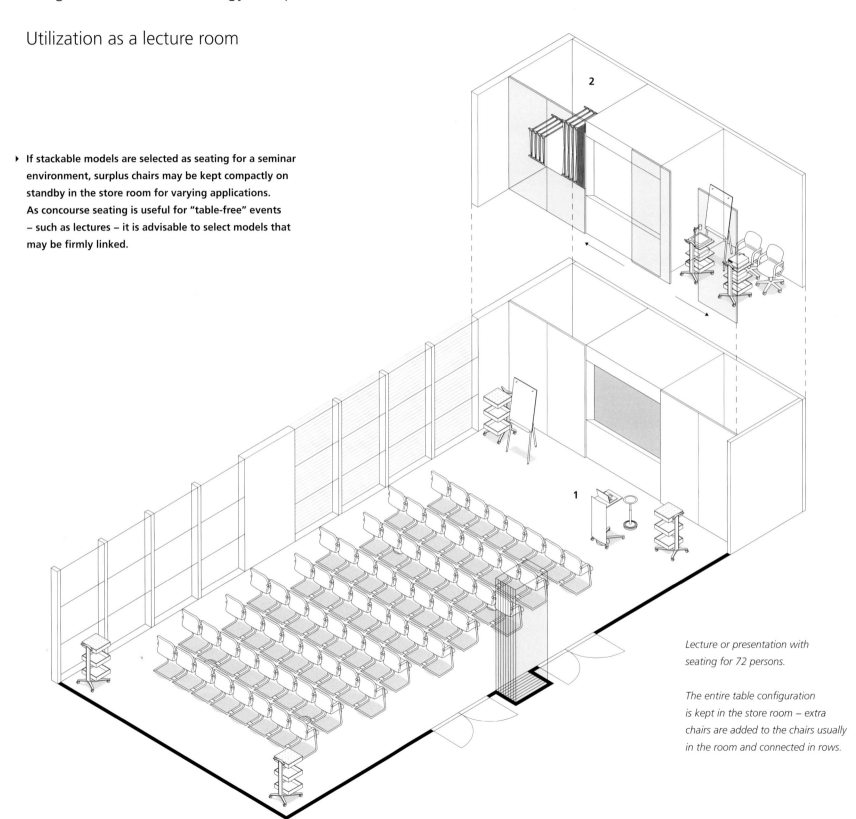

Lecture or presentation with seating for 72 persons.

The entire table configuration is kept in the store room – extra chairs are added to the chairs usually in the room and connected in rows.

Scale 1:100 / dimensions in cm
(1 cm = 0.39 inches)
Area 118 sqm
Effective area 105 sqm
Store 13 sqm

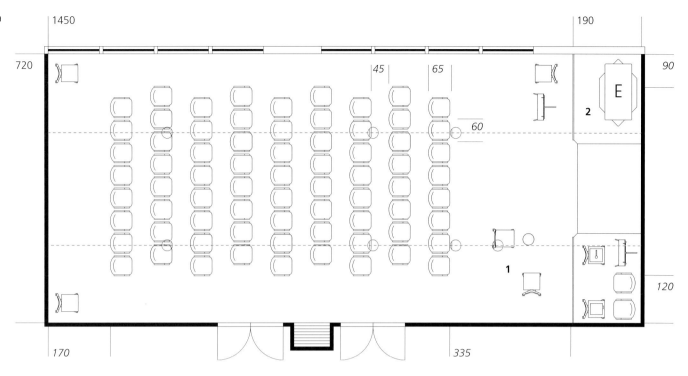

1   Lectern and leaning aid for the speaker
2   Tables and extension elements kept in the store

For events with a lecture character it is generally sufficient to equip the room with concourse seating. Should it be necessary for participants to take notes during such an event, chairs may optionally be fitted with writing tablets that can be easily clamped onto armrests. Row connectors are useful to keep a tidy appearance. Such connectors are often a legal requirement as panic safety measures for events with more than 200 seats.

For the speaker at presentations and lectures the following is on standby from the store room: a lectern with a slot-in microphone, if possible also pre-fitted to take a portable computer, and a convenient leaning aid.

If tables that are not required for furnishing a room for a lecture scenario have a folding mechanism for the table frame or legs, they may be stored compactly on a stacking trolley in the store room together with extension elements.

Seminar room with variable interior, integrated media technology and partition

Utilization of partitioned rooms for conferences, presentations, training with interaction and instruction

▸ The reconfigurability and usability of a seminar room will increase substantially if materials and technical equipment are kept on standby on mobile trolleys allowing flexible positioning as required.

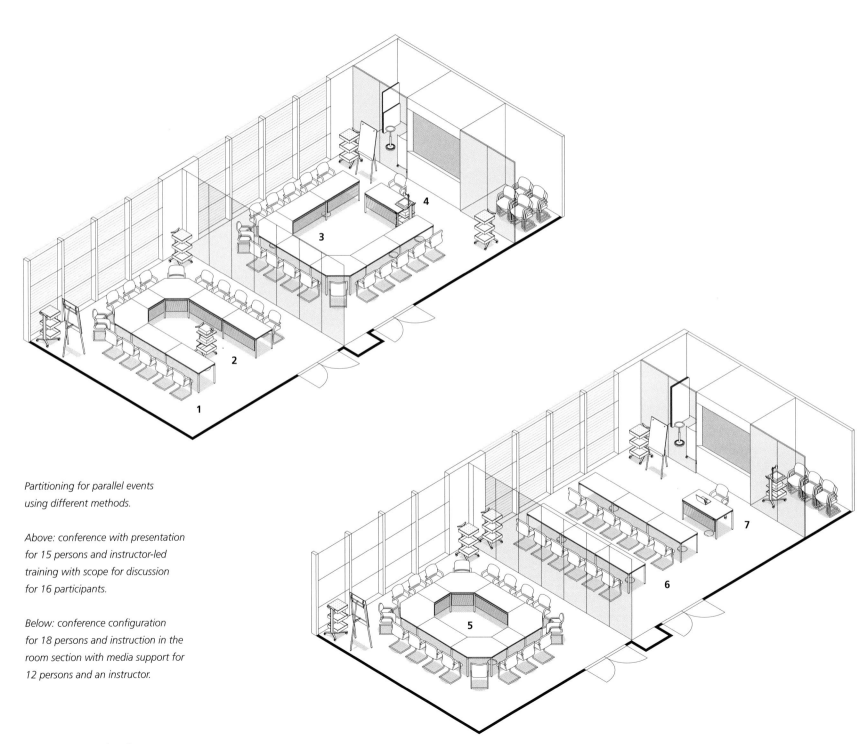

Partitioning for parallel events using different methods.

Above: conference with presentation for 15 persons and instructor-led training with scope for discussion for 16 participants.

Below: conference configuration for 18 persons and instruction in the room section with media support for 12 persons and an instructor.

Not only tables and chairs, but also conference and training materials and utensils, as well as media technology for variable applications, should be easily available and be capable of being allocated to table configurations. Trolleys for transport and technical equipment are an ideal solution: such "servers" allow the instructor to position an overhead projector or a visualizer as a video-electronic equivalent adjacent to the table so that the table itself remains uncluttered.

It is optimal to select a mobile frame structure that may be equipped to suit varying requirements, for example, with shelves, boxes and drawers for writing utensils, documents or catering materials. This ensures that participants have everything they need in a seminar at their fingertips as materials may be kept on standby. And such a coherently designed system of "servers" creates a high-quality environment and helps to prevent a chaotic appearance invariably caused by a conglomeration of different modular furniture units and technical equipment.

Flipcharts should also be easy to handle and transport, and be coordinated with the general design theme.

The seminar room may even be used for PC training courses with relatively little additional cost and effort. In view of ongoing miniaturization of high-performance hardware, several computers – for example, either models integrated into flat screens or portable computers – may be kept on standby on such transport trolleys and easily moved over to tables as required. Cabling can then be independent of table frames – providing that such "server frames" can be equipped with power supply fittings.

Such system solutions have the advantage that the same types of server can be used for varying applications – for several seminar rooms too as it is rarely the case that all elements will be needed simultaneously. This increases flexibility, supports coherent design and saves costs.

Whatever the intended use of a variably partitionable seminar room, it always makes sense to equip the room with floor ports for power and possibly networks connections. To achieve optimal space utilization, including connectivity equipment, it is advisable to coordinate the specific installation grid with various application scenarios in the planning stage.

Scale 1:200 / dimensions in cm
(1 cm = 0.39 inches)
Area 114 sqm
Effective area 100 sqm
Store 14 sqm

1 U-shaped configuration for conferences and presentations
2 Portable data projector on mobile server
3 U-shaped configuration for training course
4 Instructor's table with mobile server at the side for a visualizer, connected to rear projection device

5 Conference configuration
6 Linear layout for training without interaction among participants
7 Instructor's table with computer, connected to rear projection device

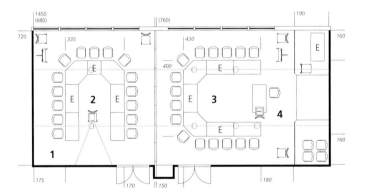

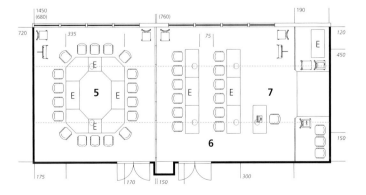

Variable table systems for seminar and training environments

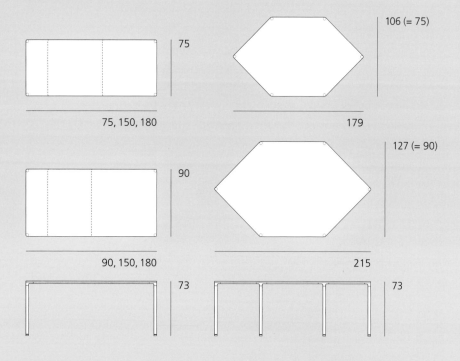

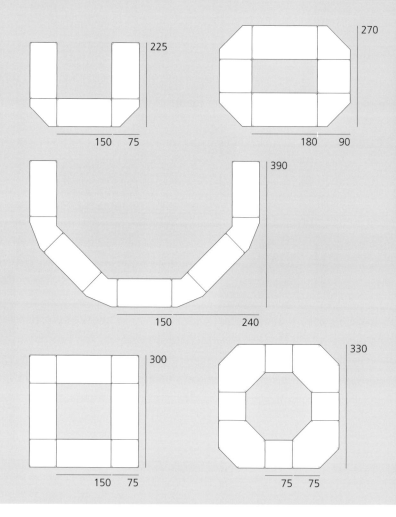

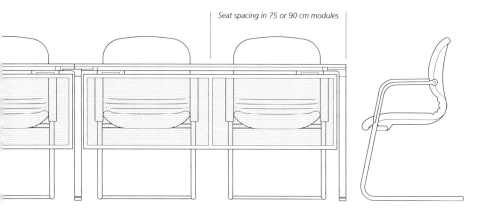

Seat spacing in 75 or 90 cm modules

For U-shaped or open-centred table configurations, modesty panels are recommended that may be easily slotted into the metal underframe of the tables and extension elements on both sides.

Variable conference table systems

Conference table systems for multi-functional conference and seminar environments comprise single tables, optionally with folding legs, and extension elements. They should allow simple configuration: for example, by means of connecting mechanisms that are permanently integrated into the underframes of tables and extension elements. This ensures zero component loss and an absence of tools required for reconfiguration. The same applies to the stackability of unused extension elements or folding tables: integral separators ensure safe stacking and protect against pressure marks from the stacking process. Another important aspect for easy handling is reducing weight, for example, by using aluminium frames and light sandwich panel for table tops which reduce weight by up to 30 per cent while providing the same degree of stability as conventional table top materials.

There is even greater scope for combining tables if extension elements may be added at both sides of a table. Three table top formats generally suffice for providing full flexibility: square, rectangular and hexagonal. For example, four hexagonal tables create a spacious configuration to accommodate twelve persons and can even be extended quickly and easily by inserting additional table tops. The fewer different forms and formats used, the easier it is for maintenance crews and the more versatile the scope for combination.

1–3

Twist table legs, extend, fold up and lock into the retention mechanism integrated underneath the table top. Integral separators provide an anti-slip surface for stacking table tops.

Swivel adjustable glides at base of legs for levelling out floor irregularities

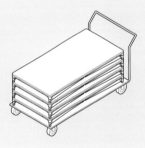 

1–4

Activate the swing-out plate of the retention mechanism at top of table leg and insert the plate of the extension element into the multiple connector.

5

Rotate the connector plate by a further 90° to insert two extension elements.

Intelligent construction of details ensures a high degree of reconfigurability: no parts can be lost as all mechanisms are integrated into the frame: the retaining clamp for pivoted table legs, the retention mechanism for extension elements, the stacking buffer and separator to protect table edges …

Specifiers' option:
Contas table system; cantilever models from the FS-Line chair range

An edge length per person of 75 cm provides sufficient space for participants and allows compact configuration for optimal space utilization.

Single tables may also be stored compactly on standby due to the pivoting mechanisms of the table legs. Stacking trolleys should be available to facilitate transport and storage of tables not in use.

If open-centred table configurations are frequently required, it is advisable to fit modesty panels that are easy to insert without the use of tools, and that match the tables. Table-to-table connectors that are simply slotted into underframes when single tables are linked are as useful as other accessories that include flexible power supply fittings, for example, storage nets for socket strips, network adapters and surplus cables that are simply inserted underneath table tops as required without impairing the stackability function.

Materials and surface finishes
Variable table systems should be able to withstand frequent configuration: the frames are therefore chromium-plated or with a hardwearing coating: distortion-free lightweight sandwich panel is recommended for table tops. Table surfaces are finished with high-quality laminates and protected by separators mounted onto the under-frames.

Multi-purpose room with mobile furniture and partition

Utilization for a conference group and training course with discussion

▸ For flexibly used, multi-purpose interiors without a store room, tables with mobile frames and vertically pivotable tops are an ideal alternative to variable table systems. They combine maximum variability with facility management benefits as only one person is required to prepare a room or participants can even arrange their individual setup themselves. Tables not in use can be stacked compactly on standby in the room itself – providing their design is correspondingly high-quality and attractive.

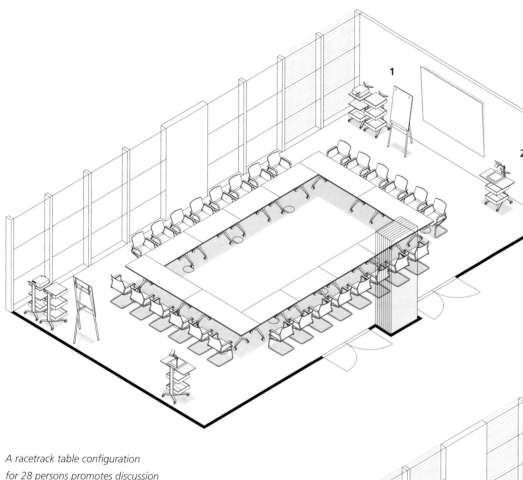

A racetrack table configuration for 28 persons promotes discussion among participants.

For training courses or seminars it is an excellent idea to select a U-shaped configuration (for 26 paticipants here) if discussion among participants is expected as such a layout allows eye contact.

The benefit afforded by mobile tables in terms of facility management contrasts with the disadvantage that non-rectangular configurations are only possible to a limited extent. In such cases it is necessary to weigh up the importance of facility management aspects, required table layouts and the aesthetic appearance of the interior.

If a multi-purpose room also has an additional store room, all furniture units – chairs, tables or media equipment – can be kept there conveniently on standby. For such applications, attention should therefore be paid to specifying hardwearing frames, table edging and surfaces that do not impair the aesthetic quality. As nothing can be stored out of sight, any elements that are not in use at a particular time also shape the overall appearance of the interior. If the rotational movement of the foot sections is automatically activated when the top is pivoted, tables may be compacted neatly in attractive, ordered columns.

A 150 x 75 cm model provides sufficient work surface and may be extended either in width or depth as required. This table depth can also be combined with wider tables to accommodate three persons per segment.

It is not absolutely necessary to have stackable chairs but this feature creates additional space if spare chairs are stored compactly in the corner.

Comfort, weight, durability and high quality are relevant functional criteria that should be considered in the planning stage. Lightweight cantilever versions, if possible to match tables, are therefore an excellent choice.

Scale 1:100 / dimensions in cm
(1 cm = 0.39 inches)
Area 100 sqm

1   Flipchart for documentation of group discussions and as visual support for elaborating on topics
2   Server for materials and overhead
3   Instructor's table with data projector on mobile server

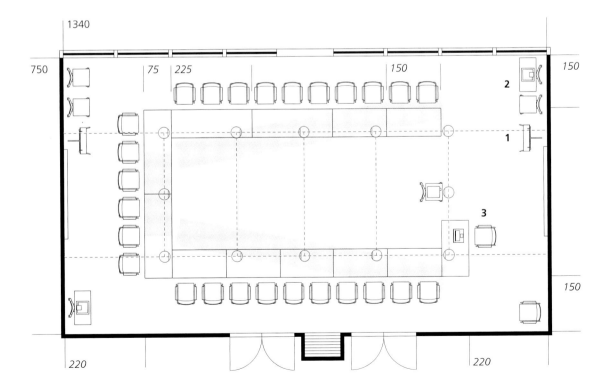

Multi-purpose room with mobile furniture and partition

Utilization of partitioned rooms for training courses, lectures and conferences

‣ When rooms are partitioned, attention should be paid to creating two equally large room sections as well as to retaining all functional aspects – such as projection areas, media equipment and corresponding mobile media servers.

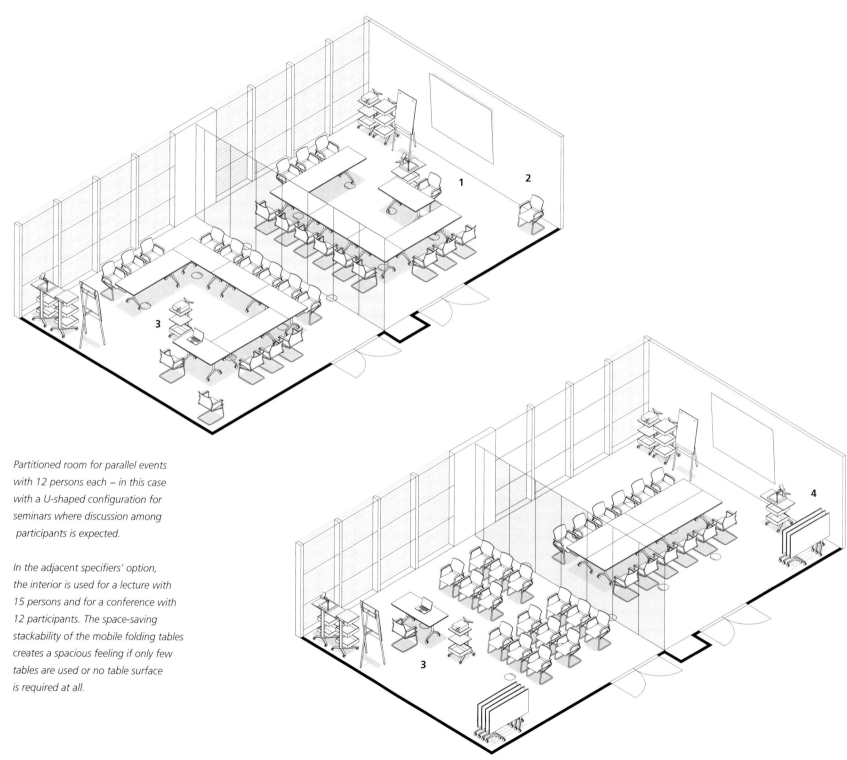

Partitioned room for parallel events with 12 persons each – in this case with a U-shaped configuration for seminars where discussion among participants is expected.

In the adjacent specifiers' option, the interior is used for a lecture with 15 persons and for a conference with 12 participants. The space-saving stackability of the mobile folding tables creates a spacious feeling if only few tables are used or no table surface is required at all.

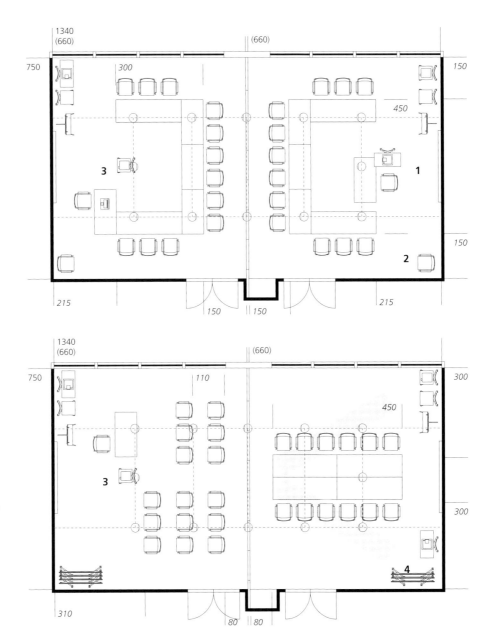

1   Instructor's table with overhead projector
    on mobile server

2   Spare chairs remain in the room on standby

3   Data projector on mobile server

4   With pivoted tops and stored in ordered columns,
    spare tables are kept on standby in the room

Partitioning a room, into two equally large sections opens up wide application scope. If projection screens are installed along the shorter sides of the room, for example, at a 90° angle to the side with windows, front projection technology may be used in both room sections.

This doubles requirements for transport and media furniture units: each room section needs a flipchart, two servers each for incidentals and catering materials, and one server each for an overhead or data projector and a video projector.

Multi-purpose room with mobile furniture and partition

Utilization for training course with tuition and for teamwork

Configuration of tables in rows is used for training and lecture applications for 24 persons when the focus is on conveying knowledge and information and participants require more spacious surfaces work and storage.

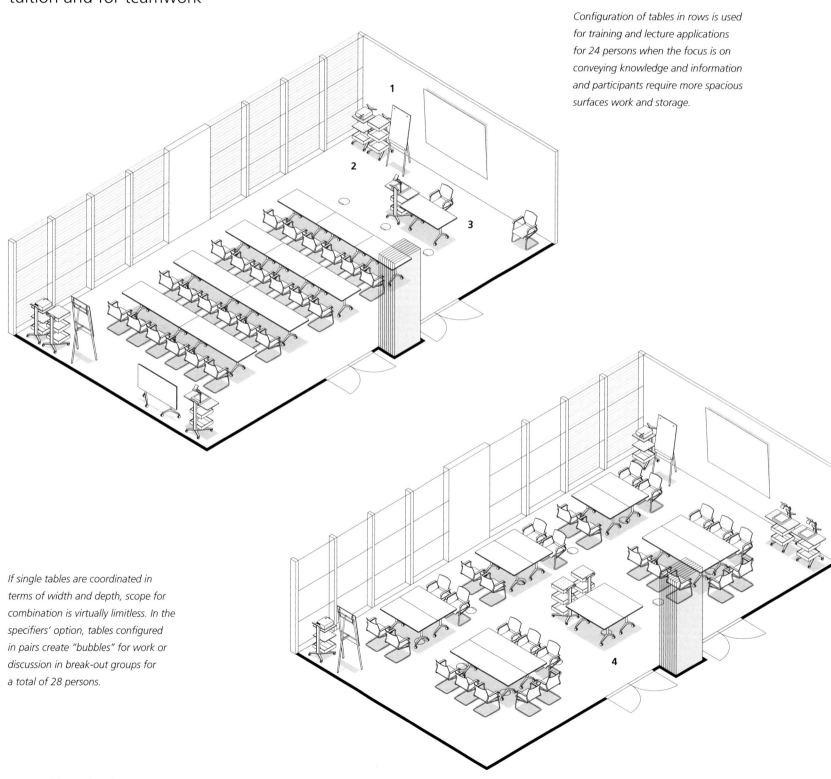

If single tables are coordinated in terms of width and depth, scope for combination is virtually limitless. In the specifiers' option, tables configured in pairs create "bubbles" for work or discussion in break-out groups for a total of 28 persons.

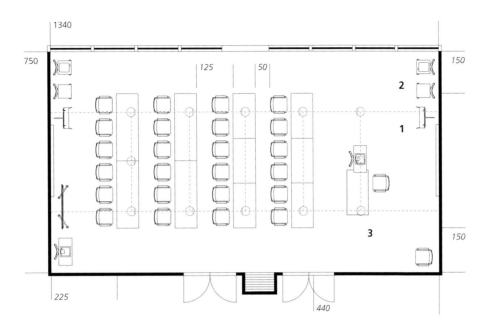

Scale 1:125 / dimensions in cm
(1 cm = 0.39 inches)
Area 100 sqm

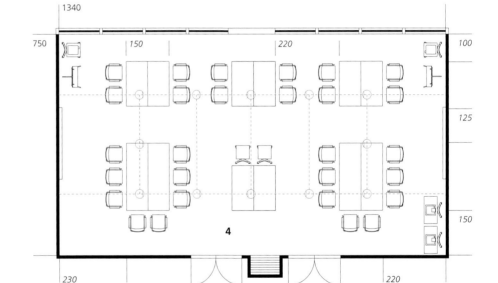

1 Flipchart for documentation of group discussions
   and as visual support for elaborating on topics
2 Server for materials and overhead
3 Instructor's table with overhead projector
   on mobile server
4 Table configuration for teamwork
   or for a celebration

As tables are positioned with no defined seating direction and
table geometry is coordinated, the room may be utilized for
almost any application. In addition to teamwork, a further
application scenario is possible, for example, for company events
such as jubilees or departmental celebrations. Tables are then
grouped longitudinally in pairs, thus providing space for up
to eight persons per configuration. Spare tables may be used
as a sideboard for a buffet.

Mobile, pivotable single tables for multifunctional training and seminar environments

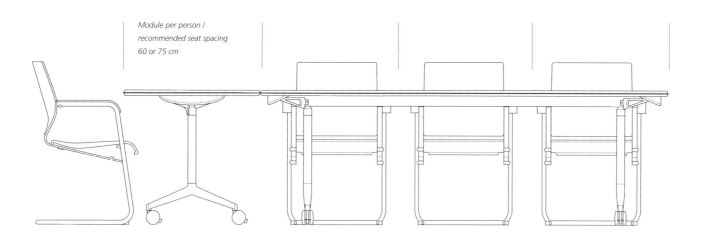

Module per person / recommended seat spacing 60 or 75 cm

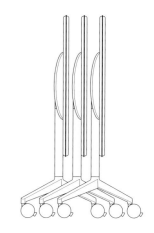

Mobile single tables and vertically pivotable table tops

In interiors with changing applications as well as in daily office life there are often situations where universal single tables are preferred to system tables or permanently installed table configurations. Single tables may be reconfigured quickly – for example, to meet specific requirements of a seminar or a spontaneous workshop, but also for a company celebration requiring an elongated table layout for a buffet or groups of tables for catering materials.

For all occasions, an edge length of 75 cm per person provides a balanced ratio between the size of an individual place at the table and the floor space required. If tables are only to provide seating along one side to be used exclusively in a seminar setting, an edge length of 60 cm is also sufficient. Otherwise it should be possible to use all sides of a table without under-frames or table legs being in the way. Tables with centrally positioned frames that are sufficiently recessed are an advantage for such layouts. Specifying lockable castors that enable tables to

overcome thresholds and uneven floor port covers serves to increase mobility and safety, simplifies regrouping and allows rooms to be equipped from one central store room. For the purpose of linking tables, an integrated table-to-table connector should be included in the accessories list as well as slot-in modesty panels for open-centred table configurations, for example, U-shaped layouts.

1–3
Table-to-table connector for positive linking and levelling at long and short edges.

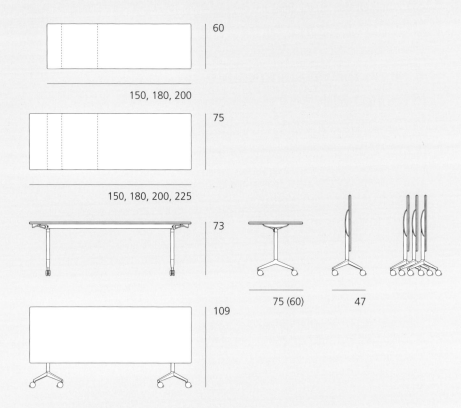

60

150, 180, 200

75

150, 180, 200, 225

73

109

75 (60)   47

2

If table tops are fitted with a pivoting mechanism, they may be transported through narrow doorways, lifts or corridors and reconfigured conveniently by one person. In rooms without a store room it is advisable to specify tables that can be compacted in optimally space-efficient columns.

Materials and surface finishes
Mobile tables must be hardwearing to allow such flexibility. In contrast to variable table systems, which should be as lightweight as possible, they must be heavy enough to guarantee tilt resistance and stable transportability on castors. Frames and foot sections are in steel, alternatively in aluminium for higher quality versions, as this material provides an equally high degree of stability, workmanship and surface finish.

Table tops finished in hardwearing laminate are an excellent solution for multi-purpose applications. A choice of veneers, which can be coordinated with an interior design theme, should be available for high-quality and prestigiously furnished environments. Impact-resilient edge profiles protect tables during configuration or transport, and interior fittings too.

109

Multi-purpose and seminar room with multifunctional furniture

Utilization for a training course and group work

▸ For interactive, self-organized changes in working methods within the same room, it is advisable to specify universally usable, modular single tables in sitting and standing height that provide creative and innovative scope for furnishing multi-purpose and seminar environments. Coherent design, specific surface proportions and easy handling allow virtually limitless scope for application for varying forms of work.

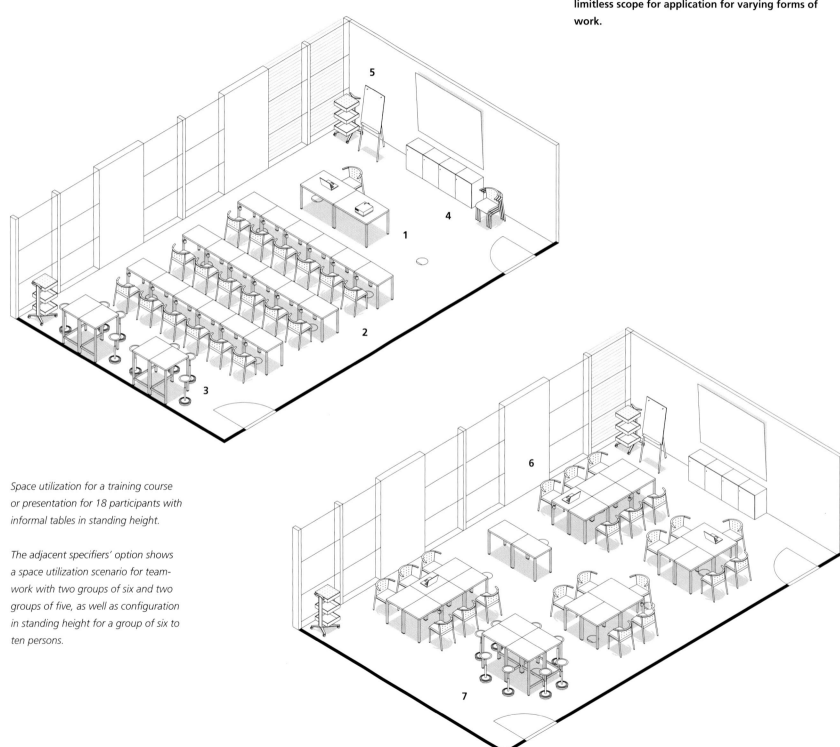

Space utilization for a training course or presentation for 18 participants with informal tables in standing height.

The adjacent specifiers' option shows a space utilization scenario for team-work with two groups of six and two groups of five, as well as configuration in standing height for a group of six to ten persons.

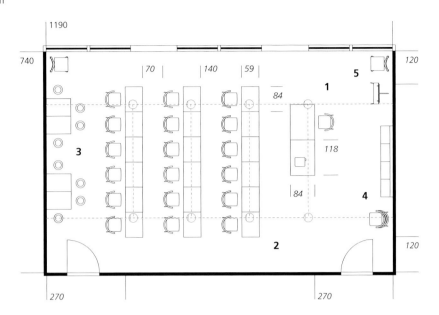

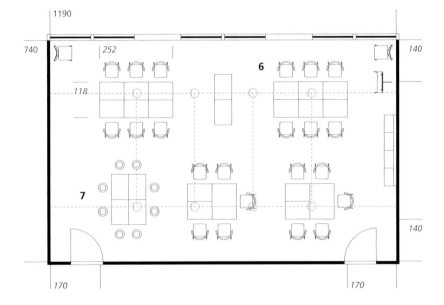

1 Two single tables for an instructor and a data projector
2 Single tables configured in rows, for one person each
3 High tables with leaning aids
4 Mobile storage units for technical equipment,
   training incidentals, tableware and catering materials
5 Mobile server and flipchart

6 Single tables configured as teamwork places
7 High tables in block configuration with leaning
   aids for meetings

The use of four-leg single tables in sitting and standing height is an ingeniously simple and versatile concept for variable furnishing of multi-purpose and training environments. Such furniture units are reduced to essentials and allow virtually limitless configurations and multi-directional use.

The modular principle of such tables allows participants to transport their workplace themselves and re-group them. In addition, the proportions, quality and archetypal design of the tables ensure a calm and harmonious appearance while providing high versatility in terms of configuration.

The balanced ratio of $1:\sqrt{2}$ has been used instead of the usual depth and width proportions of 1:2. The next largest table format has the same proportions, but double the surface area. This means that any combination results in harmonious dimensions.

Slot-on table clips, optionally with data and power connections, provide a firm linking mechanism and also power supply options on any table leg.

Multi-purpose and seminar room with multifunctional furniture

Individual table setup for a closed conference and utilization for a celebration with a buffet

▸ Proportions and surface ratios are designed in such a way that any element may stand alone or be combined as required. Reduction to one multi-directional basic form maximizes versatility in terms of application – it is only specific grouping of chairs that defines the purpose of a table.

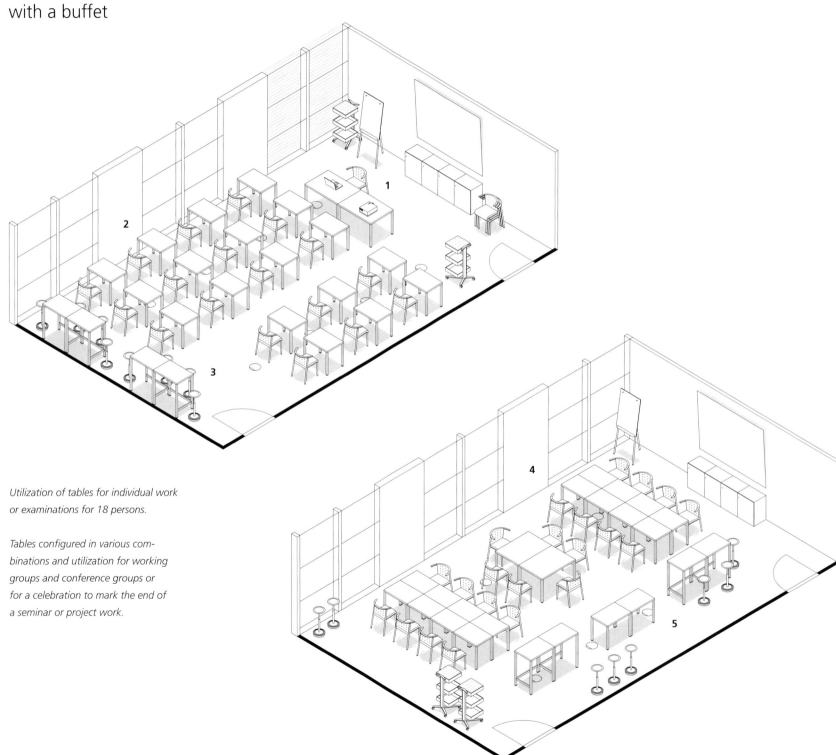

Utilization of tables for individual work or examinations for 18 persons.

Tables configured in various combinations and utilization for working groups and conference groups or for a celebration to mark the end of a seminar or project work.

An interior with multi-purpose tables in sitting and standing height covers a wide application spectrum: ranging from formal and aligned concourse layouts to highly interactive, compact arrangements for meetings and conferences.

High tables encourage the highest degree of interaction and participation. At the same time they may also be used as presentation surfaces for models or for catering materials during short breaks. A changeover from sitting to standing height also promotes necessary changes in posture and physical movement.

An ideal seating solution is a four-legged chair with armrests, preferably stackable and coordinated with the interior design theme that can even be positioned along the shorter edges of the small table format. The chair should be robust enough to allow the backrest to serve as a support for the user when discussions take place standing up, and on the other hand be light enough to be grasped by the backrest or the curved armrests and transported.

For longer periods of work in a standing position, it is advisable to select height-adjustable leaning aids that tilt in any direction while relieving physical strain and encouraging movement.

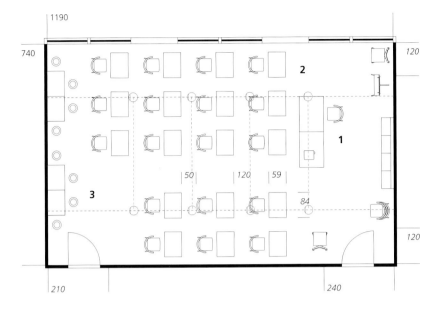

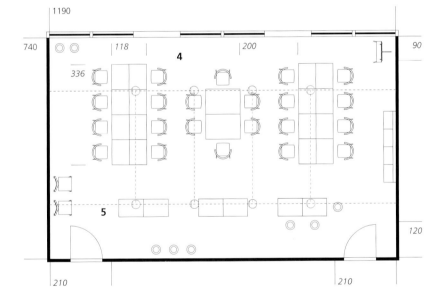

1　Two single tables for an instructor and a data projector
2　Separate positioning of single tables, each for one person
3　High tables for examination papers

4　Single tables in an elongated configuration
5　Single tables and high tables configured in rows for a buffet

Flexible interior with compact table units

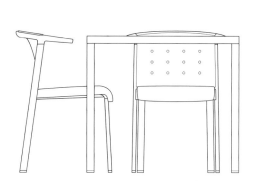

Multi-purpose single tables are reduced to essentials in terms of construction and design: the four table legs, flush-mounted at the corners, and a rectangular table top allow a host of different applications. These tables are perfectly multi-directional. A specific application is only defined when combined with chairs and accessories. To allow versatile configuration, a size should be selected that is easy to handle, and dimensions should be effectively coordinated. Aesthetic excellence combines with spacious legroom if table frameworks have slender dimensions and are visually embedded.

A particularly high degree of flexibility and a calm, harmonious impression are created by rectangular formats with well balanced surface proportions that form a contrast to conventional office and conference table formats.

DIN A paper format functions as an ideal principle upon which to base proportions of table depth to table width. The balanced proportions of 1:√2 dates back to the Greek philosopher Plato, and was used by master the builder Vitruvius in the era of Emperor Augustus as the basis of urban development in Rome. During the Renaissance it was celebrated as an architectural principle in the "I Quattro Libri dell'Architettura" from the year 1570 by Andrea Palladio, master builder in Vicenza – long before the paper industry discovered the benefits of this format. In addition to a harmonious appearance, there is a further inestimable advantage: halving or doubling the size results in constant proportions. By means of simple addition, one basic form can thus be used to create formats of varying size that are all inherently related. Even if tables are positioned in a non-aligned manner they will create a coherent,

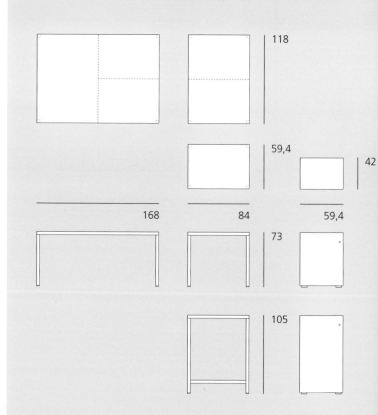

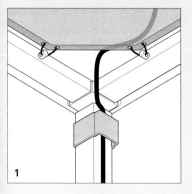

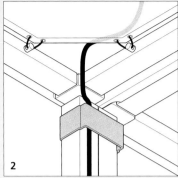

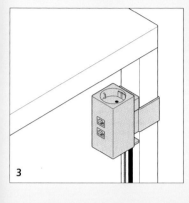

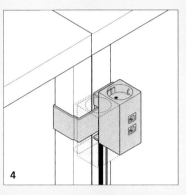

Specifiers' option:
Tables from the DinA range (1);
Confair seminar chair (2)

1
A flexible storage net in polyester attached to fittings on the underframe creates a second, flexible level directly underneath the table surface to hold power adapters, surplus cables and documents not required at a particular time.

1 + 2
Cable clips in plastic for cable management on the table leg and in double width also usable as a table-to-table connector.

3 + 4
A socket box, optionally also pre-fitted for network and VGA connections, may also be inserted into the cable clip for power supply on the table. When using table-to-table connectors, there should be sufficient space to accommodate two adjacent socket boxes.

ordered impression. With a view to promoting changes in posture and allowing various forms of interaction, tables with the same proportions should be available in both sitting and standing height (table height 73 and 105 cm).

These qualities are particularly valuable in multifunctional areas: instead of having to keep various table forms on standby, one or two table formats can be used to create virtually limitless configurations, and self-organized changeover in furnishing layouts never results in a chaotic spatial impression.

Materials and surface finishes
The more the multifunctional the application, the more neutral materials should be. Frames should be in steel and screw-fitted to guarantee stability and firm and secure precision joints. As an alternative to steel with a coated finish, table legs in shot-blasted stainless steel provide a finish that is higher quality and more hardwearing. Chromium-plating of square table legs and underframes is not advisable as even minimal polishing marks are visible on the material.

Table tops and surfaces should also meet the requirements of varying applications. Veneered surfaces may soon show unattractive signs of wear when subjected to the demands of seminar use, and joints at 90° angles cannot be produced with a seamless finish using laminates, which in turn do not create the desired degree of high quality. Through-dyed panel comprising derived timber products, such as MDF panel, are a convincing alternative. The material structure provides a striking and lively finish with a pleasant tactile quality, and scratch marks remain almost invisible as there is solid colour all the way through. Panels should be effectively sealed to prevent humidity penetration so that no ugly "ring marks" or stains are left by spilt refreshments.

Training room with integrated, interactive media technology

▸ The furnishing layout of training environments with sophisticated media technology should also be adaptable to varying work methods for optimal support of a specific learning process. An excellent solution may be achieved by using an intelligent combination of static and partially mobile table units with coherent design and simple, plug-in cable systems that, like display screens, are also integrated into table units.

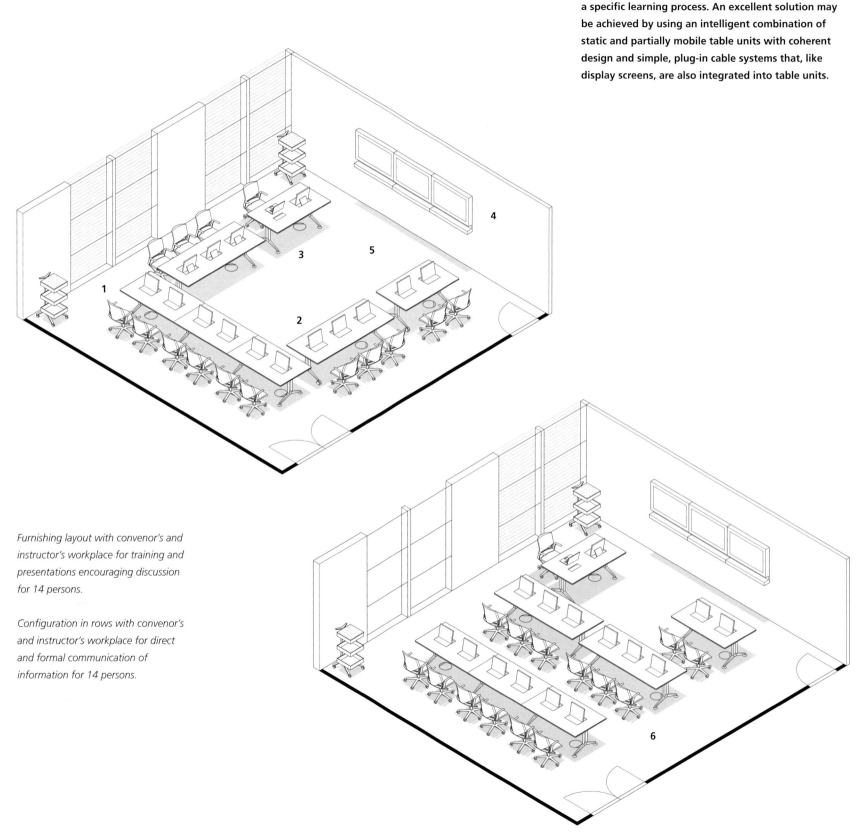

Furnishing layout with convenor's and instructor's workplace for training and presentations encouraging discussion for 14 persons.

Configuration in rows with convenor's and instructor's workplace for direct and formal communication of information for 14 persons.

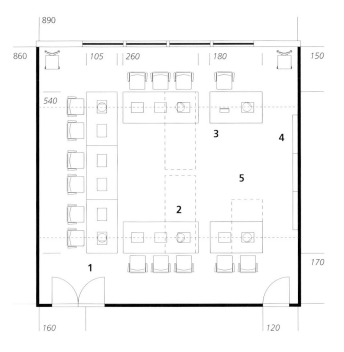

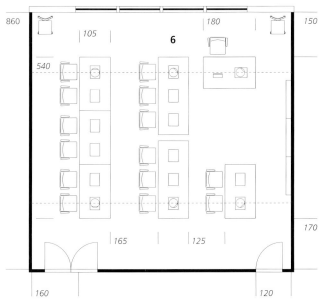

Scale 1:125 / dimensions in cm
(1 cm = 0.39 inches)
Area 76 sqm

1 Permanently installed table configuration with integrated display
2 Partially mobile single tables, pivotable by 90°, with integrated display
3 Permanently installed single table as an instructor's workplace with
  integrated display and additional connections for portable computer
4 Wall-mounted, interactive flat displays
5 The U-shaped table configuration leaves plenty of space for the instructor
  and participants to work at the interactive wall displays in parallel
6 Partially mobile tables configured in rows

In view of the rapid change in information and communication technologies, it is particularly useful for larger companies and educational institutions with correspondingly high space utilization rates to have permanent facilities especially equipped for computer training courses with integrated media technology. As in any other seminar environments, the focus in such facilities should be on interaction between the instructor or seminar leader and participants, and if required, among participants too, as it is this very kind of communication and interplay that is highly relevant for transferring information into knowledge and skills. Otherwise such courses could just as well be "attended" via the internet from any location. For this reason it is of paramount importance to ensure the most natural and effective integration of media technology and the adaptability of furniture and equipment to varying learning processes.

Flip-up and retractable displays are integrated into tables to meet such demands for communicative interaction. They may be fully retracted into the table surface to allow "barrier-free" communication among participants. Such displays are also connected interactively to shared displays on the wall. This allows participants to elaborate on any material they wish to contribute by means of sharing text and image support with all other members of the group from their individual workplace. Wall displays are touch-sensitive and thus interactive to allow the instructor to work direct and realistically as on a conventional board. Depending on specific contents and instruction methods, various settings for digital networks and configurations may be activated via corresponding programming from the convenor's workplace.

Whereas training interiors used to have static table configurations connected up by means of complex cable harnesses, combinations of coherently designed, permanently installed table configurations and partially mobile single tables may be now teamed with efficiently positioned floor ports to create variable, easily reconfigurable table layouts. The permanently fixed element defines possible connection points and configuration options, acting as a structural core, while the partial mobility of single tables permits a changeover of layout that does not require a new cable setup each time.

If multi-specifiable and easy plug-in cable systems are used in addition, which permit flexible table-to-table connections for power and data, there is virtually limitless scope for combination. Such solutions are admittedly more complex as the entire cable technology for varying scenarios is no longer located in a floor port but integrated into tables. On the other hand, it is only necessary to include a connectivity panel for power input in the space planning stage and this can lead to subsequent corresponding savings. For installations in interiors without a raised floor in particular, for example, in existing buildings or listed buildings, this may be a decisive advantage. It is important to weigh up various options quite carefully.

1

100   128

73

105

Furnishing an interior for multimedia interaction

Table-integrated displays

For seminar and training environments with sophisticated media technology, a choice of table-integrated displays is available that differ in terms of design quality and user friendliness. The spectrum ranges from manually operated flip-up displays to electromotive flat displays that slide back in vertically at the push of a button, or horizontally retractable models, and from simple plastic casing to high-quality stainless steel. The same applies to keyboards which may optionally be integrated into the retracting mechanism and simply "disappear" into the table surface when not in use. Which solution is right for you depends on individual user requirements in terms of design and prestige.

Interactive wall displays

Modern LCD displays or plasma screens provide a range of different qualities, particularly with regard to image resolution, for wall-mounted, shared displays too. A system that is adequate for video and DVD presentations is not suitable for training applications. In such cases it is absolutely necessary to have a minimum resolution of 1280 x 768 pixels to ensure a clear image from a short distance as well.

It is equally important to specify the feature of variable connectivity of up to three displays and a touch-sensitive panel that allows direct interaction by pen or finger on the display. The principle for such a scenario: the more direct and realistic the interaction, the more efficient participation and learning progress are.

In view of the high cost of seminars, where individual working periods are multiplied by the number of participants, all possibilities should be exploited to increase progress and success. There should be no economizing when it comes to the quality of furniture and equipment.

When specifying technical equipment and setting up a concept for the development, programming and cabling of such application scenarios, it is absolutely necessary to work closely with the IT department of the organization, with those responsible for further training measures and with a media specialist.

See also page 192, 202.

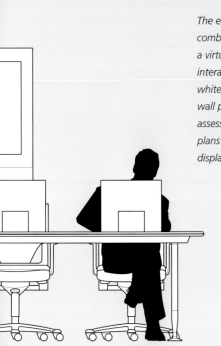

The electronic, interactive "wall panel" combines all the advantages of a virtual environment with conventional interaction tools such as a pinboard, whiteboard or a flipchart. The digital wall panel can be used to present, assess and edit graphics, network plans and websites in parallel – on the display direct using a pen or fingers.

260

2

3

Specifiers' option:
interactive, wall-mounted Commboard display (1,2);
table-integrated NoTable display screens (2,3)

Tables for media integration

When specifying tables, manufacturers should be selected who have a wealth of experience and equivalent know-how with regard to combining high-calibre design quality with perfect, tailored integration of media technology.

Tables should have a minimum depth of 90 cm to ensure an ergonomically effective viewing distance to the display.

Models from table ranges are recommended that include both statically linkable table configurations and also optionally mobile single tables to achieve a coherent design language throughout.

It would be ideal to select modular frame structures that due to the different lengths of uprights may optionally be fitted with adjustable glides or swivel castors. This allows partially mobile units to be produced in series quality without having to do a lot of "fine-tuning".

In terms of frame construction, table top geometry, materials and surface finishes the same demands apply as for multi-purpose interiors with mobile furniture, the difference being that table tops do not need to have a pivoting mechanism for such a scenario. On the other hand, it should be ensured that no central pedestal frame prevents the integration of a display.

Seating in seminar and training environments

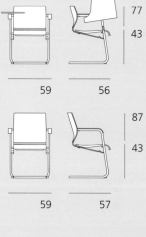

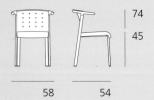

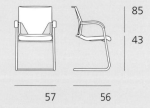

Stackable, four-legged chair with arms

The chair should be suitable for frequently changing configurations and therefore have stable and appropriate design: stackable and easy to handle – for example, due to a backrest rail that functions as a "grip" or as a tactile armrest when sitting in a "straddling" position, and even provides a support to help the user stand up. The chair can thus be carried and transported using one hand, for example, during a changeover from a plenary session to break-out groups.

Armrests have a slight outward curvature providing room to manoeuvre and making it easier for the user to turn round to address his or her neighbour.

If chairs are adapted to the height of the table edge, this will facilitate tidying up at the end of the event and give the interior an orderly appearance as chairs may be pushed in so that armrests rest against the table edge.

Materials and surface finishes
The back shell comprises easy-to-clean, recyclable plastic with a raised texture for better rear ventilation. The covers of the upholstered seat platforms should be in polyester or pure wool and removable. The frame in aluminium profile or die-cast aluminium is designed to be low-weight with high constructional stability. It is advisable to select either a hardwearing chromium-plated finish, or anodizing or powder coating to match the specific coating of the table frame.

Cantilever chairs

Cantilevers models are ideal for multi-purpose applications, and should ideally be from an extensive chair family that also comprises chairs for meetings and conferences, possibly even office swivel chairs or at least one that forms a good match in order to create a coherent appearance that supports corporate design.

The resilient frame of cantilever models allows sufficiently relaxed sitting even for longer conferences and seminars. An ergonomically designed backrest as on a swivel task chair provides the necessary degree of support for the spine in the lumbar region. Stackable cantilever chairs are a useful option for multi-purpose environments with varying applications.

The frame principle is similar on virtually all cantilever models – depending on the specific construction, they differ in terms of tube dimensions and thus in resilience, with regard to the maximum number of chairs in a stack and the degree of precision with which they may be stacked, and last but not least, in terms of aesthetic finish. However, there are greater, more significant differences with regard to the design of seats and backrests: if a suitable form and quality of material is selected, one-section seat and back shells offer a high degree of flexibility and adjustment to varying sitting positions and body dimensions and heights. If the shell is correspondingly spacious and has an upholstered edge, the backrest may also be used as a convenient armrest when sitting in a straddling position. A one-section shell conveys a feeling of comfort and protection, and it has a compact and coherent appearance, particularly from the back.

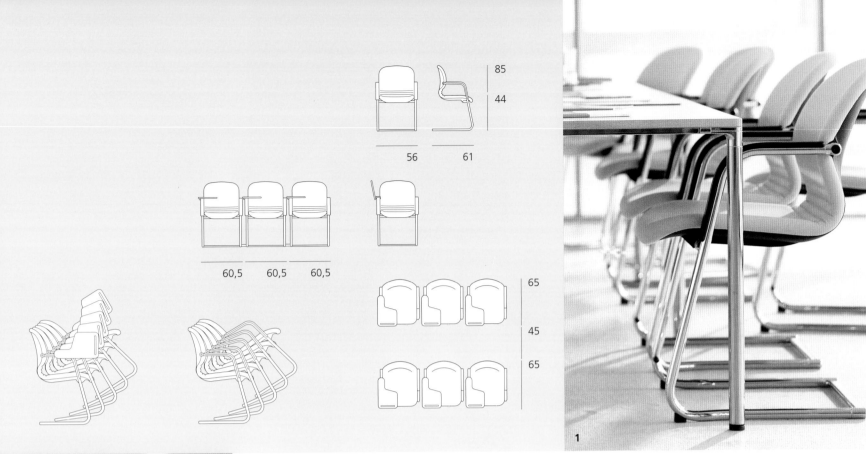

Two-section shell constructions on the other hand improve rear ventilation for the user but they are not as flexible due to their modular construction unless they are inserted into the frame as cantilevered and thus resilient elements. Viewed from the back, they have a less compact but lighter appearance and, in addition, allow various backrest heights and a host of upholstery variations.

Combinations of a seat shell and a fork-shaped, covered backrest frame are however more static in terms of the seat platform, but extremely comfortable in the back section with regard to self-adjustment and rear ventilation. If a semi-transparent fabric is used, optimal rear ventilation combines with a graceful appearance.

The decision as to which type of shell is the best depends on individual preferences and on the corresponding ranking of specific ergonomic, psycho-logical and design factors in relation to the overall design concept. In addition, it is important to select accessories in line with the specific application profile.

In high-density arrangements, e.g. in press conferences, lectures or presen-tations where no tables are required, it is advisable to be able to link chairs in rows, to add seat and row number-ing and slot-on writing tablets. Fold-up writing tablets make it easier for the user to sit down. And chairs should remain stackable even when fitted with writing tablets.

Materials and surface finishes
The seat and backrest should be upholstered with an exchangeable cover in pure wool or synthetics such as Trevira. A high degree of seated comfort is provided by a backrest that is designed as a frame construction and covered with a viscoelastic, stable synthetic material. An additional cover should also be specifiable.

One-section or two-section, upholstered seat and back shells in through-dyed plastic with covers in pure wool or synthetic fibres such as Trevira are suitable for a high degree of wear and tear. In such a case, the backrest may optionally also be non-upholstered, which has advantages in terms of cleaning but at the same time reduces the comfort aspect in terms of rear ventilation and due to the hardness of the backrest.

The frame in steel tube is chromium-plated or powder coated. Matt chromium plating or surfaces coated in the colour silver team well with polished or clear anodized table frames. Stackable versions should always be specified with a chromium-plated finish as they are subject to more wear and tear.

Conference workshop

▸ In view of the increasingly dynamic development of the general conditions and the competitive situation, change and innovation ability are becoming the core competences of virtually every organization. For the purpose of joint initiation, preparation and implementation of such concepts, a host of new interactive conference methods have therefore been developed in recent years that work on the assumption that it is only through the participation of all those involved that the degree of identification with change processes can be achieved which is necessary for efficient implementation. In addition, the active involvement of the experience potential of employees in preparation of product and process innovations leads to much better results in terms of contents too.

The furnishing of an interior reflects the principle and method of active participation in the concept of self-organization: similar to a workshop scenario, a set of modular, mobile furnishing elements, especially designed for dynamic work methods, are available which conference participants use to configure the specific interior layout they themselves require.

Dynamic conferencing:
from a workshop to moderation techniques

Only by drawing on the combined brain power of all its employees can a firm face up to the turbulence and constraints of today's environment.
Konosuke Matsushita

Conference forms between familiarity and change

Parallel to the shrinking "half-life" of guaranteed knowledge, corporate processes based on such knowledge are also subject to an increasingly faster need for change and adjustment. Although until just a few years ago it was believed that a state of longer term stability could be achieved following reform and restructuring phases, nowadays globalization with all its complex interrelations requires prompt reaction to dynamically changing general conditions and the competitive situation.

The much praised vision of structural change in enterprises and organizations frequently only gets off to a slow start. There are repeated complaints that although process innovations and suggestions for improvement are initiated quickly, they often take too long to become effective within a company. Recent studies have shown that the reasons for such shortcomings may often be found in initial meetings and conferences – and that the roots lie in the inherent instincts and forms of communication that have evolved within human communities over centuries: while stability and sense of identity are manifested in formal methods of communication, which continue to project existing organizational structures, innovation and change processes questioning the status quo have always evolved in informal circles, far apart from any official communication structures. Instead of transparency and predictability, those facing change – who have invariably not been involved in determining it – only feel a sense of uncertainty and vulnerability that takes on the form of fear and mistrust, even extending from blunt refusal to destructive opposition.

A thorough analysis of communication and decision processes therefore helps to establish the causes of the greatest barriers and obstacles. Besides psychological aspects, there are today quite concrete findings that give us every reason to involve people in determining the contents of innovation and change processes: the consequences of business decisions have become so complex that it has long since become impossible for them to be monitored and assessed by a small group taking "armchair decisions". The chance that new models, processes and structures really work in practice is therefore increasing to the extent in which we succeed in involving the special skills and potential of those who are responsible for implementing the same.

The same applies to middle management that often suffers from being over-involved during such processes. Many studies confirm that managers do not spend the greater part of their working day at the desk, but in meetings and conferences. But on the other hand, it also appears that such events are being regarded more and more as frustrating and a waste of time.

Answering questions concerning conference culture, executives have listed deficits and shortcomings in meetings which they regard as being responsible for people becoming weary of conferences:

• Participants are frequently not informed about the concrete contents and prepared accordingly before a conference appointment. This serves to expand the duration of the conference unnecessarily and results in participants feeling overwhelmed by suggestions available prior to a decision being taken.
• Ideas contributed and objections are often not acknowledged, special skills are often ignored and subsequent questionnaires frequently turn out to be "alibi events".
• Many participants do not say anything at all – perhaps because they are not involved in the topic in any way or because they had had a bad experience with the consequences of ideas they put forward in the past.

- Discipline in terms of contents and time leaves a lot to be desired and leads to many meetings ending without any concrete results – which means that the topic has to be broached at the next meeting anew.
- Factual issues are increasingly superimposed by squabbles about the in-company "pecking order".
- As a documentation of results, minutes of a meeting – providing they are recorded at all – are often sent too late, are incomplete and biased.

Not only is precious time lost due to such shortcomings in procedure, but the latter often do not achieve what is intended but invariably the opposite:

- Authoritarian enforcement of individual opinion instead of bringing creative skills together.
- Exhausting, entrenched struggles involving the "bonfire of the vanities" instead of focusing on a common goal.
- Constantly filing minutes of meetings, frustration and mentally logging off instead of motivation and readiness to embrace change.

Classic conference methods are primarily suited to predictable and preserving contents. These are however counter-productive if topics have to be dealt with which do not require the authority of hierarchical structures, but personal, individual competence and committed involvement of every single participant, irrespective of rank or status.

In order to initiate creative processes, to collect ideas and solve problems jointly, many different types of conferences have been developed which may be called "dynamic" or "interactive" forms of conferencing due to the active involvement and self-organization of participants.

Organizational forms: equal status, dynamic, participation-oriented

Methods used in conferences with a dynamic character quite intentionally aim to avoid the negative factors mentioned above: they focus on equality instead of hierarchical demarcation, on active participation instead of transmitting information with acknowledgment of receipt and notification of completion, on factual orientation instead of on individuals asserting themselves and on documentation, discussion and appreciation of all ideas put forward instead of subjective, sometimes even deliberate, filtering by means of the one person writing the minutes.

The main goal should therefore be to mask out the frequently unconscious roles of participants within an organizational structure in order to place the main focus on contents and factual issues, to motivate those involved to participate actively and be as committed as they quite naturally are in informal talks, and also to guarantee targeted positioning of communication processes. This combination of informal and formal elements as a cultural skill has to be learnt and trained as these are neither entrenched in our instinctive behaviour nor in most family and educational systems. The challenge for convenors of conferences with a dynamic character and the procedural preparation of such communication-oriented forms of work are therefore correspondingly high.

It is not for nothing that "process design" for innovation and change processes in terms of participants, time scheduling, various phases of changes in methods should be drawn up beforehand and laid down with great care. Intentional use is made of certain rituals in order to promote the feeling of social togetherness and to establish teamwork within groups that often comprise participants from different corporate fields. Such procedures include a kick-off meeting in which specific process design is explained and elucidated so that every participant can understand what is intended, as well as joint celebrations following successful interim steps and at the end of a project before implementation within the company starts with the roll-out itself.

The ideal size group for dynamic forms of communication may be correlated with the instinctive behaviour of the entrenched size of tribes. While larger numbers are quite possible for plenary sessions – for example, for open-space events – committed teamwork should be limited to twelve to fifteen participants. Any numbers above this level will invariably lead to sub-groups being formed which may have a negative effect on the factual level of the topic. Medium-sized rooms or spaces are therefore recommended for such groups. While meeting rooms and highly frequented seminar rooms should be close to workplaces, it is advantageous for conference workshops to be located away from participants' usual working environment in order to remove the focus from this temporarily. As for seminars, it is necessary to have plenty of daylight, a bright and friendly interior, subdued acoustics and adjoining spaces for intervals to allow participants to go out into the fresh air to recharge their batteries and gain inspiration for new ideas. The open-space concept already mentioned above combines the advantages of dynamic forms of conferences with a large number of possible participants: various topics are presented in a plenary session and then break-out groups of about 15 strong are formed, each with its own convenor, for subsequent discussion, processing and preparation of results ready for presentation. Participants may however change over to other groups at any time, listen in on other groups and cooperate where they find it interesting. When the defined length of the teamwork session is over, the results of all working groups are presented to the entire plenary meeting.

Furnishing and equipping a conference workshop: modular, mobile and self-organized

In addition to psychologically relevant factors of participation, verifiable findings on learning play a key role: on average, we retain 10 per cent of what we read, 20 per cent of what we hear, 30 per cent of what we see, and 50 per cent of what we both hear and see, and 70 per cent of what we say ourselves. But we can recall 90 per cent of events in which we were involved using our own motor activity. The fact that different types of rooms and furnishing are required for this purpose other than in classic conference environments almost goes without saying. Instead of

a prestigious room with a permanently installed , static system that is dominated by a table configuration as the fulcrum, a conference workshop is necessary for dynamic conferences where participants can adapt the interior themselves interactively to changes in methods and procedures. This distinguishes a conference workshop from traditional seminar environments too: in such cases, the instructor or facility management prepares the furnishing layout for a defined method of work, whereas in a conference workshop participants organize necessary equipment themselves by drawing on a "tools store" that is located in the room on standby. In comparison with a scenario where all participants start by sitting down and sit passively awaiting what is in store for them, everyone is challenged from the very beginning. This reduces warm-up phases considerably. Individual, modular, mobile furniture elements are like mosaic stones that may be reshuffled continually to create new scenarios of conference work: from a plenary session to break-out groups, from a discussion to a presentation, from a lecture to a seminar. In a conference workshop, all necessary tools should be kept clearly structured on standby ready for spontaneous use: partially mobile, stackable desks, a lectern, pinboards, flipcharts, servers for projection equipment, writing utensils and catering materials or mobile tables with a pivotable top. New media technology has become an integral part of such creative workshops in addition to "analogue" visual presentation media. In line with this development, power and data connections, if possible with internet access and projection areas, should be specified at the very beginning.

In addition to the psychological involvement and stimulation of staff potential, the principle of "self-organization" of the interior has a further concrete advantage: maintenance crew costs can be reduced considerably as facility management capacity is not necessary for changes in methods of work.

The impression created by tools and the specific media technology required may range from robust multi-purpose utilization and simple front projection of digital data to prestigiously furnished and sophisticatedly equipped, interactive command centres. In view of rapid changes and complex tasks, creative joint solutions are long since not only required on staff and middle management levels, but also within top management …

At a glance:
a day in a conference workshop

Conference workshop with a dynamic interior

Interactive change in methods is an integral part of participation processes: in the plenary session, the topic is introduced and ideas are collected; work in break-out groups can be dynamic and table-oriented, (intermediate) results and group-dynamic topics are either discussed in a barrier-free forum or – more formally – at open-centre table configurations. For lectures and presentations, either no writing facilities are required or small mobile desks or rows of tables are used, while decisions regarding further procedures are generally made, announced and documented in a more formal conference environment.

Page 128-135

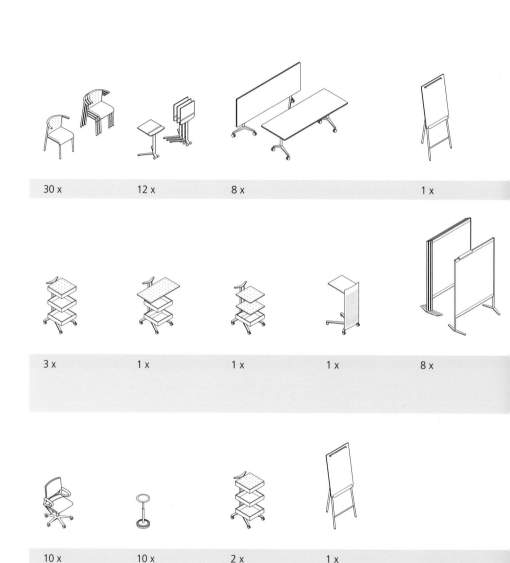

30 x	12 x	8 x	1 x

3 x	1 x	1 x	1 x	8 x

Interactive command centre

In line with the outstanding importance of strategy development or also of crisis management, top management has a special conference workshop that combines a high level of requirements in terms of prestige quality with state-of-the-art, interactive, media support and – optionally – global networking. The interior allows various settings for different phases in this case too: ranging from an introductory presentation to idea generation at an interactive high table, and announcement of final decisions.

Page 142

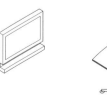

10 x	10 x	2 x	1 x

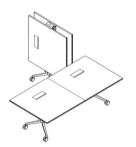

3 x	1 x	3 x

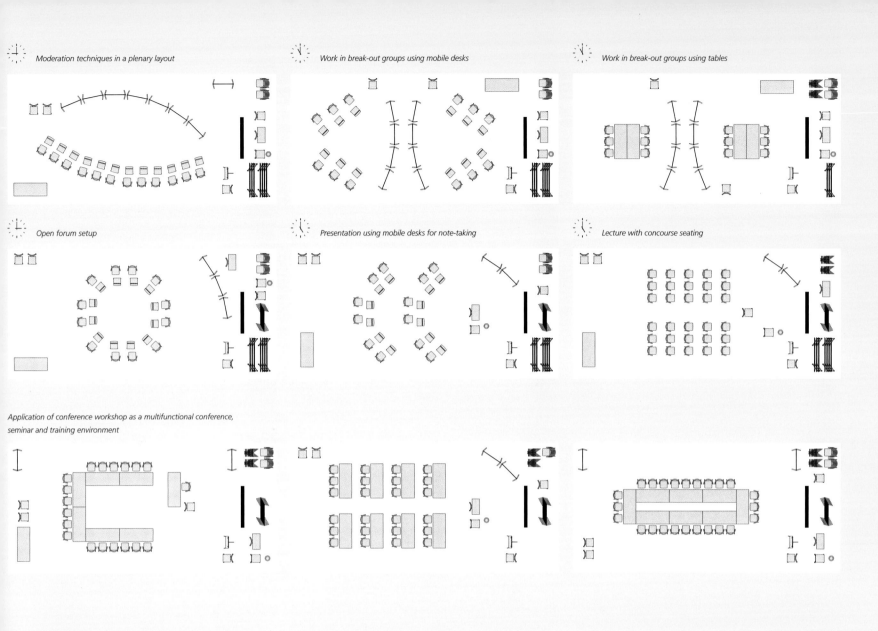

Moderation techniques in a plenary layout

Work in break-out groups using mobile desks

Work in break-out groups using tables

Open forum setup

Presentation using mobile desks for note-taking

Lecture with concourse seating

Application of conference workshop as a multifunctional conference, seminar and training environment

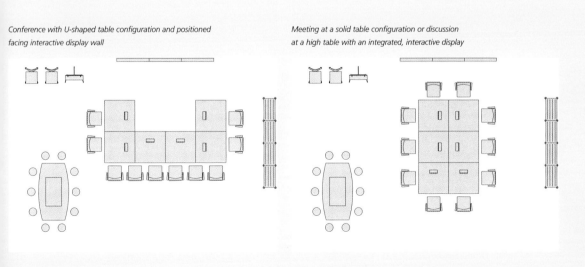

Conference with U-shaped table configuration and positioned facing interactive display wall

Meeting at a solid table configuration or discussion at a high table with an integrated, interactive display

127

A day in a conference workshop

9 am: moderation techniques in a plenary layout

▸ **Moderation techniques mark a particularly sustainable method of promoting creative processes, involving employees in decision making, and of achieving concrete results as well as commitment by means of clear consensus. Such techniques are called "written discussions" where results are not reached at shared tables but by using moderation walls.**

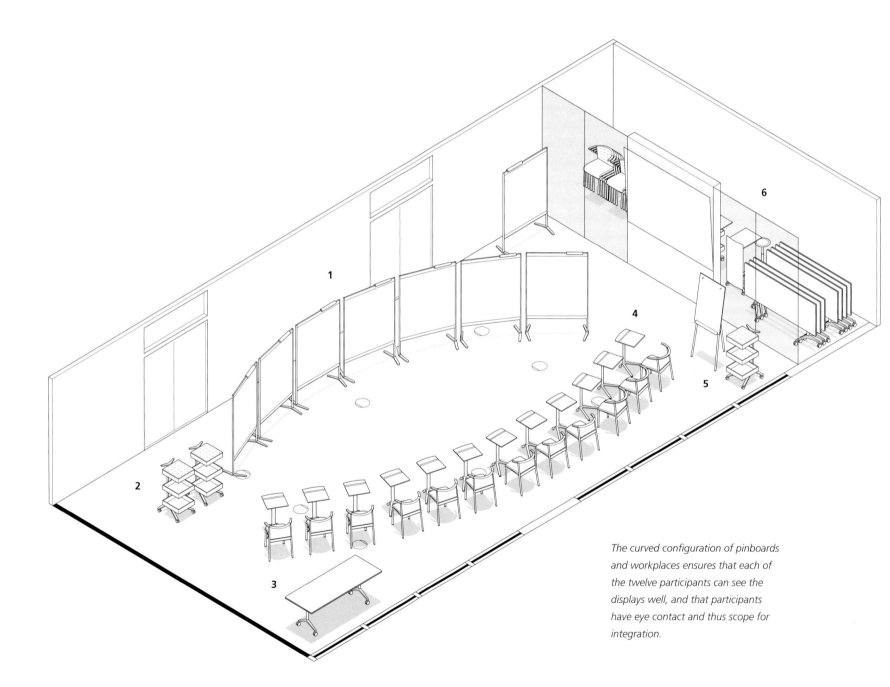

The curved configuration of pinboards and workplaces ensures that each of the twelve participants can see the displays well, and that participants have eye contact and thus scope for integration.

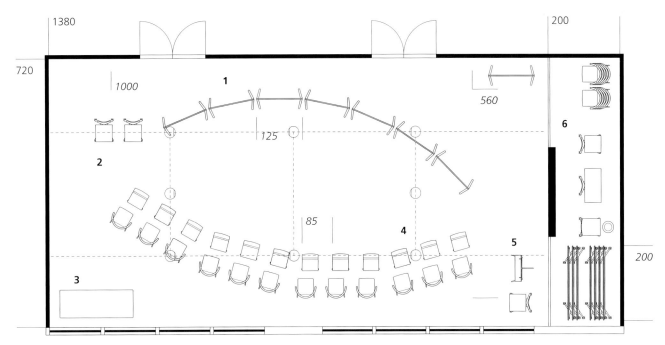

Scale 1:100 / dimensions in cm
(1 cm = 0.39 inches)
Area 114 sqm
Effective area 100 sqm
Store 14 sqm

1 Pinboards
2 Server for moderation materials
3 Mobile side table for storage and
  preparation of pinboard paper
4 Mobile desks and seminar chairs
5 Flipchart and materials server
6 Store room

A moderator leads the workshop. He or she is responsible for everyone keeping to the rules of the game and time constraints but is neither personally nor factually involved in the topic or the group. This avoids subsequent accusations of being biased and acting out of self-interest from the very beginning. The moderator starts off by explaining the tasks and goals of the session, possibly supported by an introductory presentation. Moderation techniques therefore generally start with a "plenary layout".

There is no table configuration as this would only be in the way. Participants should preferably sit in a curved constellation. This ensures that every person sits at an equal distance to the moderator and can see the other participants well.

The vertical pinboards form the shared work surface and are also positioned in a curve for everyone to see. First of all, opinions and comments are written on cards and material is then collected to which everyone may contribute. Contributions are thus "anonymous" and are then immediately displayed on the pinboards in full. It is superfluous for minutes to be taken. Cards and pens are kept on standby on the materials server. Writing surfaces comprise small mobile desks which, in contrast to writing tablets permanently mounted on the chair, have writing tablets that may be fitted on either side of the chair thus allowing them to be used by left-handers and right-handers – and also provide plenty of space for the user to manoeuvre as the depth of the tablet is adjustable as required.

A day in a conference workshop
11 am: work in break-out groups
3 pm: open forum

▸ The conference room may be compared with a work-shop in which all necessary tools are on standby and may be used as required. These tools include pinboards, light stacking chairs, writing facilities and mobile storage units for various moderation materials such as cards, stickers, pens, pins and scissors. Other useful aids are pivotable or folding tables, flipcharts and mobile servers for catering materials.

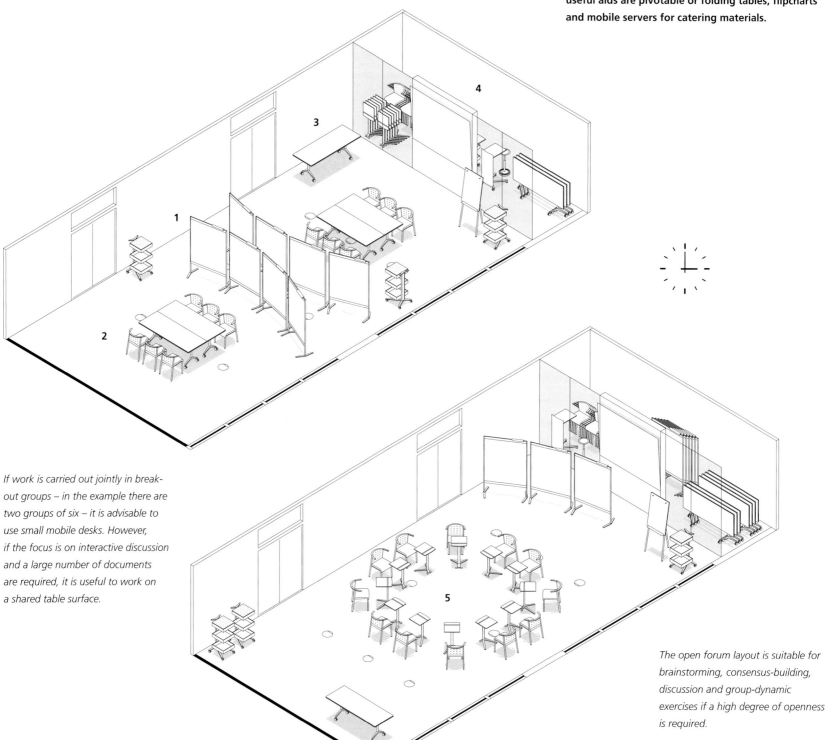

If work is carried out jointly in break-out groups – in the example there are two groups of six – it is advisable to use small mobile desks. However, if the focus is on interactive discussion and a large number of documents are required, it is useful to work on a shared table surface.

The open forum layout is suitable for brainstorming, consensus-building, discussion and group-dynamic exercises if a high degree of openness is required.

Scale 1:100 / dimensions in cm
(1 cm = 0.39 inches)
Area 114 sqm
Effective area 100 sqm
Store 14 sqm

1 Pinboards as partitions and work surfaces
  for break-out groups
2 Mobile, folding tables for 6–8 persons
3 Mobile, folding table for storage and
  preparation of pinboard paper
4 Storage space for conference tools that
  are not in use
5 Mobile desks in an open forum layout

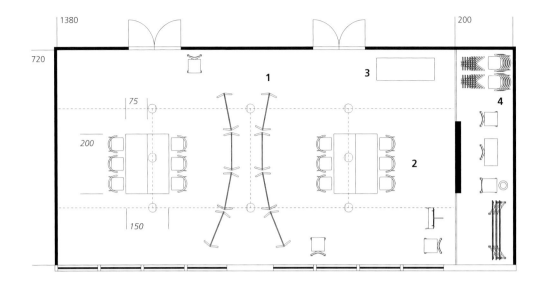

When the task areas developed in the plenary session have been sorted, described and given headings, break-out groups are formed for work on sub-tasks. Results are then presented in the plenary session, discussed and finally summarized in a catalogue of measures that is agreed on jointly. In addition to scenarios involving a plenary setup, break-out groups and discussion, a moderation session may also involve introductory lectures in order to establish a joint level of information, presentations of intermediate results or training elements for the purpose of communicating new skills to participants by means of written and vocal exercises. At the end of a moderation session where a clear method has been applied there are thus answers to simple, yet decisive questions: who has to do what, with whom and by when?

Conferences using moderation techniques are not only extremely efficient but they do not require any great effort in terms of space planning and design either, providing appropriate conference tools are at hand. By limiting numbers to a maximum of twelve to fifteen participants, medium-sized rooms are quite large enough.

Besides good daylight and a bright and friendly colour scheme it is particularly important to ensure subdued acoustics so that smaller groups could also work in the same room. The felt-covered pinboards do not only serve as work surfaces but also as partitions and acoustic elements. Pinboards, specified on one side as a whiteboard, extend scope for visual presentation. Pre-installed projection areas and efficiently positioned connections for power supply, preferably also for data, integrated into the floor, show upfront consideration for the fact that today digital media are also being increasingly used in group work – and that they ensure spontaneous access to information filed in the network.

Otherwise, neither sophisticated technical equipment nor store rooms or reconfiguration by maintenance crews are required. One decisive didactic advantage of such sessions is the self-organization of the group. Participation does not only take place mentally but also includes a real hands-on activity for partitioning the room, for example, when changing over from a plenary layout to a break-out group or for setting up the final open forum. A circular configuration of chairs is also most conducive to group-dynamic exercises and brainstorming. If all participants sit face-to-face this will allow the most direct form of contact and maximum scope for interaction. Tables would only create obstacles – both in the spatial and in the figurative sense. Small, mobile desks are therefore ideal for taking notes. Furniture units not in use are lined up along one of the short sides of the room. If required, pinboards may be positioned in front of the store to screen it from view.

5 pm: presentation

▸ Not only moderation techniques with their dynamic conference forms, but also conventional seminar methods may be used in a conference workshop. In this case, changeovers from lecture, joint plenary work, break-out groups, presentations and discussion do not only focus on different contents. They ensure stimulating change. Movement and changes in posture in group work are closely interrelated with mental agility and creativity.

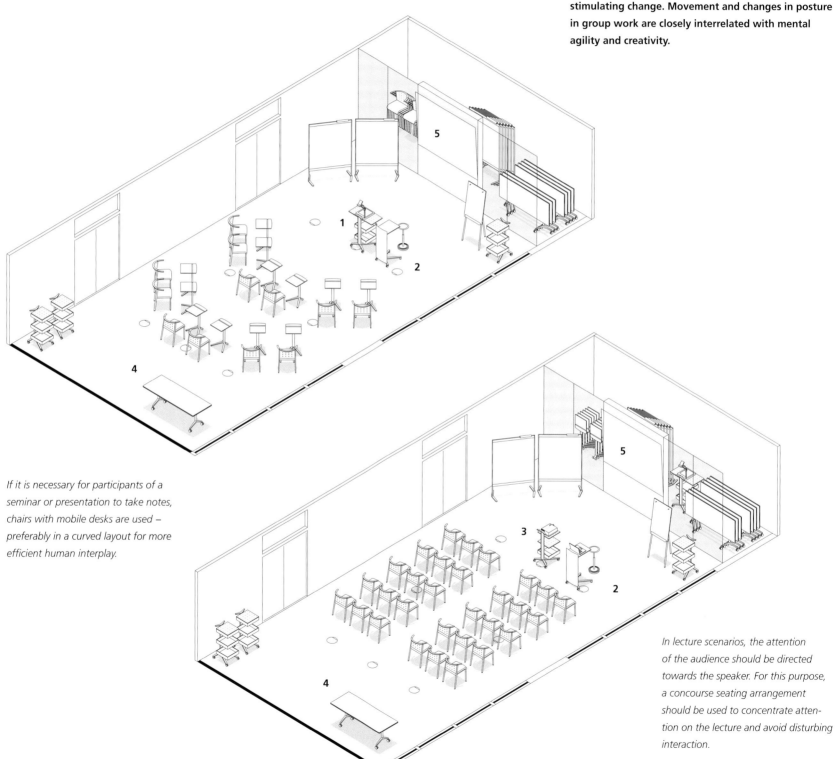

If it is necessary for participants of a seminar or presentation to take notes, chairs with mobile desks are used – preferably in a curved layout for more efficient human interplay.

In lecture scenarios, the attention of the audience should be directed towards the speaker. For this purpose, a concourse seating arrangement should be used to concentrate attention on the lecture and avoid disturbing interaction.

(1 cm = 0.39 inches)
Area 114 sqm
Effective area 100 sqm
Store 14 sqm

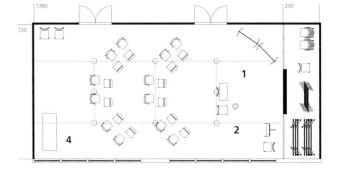

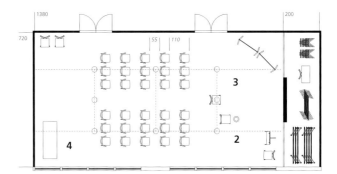

1 Mobile server for overhead projector
2 Lectern and leaning aid
3 Mobile server for data projector
4 Mobile side table for conference documents
5 Permanently installed projection area

Lectures or presentations are often an integral part of a complex working conference, for example in order to bring all participants up to the same information level or for visual elaboration of a subject. Appropriate media equipment such as a data or overhead projector on mobile equipment servers should be available if the session is to kick off with a lecture as an introduction to the topic. A lectern with sufficient space for a notebook, accompanied by a leaning aid, is useful for such a scenario.

All tools should be as light as possible and easy to handle; they should allow compact and neat standby storage, as well as be designed in a coherent, aesthetic quality. As with general tools, it is the utility quality that largely determines the

entire work progress: although procedures used in conferences with moderation techniques may be well coordinated, furniture and equipment are often inadequate for the designated rooms.

The method of reasoning according to which a provisional character serves to promote creativity is often merely a feeble attempt to make a virtue out of necessity. For model workshops are characterized by highly consistent functionality and work-focused design. After all, inventiveness should be related to work and not to compensation for shortcomings. And: the value that is assigned to such processes within the company, on the part of employees too, is to a large extent influenced by the quality of interiors.

A conference workshop as a multifunctional environment for conferences, seminars and training

▸ **From the point of view of saving on additional space capacities with corresponding furniture and equipment, a conference workshop offers some interesting potential. If it is furnished and equipped in a high-quality way, such a room may not only be used for dynamic, interactive conference methods such as workshops and moderation techniques, but also for all forms of conferences, training and seminars due to its modularity, flexibility and mobility.**

If table surfaces are required for storing large quantities of materials in conferences and seminars where interaction among participants is desired, it is useful to use a U-shaped configuration. This improves eye contact too.

For training courses with a lecture character and little interaction among participants it is recommended to configure tables in rows to focus attention on the speaker.

Scale 1:200 / dimensions in cm

(1 cm = 0.39 inches)

Area 114 sqm

Effective area 100 sqm

Store 14 sqm

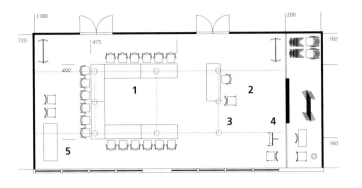

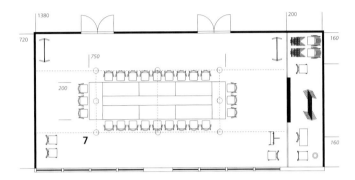

1 Six mobile, folding tables
   in typical U-shaped configuration
2 Single table as convenor's workplace
3 Mobile server for data projector
4 Permanently installed projection area
5 Mobile side table for conference documents
6 Lectern and leaning aid
7 Eight mobile tables in elongated
   configuration for 24 persons

If tools in a conference workshop have attractive, high-quality design this will not only serve to strengthen users' self-esteem and significance within a company: it opens up the possibility of using the room for conventional types of conferences and seminars too. This additional application scope allows optimal utilization of space and correspondingly high saving potential as no facilities specifically furnished for conference and seminars have to be kept in reserve.

At many locations, such as in metropolises throughout the world with high rents for commercial space, many conference and seminar rooms are today equipped with mobile and dynamic interior concepts. The room itself is then not self-organized but prepared by maintenance staff – but such an option also involves less cost and effort: reconfiguration can be carried out by one person. However, in such

cases the store room should be screened off so as not to disturb the formal character of the conference.

Depending on the desired degree of interaction in conferences and seminars, mobile tables equipped with a pivotable top are configured either in a U-shape with a separate convenor's workplace, as rows of tables with a lectern for lectures and presentations – optionally with media technology – or in a racetrack conference layout.

The room used for a conference workshop may also be used as a recreation space for breaks or for celebrations. For varying applications, it is therefore advisable to have rehearsed and repeatable configuration plans to facilitate re-arrangements. A room reservation book may be used to underline the joint responsibility for tidying up the conference workshop at the end of the event. Self-organization also covers responsibility, a process that needs to be learnt.

If the room is used exclusively as a workshop and seminar environment, it is advisable to specify tools with coordinated, hardwearing and tough surface finishes and materials. If additional applications are intended, prestigious veneers should also be available. The same applies in this situation as to any other design issues: the better and higher quality the furnishing of a room, the more carefully users handle the contents.

As in any other conference rooms, the location in the building within easy access of areas for breaks and relaxation is of paramount importance. The same applies here as in more formal environments: concentrated conference work requires regular breaks for which a change of location, preferably out in the fresh air, should be included.

See also "Foyer in a seminar area", page 284.

Furniture for a conference workshop:
chair, mobile desk, mobile table

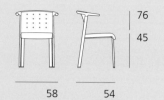

76
45

58   54

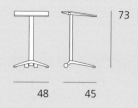

73

48   45

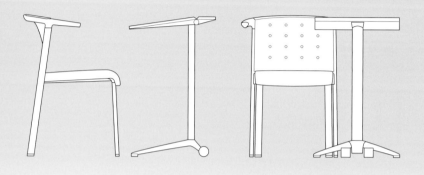

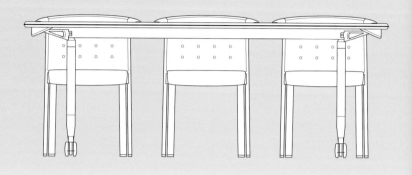

The chair

used in a conference workshop should be able to withstand frequent reconfiguration and be designed accordingly: stackable, stable and easy to handle – for example, by a backrest rail that serves as a handle, and at the same time functions as a pleasant armrest and also provides support for the user when standing and engaged in informal talks during breaks. Chairs can thus be carried and transported by users themselves, for example, during a changeover from a plenary layout to break-out groups. The armrests are cantilevered allowing room to manoeuvre, for example, when sitting in a straddling position or turning round to one's neighbour.

Materials and surface finishes
The back shell comprises easy-to-clean, recyclable plastic with a raised texture for better rear ventilation. The covers of the upholstered seat platforms should be either in polyester or pure wool, and exchangeable.

The frame in aluminium profile or die-cast aluminium provides maximum constructional stability with low weight. Depending on the degree of use and care, surface finishes should be either bright chromium-plated, anodized or powder coated, coordinated with the finishes of the frames of the mobile desks and tables.

The mobile desk

A mobile desk is used for lectures, presentations and moderation techniques; it should provide a sufficiently large space for note-taking without restricting room to manoeuvre. A robust, yet graceful frame construction, partially with castors, is therefore recommended. To meet mobility requirements it should be light and stable enough to serve as a solid writing surface. This is possible if foot sections are designed to provide the user with a flat, slightly slanting footrest: if pressure is applied to the foot section by one foot, the desk is automatically stable. As the writing surface projects slightly, the foot sections are not in the way when the desk is pulled towards the user. Compared with permanently mounted writing tablets, mobile desks have the advantage that they may be positioned slightly to the side of the chair and are therefore equally suitable for left-handed and right-handed users. Besides, the chair remains "neutral" and thus flexible for other applications, for example, at a table.

A writing surface measuring A3 across is sufficient. It should have a slight inclination, raised lipping and also be equipped with a small ledge at the rear – for example, for accommodating refreshments or for pens and conference incidentals.

It is useful if the mobile desks can be compacted neatly with writing tablets folded up and optionally stored on a matching transport trolley.

Materials and surface finishes
Laminated wood for the writing tablet guarantees high load stability with slender table top dimensions. Laminates and veneers are suitable finishes.

Columns in aluminium and V-shaped foot sections should be anodized and coated, polished or bright chromium-plated to match tables and chairs.

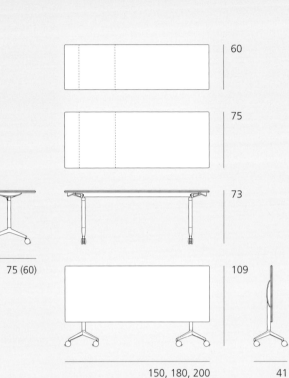

	60
	75
	73

75 (60)

	109

150, 180, 200   41

Specifiers' option:
Compacted mobile desks (1) as well as chairs and mobile
desks (2) from the Confair conference range

Mobile tables with a pivotable top provide maximum flexibility for adapting the furnishing layout to specific work phases in the conference workshop. On folding tables it is the frame that is pivoted: for this purpose they have to be placed top down, requiring two persons for handling and horizontal storage or a transport trolley for vertical storage. However, on a table with a pivotable top, the table top locking mechanism may be released with one swift movement and the table top is pivoted upward by means of the rotational movement. Combined with four lockable swivel castors this allows mobile handling by just one person. When the table top is in a vertical position, the table may be easily moved through doorways and narrow corridors and compacted neatly in the store room. If pivoting the table top automatically activates the rotational movement of the mobile foot sections, the frame construction becomes more slender, thus reducing the risk of "getting caught" on doorframes and corners during transport. In addition, tables may be compacted in ordered columns. The simplest mechanical functionality possible for intuitive handling is a decisive factor in terms of utility quality, particularly for a self-organized conference form: any extra mechanical step required makes operating more difficult. An integral, impact-resilient profile on the table edge protects both furniture and fittings during transport and configuration, and gives the table tops a slender appearance.

If seating is along one side of the table only a table top depth of 60 cm is sufficient; for seating on two sides or all sides it should be 75 cm. With regard to simple handling and mobility within a building, table width should be limited to 200 cm. It is also useful to have connecting plates underneath the table top to allow several tables to be linked to form table configurations.

Materials and surface finishes
In order to achieve space-saving frame dimensions and high tilt resistance, tables should be sufficiently heavy, a factor that also ensures stable transportability. Frames are therefore in steel or – for a higher quality of design and elegance – in aluminium, whereby necessary weight is obtained by means of a steel-core centre beam. For the finish of foot sections it is advisable to specify coated, polished or bright chromium-plated versions as for chairs and servers. In both cases, bright chromium plating should be preferred for areas subject to high wear and tear as it is highly insensitive to scratch marks. To match the mobile desks, table tops are either with laminate or veneer. The impact-resilient profile is integrated into wooden edging that is ideally in the same colour.

Furnishing a conference workshop: server

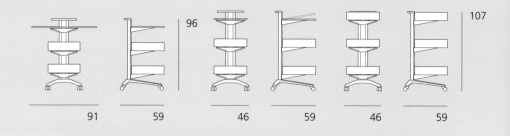

96

91　59　46　59　46　59

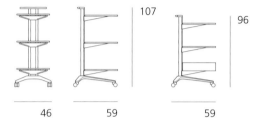

107　96

46　59　59

Mobile servers for materials and media technology

Mobile servers mark a modular system with shelves, open and closed boxes that fulfil a host of functions. With a view to meeting the requirements of different conference forms, a server family should comprise various models which may be easily "re-equipped" as necessary.

The basic models are:
servers for moderation or office materials, servers for AV equipment such as monitors, computers and video recorders, servers for overhead or data projectors, servers for catering (refreshments, snacks, tableware).

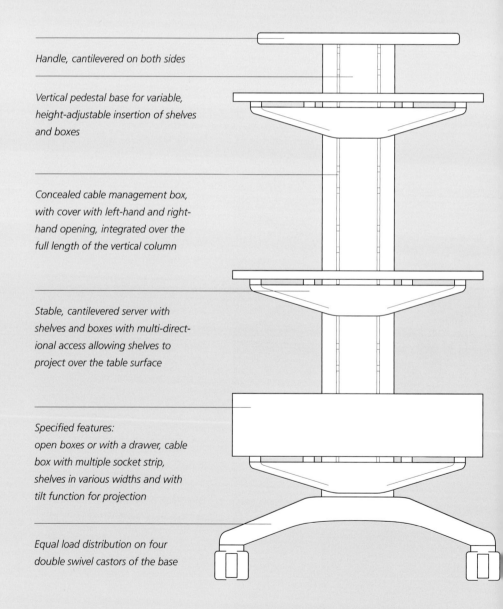

Handle, cantilevered on both sides

Vertical pedestal base for variable, height-adjustable insertion of shelves and boxes

Concealed cable management box, with cover with left-hand and right-hand opening, integrated over the full length of the vertical column

Stable, cantilevered server with shelves and boxes with multi-directional access allowing shelves to project over the table surface

Specified features:
open boxes or with a drawer, cable box with multiple socket strip, shelves in various widths and with tilt function for projection

Equal load distribution on four double swivel castors of the base

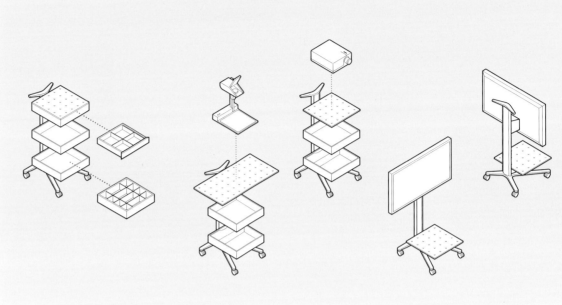

Servers for moderation materials (and catering)

These servers should have boxes for standby storage of moderation materials – such as felt pens, moderation cards and stickers, etc. It is advisable to have a flexible, slot-in set of organizer inserts for the boxes: two open boxes and one with a drawer. With such a specification, a server may also be used as a catering trolley for refreshments, cups and glasses.

Servers for media equipment

Server for overhead projector, video and data projectors as well as AV equipment should allow concealed cable management. In this case it is useful to integrate a cable management box with a multiple socket strip for internal power supply and to hold surplus cables.

Servers for overhead and projection equipment

These servers for portable projectors have a shelf as a work surface that is three times the width of the overhead projector, allowing overheads to be placed to the left and the right of the projector. Shelves should have a textured finish so that overheads can be picked up easily. Such a wide shelf also provides space for a digital projector and a notebook side by side.

Servers for projectors

As the integrated tilt adjustment function of projectors is often not sufficient for precise adjustment of the projection angle, the upper shelf of such servers should additionally have infinitely variable tiltability.

Materials and surface finishes
The vertical support structure of server frames comprises anodized or coated aluminium profile with height-adjustable positioning for shelves and boxes; foot sections with double swivel castors

are in die-cast aluminium and coated, polished or bright chromium-plated. The raw material of aluminium combines precision finishing with durability and recyclability. The cantilevered boxes and shelves are mounted on a V-shaped base, also in die-cast aluminium. The side panels of the boxes are in plywood and may be coordinated with the surface finishes of mobile desks and tables by using laminate or veneer. As one-piece sheet steel elements, the shelves with textured coating are largely scratch-resistant and should have a maximum load capacity of 15 kg.

Screen server

A screen server is suitable as a multimedia display for variable applications in presentations, videoconferences or project discussions. It comprises a flat screen, with a diagonal of up to 42 inches, that is permanently attached to a mobile server frame allowing flexible allocation to conference and work groups. As such a server is constructed in the same way as the other server

it may be moved up to tables as required and is thus a useful alternative to projectors or permanently installed displays, particularly for smaller conference and teamwork groups.

A screen server also allows a host of applications in informal environments such as lounges, relaxation areas or offices. Variable positioning and the number of shelves to be inserted in the support structure provide storage space for any necessary additional equipment such as a laptop or pc, a DVD or video player. Optionally it should also allow a camera and loudspeakers to be specified.

For more information on suitable screen technologies, see also page 202.

Visualization aids in a conference workshop: flipchart, pinboard, lectern

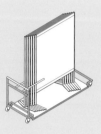

Flipchart

A flipchart is a useful and time-tested instrument used in offices and conference rooms for documenting arguments during group work for all participants to see, for visual presentation of interrelated points or for recording time schedules, action plans and agenda items.

The frame should have three legs to ensure stability, whereby the rear support should be foldable for compact storage. To accommodate users of different heights, the writing surface should be height-adjustable in at least three positions. In addition, it should be removable for easy transport. In order to ensure efficient handling the flipchart pad is locked into the paper holders by means of a clamp rail so that the pad cannot slip when sheets are turned over. It is useful to have a pentray for marker pens integrated at the lower edge of the writing surface.

Materials and surface finishes
For mobile handling it is advisable to have a frame in aluminium profile with hinges in high-performance plastic and a writing surface in light, but durable laminated wood, finished in laminate in a light colour. Veneered laminated wood, coordinated with table finishes, may optionally also be selected for prestigious environments. Surface finishes of metal parts should be specifiable in anodized, bright chromium-plated or coated to create an interior with a coherent appearance.

Pinboard

This is the key tool for moderation techniques: contributions, frequently entered on moderation cards, are often collected on pinboards. This serves to document an ongoing discussion. When changing over from a plenary layout to several break-out groups, pinboards do not only serve as a work surface but also as flexibly positionable partitions that can be used on both sides and are also acoustically efficient.

To withstand permanent wear and tear, pinboards should have a double-sided, hard wearing felt covering in which pinholes are virtually invisible. Optionally, one side may also be specified as a whiteboard for use with dry-erasable pens and magnets. The format of the board surface is based on the size of commercially available pinboard paper (at least 120 x 140 cm).

*Specifiers' option:
chairs, pinboard, folding table, mobile desks and flipchart from the Confair conference range*

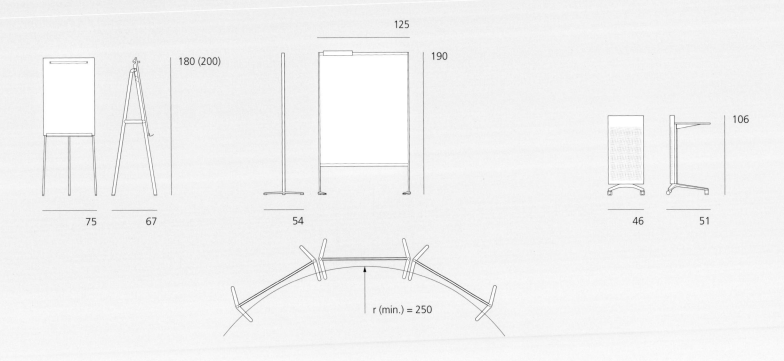

Every pinboard should have a removable pinstrip so that spare pins do not to have to be kept on the felt surface.

The frame should allow sufficient legroom so that the user may stand directly in front of the writing surface. Foot sections with flat dimensions help to avoid trip hazards and as is the case with mobile desks, a light pinboard may be stabilized if the user places one foot on the flat foot section when pinning paper and cards onto the board.

The angled positioning of foot sections allows pinboards to be arranged in a curved configuration and to be compacted neatly. A transport trolley for compacted pinboards is also a useful accessory for using in the store room.

Apart from conferences with a dynamic character, high-quality pinboards may also be used as displays for exhibitions, presentations or information boards.

Materials and surface finishes
The pin surface comprises soft wood fibreboard with a firm felt covering which makes it easy to insert pins. The frame is in light aluminium profile and foot sections are in die-cast aluminium, anodized, coated or polished to match the other furniture units.

Lectern
A lectern should also be an integral part of a conference workshop. To ensure the degree of mobility required for self-organization, the front foot sections should be fitted with double swivel castors while the two rear feet should have anti-slip rubber glides. The lectern can then be easily moved by canting it slightly. A horizontal surface provides space for a manuscript or a laptop and should optionally be specifiable with a reading light or a microphone. If the support structure has accessible cable channels, this allows clear and concealed channelling of power and data cables down to the floor. A sufficiently wide modesty panel reaching from the floor over the entire area of the lectern gives the person addressing the auditorium a high degree of psychological security. If the front panel is partially perforated this will improve acoustic performance, and the lectern will look aesthetically lighter.

Materials and surface finishes
As for servers, the vertical support structure of the lectern is in anodized or coated aluminium with flip-up cable channels integrated at the sides. The foot sections with two double swivel castors and two rubber glides are in die-cast aluminium, coated, polished or bright chromium-plated.

The modesty panel is in partially perforated powder coated sheet steel with a smooth finish for attachment of logos or magnetic plates. The shelf in dimensionally stable plywood, finished with laminate or veneer, is mounted in a cantilevered position on a V-shaped support in die-cast aluminium to provide ample legroom.

Interactive command centre

▸ Maximum participation and creative input of ideas are not only the order of the day on staff and middle management levels but are also required in top management, for example, when strategy development or crisis management is on the agenda. A spacious high table with an integrated, interactive display, various wall-mounted screens that are flexibly connectable and also touch-sensitive, and a variable setting comprising mobile, folding tables with integrated connectivity for multimedia conferences guarantee dynamic conferencing of the highest order.

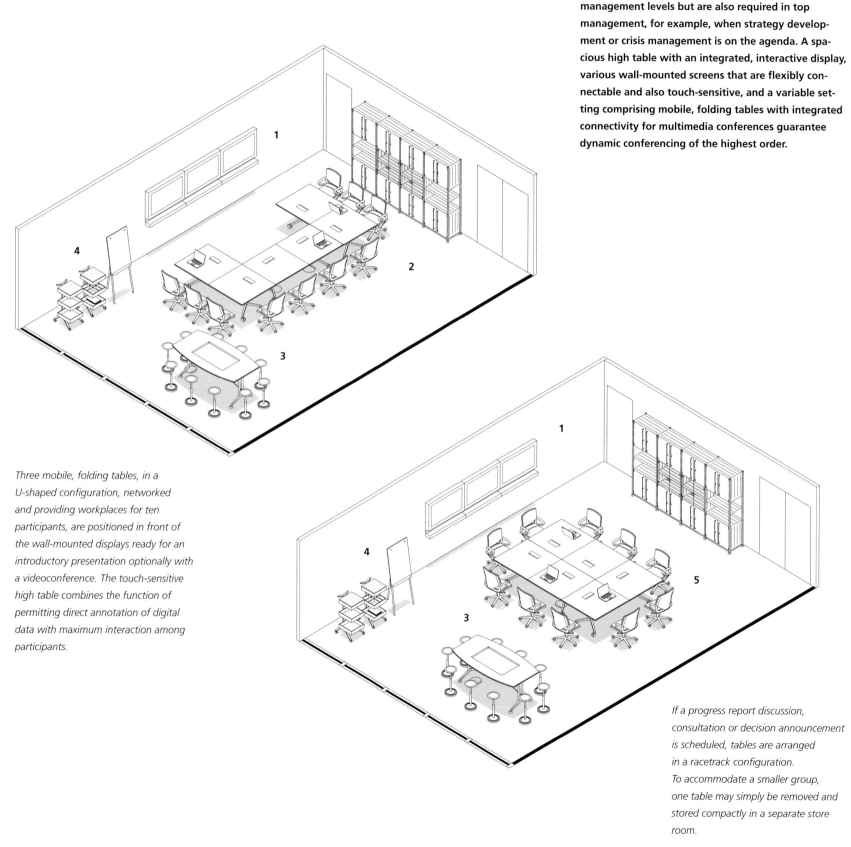

Three mobile, folding tables, in a U-shaped configuration, networked and providing workplaces for ten participants, are positioned in front of the wall-mounted displays ready for an introductory presentation optionally with a videoconference. The touch-sensitive high table combines the function of permitting direct annotation of digital data with maximum interaction among participants.

If a progress report discussion, consultation or decision announcement is scheduled, tables are arranged in a racetrack configuration. To accommodate a smaller group, one table may simply be removed and stored compactly in a separate store room.

Scale 1:125 / dimensions in cm
(1 cm = 0.39 inches)
Area 78 sqm

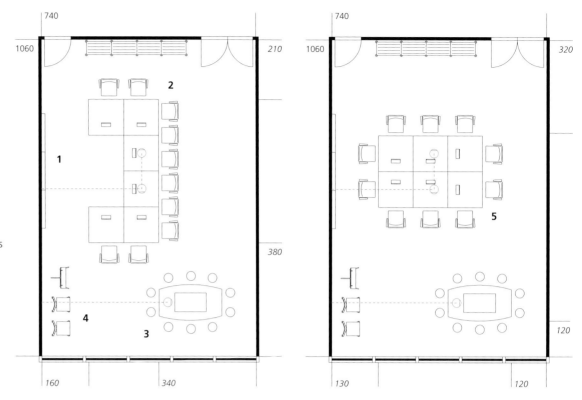

1 Wall-mounted, interactive displays
2 Mobile, folding tables with connections for technical
  equipment in U-shaped configuration and facing displays
3 High table with integrated, interactive display
4 Mobile server and flipchart
5 Mobile tables, configured in a large conference table
  arrangement

The rapid change in the competitive situation and general conditions, and globally distributed corporate activities require the "command centre" on the one hand to be the fulcrum of creative collaboration of top management, on the other hand it should be directly networked, i.e. function as a "hot line" to other linked sites within the company. A high-quality and technically sophisticated conference workshop for top management comprises a combination of mobile, folding tables providing full connectivity for multimedia support, up to three large-format, interactive wall screens and a high table with integrated, touch-sensitive display. This serves to combine clear leadership structures with dynamic input of ideas, fast deliberation and decision processes as well as global networking.

In a U-shaped configuration, the wall screens can be used for documenting explanations of the status quo and respective tasks. Wide scope for operating and networking screens allows synchronous visual presentation of up to three different sources of information, for example, for a presentation, a videoconference call and for supporting, spontaneously accessible data from the intranet.

The person holding the presentation is thus able to work from the screen direct and emphasize and annotate important aspects using a pen. But participants can also play an interactive role: participants can connect to the presentation display via a notebook from their workplace for additional info-exchange.

If creative info-exchange and the development of a joint solution are the order of the day, participants change over to the high table that provides optimal support for participation and informal interaction. Irrespective of individual "positions", everyone can add input to the shared digital display by pen or finger and discuss, reject or further develop contents. If consultation and binding decisions are required, a more formal environment is necessary in which tables arranged in a configuration communicate a hierarchical order.

The seating solution comprises comfortable to luxurious mobile swivel chairs on castors with ergonomic automatic synchro-adjustment to encourage movement and facilitate changes in position, in the figurative sense too.

Interior for interaction with media support

Interactive high table

Such a table provides the most efficient tool for solving deadlocked situations and for promoting creative potential within a group. No other setting supports interaction better than shared working in a standing position round a horizontally integrated table surface. This comprises a high-resolution display, minimum 50 inch, integrated into the table surface. Without having to "learn" how to work this, every participant can work intuitively on the digital panel. Additional information may be accessed spontaneously from the network, and results are immediately available in digital form. Simple additional programming options allow data to be rotated like an analogue piece of paper. Either a computer, preferably integrated into the table frame, or a central server function as a data source.

The table surface should be barrel-shaped and accommodate six to eight persons. A sufficiently large ledge provides storage space and support for the user when standing. If a 50 inch display is used, the table top should have a depth of 90 cm (on the shorter edge) and 120 cm (across the centre) and be 240 cm wide. A table height of 90 cm provides a convenient working height for participants of differing heights. Concealed cable management should be specified to avoid a chaotic visual impression and trip hazards.

Materials and surface finishes
With a view to creating ample legroom, and both transparency and visual lightness, the table frame should comprise a stable underframe and a techni-frame in aluminium profile. Table legs themselves should ideally be recessed and comprise uprights and foot sections both in aluminium that are fitted with adjustable levelling glides. Depending on the specific design concept, options should include coated, clear anodized, polished or also bright chromium-plated frame finishes. MDF panel is used for table tops; this material allows various types of edging to match any design theme: ranging from a straight edge profile or a double bullnose option with integral impact-resilient profile to chamfer edging that gives the table top a "floating" appearance. Various veneers or even linoleum, coordinated with the design theme, should be available as surface finishes.

Mobile, folding tables with sophisticated multimedia connectivity

These tables provide links to the multimedia world for dynamic conference forms with varying methods and number of participants too. They have permanently integrated cable management and connection points in the table frame that are accessible via one or two table portals in the table surface with a 180° hinged cover. They provide space for network adaptors, surplus cable and battery chargers so that the table itself remains "clear" and free of technical equipment, apart from connected notebooks. A show-me button in the connectivity module allows a specific notebook to be connected to the shared display panel at the push of a button, for example, to a wall display or a mobile rear projection unit.

Specifiers' option:
mobile folding tables from the Confair conference range with integrated connectivity modules for media technology (1); InteracTable with touch-sensitive, interactive flat screen (2)

At both ends of the table, cable management boxes underneath the table surface have connectivity modules, operable by untrained personnel, with input and output modules for connecting VGA, audio, USB, power and a show-me button. Up to 20 workplaces may be connected in this way, each requiring only three cables between tables and a pre-installed floor port. Optionally a network connection should also be possible. To reconfigure, disassemble or extend table arrangements, connecting harnesses are re-attached appropriately in a safe and fool-proof way.

Tables are fitted with wheels and lockable brakes, and can be folded vertically by one person with one swift movement due to an ingenious, coordinated mechanism allowing them to be easily compacted or moved through doors and corridors to store rooms. Table edges should be finished to match the other tables – for example, an interactive high table. However, it is advisable to specify double bullnose edging with integral impact-resilient profile so that table edges can withstand frequent reconfiguration and possible collisions during transport.

Materials and surface finishes
To facilitate flexible configurability, tables have a recessed frame that provides sufficient all-round legroom. In order to facilitate the folding function of the table, table underframes, the cable channel and uprights should be made from aluminium profile, a material that combines high dimensional stability and precision with low weight. Table top bearers and foot sections are in die-cast aluminium to provide necessary stability and a high quality of design. Depending on the edging, it is advisable to specify table tops either in fine particle board or MDF, and table lipping should be in solid wood. The finishes of table tops and portals should allow a coherent design concept to be achieved using an option from a wide choice of veneers or linoleum.

Wall display
An interactive digital wall display is an aid to direct and particularly authentic visual presentation of material. Up to three such networked, interactive presentation and work surfaces may optionally be hung in front of the wall or flush-mounted, depending on specific pre-installed fittings. If programmed and connected correspondingly, displays can be activated jointly or also individually to access up to three different data sources synchronously, for example, the internet, a presentation and a videoconference. A single display is suitable for use with groups of six to a maximum of ten. The screen resolution should ideally be high to facilitate precise, direct working on the display surface, which should be at least 50 inch. With an aspect ratio of 16:9, this corresponds to a screen diagonal of 127 cm. A special frame accommodates the hardware for intuitive interaction on the display surface by finger or pen. A ledge underneath the display is useful for accommodating pens or a remote control device. When specifying, it should be observed that necessary connection fittings (VGA, power, audio, interaction and possibly also network) or corresponding cable channels should be installed in time and available at the desired place.

Materials and surface finishes
If displays are flush-mounted in the wall, only a narrow edge of the frame is visible. Various frame systems provide wide scope for design: aluminium, anodized, bright chromium-plated or coated, or stainless steel. For constructions hung on the wall, the visible frame is much wider and should therefore have a matt finish, for example, in coated aluminium

For further information, see page 195, 201, 202.

Assembly halls

▸ Due to their basic function, a company restaurant, a canteen and a cafeteria are communicative places and frequently pivotal to the performance of the informal network within the company. Communal eating and chatting is invaluable. It would therefore be opportune to use these places for more far-reaching communication functions too. If space planning and furniture specifying includes corresponding flexibility, a canteen may be transformed into an assembly hall or a lecture room without any great effort. For rooms in conference centres, efficient multifunctional use is as much one of the basic requirements as the possibility of partitioning rooms to achieve a high utilization rate that is adapted to varying needs.

From eating together to conferencing together

**Without communal eating,
no human group can hold together.**
Christopher Alexander

The concept and status of work is being changed to an ever increasing extent by current structural change in industrialized countries. In view of global competition, companies rely on their employees being more strongly and efficiently committed in all corporate areas. In order to achieve greater performance potential and higher productivity, companies do in effect, have only two possibilities: either they increase performance pressure on employees as these are regarded merely as a workforce, as a "cog in the wheel" as Charlie Chaplin depicted it so nightmarishly in "modern times". This may be successful in the short term but in the long term pressure provokes counter-pressure, and an overproportional amount of energy is wasted in internal relations. The alternative is to understand employees as the most important capital a company has, to make people with all their abilities and talents the focus of attention and allow them to participate in corporate development. In the long run, such an approach promises much more success, as supporting human resources is always a much more sustainable instrument for increasing motivation, performance and quality assurance. Pressure and intimidation on the other hand frequently lead to a climate of fear, increase the sickness rate and suffocate creativity.

Regularly conducted Gallup polls prove that the greater majority of employees still "work to rule", that a substantial number have already "given notice within their mind" and only a minority work for their employer in a committed and motivated way. That is not only a pity for those concerned as they spend the greater part of their life working, but it is also a waste of money as personnel costs are some of the highest budget items. In the wake of the demographic development in some industrialized countries and the increasing shortage of skilled labour, the health and well-being of employees are becoming important for sustainable corporate development beyond such concerns: on the one hand, a longer working life and on the other hand, competition among companies for human resources simply require more quality of life in the working world. The economic theory according to which economic development occurs in long waves, so-called Kondratieff cycles, distinguishes certain basic innovations for economic development. According to this approach, we are now facing the sixth economic cycle. This differs from the five previous economic cycles, which were marked by the steam engine, steel, electrical engineering, chemistry and information technology, as this is the first time that the focus in not on technology but on human beings themselves. Key growth drivers such as health, diet, wellness and the cult of the body, including corresponding research in biotechnology, gene technology, pharmacy, etc. are primarily aimed at individual people who thus become the most important innovation driver. Endeavours to achieve a better balance between the world of living and the world of work or the globally increasing significance of stakeholders are also indicators that people themselves are moving into the centre of economic interest.

The degree to which a company appreciates its employees is shown particularly clearly in the design of time and space for leisure and breaks in the working world. For while the furnishing of workplaces is directly linked to the factor of "productivity", corporate culture can prove itself particularly in areas where performance capability is not ostensibly required but individual well-being and togetherness are the order of the day. This is about human interplay, moods, atmosphere and casual informal communication. On the one hand, the nature of informal exchange increases a sense of community and social competences but on the other hand, such encounters generate important new ideas and knowledge interfaces within corporate structures. Recent surveys show that private and job-related contents generally merge.

Canteens and cafeterias are key places in this invisible network. For eating is more than merely intake of food. Communal eating is a cultural and social act that is an inherent part of our instinctive behaviour. Nowhere else do closeness and familiarity evolve faster than during communal eating, a ritual that runs through the entire cultural history of humanity like a central thread. In his Pattern Language, Christopher Alexander puts the social aspect in a nutshell: "without communal eating, no human group can hold together." If this form of community-building is lacking, which is often connected with unconscious rituals, the bond of the community will disintegrate. A family that does not meet for communal meals, whether it is on festive occasions or in daily life, cannot hold together.

In business life too, eating plays a special role in creating confidence. In such an environment it is generally quite an essential basis for cooperation that is created, which becomes more formal later on. Within a company, communal eating involving employees from all areas is a welcome vent and invariably an impetus for new ideas. A conducive environment must be designed with a view to promoting such human interplay. Appropriate ingredients are equally important – but this is up to the kitchen. It is not necessary to describe the situation in many canteens with regard to eating culture. Just one remark is perhaps necessary: in addition to many other factors, wrong eating habits also impair health and thus performance capability. Appropriate design of the working environment also considers the inter-relations between diet and both mental and physical performance. For anyone wishing to tackle a conference or concentrated work after lunch with ease should not make life difficult for themselves when eating: light meals versus stubborn decisions.

Organizational forms: service oriented, open and multifunctional

As a hub of informal communication, a company restaurant should be open all day long. There is something "going on" all day. Such a day might last fourteen hours or longer as working hours in many administrative areas have to be more flexible due to global distribution of locations, partners and customers to guarantee accessibility from different time zones. Shift work, which has long since become the order of the day in production areas, is increasingly becoming the norm in canteen areas too. It is important for a company restaurant to be attractive and open for all employees to avoid the creation of a "class society" and to strengthen the sense of community. Production and administration areas are becoming more closely connected in any case, and for management too it is advisable to patronize communal eating throughout all corporate hierarchies. Nowhere else – perhaps with the exception of the plant gate and reception – can a more authentic impression of moods, opinions and factual estimation on the part of employees be gained. How much faster and better could wrong decisions be corrected and new ideas be implemented if relevant information from the "shop floor" were not delayed and filtered on its way to executive floors?

If the catering area is not one of a company's core competences or the business is too small to allow professional catering, it may be useful to lease such premises to external caterers. This is also advisable when working hours required on the part of catering staff do not coincide with those usual within the company. A company restaurant could also be opened to guests, visitors and external users, such as employees from institutions and businesses in the immediate vicinity, to increase utilization capacity and make leasing this business more attractive. The arrangement that is usual in conference centres, namely linking catering with conferences, could also be useful to companies themselves. Why should a company restaurant not be furnished in such a way from the very outset that allows it to be used for lectures, presentations or a company plenary assembly if the latter addresses a large part of general, in-company public? Such a solution is always more cost-effective than keeping special, generally infrequently used areas for this purpose, and it is much better than holding such events in provisionally unused production or dispatch facilities as is often the case. If rooms are furnished with this in mind, the organizational effort for temporary use is assessable. In addition, gastronomy operators have enough experience with adapting their facilities to customers' wishes – for example, for family gatherings, club or even conference events.

The furnishing solution: easy-care, high-quality and flexible

The location of a company restaurant within a building is quite decisive for the user groups who frequent it. If a good cross-section of staff is desired, it should be centrally located so that it may be reached quickly. If it is to be open to external people, an outer access should not be forgotten and entry into the company building would be via corresponding access and security systems. It should look out onto an outdoor area, ideally with natural landscaping, and an outdoor patio for catering purposes in good weather will help to create a high quality of relaxation and regeneration. A short walk after lunch is not only recommended for health reasons, but also gives people the chance of conversing in private.

The spatial structure should allow standby use for various applications: lively and quiet areas, small sections with semi-public corners and large displays which may be reconfigured quickly as the need arises. In a nutshell: this environment should provide all those qualities that are typical of busy places – space for being alone in society, as well as for large events, for a quick snack or for lingering with an espresso.

Central or decentral cloakroom elements can cater for changes in weather conditions. Wall newspapers and bulletin boards provide information on current events and activities; shelves or newspaper stands are used to accommodate daily newspapers, magazines and company-related literature. Wall-mounted screens allow special media events such as sports to be enjoyed jointly. However, a television channel should only be used by way of exception and in very limited amounts so as not to impair desired interaction among visitors.

Furnishings should maintain an appropriate balance between informal and professional use. Easy-care flooring but with a high-quality appearance, a light and friendly colour scheme, plenty of daylight and variable lighting control technology create a professional atmosphere. Appropriate acoustics should also be ensured as time spent in a busy company restaurant could easily result in annoyance due to a high level of noise.

Window blinds, projection areas, a ceiling-mounted digital projector and an integrated sound system allow the room to be used for more formal conference forms with many participants too.

The interior should include: light, yet comfortable, ideally stackable chairs that are easy to clean, and multidirectional, single tables – with a hardwearing finish to meet demands for high wear and tear – quickly configurable into elongated arrangements or capable of being stored compactly, combine restaurant qualities with flexible space utilization.

Why should lunch with colleagues or business friends not simply merge into a scheduled meeting – and a changeover to a conference room becomes superfluous? Such communal eating areas should however be specified to include power and data connection points to allow media technology to be used if needed. This opens up yet another interesting perspective: how often does it occur that an interesting conversation evolves out of a more or less coincidental encounter in the company restaurant and people then arrange to meet again as it is not possible to access information, that is generally digital, on the spot? Such processes could be simple and efficient if small corner tables with interactive displays were also available for spontaneous visual presentation of information from the network or from a digital "workplace", or if sections of the company restaurant could also function as an internet café, equipped with technology that promotes human interplay efficiently. Power, data and internet connections should at least be specified in this interior as in any other communication environment. Scope for using a company restaurant as a real central hub within a company's communication network is far from exhausted.

At a glance: company restaurant and assembly hall, partitionable rooms for conference and seminar applications

From a company casino to an assembly hall

A company restaurant is one of the most important planning tasks if encounters, communication and networking are to be promoted within a company. The interior should provide spatial facilities for various dialogue scenarios, meet specific requirements in terms of hygiene, air conditioning and lighting technology and should also allow use as a multifunctional events centre for company plenary sessions.
To meet these requirements it is necessary to specify both the integration of multimedia technology and variable seating and flexible tables which may be kept compactly on standby in the store room.

Page 152–155

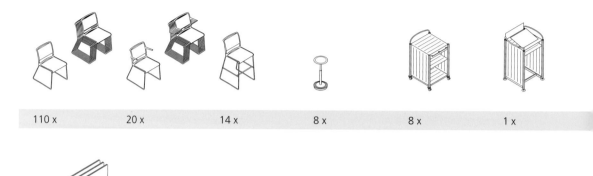

| 110 x | 20 x | 14 x | 8 x | 8 x | 1 x |

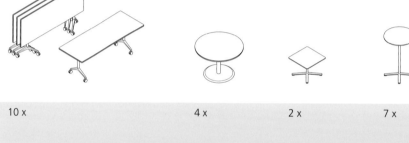

| 10 x | 4 x | 2 x | 7 x |

Multifunctional, partitionable conference and congress centre

Combining gastronomic use with conference and congress quality is the core task in specifying congress centres. Application scope ranges from lectures and presentations with a plenary layout, seminars and conferences to shareholder meetings or celebrations such as company jubilees and weddings. The combination of intelligent, variable space partitioning, sophisticated room control and media technology and high-quality, flexible furniture helps the company to position itself in the market with an ambience that is always a convincing and professional solution, and also to reduce follow-up costs for reconfiguration and storage space.

Page 156–161

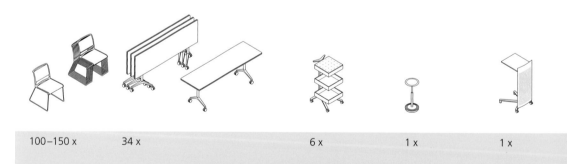

| 100–150 x | 34 x | 6 x | 1 x | 1 x |

Company restaurant with mobile furniture (page 152–155)
Area 196 sqm / Store 16 sqm

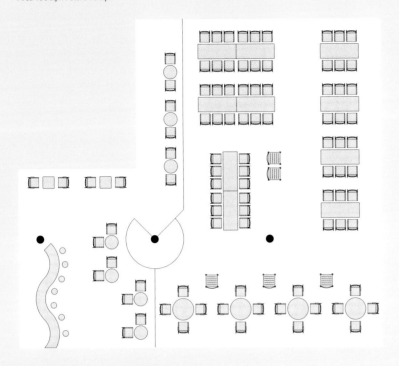

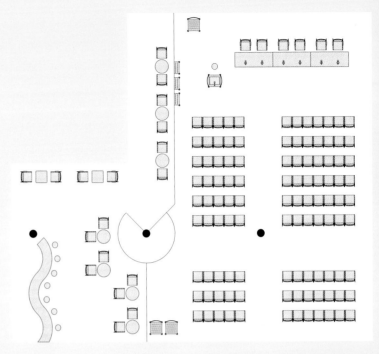

Dining room with restaurant and bistro sections,
as well as adjoining cafeteria gallery, with a total of 94–108 seats

Utilization of dining room as an assembly hall
with a stage and concourse seating for 108 persons

Multifunctional and partitionable conference and seminar rooms with mobile furniture (page 156–161)
Total area 210 sqm / Store 15 sqm

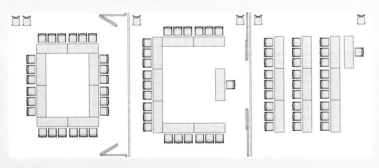

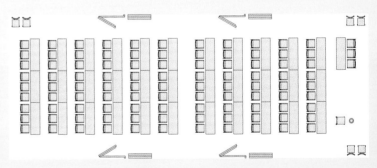

Utilization of partitioned rooms: conference for 24,
seminar for 21 and training for 27 persons

Utilization of the whole space for an assembly
or a congress for 99 persons

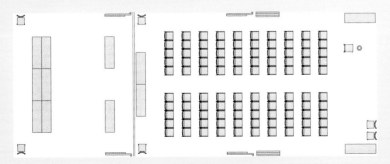

Utilization in partitioned, two-thirds section: lecture with concourse seating for 100 persons
and subsequent reception with buffet in the smaller section of the room

Utilization of the whole space for a banquet
with a buffet and dance floor for 72 guests

From a restaurant environment …

Bar and cafeteria on gallery level offer a good overview without being in the limelight. Both have different seating and high table arrangements.

If the canteen is the communicative fulcrum of the company, it lends itself to using these facilities for events as well, such as an assembly or celebrations involving the whole of the company. For this is undoubtedly the place within the company where employees and management meet on equal terms – and with the same basic human needs. For the purpose of the partnership described at the beginning, the "dining room" is therefore an ideal place for creating a sense of community. To meet these demands, the planning stage should combine atmospheric criteria with the functional aspects of a variable interior in the most effective way.

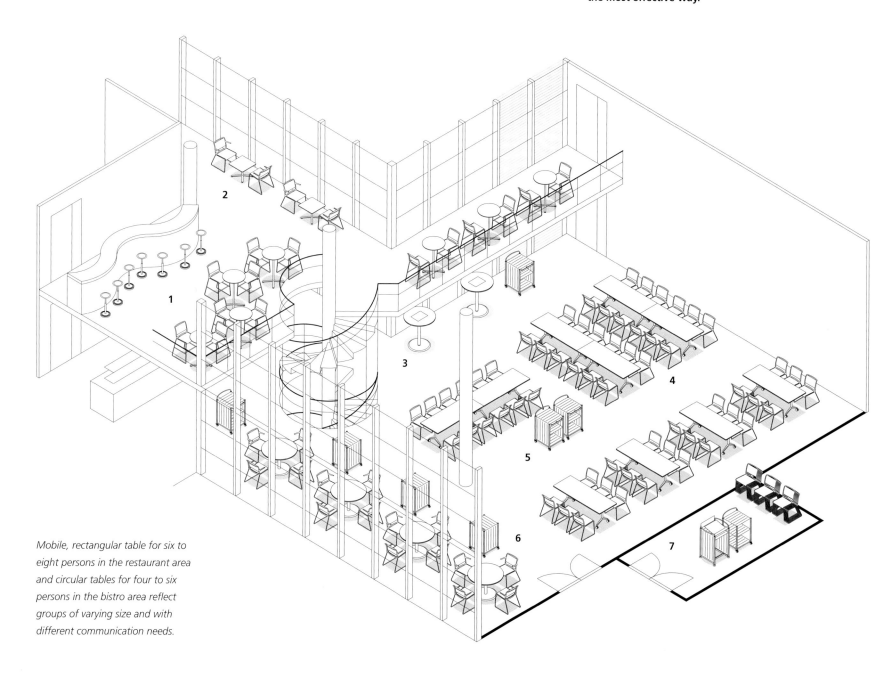

Mobile, rectangular table for six to eight persons in the restaurant area and circular tables for four to six persons in the bistro area reflect groups of varying size and with different communication needs.

Scale 1:125 / dimensions in cm
(1 cm = 0.39 inches)
Restaurant area 196 sqm
Store 16 sqm

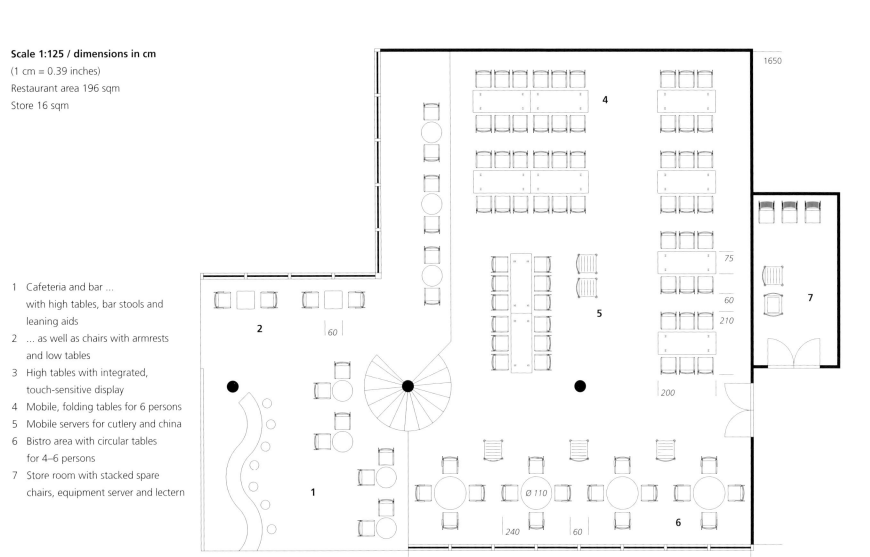

1 Cafeteria and bar ...
   with high tables, bar stools and
   leaning aids
2 ... as well as chairs with armrests
   and low tables
3 High tables with integrated,
   touch-sensitive display
4 Mobile, folding tables for 6 persons
5 Mobile servers for cutlery and china
6 Bistro area with circular tables
   for 4–6 persons
7 Store room with stacked spare
   chairs, equipment server and lectern

The quality of the space itself and the furniture of a company restaurant should reflect and support its great importance. A two-storey structure with a gallery and correspondingly coordinated furnishings allows clear differentiation in terms of various communication needs and catering options while conveying an impression of spaciousness. The central eating area is thus furnished with tables for six persons that may be quickly arranged in an elongated configuration if required. Around the perimeter there are circular bistro tables for small groups of up to six for communal eating and also for more confidential talks. For such purposes, it is therefore ideal to select premises that are not horizontally structured but have several floor levels.

Mobile servers on castors for spare cutlery and napkins may additionally be used to partition areas optically and should be positioned conveniently within reach of tables. The cafeteria area is clearly separated from the dining room and furnished with a high counter and bistro tables that provide an environment for different types of communication and privacy. Two high tables with an integrated, touch-sensitive display permit spontaneous access to data from the network or the internet.

... to an assembly hall

▸ With a view to allowing the dining room to be converted into an events space with little effort, tables should be specified that can be simply removed and stored compactly on standby. It is particularly useful to have a store room close to the canteen to keep spare chairs, tables not in use, a lectern and mobile media storage units on standby for assemblies.

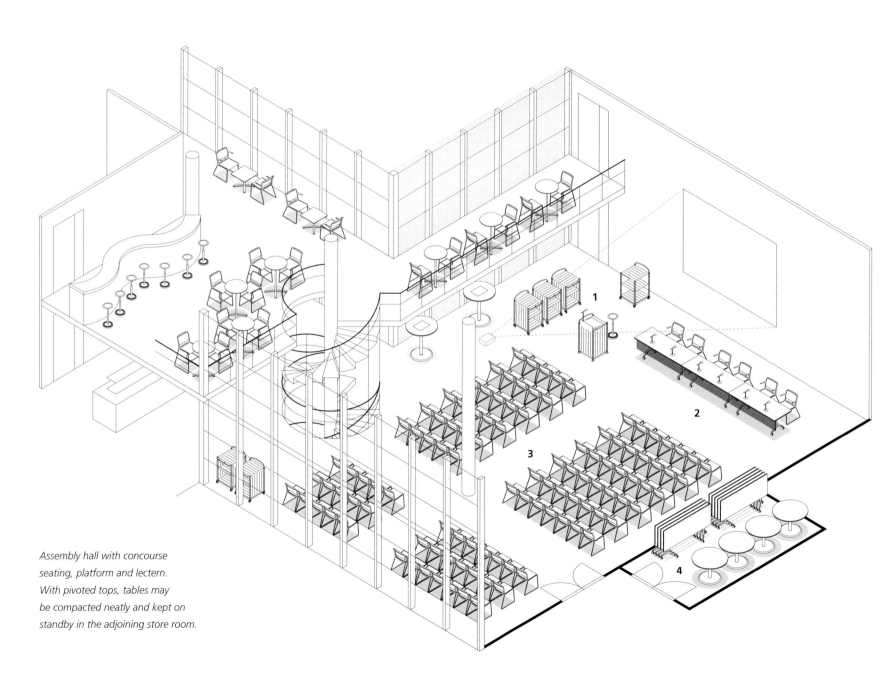

Assembly hall with concourse seating, platform and lectern. With pivoted tops, tables may be compacted neatly and kept on standby in the adjoining store room.

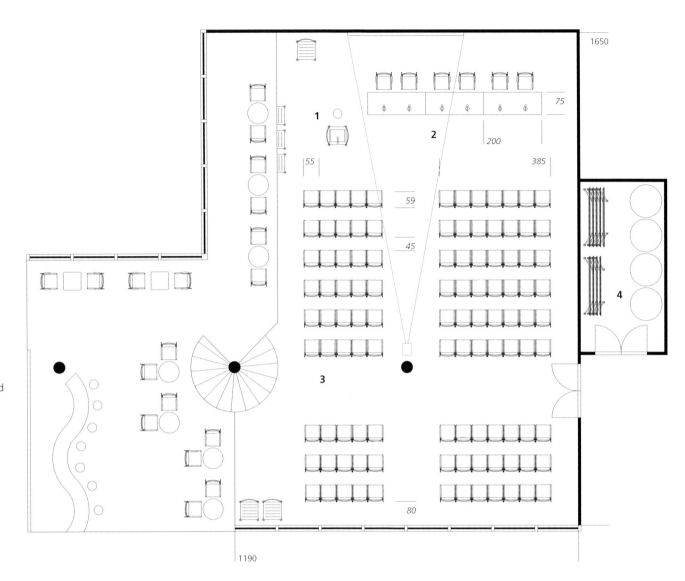

Scale 1:125 / dimensions in cm
(1 cm = 0.39 inches)
Restaurant area 196 sqm
Store 16 sqm

1650

75

1   200

55   385

59

45

80

1190

1   Lectern with microphone
and leaning aid

2   Platform comprising tables linked
in rows, with modesty panels and
microphones

3   Bistro chairs linked by means
of row connectors

4   Store room with neatly compacted
tables with pivoted table top

The room height afforded by such a two-storey structure is a
great advantage for varying applications including a setting for
assemblies, presentations, films and lectures: a large projection
area can be created which may be seen well from every place in
the room. A digital projector, mounted underneath the ceiling
or integrated into the ceiling, is used for projection. If compact,
stackable chairs with row connectors are used as a seating
solution extra chairs simply have to be brought from the store
room and linked.

It is particularly practical to be able to link chairs without the
use of tools or additional, loose connecting parts, some of which
invariably disappear over the course of time. Connecting elements
integrated into chair frames are therefore ideal. Chairs should
combine a comparatively high degree of seated comfort with
low weight and easy handling. It should be remembered that in
many countries it is compulsory for concourse seating with more
than a certain number of linked chairs – in Germany it is 200
upwards – for individual rows of chairs to be anchored to the
ground as a panic safety measure.

The platform for six persons can be configured using existing
tables. If modesty panels are required on this row of tables for
psychological reasons, it is advisable from the very beginning to
select a variable table system also used in the training and seminar
area that includes such accessories. Media servers and a lectern
are best selected from a furniture range that is also used in
conference and lecture rooms.

Multifunctional and partitionable conference and congress centre

For example: conferences, seminars and training

▸ Congress centres in attractive locations and at central traffic junctions are becoming increasingly important as they allow companies to hold large scale events with overnight accommodation without having to keep such facilities on standby themselves. With a view to being able to rent out such facilities for a wide variety of applications and utilize them profitably, the focus should be on professional utility and design quality as well as on a welcoming atmosphere.

Although the importance of congress centres may be increasing, the quality of their interiors is frequently lacking. Dim lighting, improvized media technology, highly uncomfortable and obviously cheap chairs, as well as unstable folding chairs, tediously camouflaged with loose covers, sometimes form a strange contrast to the high standard that is conveyed by the design of the entrance area, foyer or guest rooms. Furniture and equipment are after all an easy means of distinguishing oneself from the large number of rival conference hotels and centres and positioning oneself at the top.

The basics for creating a professional "feel-good" atmosphere include a front terrace on the ground floor for relaxation in the fresh air, plenty of daylight with variable illumination control when using media technology, sufficient room height that also conveys a feeling of spaciousness in a plenary layout and intelligent installation of media technology and furniture that is both high-quality and practical, which may be stored compactly on standby and configured for varying space applications in a cost efficient way. After multi-purpose rooms have been partitioned, modern media technology may also be used due to a simple but intelligent grid of floor ports for power, data and internet connections. Flat screens, permanently mounted on sliding and pivotable frames, provide a practical solution for presentation requirements. And last but not least, mobile tables with pivotable tops, as well as chairs in compact stacking heights allow spare furniture to be stored close by in medium-height cupboards instead of in separate store rooms. These cupboards may in turn be used as a storage surface for tableware or catering materials in convenient standing height whenever the area is used for breaks.

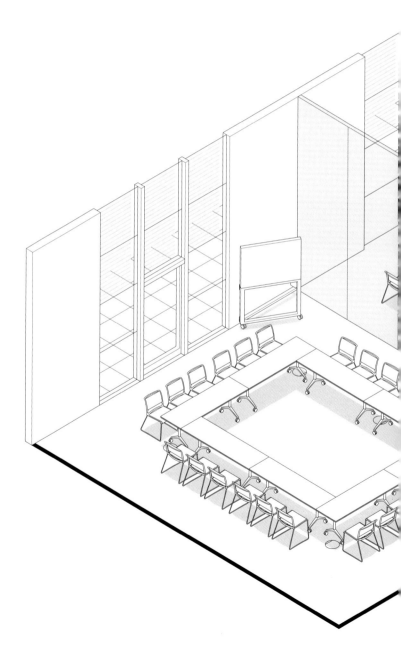

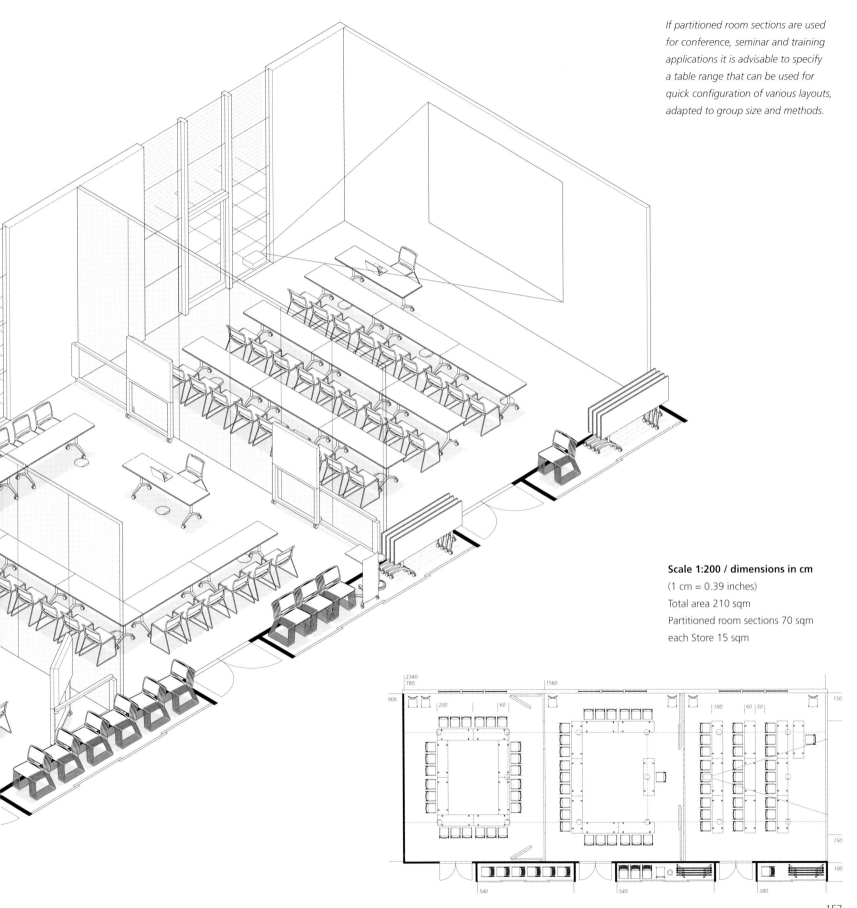

If partitioned room sections are used for conference, seminar and training applications it is advisable to specify a table range that can be used for quick configuration of various layouts, adapted to group size and methods.

Scale 1:200 / dimensions in cm
(1 cm = 0.39 inches)
Total area 210 sqm
Partitioned room sections 70 sqm
each Store 15 sqm

Multifunctional and partitionable conference and congress centre

For example: assembly and lecture scenario with a reception

▸ The room is opened fully or partially for large gatherings or plenary lectures. Lighting, air conditioning and AV media technology in partitioned room sections can therefore be operated individually or centrally. Preparation and configuration times and storage space can be reduced considerably if mobile, pivotable tables and comfortable, light and compactly stackable chairs are used.

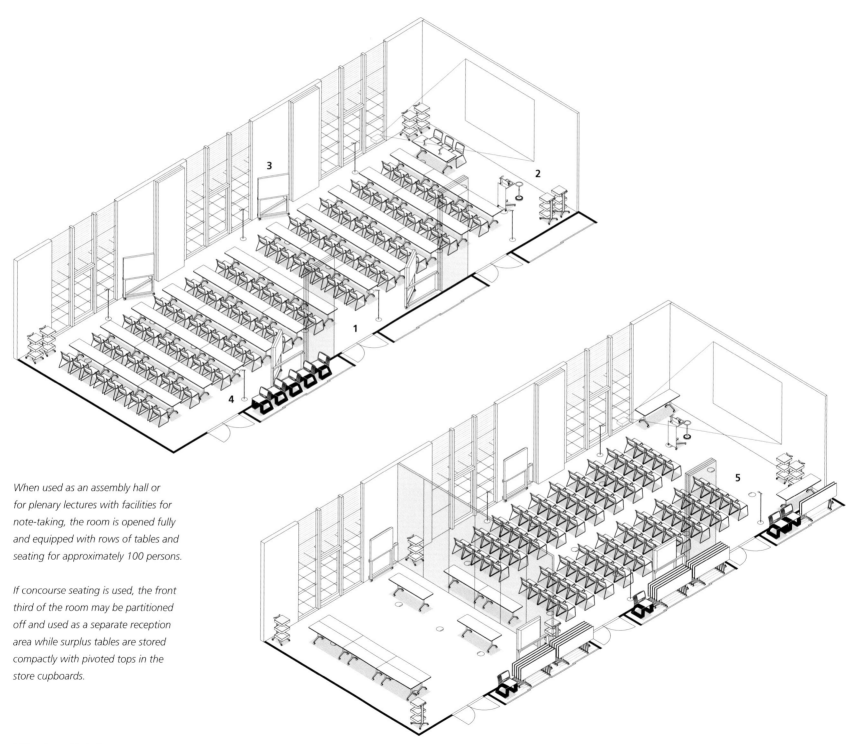

When used as an assembly hall or for plenary lectures with facilities for note-taking, the room is opened fully and equipped with rows of tables and seating for approximately 100 persons.

If concourse seating is used, the front third of the room may be partitioned off and used as a separate reception area while surplus tables are stored compactly with pivoted tops in the store cupboards.

Scale 1:200 / dimensions in cm

(1 cm = 0.39 inches)

Total area 210 sqm

Partitioned room sections 70 sqm

each Store 15 sqm

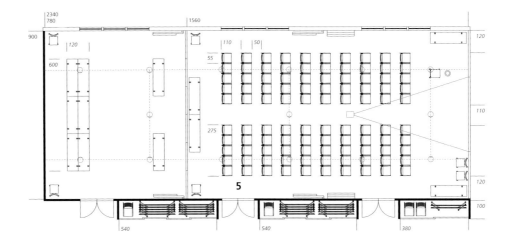

1 Utilization of total area with rows of tables
2 Lectern with connections for a laptop
3 Pivotable, wall-mounted flat screens to support visualization of presentations for back rows
4 Microphones for questions from the auditorium, positioned at the sides and close to floor ports
5 Two-thirds section of partitioned room and utilization for a lecture with concourse seating

Large-scale assemblies, particularly shareholder meetings or celebrations, are frequently held in external conference centres with an adjoining hotel. Depending on whether note-taking is required, the room is opened fully and equipped with rows of tables with corresponding seating or with concourse seating. When the total area is used, the room height – in the specifiers' option it is 4.80 m – is not only important in terms of proportions and a feeling of spaciousness, but it also permits a sufficiently large projection area that can even be seen by back rows of chairs and tables.

Additionally, presentations may be followed via the flat screens that have now been shifted to the outside and tilted and are connected in series for this purpose. This provides quite useful support in terms of visualization for rear peripheral areas in particular. Microphone stands are positioned at the sides close to floor ports to ensure that questions from the auditorium are audible for all participants.

If no surfaces are required for note-taking or refreshments, table tops may be pivoted and all tables may be moved to store cupboards outside by just one person within a few minutes. If the pivoting mechanism on the table tops activates the rotational movement of the foot sections, tables may be compacted in ordered columns. Due to high-density concourse seating, the front section of the room may be partitioned off, for example, for cocktails or a buffet.

Multifunctional and partitionable conference and congress centre

For example: banquet with a buffet and dance floor

▸ In addition to more formal types of conference, events with informal elements may also be held in conference and congress centres with a multifunctional interior. If an interior with correspondingly variable partitioning elements, intelligent room control technology, multi-media technology and flexible furniture has been specified, the changeover from formal to informal event elements is child's play.

For festive events with a subsequent informal programme, for example, a banquet and dancing, partitioning elements can optionally be opened halfway. Due to the installation grid of the floor ports, the disc jockey located in the central dancing and buffet area can connect to multi-media and sound technology.

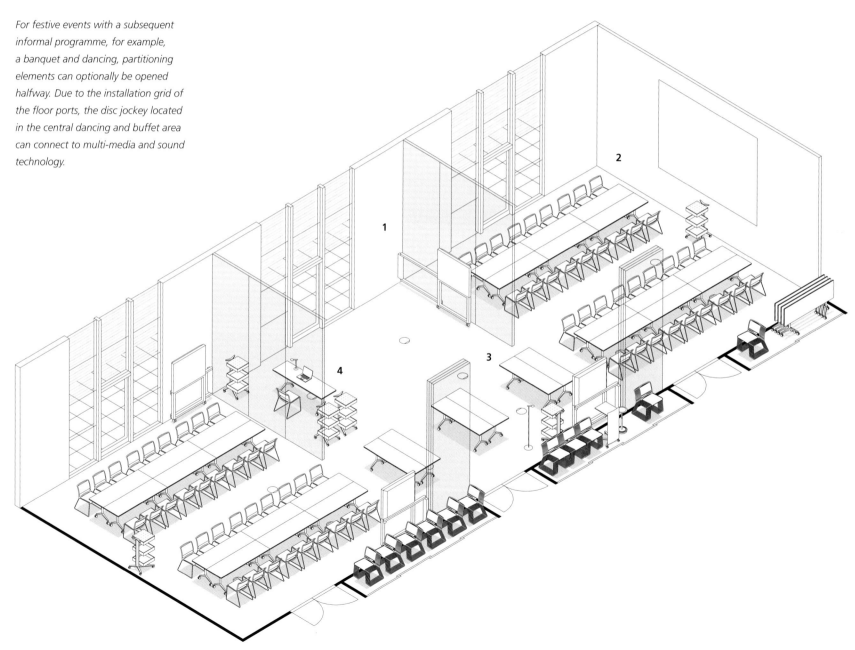

Scale 1:200 / dimensions in cm
(1 cm = 0.39 inches)
Total area 210 sqm
Partitioned room sections 70 sqm
each Store 15 sqm

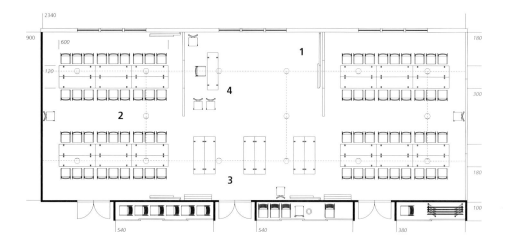

1   Zoning of total area into partly separated areas
    for dining area, buffet and dance floor
2   Linked, elongated table configuration for banquet
3   Tables configured in twos for buffet
4   Place for the DJ, connected to available
    media technology

Particularly festive events that go on for a longer time "thrive on" the changeover from more formal programme elements, such as presentations and lectures, and subsequent informal elements allowing deeper conversations or high-spirited celebrating. Whether for a lecture by a keynote speaker followed by a banquet or a wedding with contributions by guests, communal eating and dancing – the room should provide a suitable solution for any occasion that may be configured easily and quickly.

Partitions are very important for such scenarios: they should not only be acoustically efficient but also allow optimal variable zoning. Solutions that close off half the room from either side provide advantages in terms of handling, distribute floor space required for the partitions to two sides when fully opened, and allow visually and acoustically coordinated partial areas to be created without separating them completely. The same applies to AV media: if correspondingly programmable and operable, this allows variable utilization of image and sound in partial room sections.

The furniture should also combine a high-quality appearance with professional utility quality and practical advantages. For seating, it is ideal to select models with resilient seat and backrest covering that provides a comparatively high degree of comfort, are easy to clean and may be stacked precisely and compactly. Similar criteria should apply when selecting mobile table models. Hardwearing surface finishes, stable, high-quality frames, easy operation of swivel mechanisms, edging with impact-resilient profile and space-saving stackability give the interior a prestigious character and, due to high functionality, also reduce facility management costs.

Variable furniture for a company restaurant, assembly halls and congress centres

Chairs, stools and leaning aids

Chairs should be easy to clean and handle with, for example, the upper edge of the backrest designed as a grip for convenient lifting, carrying or correct positioning. Firm upholstery provides adequate support for an average sitting period of two hours. In this case non-upholstered plastic shells are suitable for the backrest or synthetic and viscoelastic fabric netting for both the seat and backrest. The design of the chairs should allow different sitting positions; armrests with an outward curvature are therefore recommended for this purpose.

In a multifunctional restaurant area, furniture must be reconfigurable without any great effort. In this case, chairs should be easily, precisely and compactly stackable for keeping spares on space-saving standby. Assembly and disassembly are much easier if chairs can be transported on a matching stacking trolley. Skid-base chairs with flexible seat and back frames are ideal, extremely light constructions.

If chairs are used for events in concourse layouts they should be linkable by means of row connectors. Instead of loose connecting elements it is advisable to specify integrated connectors form the very beginning. For the purpose of configuring high-density rows, models with armrests should alternate with models without armrests when linked.

Materials and surface finishes

Synthetic materials are particularly suitable for backrests due to their easy-care properties. They should however be in perforated or netting material to ensure efficient rear ventilation. Constructions should prevent marks being left by the stacking process. If models with seat covers are used these must be easily removable for cleaning purposes. For frames, materials such as bright chromium-plated round tube or rod are recommended which can withstand rough handling. For stone and wood flooring, integrated felt glides should be specified which do not leave any scratch marks and are not worn down by the chair being shifted.

Low, sitting and standing height tables

Different points of functional focus may be set in a canteen interior: the restaurant area generally requires rectangular or square tables; in the case of self-service, the table top format should be coordinated with the dimensions of the trays used.

For the cafeteria or bistro area on the other hand, circular tables allowing variable seating are advisable as users spend a shorter time there.

A stand-up café with high tables and matching stools provides the right ambience for a quick snack.

And leaning aids are suitable for chats and refreshments at the bar. If high tables are to be temporarily stored in a space-saving manner, it is advisable to select models that have a slot in the top surface allowing them to stack compactly as an aesthetically attractive and practical solution. Bar height stools should have a footrest to relieve pressure while it has proven to be useful if self-righting leaning aids are both height-adjustable and mobile in all directions to adapt to various postures.

Materials and surface finishes

For square and circular tables it is advisable to select modules with a pedestal frame with flat foot sections or a disc base in die-cast aluminium to provide maximum legroom. Foot sections may have a bright chromium-plated finish and therefore be extremely hardwearing; this finish is however not recommended for a disc base due to the mirror effect. Table tops should be both hardwearing and graceful, for example, by means of slender tops with a chamfer edge. For this purpose, through-dyed materials such as HPL provide solutions that are both elegant and lastingly aesthetic.

Tables fitted with interactive displays, see page 195.

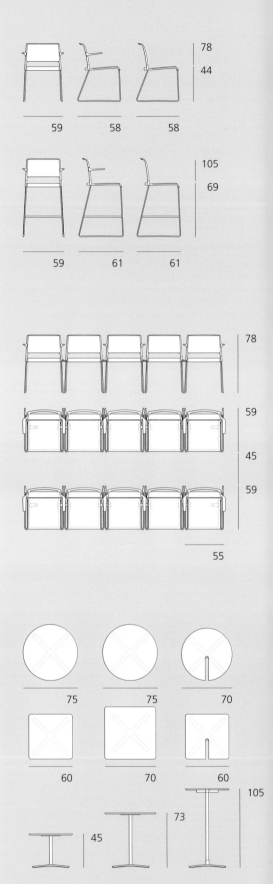

Rows of chairs can be connected extremely easily using integrated connectors: present the keyhole, lock in the next chair – that's it. No loose parts, no assembly effort.

A slot in the top surface allows up to three high tables to be stacked compactly.

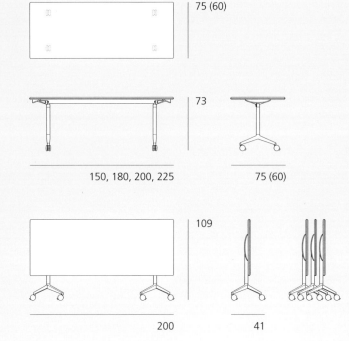

75 (60)

73

150, 180, 200, 225   75 (60)

109

200   41

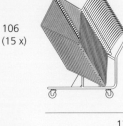

106 (15 x)

153 (25 x)

98   121

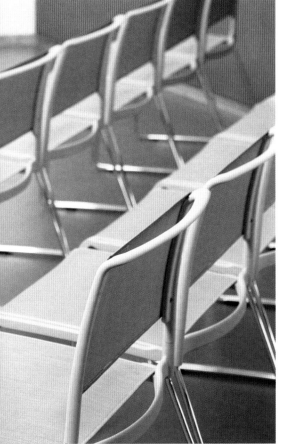

Specifiers' option:
stackable chairs from the Aline range

Mobile tables with pivotable tops

To transform a company restaurant into an assembly hall, tables should allow easy transport and compact storage. Various solutions are possible: stackable or collapsible, as well as folding tables. Mobile single tables which may be kept compactly on standby by folding or pivoting the table top are however extremely practical for such purposes. This allows the table to be compacted and transported easily just by one person. For space-saving intermediate storage, tables should allow efficient compacting. Table-to-table connectors for linking longer configurations or modesty panels when tables are used on a stage are useful accessories. If the same table models can be used as in seminar applications, in which similar demands are made on functionality, utility qualities and surface finish, specifying coherent models from one product family will incorporate all the advantages of standardization, and last but not least, allow more flexible facility management.

Square tables for restaurant interiors with self-service should provide an edge length per person of at least 60 cm. In the specifiers' option for six persons this produces table dimensions of 75 x 200 cm. If table legs, underframes, frames or foot sections are sufficiently recessed, the shorter sides of the table may also be used for seating on such a format without it becoming too narrow.

Materials and surface finishes
Frame materials and finishes should be able to withstand a high degree of wear and tear while providing a high level of design quality. Foot sections in bright chromium-plated or at least polished die-cast aluminium are an adequate finish. It is however not advisable to specify a coated finish as this shows scratch marks easily should small stones be brought in from outside on the soles of shoes. Table tops require a laminate finish in hardwearing kitchen worktop quality to withstand wear and tear from simple catering tableware too that is frequently not polished at the base. And last but not least, it is useful to specify table lipping with an impact-resilient profile to protect table tops against damage during transport and when placed together.

Auditorium
and plenary assembly hall

▸ An auditorium for plenary assemblies is one of the central, often highly symbolic places of communication within a community. A parliamentary plenary assembly, a lecture hall or congress hall – nowhere else are building planning, technical equipment and furniture specifying as closely linked as here. They are therefore some of the most challenging planning tasks. Space dimensions and geometries, utilization concepts, room control technology and furnishing are closely coordinated from the very beginning; subsequent changes are only possible with considerable effort.

Lecture and debate – dialectic conflict culture or the search for consensus?

Architecture is a kind of eloquence of power conveyed through forms.
Friedrich Wilhelm Nietzsche

No study has been carried out on seating orders in parliament. It is beyond doubt that the three basic models – circle, semi-circle or, as in British Parliament, two blocks facing each other – affect the procedure and the atmosphere of parliamentary debate.

What distinguishes the identity of British Parliament is the idea of "Government by discussion". The architecture of the British House of Commons fulfils these requirements quite uniquely: Members of Parliament speak from their seat and hardly have to raise their voice to be heard. They can keep their eye on their political counterpart – quite literally – whom they have to criticize and convince. Therefore, the dialogue between Government and Opposition is often interrupted by spontaneous heckling. The British do, in fact, owe this traditional debating form to a decision by Winston Churchill. After Parliament was destroyed in 1943, Churchill decided in favour of reconstruction in the traditional form:

"If the House is big enough to hold all its Members, nine-tenths of its debates will be conducted in the depressing atmosphere of an almost empty or half-empty Chamber. The essence of good House of Commons speaking is the conversational style, the facility for quick, informal interruptions and interchanges. But the conversational style requires a fairly small space, and on great occasions there should be a sense of crowd and urgency."

This was indeed an interesting, if somewhat patriarchal decision. Building in the name of democracy does not always produce such a clear decision. During the dispute on the allocation of seats in the German Bundestag, Carlo Schmidt, an architect himself, was so fascinated by the British idea that he wanted to superimpose it on Bonn: "It would be good if the incumbent Chancellor sat facing the incumbent Leader of the Opposition, so that they could see the white of each other's eyes. A lot of things would be said differently to how they are expressed today."

Things did not get that far in Germany. Following the intermezzo of the new construction of the bright and transparent parliament building in Bonn, boasting an overall architectural principle that should quite intentionally mark the image of an open democracy, the old Reichstag building was refurbished by British architect Sir Norman Foster ready for housing the German Parliament when it moved to Berlin. It is up to the individual to decide whether the resolution to move the seat of the German Parliament into the historic building from the later 19th century was right, and whether the synthesis between old and new which Sir Norman Foster envisaged was successful... One thing is for sure: the building and space structure of a parliament building have considerable symbolic significance, and influence the style and intensity of interaction. This applies on both a small and large scale: in a university lecture hall, a company auditorium or a training centre – a symbolic location, space dimensions and forms, and an appropriate arrangement of seats are able to promote or impair a culture of argumentation and discussion. The same applies to the way it is used: a virtually empty lecture hall is as disheartening for the auditorium as for the speaker.

On the other hand, an overcrowded room may be quite conducive to real discussion – providing every participant can find a comfortable seat and the hall has adequate lighting and air conditioning.

Organizational forms:
ritualized, focused and planned

The higher the number of participants in an event, the more important it is to have clear rules of the game. Parliamentary work, for example, follows fixed rules and rituals which are monitored by officials especially appointed for the purpose. If one of the rules is not observed, officials call for order and give reprimands or warnings, and if necessary may also dissolve a plenary assembly. The distribution of roles in a parliament are reflected in the seating order too: parliamentary parties are divided according to blocks, if it is a democratic parliament, and within the parliamentary party the highest ranking members sit on the front seats, while "backbenchers", who still have to earn their merit, have to take the back rows as their name implies. Both time schedules and the agenda for sessions are defined in advance. What is to be discussed and passed is announced publicly beforehand.

In training centres and institutions of higher education on the other hand, a plenary assembly hall or lecture hall is used by various groups. Rooms are firmly booked for user groups too, for example, for the duration of a semester, and lectures and seminars are detailed in the prospectus. There are also pre-defined roles: assistants generally prepare lectures and media technology support, the lecturer or sometimes a guest or a specific speaker from the auditorium presents the material, while the listeners – as the name of auditorium suggests – are generally restricted to the passive role of absorbing information and note-taking. Interaction between the person lecturing and the auditorium only takes place if someone catches the speaker's eye and is invited to speak.

Within a company, regular use of an auditorium in the sense of ritualized imparting of information is however more the exception, unless it is a large company with its own training centre and a large number of participants. Such rooms are mostly used for presentations, for example, showing films, for groups of visitors, press conferences and special lecture events.
As the utilization rate is correspondingly low, many companies have started opening up or renting out such rooms to external users too on an hourly basis.

Room and furniture:
from a "theatre layout" to a "cinema"

Whilst plenary sessions are the order of the day in politics, debates and discussions in front of the entire plenary assembly are less important in companies. However, anybody who frequently holds symposia, lectures and presentations in front of a large audience and is planning a large central hall for the purpose is well advised to consult the architecture of ancient theatres. For such purposes, the size is less decisive than having a semi-circular to three-quarter circular seating arrangement. Such an arena layout with ascending rows of seats ensures a good view and acoustics from every seat and facilitates discussion with one's immediate neighbour. If interaction within the auditorium is only of minor importance, orthogonal room forms are useful as used in cinemas. Seat rows are configured with an ascending elevation in this case too, but the viewing direction is exclusively focused on the front stage. To achieve necessary height to accommodate ascending seat rows, auditoria are in any case generally located in ground floor areas with corresponding height or in a two-storey construction.

Depending on whether such facilities, including foyer, cloakroom, sanitary installations and equipment rooms, are also rented out to external users, there should also be a separate means of access from the outside in addition to internal access arrangements to allow inside areas to be screened off easily.

Auditoria are frequently located in the basement area of the building and do not have any source of daylight. That is quite useful if a lecture hall is to be used exclusively for presentations with media support, for film shows or for artificial light performances which would otherwise require a complex system of electric blinds to prevent daylight flooding into the room. For events that take place over a longer period of time and that allow interaction amongst participants themselves or with the podium, lack of daylight does however have a rather negative effect: Having to focus one's attention constantly in one direction is tiring and the exclusive use of artificial light has a similar effect.

With a view to optimally versatile and thus frequent utilization of such facilities, these should be equipped with everything that is necessary for different types of events: a podium, stage elements, store rooms, comfortable seats and note-taking facilities. This also includes a large screen and such installations as are necessary for using modern media technology. Room areas and heights require air conditioning, lighting and acoustics to be planned with care, for which purpose professional specifiers should be consulted.

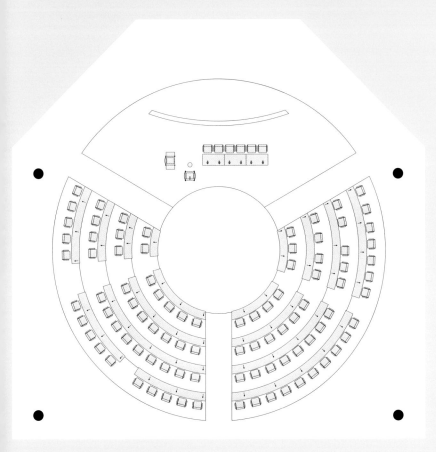

Plenary assembly hall with 94 seats (page 168)
Area 550 sqm

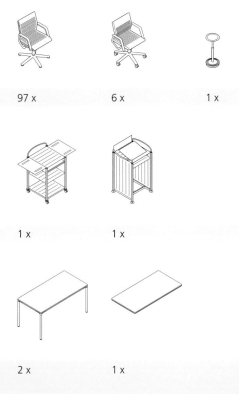

97 x   6 x   1 x

1 x   1 x

2 x   1 x

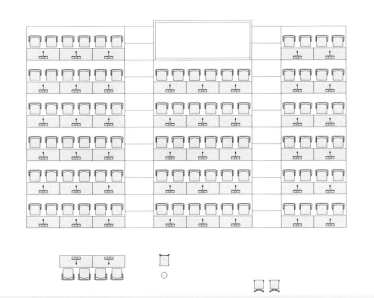

Auditorium with permanent seating
and system tables for 90 persons (page 170)
Area 335 sqm

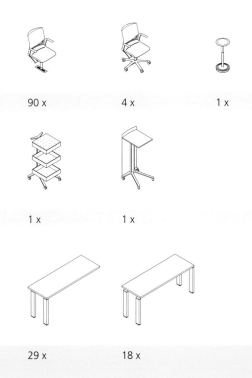

90 x   4 x   1 x

1 x   1 x

29 x   18 x

Plenary assembly hall

▸ For plenary assembly and lecture halls involving discussions, it is advisable to select interiors with a semi-circular to three-quarter circular seating arrangement. They combine good eye contact for participants with a concentric focus on the podium and the stage. With suitable technical equipment, such an auditorium may be used for a host of different types of events.

Plenary assembly hall for 94 seats at tables, a lectern and a podium with multifunctional application scope – from a presentation and a debate to theatre and a concert.

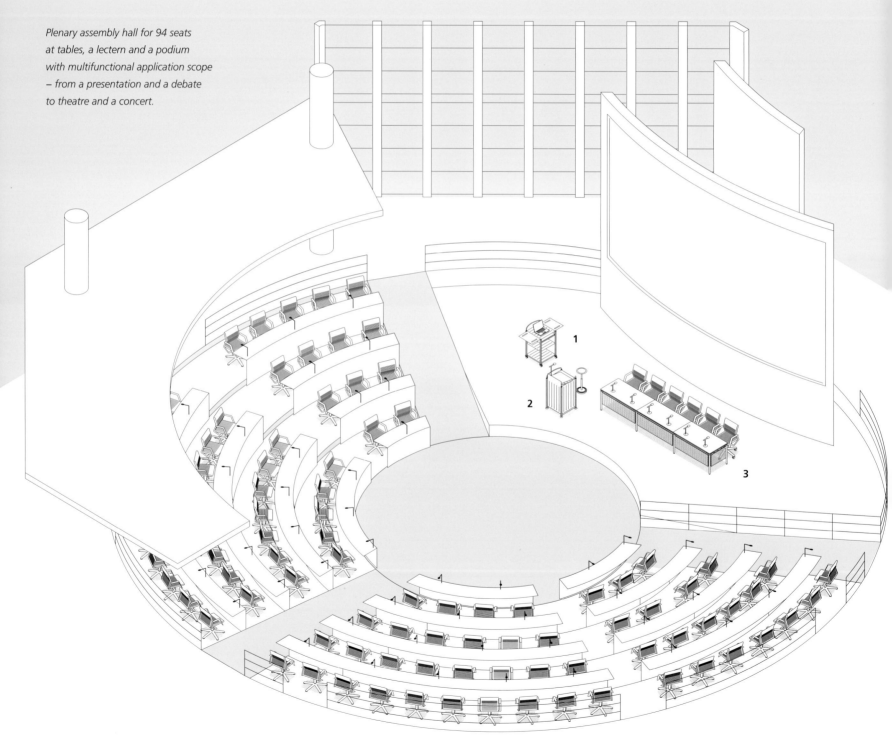

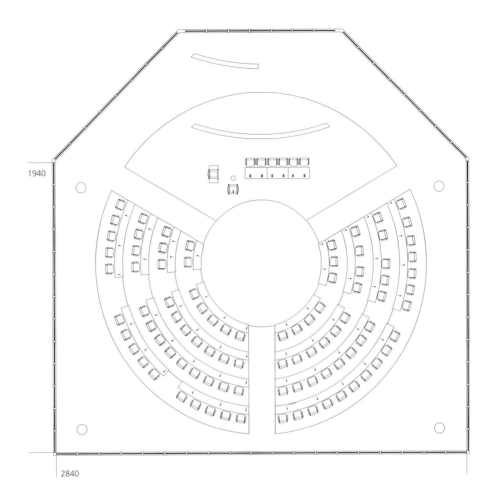

1   Mobile server with laptop
2   Lectern with leaning aid
3   Podium comprising conference tables
    with modesty panels

Auditoria, which are intended to promote discussion and info-exchange, are based on the form of an ancient theatre. In those times it was already possible to optimize acoustics by means of space geometry and materials in such a way that every word from the stage could even be understood in the back rows – without any means of sound amplification. Modern sound and media technology means that the choice of room forms and geometry is much more flexible today. If the room has a daylight façade, its form also shapes the outer cubature of the building due to its cantilever structure. Auditoria with parliamentary seating also allow flexible

application: an event space can become a multimedia centre if, in the building stage, platform elements, intelligent lighting technology, modern AV media and a curved rear projection area are specified in addition (as in the specifiers' option). Theatre performances and concerts may be held besides lectures, presentations and discussions – providing room acoustics have been specified with care. If there is corresponding space planning with communally used facilities and cloakrooms, such an auditorium may also be rented out to external users for efficient utilization.

When specifying furniture, special attention should be paid to the ergonomic quality of seating. Anyone constantly having to look for comfortable posture will have difficulty in finding the right mindset too. Should it be necessary to specify scope for variable configuration of "seating blocks" with a constant total number of participants – for example, to accommodate the current strengths of parliamentary parties following an election – it is advisable to select swivel chairs with a star base instead of chairs with swivel columns anchored into the floor. The same applies to tables which as system solutions may be extended or downsized.

Auditorium with permanent seating and system tables

Lecture hall with 70 places at tables, a lectern and a podium for lectures, presentations and film shows. In the rear, centrally located equipment room there is space for a projector, a sound system and room control technology as well as for any necessary interpreters' booths.

▶ **If used exclusively for lectures, presentations and film shows, it is advisable to choose an orthogonal form for the auditorium without any daylight, with ascending rows of seats and tables which are permanently installed and positioned directly facing the presentation area. For table configurations in particular, modern work procedures such as note-taking or showing presentations should be taken into consideration: a personal laptop is nowadays as usual for congress delegates as in a training centre or a university.**

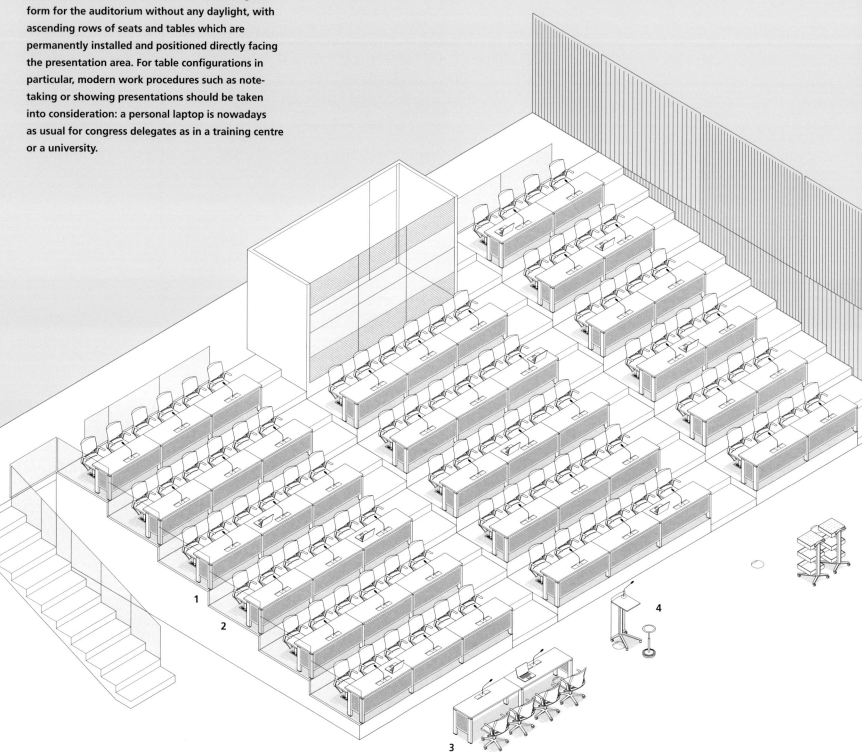

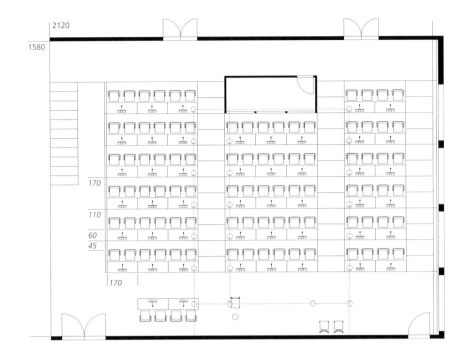

1 Rows comprising system tables
   with tops in a special format
2 Swivel chairs with fixed floor anchorage,
   but with adjustable seat depth
3 Platform with the same type
   of system tables as in table rows
4 Lectern with leaning aid

Events in lecture halls generally focus less on info-exchange on the part of participants but more on the front display surface and the speaker. For this purpose it is therefore possible to use linear configurations of rows of tables and chairs in a compact, rectangular room form with correspondingly good space utilization and simple integration into standardized building structures. Not only is daylight unnecessary, it would even be a disturbing source of light for front projection. A lecture hall can therefore also be located in a basement area that does not have any façade elements.

In order to stay abreast of changing work procedures with mobile information and communication technologies, a future-proof lecture hall equipped should have an intelligent installation grid for power, microphone, headphone and data connections integrated into the floor so that rows of tables may be linked to the power supply with ease. If connection points in table surfaces are networked with the presentation medium, presentations may be shown on laptops direct and do not have to be supplied or sent to participants subsequently as is usual today.

In addition to real buildings, an increasing number of universities and teaching institutions have a "virtual campus" which may be integrated into a real lecture in this way. At the same time, the number of events attended "virtually" from distributed locations is increasing. It almost goes without saying that a modern lecture hall should therefore be equipped with internet access, videoconferencing facilities and full multi media technology.

Firmly anchored swivel chairs, adjustable in depth, with automatic synchro-adjustment help to prevent early signs of fatigue and they promote mental agility too by providing physical support.

Seating in a plenary assembly hall and an auditorium

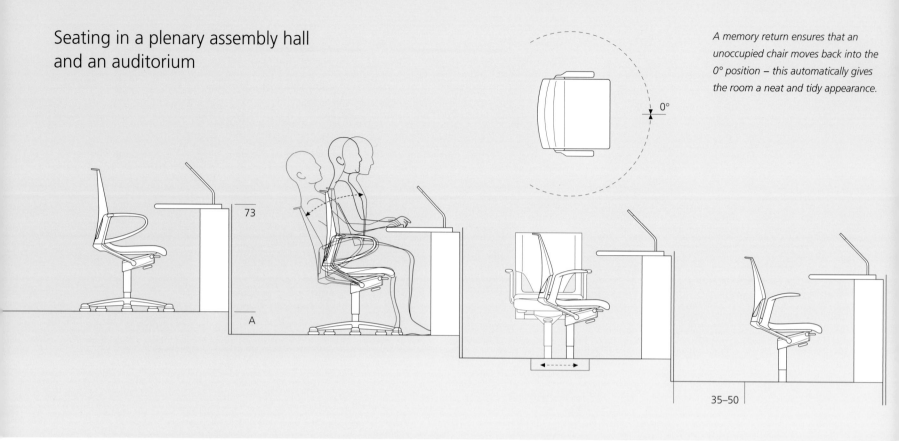

A memory return ensures that an unoccupied chair moves back into the 0° position – this automatically gives the room a neat and tidy appearance.

Swivel chairs

Swivel chairs used in a plenary assembly hall or a prestigious auditorium should, like swivel chairs at the workplace, ensure a coordinated seat and backrest tilt for ergonomically correct seating with the aid of an automatic synchro-adjustment mechanism which promotes frequent changes in posture. In this case, users themselves should be able to adjust the counter-pressure of the backrest easily and intuitively to their individual body weight and the length of their upper body leverage. Depending on the application and prestige requirements, models with standard to spacious set widths should be used.

While seat widths of 60–64 cm are fully adequate in lecture halls and training centres, swivel chairs in prestigious environments should have a seat width of at least 67 cm.

In addition to a flexible arrangement of swivel chairs on a star base with glides, it is also suitable to have floor anchoring for swivel columns for permanently installed concourse seating in an auditorium. The mounting device should however allow the chair to be adjusted in depth for the user to sit down with ease and for individual selection of the distance to the writing surface. A memory return in the swivel joint ensures that the chair automatically returns to a position parallel to edge of the desk. If required, this mechanism should also be integrated into models with glides. Whether chairs should be adjustable in height too is a matter of choice: ergonomically better adjustment of the seat height versus a much less calm and orderly ambience due to unused chairs having varying heights.

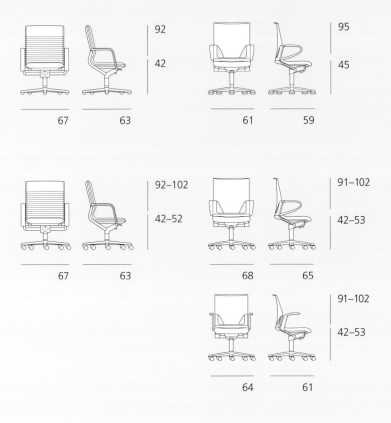

Specifiers' option:
swivel chairs from the Modus swivel chair range

Materials and surface finishes
For a prestigious environment, fine textiles or high-quality leather are an excellent upholstery option. The seat platform should be fully upholstered and covered on the back section too, to create the most optimal sound-absorbent impression. Attention should be paid to specifying a firm and air-permeable cushion providing both support and a good sitting climate. Alternatively, open frame constructions are suitable for the backrest, optionally also with a semi-transparent covering in stretch material. They are as acoustically efficient as a fully upholstered seat platform, they adjust to the individual user and changes in posture like a second supporting skin, and ensure optimal rear ventilation. Such constructions convey a much lighter and more transparent impression than voluminous seat platforms.

The choice depends on what furnishing character is to be conveyed in terms of the general design theme of the interior: more conservative and dignified or modern and dynamic.

The surface finishes of frame components and visible mechanism components should be chromium-plated or polished to withstand constant wear and tear. Colour-coordinated powder coating can enhance the coherent overall appearance, but it is much more scratch sensitive.

Table configurations
with media integration
in an auditorium

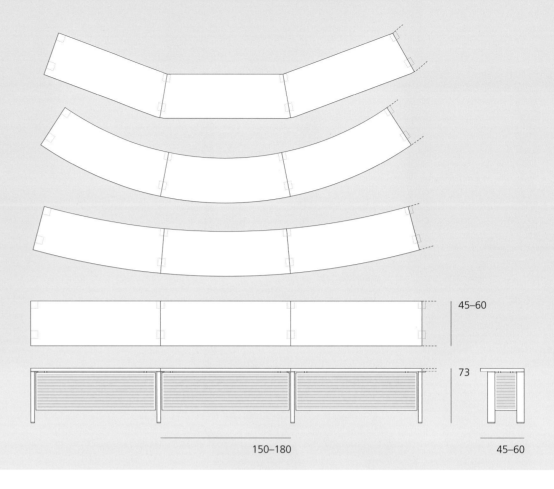

45–60

73

150–180

45–60

System table configurations

In contrast to specially developed products, such configurations have the advantage of providing high finishing quality at a comparatively favourable price due to using standardized frame elements; and it is easy to add to or exchange table tops should this be necessary. This requires such a table system to allow a high degree of individual adjustment to application and space profiles in terms of table top forms and geometry and also with regard to technical equipment. Table ranges permitting tops to be used in various forms and sizes without any necessary complicated frame adjustments are an excellent choice. If such a system comprises mainly bending-resistant table tops which are linked to table legs by means of an integrated connector, the same frame version may be used to coordinate the radii of table top forms within statically acceptable dimensions in virtually limitless configurations. A construction without an underframe provides more legroom and allows free positioning of cut-outs in the table top for connectivity modules. A further advantage of such a principle is that table legs also function as a means for linking table tops.

Connectivity modules in table tops may be configured as required: retractable modules for plug-and-play connections but also modules that are integrated into a cable channel underneath the table top and accessible from above by means of 180° hinged table portals. The latter have the advantage that the table surface does not become less spacious due to network adaptors, surplus cables and battery chargers as these can be stored in the cable channel. Such table portals may also be finished to match table finishes to create a coherent surface. If connectivity modules are configured in series via a simple plug-in cable between table tops, both the number of floor ports and the volume of cable channelled underneath tables may be reduced considerably.

A table depth of 60 cm is sufficient for using a laptop. The front table legs should be recessed and optionally have circular, rectangular or square material cross sections to relate to the interior design theme and table top geometry. The same applies to the front table edge profile which should be either straight, double bullnose, undercut or chamfer. The ascending layout of the tables definitely requires modesty panels at the front; it is also advisable to specify side panels at the end of rows.

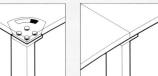

System tables are an ideal solution for planning special table configurations in auditoria; table top forms can be selected largely independently of frame constructions.

In the specifiers' option, tables individually configurable in terms of form are linked by means of a bayonet connector at the top of the table legs. This allows the firm and secure joint to be locked and released with one swift movement.

When using such a linking principle, table tops should be sufficiently bending-resistant to make additional underframes superfluous – and the

latter would only serve to restrict legroom in any case. Adjustable glides for levelling out floor irregularities are necessary for the purpose of aligning table rows.

There is more scope for individual design concepts if the connector is suitable for accepting different types of table legs.

In an auditorium layout with ascending rows of seats and tables, it is necessary to specify modesty panels which are mounted under the front edge of the stable table surfaces.

If media technology is to be integrated, individual table tops should be equipped with table portals and flat cable channels in light, but stable extruded aluminium profile. Any necessary modules for microphones, headphones and a laptop with connection points for power and data should be permanently installed in such table portals and cable channels.

Cable channels should be linkable laterally via connectivity modules using short connecting cables. Up to forty workplaces can thus be connected in series without any quality loss in transmission.

In order to avoid trip hazards, but primarily to ensure perfect functioning, vertical cable channels to individual table rows should be mounted in a concealed manner, for example, in the profiles of table legs, providing the cross section of the legs is sufficient for this purpose.

For integration of media technology into table configurations, see also page 192.

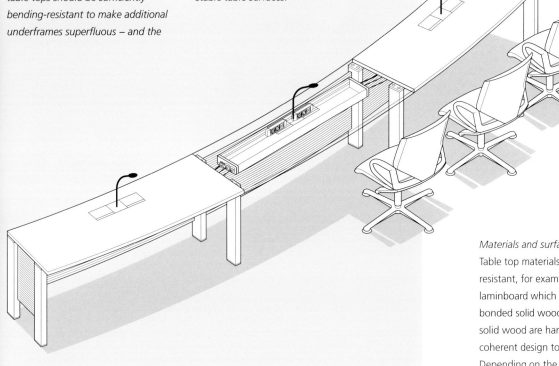
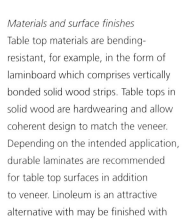

Materials and surface finishes
Table top materials are bending-resistant, for example, in the form of laminboard which comprises vertically bonded solid wood strips. Table tops in solid wood are hardwearing and allow coherent design to match the veneer. Depending on the intended application, durable laminates are recommended for table top surfaces in addition to veneer. Linoleum is an attractive alternative with may be finished with a visible lipping in solid wood.

Table legs comprise round tube or square or rectangular profiles that are made from tough and dimensionally stable materials such as steel or aluminium. Easily adjustable glides should be used to level out floor irregularities. Surface finishes of table legs should match chair frames. Bright chromium plating is however not recommended for rectangular or square cross sections as the smooth surface may produce an unwanted mirror effect. In this case, anodized or coated finishes are the better choice.

Planning guide
and media selection

▸ In addition to factual goals and objectives for conference and communication environments, planning and specifying must consider the number of participants, seating orders and requirements, distances between furniture units and equipment and edge lengths per person and statutory requirements. When integrating media equipment, room dimensions, the number of participants and the character of the conference should be determined from the very beginning so that corresponding technical connections, floor space, store rooms or special rooms for technical equipment may be included.

Where images speak …

If you can't talk about, point on it.
Laurie Anderson

Language is the first means of putting thoughts into the world so that communication can evolve out of the thinking process. Thoughts continue to develop in the course of a dialogue. Argumentation is expanded, reviewed and modified; or as Heinrich von Kleist put it: thoughts are produced in the course of speaking. And while listening. Whether real interaction evolves is determined by mutual pre-knowledge, social dependencies, the formal method of communication, the number of participants, by acoustics and the spatial arrangement of dialogue partners who have a decisive influence on the degree of potential interaction. Seating order and table form define the framework in which communication can develop.

The rhetorical talent of "communicators" as a complex interplay of body language, the pitch and modulation of the voice, syntax and choice of words should not be ignored either. Language is therefore a flexible medium and verbal communication is a dynamic, interactive process between the sender and recipients. Although this process invariably involves data and facts as the main "actors", but they do not determine the "stage setting". Graphic language is pictorial language: data and facts are embedded in narrative situations. Before the written word was invented, storytellers were responsible for passing down traditions and knowledge, and through the power of their language they inspired their listeners to create their own mental images.

Images as language support

Other vehicles aid the communication process if language is not sufficient. Whether they are gestures, graphics, images or objects – they are all a means of enriching verbal communication by adding unambiguous points of reference or – depending on the individual point of view – of limiting it too.

It is a popular saying that "A picture says more than a thousand words". To elaborate: it is the task of visualization to facilitate the act of understanding, grasping or recognizing. It can clarify imagination, insight and concepts and illustrate both objects and processes. Visualization is therefore primarily used where the spoken or written word needs additional media support: for presenting and "recording" abstract, theoretical thoughts. For images, drawings, graphically represented statistics, models … can clearly enhance the process of learning and understanding and also shorten it in terms of time.

According to statistics from Harper's Index, people can remember 90% of what they have done, 70% of what they have said and 20% of what they have heard! So much for the statistics side. How individuals react varies considerably: one person understands best what he sees; another person what he reads; and the third only what he has written down. There is not only one way of conveying knowledge. Not everyone understands the same method of explaining something. Holistic concepts of teaching and learning take this realization into consideration by conveying knowledge "via many different channels", by involving several different senses. As usual, the key to success is the right dose: the flood of images of our media age with the visual stimulation it entails can lead to hebetude and overstrain; vice versa, extremely rich, inner images can evolve in an understated, contemplative environment.

Multimedia communication with all one's senses

Language is accompanied by image information and sounds, but also by experiences, games and various forms of interaction. The nature of the information to be conveyed and methods employed should determine what kind of support or media are preferred. It is frequently the case that technical equipment available in the communication room which determines the nature of such support – and this, in turn, either promotes or impairs learning performance. Arbitrarily exchangeable, standardized "PowerPoint battles" can be as tedious as dry, endless monologues. And sometimes the virtually limitless possibilities afforded by multimedia communication seem to be bent on merely concealing lack of factual content.

If speakers concentrate more on presentation technology than on listeners, if there are delays due to technical hitches and if there is no interactive adaptation to a current situation due to the rigid order of overheads, then digital media technology support will even be a step backward compared with traditional media, such as an overhead projector. Using such equipment, the speaker interacts with the medium direct; he or she can omit individual overheads or repeat them and even emphasize certain information spontaneously by marking them with a pen.

Coordinated choice of media and media integration

There is thus no patent solution for the right use of media technology. It is more important to select media that suit specific requirements, differentiated according to communication forms, contents, space dimensions and structure, number of participants and furniture. A flipchart might be the best solution for spontaneous visual presentation in small groups; pinboards can be easily aligned and re-grouped in a workshop environment.

Training programmes thrive on active exercises and games, and digital media are particularly important whenever there are large numbers of participants or spontaneous access of data on the internet or network for work in smaller groups is desired. In spite of many different scenarios involved, there are some common rules: the focus should not be on media per se but on information and interaction. This is supported by natural, and in the case of technical equipment, ideally invisible integration into the interior design theme by means of simple, intuitive operability and functionality allowing spontaneous control and editing to create an authentic situation between senders and recipients. The more efficiently the digital world is integrated into the real environment and the closer the virtual simulation of, for example a video-conference, is to the concrete world of experience, the greater the likelihood of acceptance will be. Digital and media networking of globally distributed locations will then be able to combine substantial economic benefits with the reduction of negative ecological impact – for example, due to fewer business trips.

Outlook: invisible technology for supporting communication and cooperation

When starting a modern car nowadays, the ignition activates a number of invisible small computers, processors and sensors that prepare to function, and which, for example, are operated by pressure upon control surfaces or even perform automatically as the situation requires. Translated in terms of buildings, this concept points to many possibilities for adapting building and media technology such as lighting, electric blinds, air conditioning, sound and image systems to user requirements.

Easy-to-operate touch panels with which the entire conference room technology is controlled nowadays mark an initial step in the direction of buildings that "behave" cooperatively towards users. Connection and signal technologies that allow users to present their individual data on a shared display at the push of a button from any conference workplace are already available, as are conference tables with table tops that form a large-format interface, or touch-sensitive wall-mounted screens. Digital paper that can be written on quite normally will become part of daily routine in the not too distant future, perhaps including electronically equipped information walls that "recognize" the user profile of an interested party and transmit relevant information proactively. Vast, international research projects on invisible computing and ubiquitous computing point to developments of the future: the former promotes the idea that technology should be active completely behind the scenes and its functionality should be quite naturally available, while the latter examines the possibilities of providing access to an immaterial, digital information and communication space from any location and from any room.

In areas focusing on communication and cooperation it is decisive for technology to serve people and not vice versa. Otherwise everything will be thwarted that accounts for the very special quality of human interface: group dynamics, building up trust, spontaneity, info-exchange and joint idea generation within the complex human interplay that involves all the senses.

Overview of tables and table configurations

The table is the fulcrum of conference and meeting environments. Its dimensions, form and frame construction define the possible number of participants, the degree of interaction among participants and the means of differentiating workplaces. However, one general rule applies: the smaller the table, the greater the degree of interaction; the more circular the table, the more variable the number of places and the more equal these are; the more elongated and straighter the form, the more regimented the seating order is. Recessed table frames increase the variability of the number of seats, while edge-flush table frames that can be linked allow are more versatile. Solid table surfaces focus on a communal platform while open-centre configurations personalize individual sections of the table top and create a distance to those facing.

 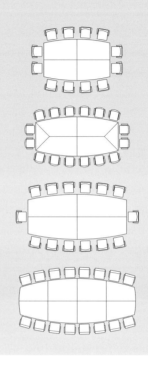 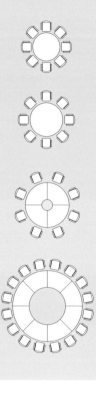

Number of places at table	4–10	10–20	8–16
Degree of interaction	Circular tables: very high, equal positions and eye contact. Barrel-shaped, boat-shaped, oval, elliptical: high, facilitates changes in positions.	The more compact, the higher. Shared surface as an element that connects people. Decreases with more than 12 participants.	Very high, decreases with more than 16 participants.
Flexibility of number of places	High in combination with recessed frames. Increasing and decreasing density of chair arrangements by 30% to 50% possible.	Medium high, increasing and decreasing density of chair arrangements by a total of up to 25% along curved edges and short sides.	High, increasing and decreasing density of chair arrangements by 30% to 50% with recessed frames possible.
Space utilization and media technology selection	Constant with a static table, high if a mobile table is used. Power and data connections in centre of table useful.	Constant, static. Power distribution and data connection points useful.	Constant, static. Power distribution and data connection points useful.

Table widths:

min. 75 cm edge length per person = edge length grid 75, 150, 225 cm or 90, 180, 240 cm

Table depths:

with seating on one side: min. 60 cm (training environment), 75 cm (conference), 90 cm (conference with integrated technical equipment); with seating on both sides: min. 105 cm, with integrated technical equipment min. 120 cm

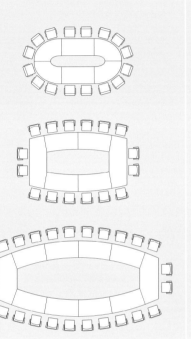

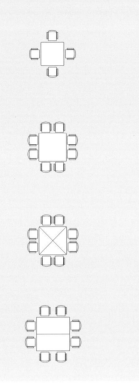

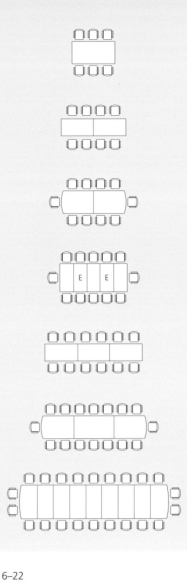

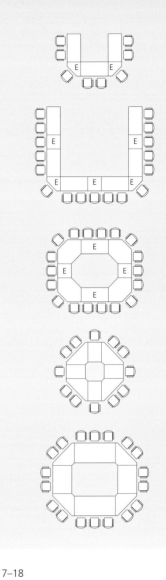

16–24	4–8	6–22	7–18
High to medium high, depending on radius, decreasing with more than 16 participants.	High, with equal sitting positions.	High to medium high due to shared surface, but the more elongated the rectangle and the more participants, the lower. Emphasized places at centres of tables and on short sides.	High, due to good eye contact and equal places, with U-shaped form optionally facing vertical presentation surface.
Low to medium high, depending on radius, increasing and decreasing density of chair arrangements by a total of up to 20% along curved edges and short sides.	Low to very low.	Very low to low (for compact forms with curved short sides).	Very low to low, angled corners allow variable seating.
Constant, static. Power distribution and data connection points useful. Microphones advisable with 20 participants upwards; necessary for a distance of more than 12 m.	Variable due to connectability in rows. High flexibility if comprising two rectangular tables. 1–2 optional power and data connection points.	Constant for statically assembled configurations. Variably divisible for system tables. Power and data connection points useful.	Constant with statically assembled configurations. Variably divisible and configurable for system tables. Power and data connection points useful.

Overview of seating

Due to the increasingly stronger links between communication and work processes (e.g. in project work), office swivel chairs are being used in meeting and conference environments as these support facility management (standardization, easy handling due to castors). This does however, result in the appearance of conference and meeting rooms becoming less harmonious and more complex, and the storage space required for extra chairs increases due to lack of stackability. The choice of the right type of chair should therefore consider facility management, the area of application and sitting dynamics coordinated with the length of sitting in addition to aesthetic criteria.

	Cantilever chairs	**Four-legged chairs**	**Skid-base chairs**

Maximum recommended uninterrupted period of sitting	Up to 90 minutes depending on upholstery	Up to 75 minutes depending on upholstery	60-75 minutes depending on upholstery
Sitting dynamics	Slightly resilient effect due to cantilevered steel tube frame. Change in posture possible depending on spaciousness.	Static frame, back adjustment with flexible constructions or with stretch material. Change in posture, such as straddling, possible with cantilevered armrests.	Slightly resilient circular rod frame with slender cross-sections and elastic materials; back and seat adjustment with frames with stretch material. Change in posture, such as straddling, possible with cantilevered armrests.
Area of application	Conference and meeting room; training, seminar and lecture room	Conference and meeting room; seminar and lecture room	Multi-purpose and assembly rooms, cafeteria, skid-base chairs in lounge and foyer
Space utilization	Constant position and number of places, variable in terms of number of seats and position with stackable models, optionally with writing tablets or row connectors.	Constant with same position and number of places, also variable with changing numbers of places for stackable models.	Chair: constant position and number of places; stackable models: highly variable; varying number of places and position; optional row connectors/numbering.

Swivel chairs
without synchro-adjustment

Swivel chairs
without synchro-adjustment

Swivel chairs
with synchro-adjustment

Swivel chairs
with synchro-adjustment

75-90 minutes depending on construction/upholstery of seat and back	90 minutes depending on upholstery technique	120 minutes depending on upholstery technique	120 minutes depending on upholstery technique
Swivel, with elastic constructions or ones with stretch material, and cushions Mobility and adjustment of back and seat. Change in posture, such as straddling, possible with cantilevered armrests.	Swivel, with elastic constructions or ones with stretch material, and seat cushions Mobility and adjustment of back and seat. Change in posture such as straddling possible with spacious models.	Swivel with body-synchronous inclination, with elastic constructions or ones with stretch material, and seat cushions. Adjustment of back and seat. Change in posture such as straddling possible with cantilevered armrests.	Swivel with body-synchronous inclination, with elastic constructions or ones with stretch material, and seat cushions. Adjustment of back and seat. Change in posture such as straddling possible with spacious models.
Conference and meeting rooms; consultation places and show rooms	Conference and meeting rooms	Conference and meeting rooms; workplaces, consultation places	Conference and meeting rooms; workplaces
Constant, same position and number of places with glides; variable position with swivel castors.	Constant with same position and number of places.	Constant or changing with constant number of places and variable position depending on table range.	Constant or changing with constant number of places and variable position depending on table range.

Minimum distances
from table edges to walls
or to permanently installed
furniture units

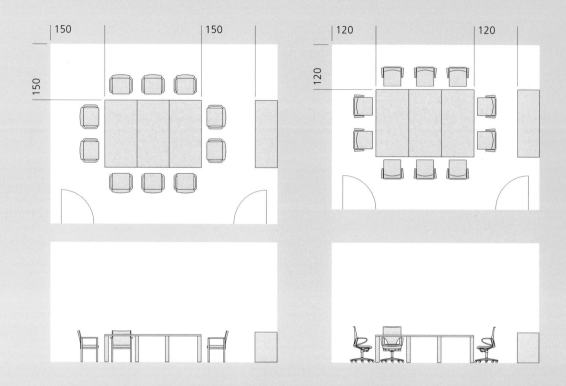

Specifiers' option: scale 1:100

If chairs with a non-swivel frame are used,
a minimum distance of 150 cm to table edges,
shelf units or walls should be observed. This
leaves plenty of space around the table to move
chairs away from the table for the purpose of
sitting down or standing up.

A distance of 120 cm is sufficient if chairs are
swivel. However, it should be observed that the
opening radius of doors and space required for
chairs do not coincide.

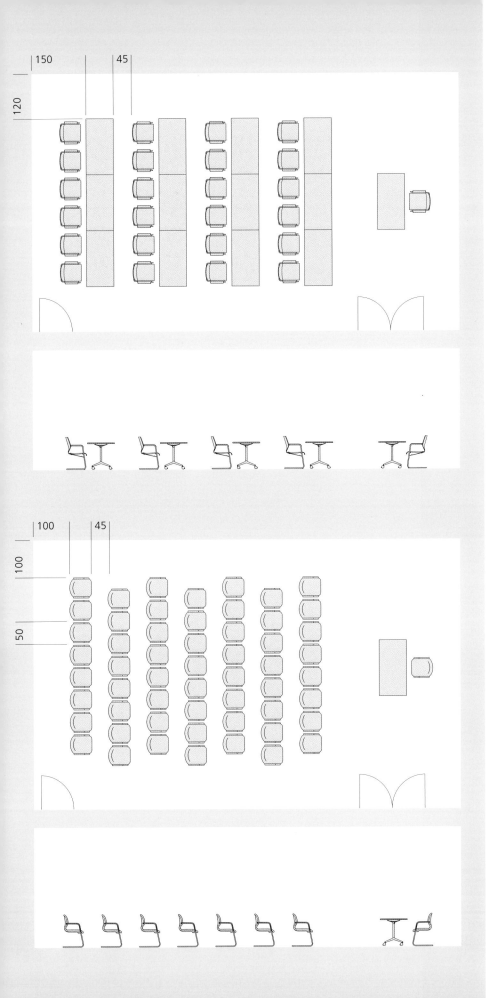

Minimum distances
for rows of tables and chairs

There should be a minimum passage way of 45 cm between the backrest of an occupied chair and the next table edge when tables are configured in rows in a training room.

In lecture or assembly rooms, in which concourse seating is only used occasionally, rows of chairs must be firmly connected as a panic safety measure depending on regional and national requirements. In Germany, for example, this applies to more than 200 seats. There should be a staggered arrangement of rows to provide an unobstructed view to the front.

If there are only few seats, it is sufficient to use row connectors to achieve neat alignment. It is useful to specify numbering of rows and seats if seats are allocated for specific events or a quick overview of the number of participants is required (e.g. to comply with fire precaution rules). A minimum passage way of 45 cm between rows is required. The minimum width per seat unit is 50 cm.

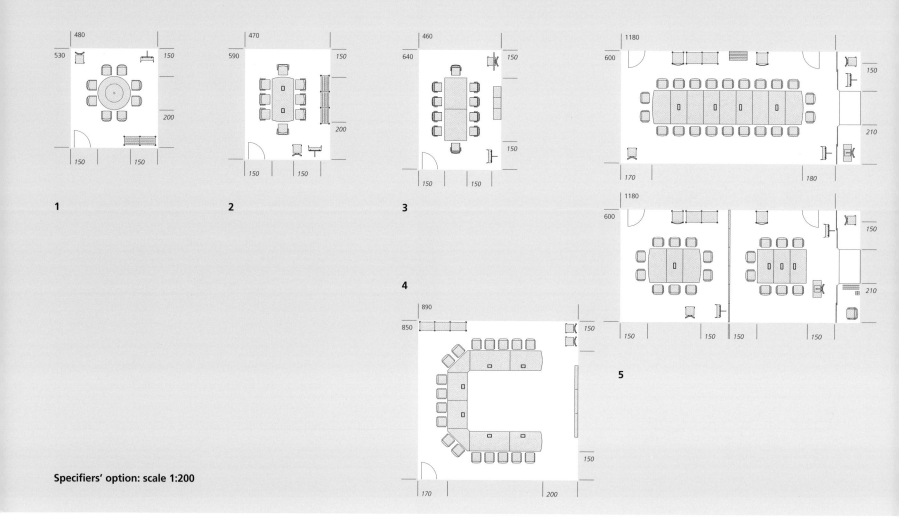

Specifiers' option: scale 1:200

1   Meeting room for 8 persons
with circular single table,
25 sqm = 3.1 sqm/person

2   Meeting room for 8 persons
with rectangular single table,
27 sqm = 3.4 sqm/person

3   Meeting room for 10 persons
with flexible single tables,
29 sqm = 2.9 sqm/person

4   Conference room for 18 persons,
U-shaped table configuration,
edge length per person: 75 cm,
75 sqm = 4.1 sqm/person

5   Partitionable conference room
with media wall and store room
for max. 22 persons,
variable table configuration,
edge length per person: 90 cm,
70 sqm = 3.2 sqm/person

6   Conference room with elliptical
table configuration for 32 persons,
permanently installed configuration,
edge length per person: 90 cm,
158 sqm = 4.9 sqm/person

7   Multi-purpose room for conference
and seminar applications
with integrated media technology
and partition for max. 34 persons,
mobile single tables or variable table
configuration,
edge length per person: 75 cm,
105 sqm = 3.0 sqm/person

8   Workshop room for conferences,
training, seminars and workshops
with moderation techniques;
utilization for 12 persons
with interactive conference forms;
for 30 persons for lectures
or presentations,
105 sqm = 8.0 or 3.5 sqm/person
respectively

6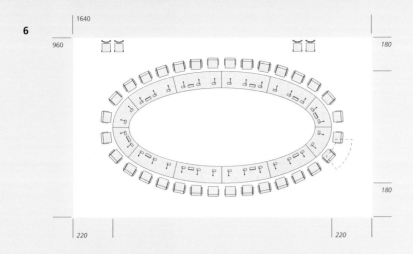

7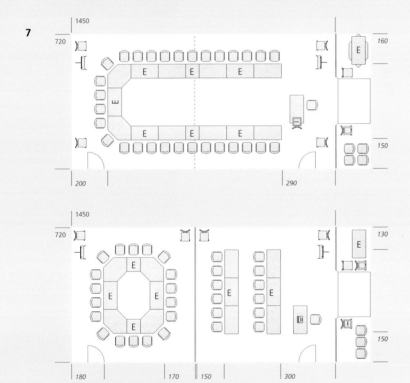

8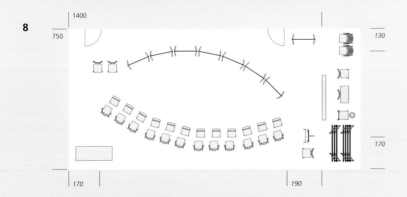

Space requirements in conference and training rooms

The choice of table configurations in a conference or training room should be based on space geometry and dimensions, the desired number of participants, the required and envisaged form of communication and the utilization rate. Depending on these factors, the focal point of planning is on the degree of interaction, a shared work surface, equal sitting positions, positioning facing presentation surfaces or variable space utilization for different purposes. The more compact the table form, the more equal the places around the table and the higher the degree of interaction; the more elongated the table form, the more exposed central places and shorter sides are and the more restricted the "communication radius" of participants is.

Floor space of 2.5 sqm (including passage ways, rear space, space for sitting places and related table surface).

The ground plans in the specifiers' options show frequently occurring table configurations with corresponding seating orders and space requirements taking the before-mentioned minimum distances to surrounding furniture units or walls into consideration. The required floor space for accompanying conference furniture units are included in the space requirements per person.

Planning guide
for media selection

Depending on room dimensions and form, furnishing concept and the technical complexity of functions, media technology application in conference environments may be planned by businesses themselves or the expert skills of specifiers is required. Analogue media are low-complex and as easy to plan as to operate. Wall boards, pinboards or flipcharts simply need corresponding wall brackets, floor space and storage facilities. Analogue projection equipment such as slide or overhead projectors are equally easy to plan: it is generally sufficient to include projection areas of suitable size, electric blinds, mobile equipment trolleys or static brackets and integrated solutions, as well as any necessary cables and correctly positioned power connection points.

As analogue AV media are being complemented or replaced to an ever increasing degree by digital media, every conference and meeting room today should, however, be equipped with correspondingly necessary cables and power connection options. Double floors allow retro-fitting compared with the acceptable amount of cost and effort, but do require higher pre-investment and reduce the usable height of storeys.

This is important to the extent that the height of the room limits the possible size of the projection area. Alternatively, cable channels with integrated connection points and hinged floor ports can already be specified when laying the floor. It is advisable to go through various utilization scenarios with corresponding furnishing layouts in advance in order to develop a useful installation grid for this purpose. If walls are to serve as surfaces for electronic displays, such as wall screens, corresponding connection points must also be specified there. Supplementary channels are not a satisfactory solution as cables are then channelled into the depth of the room which, in turn, can result in precarious and frequently also prohibited trip hazards. A ceiling is also unsuitable as a "distributor level" as vertical lead-aways obstruct the view and impair the appearance of the interior.

If digital media should not only function in the room as self-sufficient solutions but also be integrated into networks, IT specialists and system administrators of the respective company are also needed and should be involved in addition to the specifier.

Relevant areas for specifying
The planning guidelines presented and described here can in no way replace the competence of specifiers and IT specialists. They are intended to provide a basic understanding and to make companies aware of key tasks with a view to achieving holistic solutions.

Acoustics

Noise emissions are now some of the greatest impact factors in the work environment. In addition to noise development from technical equipment and high sound peaks from telephone calls and conversations in the immediate vicinity, this is also connected to the frequent lack of consideration for room acoustics. What is harmful to health at workplaces impairs the key function of the room in conference and communication environments: to make the spoken word or sound reproduction as audible as possible without any distortion and interference. Room dimensions, geometry, materials and surface finishes of floors, walls and ceilings, as well as furniture and last but not least, the number of persons influence sound reflection and thus reverberations as well as absorption. Digital simulation programmes offer the possibility of including these parameters in the planning stage and of checking and optimizing the acoustic effect of a room.

Audio transmission

Technical amplification of voice and sound reproduction is necessary for distances exceeding twelve meters. However, microphones, amplifiers and loudspeakers cannot compensate for poor room acoustics – on the contrary: negative aspects are also amplified. Besides correct operation, the choice of the right technology also plays a key role to prevent, for example, dreaded acoustic feedback effects. There are repeated problems with clip-on microphones in particular. They generally stem from poor planning, wrong choice of loudspeakers or improper use. Sound transformers and line sources are systems that are available for small and medium-sized conference rooms that combine transmission quality with functional reliability. Such loudspeaker systems can be integrated invisibly into surfaces and walls, but they do require special control technology and adjustment to achieve satisfactory acoustic results.

Lighting and electric blinds

Light, in particular daylight, is decisive for human vitality and biorhythm. Light may however become an interference factor with regard to the reproduction quality of projected images and films. For that reason there is often no incidence of daylight in theatre cinemas and many lecture halls. However, in conference and communication environments, darkness or the exclusive use of artificial light have a tiring effect and prevent active info-exchange. In such cases it is necessary to find a satisfactory compromise for variable ways of darkening the room that is influenced by the incidence of interfering light, the light intensity of projectors, the projection concept and the size of the projection area. But: no projector is able to compensate for direct incidence of daylight or even sunlight on the projection area – it is therefore absolutely necessary to have some method of darkening the room.

Projection area in relation to room dimensions

A planning aspect that is frequently neglected is the question of the relation between the possible projection size and the maximum viewing distance which ensures that projected data and images are easily recognizable and legible. The minimum viewing distance is one-and-a-half times, the maximum viewing distance is five times, and with films it is six times the width of the projected image. The lower edge of the image should be on a level of 120 cm (eye level of viewers when sitting) to provide a good view. In the case of large room depths, the bottleneck is therefore less potential projection widths but more the height of the room in order to produce the required projection area.

Planning advice for installing floor connections

In multifunctional, optionally also partitionable training rooms, a number of different events can take place such as conferences, lectures, presentations and seminars for which coordinated and flexible application of media technology should be specified. Possible scenarios involving varying table configurations should be gone through in the planning stage. This will supply information for positioning conference media – such as overhead or slide projectors and if necessary also mobile digital projectors and corresponding control equipment such as laptops, PCs or a video recorder.

Various ground plans may then be used to create an efficient grid for the installation of floor-integrated connections for power, data, network, AV or also telephones. This is particularly advisable in the case of new buildings.

If existing facilities are converted to new use where floor installations are only possible at great expense, the number of connection points can be substantially reduced by specifying table ranges which allow horizontal cable management within tables themselves.

If the room is partitionable in two equally large sections, installations should be carried out symmetrically along the dividing line to have the same utilization options available for both sections of the partitioned room.

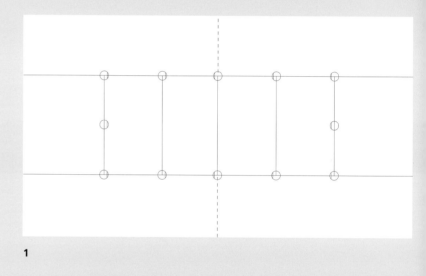

1

1   Installation grid for floor connections, coordinated with the utilization scope shown here. There are projection areas along the shorter sides of each room, thus allowing media support after partitioning in both sections.

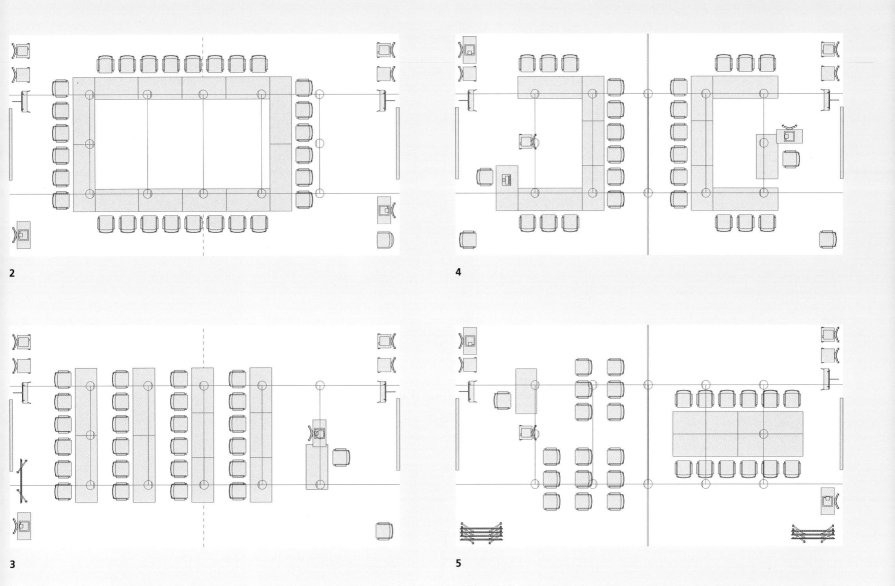

2 Utilization of room for a large
conference without media technology.

3 Lecture, seminar or presentation
with projection while using the
entire room.

4 Partitioning of room for events taking
place in parallel. The specifiers' option
shows two training scenarios, each
using a projector.

5 Utilization of partitioned room sections
for a lecture with projection as well
as for a meeting.

Technical equipment integrated into tables and table configurations

It is not only general media technology that should be considered in a conference room but also diverse electronic equipment used by participants. The use of laptops, mobile phones or multimedia handheld computers such as PDA (persona digital assistant) has become an integral part of daily routine in such environments. That is why more and more technical equipment is being directly integrated into table and table configurations: this ranges from simple plug-in cables and concealed storage space for network adaptors and surplus cables, new facilities for connecting the contents of screens interactively on the general projection area to integrated microphones and connectivity modules for telephone conferences and videoconferencing or integrated digital projectors and monitors.

Modules for power, data connections, VGA and sound (stereo jack plugs) are indispensable basic features of conference tables. Easily accessible cable management systems on or in the table are as important as corresponding pre-installations in a conference room with correctly positioned connection points in the floor. The question as to whether technical equipment should be integrated into the table depends on individual weighting of pros and cons.

The following general principle applies: the more additive connectivity modules are, the more cost-effective and versatile future adjustment scope and table application are, the more integrated the solutions, the less technology disturbs group-dynamic communication processes.

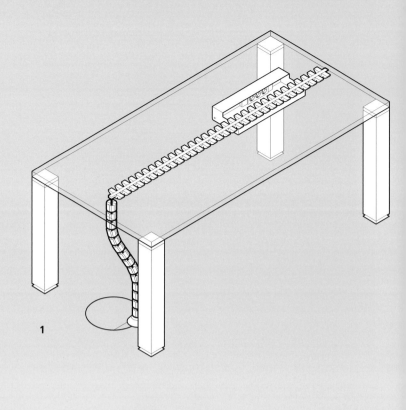

1

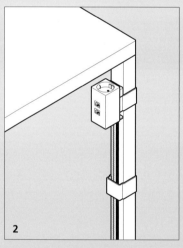

2

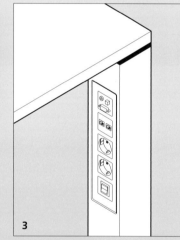

3

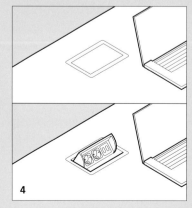

4

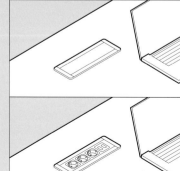

5

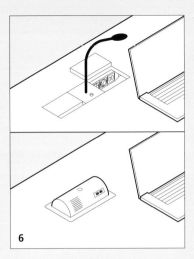

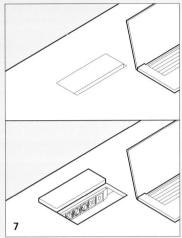

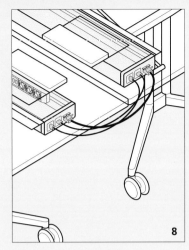

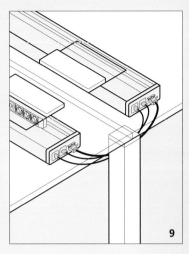

6 **7** **8** **9**

Additive modules for cable management and installation

(1) The advantage of additive power modules is being able to retain the neutral function of the table and thus allow varying applications, and to carry out subsequent changes with ease. Vertical cable channelling is on the table leg itself, for example, using slot-on clips or link chains that may be fixed individually underneath the table top. For horizontal integration, cables are channelled in detachable cable tracks or inserted cable nets to accommodate network adaptors, socket strips and surplus cables. Alternatively, fold-down cable trays may be used. It is disadvantageous to have awkward plug-ins, possible restriction of legroom and longer, disturbing cables to equipment lying on the table surface.

(2, 3) Additive installations are recommended for variable and multi-functional tables and table systems. A semi-integrated solution permits variably positionable table legs with integrated cable management and connectivity modules.

Hinged techni-stations, visibly integrated into table tops

(4, 5, 6) Individually specifiable techni-stations in plastic or aluminium may be integrated into table tops direct for quick and simple operation. They are accessible via hinged covers or may be flipped up or rotated to expose. Configuration scope ranges from usual power, data and audio connections to complete modules for a telephone conference, including microphones and loudspeakers. Attention should be paid to modular configuration to allow subsequent adaptation of connection technology without having to exchange the entire techni-station. Vertical input cables should be in the foot section of the table; horizontal cable management should be underneath the table top by means of permanently installed cable trays or baskets. It is however a disadvantage that plastic or aluminium cladding impairs the coherence of the table surface and surplus cables as well as network adaptors are "stored" on the table surface.

Techni-stations are advisable for statically installed table configurations or optionally mobile single tables if quick availability of functionality (plug and play) is more important than invisible technical connections.

Technical connections integrated invisibly underneath the table surface

(7) With such solutions, all cable management elements and modules are integrated into fold-down table trays as a separate level of technical equipment underneath the table top. This also includes power supply for clip-on microphones. Access to socket strips or equipment consoles with individually specifiable modules is via table portals with brushed profile which are coated or veneered to match the table surface. The back panel of the cover should also be finished accordingly. If the portal has an integral hinged cover with a 180° opening function, plug-ins are fast and simple. A sufficiently spacious table tray allows storage of surplus cables, battery chargers and network adaptors too.

New signal technologies permit data connections to be combined with a "show-me button". This allows up to 20 users to show their sources of data, for example laptops, on the shared presentation medium such as a digital projector or a large-format screen at the press of a button to make a spontaneous, visually supported contribution.

(8, 9) If technical equipment is permanently installed for each table unit and if cable trays have corresponding table-to-table connections, this technology may not only be used for static table configurations but also for table systems and mobile, single tables for variably used rooms.

In old and existing buildings, it is often the simplest solution to include the installation level for integrating modern media technology underneath table surfaces rather than in the floor. Extra investments required will soon pay off as higher density interior arrangements are possible and pre-installation costs in buildings can be considerably reduced.

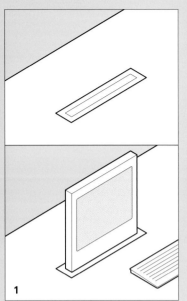

1

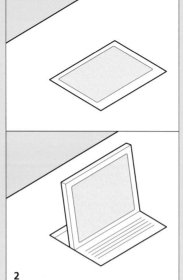

2

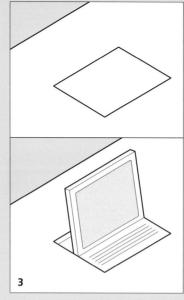

3

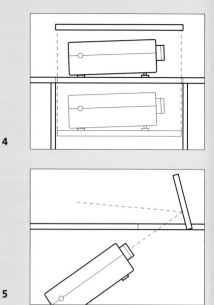

4

5

Integration of retractable monitors and projectors into tables and table configurations

Heavy equipment such as flip-up or retractable monitors or digital projectors can also be directly integrated into the table surface. It should however be ensured that monitors are supported by the frame structure using suitable techni-frames and not by the table top itself.

(1–3) Various electro-mechanical solutions are available for integrating such equipment: displays either slide into the table top vertically or are horizontally integrated, optionally with either the display surface facing upwards or with the rear panel facing upwards and coated or veneered to match the table surface. Horizontal integration requires a low insertion depth underneath the table which means that legroom is not restricted. A vertical solution requires modesty panels to be fitted.

(4, 5) The integration of projectors may be supported by an elevator whereby the unit emerges from the table surface vertically together with its cover; or mirror projection may be used. In the latter case, the digital projector remains in a constant position underneath the table and projects the image against a mirror that is mounted on the underside of a flap in the table surface. If the flap is opened at a pre-defined angle, the mirror directs the projection beam onto the projection area.

It is only advisable to integrate a digital projector underneath the table if the table depth is sufficiently large due to space requirements – and if the construction is not connected to the table frame and the top as otherwise even the smallest vibrations would be directly transferred to the projection.

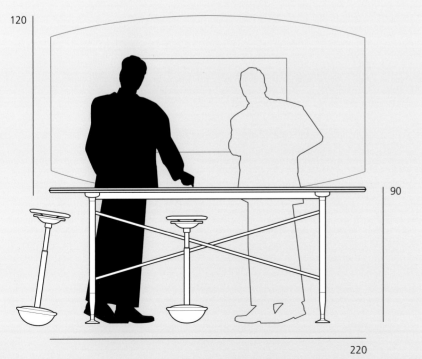

1

Ø 100

105

120

90

2

220

Interactive tables

Interactive solutions such as the ConsulTable (1) or the InteracTable (2) are designed to promote interaction in small conference groups with four to eight participants as directly as possible by providing digital media support. The electronic interface, integrated horizontally into the tables, serves as a direct, shared and interactive surface for work and visual presentation. Any information required may be visually presented there, enriched by material spontaneously accessed from the internet or the network and subsequently discussed.

Using corresponding software applications and touch-sensitive features, contents may be rotated like analogue documents and annotated using a pen to allow the benefits of the digital world to be used immediately during discussions, including saving results and email distribution. In addition, such meeting and conference tables permit synchronous cooperation of geographically distributed teams too.

A large flat screen, horizontally integrated into the table surface, serves as an interface: either a 17" screen (ConsulTable) or a 50" screen (InteracTable). These units disappear completely into the background as neither cladding nor cables are visible.

Interactive tables are particularly suitable for small meeting and consultation rooms, and also for project offices or semi-public zones with a more informal character such as foyers, showrooms and customer service areas.

See also pages 142, 144, 249, 268, 275.

Overview of media selection
for visual presentation

Media	Image size
Flipchart	70 x 100
Pinboard	120 x 150
Whiteboard	120 x 150 high
Wall-mounted board	200–300 x 120
ScreenMate (mobile plasma or LCD display)	40", aspect ratio 16:9
CommBoard, wall-mounted	50", aspect ratio 16:9
CommBoard mobile	50", aspect ratio 16:9
InterWall	70", aspect ratio 4:3
Overhead projector	100 x 100 to 300 x 300
Slide projector	150 x 110 to 600 x 400
Visualizer	Dependent on output technology (screen or projection)
Portable digital projector	150 x 110 to 300 x 225
Ceiling-mounted digital projector opened up	240 x 180 to 800 x 600
Ceiling-mounted digital projector concealed	240 x 180 to 800 x 600
Wall-integrated digital projector	240 x 180 to 800 x 600
Rear projection	180 x 135 to 360 x 270

Analogue	Digital	Interactive	Audio	Video	Static	Mobile	Open-ended	Sound development	Electric blinds	Power connection	Data connection points
●		●				●	●				
●		●				●	●				
●	○	●				●	●			○	○
●		●			●						
	●	○	●	●		●				●	●
	●	○	●	●	●		●			●	●
	●	●	●	●		●				●	●
	●	○	●	●		●		●	◐	●	●
●		●				●		●		●	
●						○	○	●	●	●	
	●	●				●			○	●	●
	●		●	●		●		●	◐	●	●
	●		●	●	●		○	●	◐	●	●
	●		●	●	●		○		◐	●	●
	●		●	●	●		○		◐	●	●
	●		●	●	●		○		◐	●	●

● applies

○ optionally

◐ partially

Flexible and mobile visualization displays

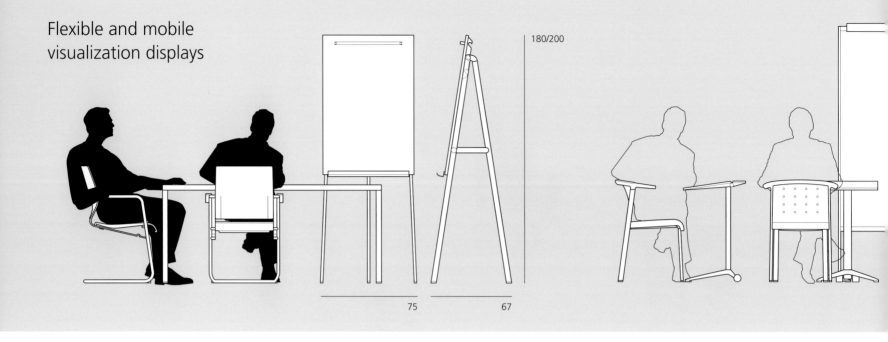

180/200

75   67

In spite of technological progress, traditional visualization media are still indispensable in smaller conference and meeting rooms.

This is connected with the following:
- Everyone has learned and has known how to use pen and paper since childhood.
- They may be positioned spontaneously within a room and used completely independently of technical connections.
- Scope for variable addition allows synchronous presentation of several large-format sets of contents.
- The medium (paper) can be separated from the medium carrier (flipchart, pinboard) and may be taken away, presented and stored individually.
- The materialization of information on paper permits greater authenticity and more direct points of reference than abstract actions by keyboard and mouse.

This is why such media are not replaced but are complemented by means of new media, such as digital wall screens and projectors.

Flipchart

A flipchart is a suitable medium for visualizing agenda points, to make more complex interconnections comprehensible by spontaneously using a sketch, to document time schedules and to record jointly discussed measures. Commercially available flipchart pads are used and large writing using thick felt pens ensures legibility up to a distance of eight metres.

While a horizontal visualization and work surface tends to support more informal, interactive and participation-oriented communication processes, a vertical information surface has a more compelling character and it promotes focussed attention. The changeover from a conference table to a flipchart therefore has an important didactic aspect too: it opens up scope for ending creative discussion phases with a concrete result.

A flipchart is therefore suitable for smaller conference and meeting groups of up to fifteen participants. Mobile flipcharts on castors are optionally available in addition to models with a foldable frame.

For materials and surface finishes, see also page 140.

Pinboard

A pinboard is regarded as a vertical surface for documentation and work in interactive conference forms in which ideally all participants are involved in collecting material, analysis evaluation and developing solutions. It is therefore used primarily in a conference workshop, but is also useful in meeting environments. The pin area is generally covered with a brown-beige sheet of paper fixed with pins. The Text is written directly onto this sheet and participants' contributions are also attached with pins, grouped and stuck on firmly in their final order for everyone to see, so that results are saved for further processing and documentation purposes. In addition, pinboards also allow complex, large-format documents

190

195

125   54   137   80

such as print-outs of project plans to be kept in sight during a conference. Last but not least, they can function as temporary screens for work in break-out groups.

Pinboards can also be positioned together to create large-format displays as required to provide information panels for all conference delegates. In this case, maximum viewing distances should be two to six metres depending on the size of the lettering.

For materials and surface finishes, see also page 140.

Whiteboards

Whiteboards may be used as an alternative to pinboards. They are available in various sizes and versions: as horizontal formats permanently attached to a wall, as horizontal and upright formats integrated into a media wall or as free-standing elements which may be flexibly allocated to a conference group like pinboards. The surface for which dry-erasable pens are used comprises a scratch-resistant, thin,

white enamel steel plate. This allows posters, graphics, plans and other large-format paper documents to be attached with magnets. The panel has a frame, generally in aluminium, with an additional pentray. The surface is cleaned after use by means of a special eraser that is also attached to the whiteboard by a magnet. In contrast to a pinboard, visually presented material is only of a temporary nature as with a conventional school blackboard using chalk. A photograph is then taken of the contents for the purpose of saving results and documentation.

Whiteboards are now also available as digitally enhanced versions. On such boards the positions of a special pen functioning as a transmitter are recognized, virtual, written lines and drawings are indicated, saved and rendered as printable data. The eraser is in the form of a virtual sponge allowing both deletion and correction. These hybrid boards mark an initial step towards digitization, yet they make use of the possibilities of integrating virtual visual presentations into interactive conference work to a small extent only.

InterWall

The InterWall is a mobile, spatially flexible visualization display that consistently combines the real inter-actions of a conference such as writing, annotating and marking with all the advantages of the digital world. It comprises a mobile frame upon which is mounted a 70", frameless glass panel that refracts the light of the special data projector integrated at the rear in such a way as to render a clear yet transparent image visible on the panel. The digital projector is controlled via a PC or a laptop allowing the InterWall to be used as a mobile rear projection unit which, when turned off, appears fully transparent above the frame.

The main benefit is however that it may be additionally equipped with interactive functionality and a digital pen. This allows projected digital documents such as pictures, plans, graphics or websites to be called up on the panel direct, presented and edited. Every step, every marking and annotation can be saved, filed in the

network or sent by email. Additionally, a neutral, virtual paper surface may be called up which may be written upon using pens in a choice of colours and thicknesses.

The InterWall marks an innovative, flexibly usable presentation and work medium for conference groups up to fifteen strong, which may also be integrated into conference environments with high-quality furniture due to its design quality.

For materials and surface finishes, see also page 85.

> ▸ Flat screens are increasingly used as an alternative
> to projection technology in small to medium-sized
> meeting and conference rooms. The technology used,
> sizes and features define not only the price but also
> application scope: possible viewing distances correlate
> with the size of the display and with the quality of the
> screen resolution, which together with characteristics
> such as touch sensitivity, in turn determines whether
> the screen can also be used as an interactive work
> medium.

Mobile and wall-integrated flat screens

Plasma screens

Screens with plasma technology can be manufactured up to a size of 120" (screen diagonal). With this technology, light is produced by means of ionized gas (plasma) similar to fluorescent tubes. In between two glass panels there are many small partial vacuum chambers filled with inert gas and one fluorescent substance each. Three chambers each with the primary colours of red, green and blue together form a pixel. One transistor per chamber ignites (ionizes) the gas specifically, thus generating coloured light. Screen proportions have an aspect ratio of 4:3, increasingly also 16:9.

The greatest advantage of plasma screen technology is excellent image quality due to high contrast and brightness. This allows plasma displays to be used in bright environments too. In addition, pixels are addressed very fast and the possible viewing angle is much wider than with LCD technology.

The disadvantages are low colour saturation in the greens, high heat emission, the risk of burning in with images left on the screen too long depending on the model, high energy consumption and weight, as well as transport sensitivity.

LCD screens

LCD technology has become known primarily due to laptop displays. Screen sizes of up to 65" screen diagonal can now also be produced which are used in meeting and conference rooms. With LCD technology, a backlight creates light that passes through a substrate containing liquid crystal material. At the same time, electrical currents cause the liquid crystal molecules to align to allow varying levels of light to pass through the second substrate. The screen is divided up into pixels by means of a fine matrix; the liquid crystal molecules address a particular pixel and form a colour point. The screen proportions also have an aspect ratio of 4:3 or 16:9.

The advantages of LCD technology are high image resolution (number of pixels), comparatively low energy consumption and low weight; flicker-free, distortion free, and sharp image reproduction, as well as long service life. The disadvantages are back-lighting and a lower level of brightness which it entails, slightly slower reaction times with moving images (films), more limited colour reproduction, smaller viewing angle, as well as substantially higher prices for large formats compared to plasma screens.

Recommendations

Due to the rapid development of screen technology and dynamic price developments, which depend to a large extent on manu-factured volumes, it is advisable to check the current status of relevant pros and cons, to compare with specific intended applications and then to take the decision. New models with LCD technology can increasingly compensate for disadvantages compared with plasma screens, but they are – still – over propor-tionately expensive.

When selecting suitable flat screens, interactive application scope should be of paramount importance in addition to the question of the most effective screen size and technology if flat screens are to be used in conference rooms. Support for communication in the form of active editing, modifying and annotating of rendered information is thus possible over and above mere visualization.

Mobile or wall-mounted integration?

Mobile flat screens can be used for several rooms. In addition, they have the advantage that they may be moved up close to the conference table if required thus making it easy to maintain the maximum viewing distance. Corresponding power, AV and optional network connections are however required at sensible positions.

Wall-mounted solutions provide the possibility of positioning up to three screens adjacent to one another, and of thus creating a large display in which screens may be controlled jointly as well as individually, for example, for synchronous visual presentation of various data sources. While the screen size should be limited to 50" for weight reasons for mobile applications, for wall-inte-grated solutions it is only the width and height of walls as well as the load capacity of the mounting bracket that limits screen size. Permanent positioning on the other hand requires coordination and alignment of the conference table configuration with the presentation surface to ensure maximum distances and viewing angles.

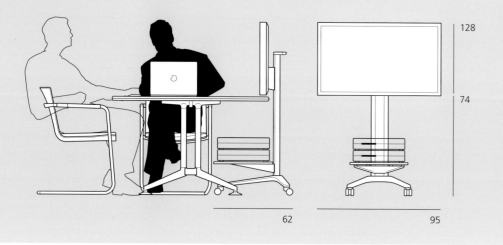

128

74

62

95

ScreenMate

The ScreenMate is an example of a mobile, medium-sized display that may be moved up to conference tables and table configurations for presentations and videoconferences. Depending on the screen diagonal, it is suitable for a group of participants of eight to six.

In this case, a plasma screen, optionally with an integrated loudspeaker system and a camera is mounted on a mobile aluminium frame on castors that is fitted with additional shelves to accommodate various output devices and with integrated cable management. The cantilevered construction allows it to be moved very close to the conference table. The maximum viewing distance is approximately 5 m for a screen with 43" screen diagonal with an aspect ratio of 16:9.

If the ScreenMate is networked with correspondingly positioned technical installations in the table configuration, then every laptop that is connected can be activated as a data source by means of a show-me button. This gives every participant the possibility of supporting visual presentations at any time in a way that is visible to all those involved, including spontaneous discussion contributions.

CommBoard mobile

Interaction scope is enhanced further if mobile, large-format flat screens are used with an interface that is inherently interactive, and operation and processing may be carried out by finger or pen on the display direct. Then, any digital documents such as images, graphics or plans may be given digitized "handwritten" markings, corrections or annotations, which may be saved online, filed in the network or mailed. If the screen can be tilted infinitely variably by up to 30° electrically from the vertical position (90°), as is the case with this mobile CommBoard, it may be used both as a shared presentation surface and as a desk-like work surface. With a 50" screen diagonal and an aspect ratio of 16:9, the maximum viewing distances for presentations is approximately 5.50 m, permitting groups of up to eight to ten persons.

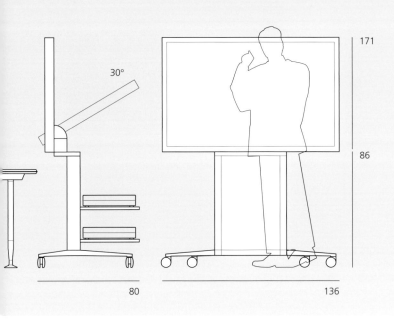

While the display size is important for the maximum viewing distance the quality of the image resolution is important for minimum viewing distance. This should be as low as possible as work may also be carried out alternatively on the display direct. An image resolution of at least 1280 x 768 pixels is therefore advisable.

Attention should be paid to the aesthetic quality of the model in addition to technical functionality as such a presentation and work medium as a conference table and chairs are a visible element of a conference interior.

CommBoard

Interactively equipped flat screens are also possible as wall-integrated solutions. For this purpose the screen is hung on the wall like a picture using correspondingly stable brackets; any power, data and network connections must be pre-integrated into the wall. It is even better, although involving more effort, to have a flush integration as only the interface is visible and not the technical device itself.

In this example, up to three such screens may be positioned side by side and networked. Such an enlarged display permits greater viewing distances. In addition, different kinds of information may be presented in parallel such as graphics, time schedules and websites and operated and edited by pen or finger.

The type of media integration determines the character of cooperation to a large extent: although the screen technologies employed by a wall-integrated or mobile CommBoard and InteracTable (see page 195) respectively are identical, they do however support quite different forms of communication. Presentations on vertical screens support focused attention, a low level of interaction amongst participants and more formal communication, while work at an InteracTable promotes above all active participation, a high degree of interaction amongst participants and informal communication due to horizontal integration in high table height.

Visualizer

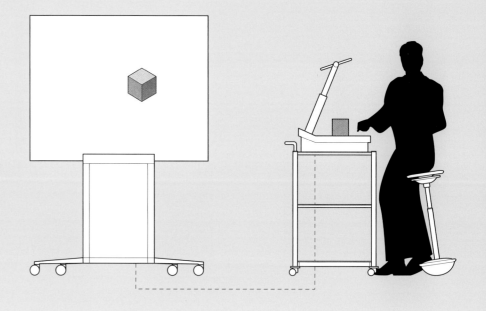

Function

The visualizer is the electronic refinement of the "overhead principle". Similar to an overhead projector, the visualizer has a work surface onto which both two and three-dimensional objects may be positioned. For a lecture or talk requiring digital imaging it is not necessary to present information on overheads: any printed matter may be used (individual sheets, brochures, books). The originals are recorded by an integrated video camera and transmitted as video signals to the output equipment – for example, a monitor or projector. As transmission takes place via cable, the location of the visualizer is not tied to the position of the reproduction surface, in contrast to an overhead projector.

Application

As the surface upon which overheads are placed is also the work surface for the speaker, it should be positioned at a height so that overheads can be written on and objects can be rotated. To the left and the right of the overhead surface there should be sufficient space for prepared or already used material.

Specifying the interior

Due to the spatial independence of the output device, the visualizer can be used in a mobile and flexible manner: at an instructor's workplace in a training environment, whereby the device should not obstruct the view of the reproduction surface or be placed immediately at a conference participant's workplace. The only prerequisites are connections for power and video cables.

Whether the room has to be darkened using electric blinds and, if so, to what degree, does not depend on the visualizer, but on whether the image is produced via a monitor, front projection or rear projection.

Accessories
Monitor, video projector
or video rear projection;
mobile server

Video and data projectors

Digital projector technology

Digital projectors can optionally reproduce analogue videos or digital data. They are available in various sizes, performance spectrums and for different utilization scenarios: ranging from a small, portable device and models that slide out of tables electrically or have a tilted mirror mounted underneath a table to large, high-performance devices that are permanently mounted or integrated on ceilings or walls.

Function

During video projection, an electronic video signal is transmitted again into light rays, by means of which an image is projected onto a white wall surface or a projection screen. The advantage compared with reproduction via a monitor is a much larger or even substantially larger image size depending on the type of device and light intensity, which allows application in front of a large circle of participants too. There are various kinds of projector technology: tube projectors, LCD projectors and DLP projectors (digital light processing).

With traditional tube projectors, the signal sources of red-green-blue are projected from three precisely adjusted tubes with one lens each in such a way that the coloured image is produced on the projection surface.

The most usual type of projectors today are LCD devices with a single lens whereby light is transformed into a coloured image within the projector by being sent through a 1.3 to 1.8 inch chip with approximately 1.3 million pixels which is in the form of the liquid crystal display. Depending on light intensity and the type of optical lens a large, wall-filling image can thus be projected. As the chip absorbs light much more light is needed in the projector than reaches the projection area. In the case of low image resolutions this may produce undesirable effects such as a so-called "fly screen".

The only recently developed DLP principle is based on a DMP chip (digital micromirror device) with approximately 500,000 tiny, moving mirrors (16 x 16 micrometres) for reproducing one pixel per mirror on the projection area. The mirrors are tilted up to 1,000 times per second by means of electric impulses. The position of the mirrors regulates light intensity per pixel on the screen. This provides natural colours, even image rendering and avoids convergence problems of colours as this technology only needs one image generator.

A video projector can reproduce image signals from different types of output devices:

- Analogue video signals from a video player or a receiver
- Analogue or digital video signals from a visualizer, which replaces a conventional overhead projector in the specifiers' option and also permit projection of smaller, three-dimensional objects
- Digital signals from DVD players and computers

There are three different technologies which are suitable for using video projectors in meeting, conference and training environments:

1. Front projection with a permanently installed video projector
2. Front projection with a mobile video projector
3. Rear projection

Front projection
with a permanently installed video projector

180

120

1.5 x projection width

Front projection with a permanently installed digital projector is the most common type of media technology in large conference and training rooms. The most suitable projection surface is a smooth wall surface painted in matt white (RAL 9003), providing the projector is sufficiently light intensive. If attempts are made to compensate for lack of light intensity by using a reflecting surface this will often result in an increase in brightness towards the centre, a so-called hot spot.

As it is not advisable to have a completely darkened room as participants otherwise tire quickly and cannot make any notes, the light intensity of the projector must compensate for the stray light of the remaining room light. For this purpose, the projected useful light has to be five times stronger than the stray light that falls onto the projection area. The light intensity of the projector is described in lumen which corresponds to one lux per sqm projection area. The required light intensity can be calculated on the basis of the size of the projection area and stray light.

Calculation example:
Projection area 4 m x 3 m = 12 sqm; 1,000 lumen luminous power is required per sqm with 200 lux stray light, that means a projector with at least 12,000 ANSI (American National Standard Institute) lumen.

The less diffused light that reaches the projection area, the more brilliant the image. The best image quality is achieved in a completely darkened room, for example, in a cinema. For rooms that require various degrees of darkening, electrically controlled blinds and lighting with infinitely variable brightness adjustability are perfect solutions.

Specifying the interior

If it is planned to use rear projection in a large auditorium, i.e. with very large image widths, a permanently installed device is advisable due to the large projection size required and the weight of the equipment. All interrelations between projection distance and the size of the projection area, as well as the tilt angle to the projection area, should be considered from the very start.

The projector is located in the auditorium – frequently integrated into the ceiling or the wall opposite the projection area – and throws light onto the projection area frontally. Video projectors with high light intensity can generate an image width of up to 12 m – providing a room height of 10.20 m is available. But: the higher the light intensity, the more cooling the digital projector requires and the higher its noise level.

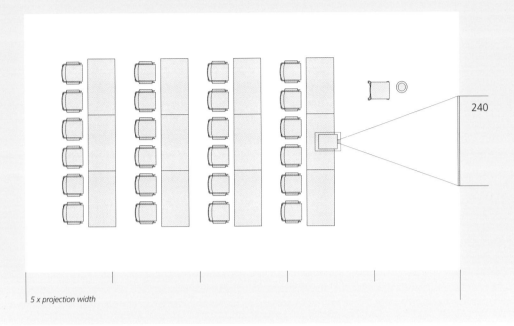

240

5 x projection width

It is therefore advisable to integrate a permanently installed digital projector into closed, noise-absorbing casing, whereby adequate ventilation must be ensured. The data source for the projector is generally located at the speaker's table, to the side in front of the projection area. A connection cable must also be available at this point. The digital projector can generally also be operated from there via a wireless remote control.

One of the most important planning parameters is the possible size of the projection area, which in turn defines the maximum possible viewing distance to ensure that projected data and images are easily recognizable and legible: in the case of fixed images, it should not be more than four to five times the width of the projected image; with films, it should not be more than six times the width of the projected image and not less than one-and-a-half times. An image ratio of 4:3 and minimum height of 120 cm for the lower edge of the image makes it easier to calculate what projection width is possible on the basis of a generally predefined room height and how great the maximum distance to the projection should be.

For example, a room height of 3 m allows a maximum projection height of 1.80 m. This produces a projection width of 2.40 m and a maximum distance of 9.60 m to 12 m; 14.40 m for films. If a minimum distance of 3.60 m is subtracted, this leaves 6 m to 8.40 m (10.80 m for films) for positioning chairs and possibly tables.

The distance may be correspondingly greater if a projection ratio of 16:9 is used. It should however be considered that most data are generated with an aspect ratio of 4:3. If data are not recalculated in terms of the other projection ratio, reproduction will be distorted accordingly.

Hints on use

Besides light intensity and maximum distance typeface and type size are also important when projecting written material. Type should be between 16 pt and 20 pt to ensure that it is legible.

Front projection with a mobile video projector

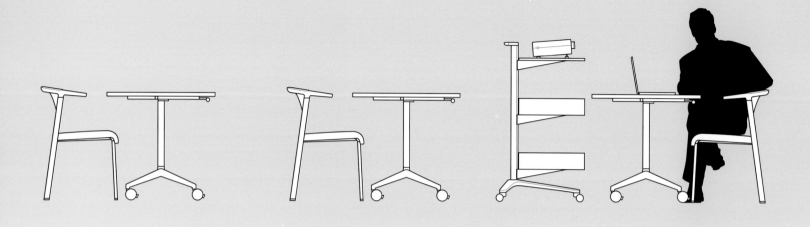

Small, portable LCD digital projectors are suitable equipment for meeting rooms and for small to medium-sized conference rooms in which media technology is only required occasionally. As portable projectors have much lower luminosity than large projectors they are only suitable for events with a limited number of participants. The brightness of the image can be enhanced by reducing the ambient light as stray light accordingly.

Kept on standby in a central store room and checked regularly for efficient functioning, they may be easily transported to the required location and installed there. By using LCD technology as compared with tube projectors, no complicated image adjustment is necessary which would otherwise have to be carried out whenever equipment is repositioned in order to synchronize the three coloured light rays. In addition, such digital projectors should have variably adjustable lenses with a focal length that can be adapted to the size of the projection area even with different projection distances. Last but least, equipment with a low level of sound development should be specified as the projector is positioned close to the auditorium.

Specifying the interior

In this case too, the most suitable projection surface is a wall surface painted in matt white. Screens with a reflecting surface, often used in the past, decrease the image quality as brightness increases towards the centre of the image.

In a conference room, a digital projector is often installed on the conference table which should be equipped accordingly with power supply, and be connected to a laptop as a data source. However, any minor vibration on the table surface is directly transferred to the projected image. If the distance to the projection area allows, the digital projector should therefore ideally be placed on a mobile media trolley equipped with a tiltable surface to accommodate the device and with additional shelves for other equipment, such as a video recorder. Such positioning is highly recommended for lecture and training applications.

With a mobile trolley and an adjustable lens, the distance between the projector and the screen can be coordinated with the size of the audience or the distance to the first row of seats. As nearly all mobile devices have parallax compensation when a slanting projection angle is used, the projection area no longer needs to have an adjustable tilt facility to ensure parallel vertical alignment of the image.

Rear projection

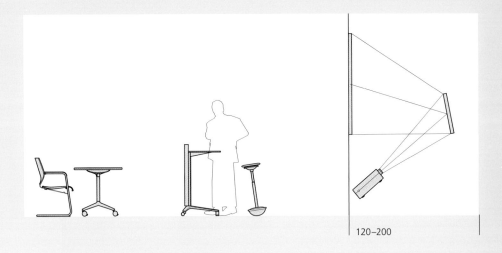

120–200

For rear projection, the light ray of the projector is reflected from the rear onto the projection area via one or even two tilted mirrors. As this rear section of the room is generally fully encapsulated and completely dark, there is no stray light and this optimizes light efficiency correspondingly. The advantages of rear projection are therefore that ambient light only has to be reduced slightly, that activity can take place directly in front of the projection area without any dazzling effects and without any shadows being cast, and integration of projectors into the rear section of the room provides acoustic insulation.

The disadvantages are loss of space, a poorer horizontal viewing angle and brightness distribution compared with front projectors, as well as relatively elaborate effort to produce of the projection area in the form of a media wall or other architectural construc-tions. Although the installation depth of the digital projector can be reduced using special lenses, this advantage is at the expense of geometric distortion and poorer distribution of the image definition.

Specifying the interior

Depending on the size of the projection area, the required installation depth for the rear projection unit is between 1.20 m and 2.00 m. If programmed accordingly, two or more rear projectors may be placed next to one another to produce one correspondingly wide image.

As rear projection units are permanently installed in the room, they are often specified as the central component of a multimedia wall. Depending on the shape of the room, multimedia walls may extend over the entire width of the room or be a corner solution. Direct incident light radiation onto the projection area from natural or artificial light should, however, be avoided.

In small rooms, the sound system is integrated into the multi-media wall itself, whereas in larger rooms additional loudspeakers (on the ceiling or on side walls) should be specified. For mobile input sources – such as a visualizer or a computer – floor sockets for power, data and AV should be specified according to a useful installation grid.

Well planned integration of media technology shortens prepara-tion time for presentations considerably and avoids waiting times – which, in the process of conference group dynamics in particu-lar, are unbearable for both the speaker and the auditorium.

Multimedia wall for front projection with a furniture store room

In multimedia conference and training rooms, multimedia walls comprise integrated modules that combine the desire for lockable storage space for mobile equipment or spare furniture units with requirements in terms of display or projection areas. Depending on the shape of the room, multimedia walls may extend over the entire width of the room or be a corner solution. The depth of the modules depends on how many are used and on how much floor space is required to accommodate conference furniture. Facing the room, the multimedia wall has two levels for sliding panels: the outer level is used to close the wall completely, while the inner level may be equipped with panels for analogue presentations – for example, whiteboards or pinboards – as well as with a central projection area.

1 Top view of panel levels and storage space
for conference furniture

2 Fully closed multimedia wall; the surface finishes
of the panels may be coordinated with the interior design
theme or material finishes by means of lacquering,
laminates or veneers

3 Outer panels, opened to allow use of the projection area

4 View of storage space with compacted mobile desks,
a flipchart, a lectern and a leaning aid, pinboards
and servers for moderation materials, for an overhead
projector, a digital projector and a visualizer

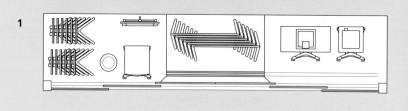

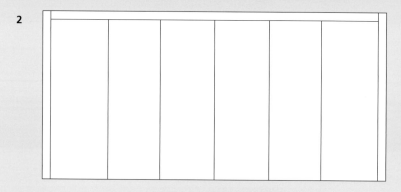

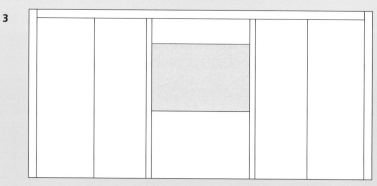

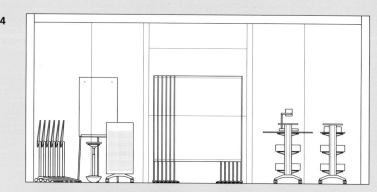

Multimedia wall with integrated rear projection unit

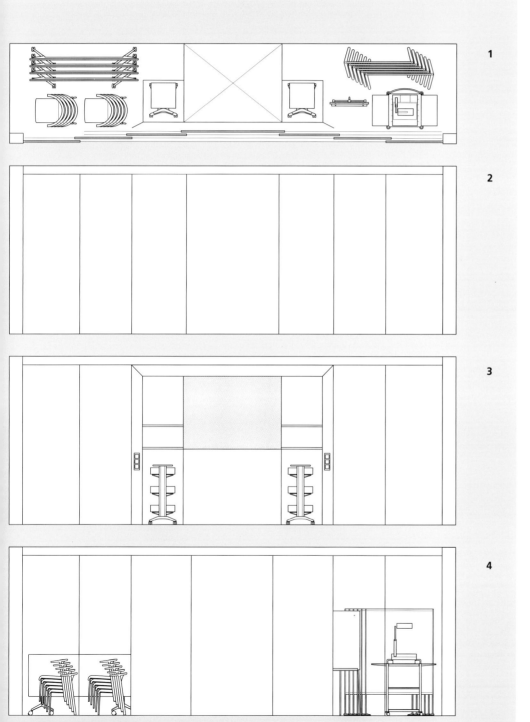

The permanently installed rear projection unit forms the centre of the multimedia wall. Video equipment and a loudspeaker system may be integrated on the left and the right. In each of the lower sections, there is space for a mobile media server or a material server. The multimedia wall may be completely closed by means of sliding panels.

The remaining space behind the panels functions as a "garage" for parking not only additional furniture, but also a visualizer which the speaker or instructor can move into the room as required.

1 Top view of rear projection unit, side compartments for control equipment and storage space for additional furniture

2 Front view, completely closed

3 Inner panels opened, for use of projection area

4 Outer panels opened, view of storage space with compacted mobile tables with pivoted table tops and stacked chairs, a flipchart, pinboards and a media server for a visualizer

Speaker's lectern, instructor's table, convenor's workplace and podium

Anyone standing in front of an auditorium or sitting on a podium as a speaker or an instructor is in the limelight. Tension is correspondingly high for the one, while expectations are high on the part of the others. Difficulties in connecting and operating media technology thus have an extremely dramatic effect: every minute of delay, any uncertainty or unsuccessful attempt to start up equipment is a false start that has a negative effect on human interplay.

A cable tangle on the floor or underneath tables may not only become a trip hazard, but it also makes an unprofessional impression. Special attention should therefore be paid to the aesthetic quality and technical functionality of such places in the limelight. Convenient allocation and easy handling of equipment, concealed cable channels and correctly positioned power and data connection points in furniture units and floors should go without saying (see also page 190, 192).

In variably used rooms, it is advisable to specify instructor's workplaces comprising mobile equipment trolleys and tables with integrated cable channels and connectivity modules, as well as storage space for surplus cables. If there is open cable channelling between the table and the multimedia server, the distance in between should be as short as possible so that cable lengths can be kept to a minimum.

Alternatively, a system table may be used from the table range specified for the auditorium, providing it may

also be equipped professionally with corresponding cables and a modesty panel for concealed cable management underneath the table top.

A speaker should stand during a lecture as his or her voice then has a fuller ring and greater dynamics of movement can support rhetoric. A partially mobile lectern with a modesty panel emphasizes the more formal lecture character while a high table creates a casual atmosphere. Both furniture units may be combined with mobile multimedia severs and fitted with technical equipment as required; the lectern may also be specified with a reading lamp in a room where electric blinds are used.

In lecture and training environments with technically sophisticated equipment, the entire media technology, including videoconferencing, optionally also lighting and air conditioning, may be controlled by means of a central interface which may be accessed via the integrated screen at the convenor's workplace and is preferably operable via touch functions.

Podium configurations should comprise variable system tables with modesty panels. As many speakers have their own laptop with them, table workplaces should be equipped with necessary data and power connection points. If the tables can be networked with one another and with the projection unit, and if the connectivity modules have a show-me function, any speaker may use his or her laptop to connect to the projector without any usual time-consuming, nerve-racking insertion or removal of plugs.

In the specifiers' option, the instructor's workplace, comprising a single system table with an inserted modesty panel, has a mobile media trolley for convenient operation of the visualizer while sitting. Data are rendered via a rear projector integrated into a multimedia wall.

Instructor's workplace, comprising a mobile table with a portable digital projector on a media server that is also mobile.

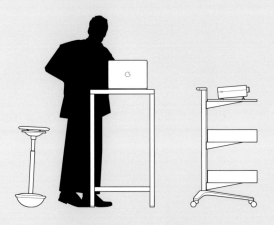

High table, functioning as a lectern, combined with a mobile media server for the portable video projector.

Podium, comprising variable tables with inserted modesty panels. Techni-stations (with microphone system) integrated into table surfaces do not only allow the speaker to network a portable computer with the projector from his or her workplace, but also allows him or her to connect a laptop to the projection area interactively via a "show-me button" as required.

Lectern with a mobile media server with a wide shelf for a portable overhead projector and shelf space for overheads at the side.

Convenor's workplace in a technically sophisticated training room with table-integrated displays. The instructor can operate all room functions from his or her workplace and display various information on the three wall-mounted flat screens.

Workplaces
for communication

▸ Studies on the work situation in management come to enlightening conclusions: managers like to take decisions within a team even if they could do it alone. The privilege of giving orders and monitoring their fulfilment is being replaced by the task of strengthening employees' identification with corporate goals and of allowing them to share responsibility. Furnishing concepts for executives' offices that adopt this impetus do not therefore focus primarily on prestige, but on openness, transparency and team thinking to create an atmosphere with an emphasis on communication.

Communication as a leadership task

Leadership is learning, not knowing. To understand
leadership as knowing (knowing it all and better) is pure
arrogance. It is a joint adventure that is pursued between
those who are led and their leaders. New discoveries.
Space for creativity. Enjoying work. Because we move
more in the direction to which we feel attracted.
For this purpose we need plenty of communication,
openness and understanding.

Rudolf Mann

Opportunities and limits for opening up the "command centre"

What all conference forms, methods and locations described
so far have in common is that they involve public or semi-public
environments which are specified as places of communication
separated from workplaces. That means participants always have
to change locations in order to communicate face-to-face at
a "neutral place". This corresponds to the instinctive, human
territorial separation of privacy and community. However,
meetings in certain business areas are quite consciously held in
the privacy of a personal workplace. This is traditionally the boss'
"command centre". In this context one is reminded of the term
of "audience" that is still used today in political and church
matters: the very question as to who summons whom and where
conveys the power relations and the behavioural role for ensuing
discussion.

It is therefore not surprising that meeting spaces at the workplace,
particularly in the case of high-ranking executives, have a long
tradition within companies themselves. If sharp tongues claim
that such areas are only necessary to furnish the empty spaces
of oversized executives' offices, this interpretation is incomplete
– which does not imply that real space requirements should not
form the basis of economically oriented architectural planning for
such areas too. An indication that the communicative function of
such an area is becoming more and more important regardless of
image and social prestige, can be seen in the rapidly increasing
amount of working time spent in meetings, particularly on the
part of executives.

They now spend 80-90 per cent of their time in various kinds of communicative face-to–face processes. Changes in the working world therefore require new leadership qualities, especially on the part of superiors. How else can leadership style and culture be expressed, fears be overcome, barriers be eliminated and employees be motivated for outstanding performance if not in the form of personal discussion with "those being led"?

At a time when the half life of sure knowledge is declining rapidly, in which data bases via the internet and intranet allow maximum transparency of knowledge and access to many groups of persons, "knowledge" as an instrument of power has had its heyday. A superior who knows everything better and surpasses the competence of his employees in every respect, either has incompetent staff or is so specialized that instead of carrying out leadership tasks he or she should assume the operative implementation of tasks and duties.

As companies today focus their efforts towards the outside on customer orientation, communication and marketability, where thinking in terms of territorial allocation used to dominate, the character of work and behavioural patterns among superiors, colleagues and staff are also changing.

Management consultant Rudolf Mann describes modern management behaviour as follows: "We need a new type of communication in which we can exchange information and points of view. No longer for the sake of being right, of winning, but for gaining insight into the other person's point of view". Beyond the ethical principle of paying due respect to employees, a cooperative style of leadership has concrete implications for corporate development too: anyone who does not promote the potential of employees forfeits the future – and in view of personnel costs, ready cash too.

The objectives and contents of discussions between management and employees may be of a varying character: they range from personal discussions about progress reports to agreement and decision-making processes, from a regular jour fixe, or a feedback discussion to project-specific talks. Besides the psychological components already mentioned, quite pragmatic aspects are also important for meetings at the workplace: any relevant documents are immediately to hand, one can save moving to a meeting room – and a straightforward and private workplace can provide a discreet and personal atmosphere in which confidential matters may be discussed more openly and with greater ease. It should not be underestimated that a "manager's office", as a territorial projection of hierarchy, has such strong symbolism for in-company ranking that factual issues may be involuntarily linked to "political", generally unconscious and unformulated aspects. A meeting "with the boss" acts as a signal of being something special, vis-à-vis one's colleagues too. To have secured an "appointment" invariably attracts a feeling of curiosity, admiration or envy, while "being called into his or her office" tends to trigger a reaction of pity or even malicious joy.

The significance of such rooms as a placeholder for the value within a hierarchy is firmly entrenched in the collective memory of a community, often even irrespective of the actual meaning of the current "cellular office occupier". In organizations that practise "non-territorial" workplace concepts, including work-places of superiors, the latter generally remain unoccupied when this person is not in the office. At most, it is "equals" who dare to occupy this space. It is therefore not surprising that any other person using this place temporarily is assumed to have higher ambitions.

The extent to which such viewpoints diverge is also shown by individual interpretations of architectural and organizational concepts. If a manager has his or her office designed in a very transparent manner to demonstrate openness and involvement, this may be perceived as exactly the opposite: the boss wants to see and monitor everything from his personal vantage point. Although the workplace of a primus inter pares in a team office is intended to be employee-oriented, it may be interpreted as permanent checking up. It is therefore extremely important to analyze management culture and its tradition within a company very carefully before implementing such design and organizational concepts.

No manner of interior design will however be able to remove demarcation – in spite of calls for collegial openness: the scope for lower ranking employees to question matters comes to an end at the latest when the competence and qualifications of the cellular office occupier are doubted, however diplomatically such questions are formulated.

As already described above, discussions in a manager's office are frequently pre-organized and an appointment is made. With a view to using a superior's scarce time most efficiently, an agenda is generally expected that relates to the nature of the appoint-ment and is usually drawn up by the person who needs to obtain consensus on a certain issue. The same applies to taking minutes of a meeting and confirming scheduled points on the agenda, whereby the lower ranking person generally is responsible for this task, with the exception of job-related discussions. As a competent style of leadership also involves preparing for such scheduled discussions, the "private" atmosphere in such talks may also ensure that after dealing with the agenda, there is often some time left for more informal conversations which are of paramount importance for the self-esteem of one's dialogue partner and better mutual understanding. A conversation that is motivating for both parties will therefore always consider the human and personal aspects of cooperation in addition to factual issues. It is generally not necessary to prepare a room especially for this purpose. To create a relaxed atmosphere it is however advisable to provide some refreshments.

Equipment and furniture:
between personal influence and corporate identity

The higher the ranking within an organization, the greater the freedom generally is to specify one's own interior – which does not necessarily result in high-quality design. Although many managers feel sure of their business decisions, they do not feel competent – quite rightly – with regard to questions of design. It is often wives or assistants who do not only choose ties but furnishings too. With increasing numbers of women in management positions, there is hope that this may result in a transfer of competence in questions of design. Management workplaces and offices should also be covered by a furnishing manual for binding corporate design to avoid conflicts between individual perception of taste and the collective corporate image, and new furniture having to be purchased with every change in management. Offering two to three alternatives and thus freedom of decision and choice is certainly much better than discussing issues of taste by giving people a free hand.

As the name of "management floor" says, offices of top management are generally located on the top floor. Hierarchical rank and spatial positioning are inextricably linked. Status is reflected by the size of the office, the location on the floor of the building – corner rooms with windows on two sides are particularly exposed – and measured by the size of the ante room with respective top secretarial staff. This is where appointment schedules are managed, documents are updated and business trips are booked, and providing sustenance is part of the service too. In middle management however, managers' offices are generally allocated to the departments which they lead. Central services often take care of back office management on this level.

The miniaturization and extended use of computer technology on management levels has led to a reduction in both storage space and desk space required in the office. The free spaces thus created may be used to generate a communication oriented ambience, even in smaller areas.

Conventional office structures with cellular offices – by nature rather narrow – where a table is extended for discussion purposes by adding a "tear-drop", do not do justice to the increased importance of communication, either psychologically or functionally. A workplace should either be designed so that a real face-to-face situation arises, but which always retains a formal character, or the room should provide space for a separate meeting table which, depending on the form of the table, supports a more formal or informal atmosphere. Last but not least, in spacious offices, high tables and corner seating may be used to provide additional, differentiated facilities for various phases of discussion.

As in other "communication environments", there should also be the possibility in an info-exchange room to have spontaneous access to data filed in a network and to present the same visually during a discussion. While the cellular office occupier has all documents at hand that might need to be consulted, this is obviously not the case with one's dialogue partner. How much more efficient could such discussions be if queries could be answered immediately by means of accessible data – and how much more confident might those involved feel if they did not have to worry about having important facts and figures at hand …

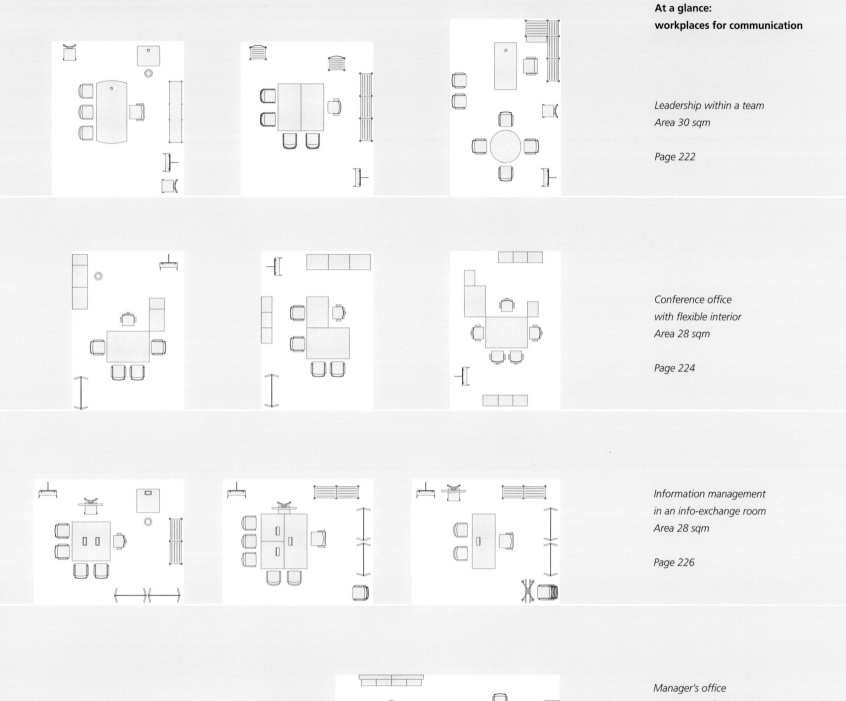

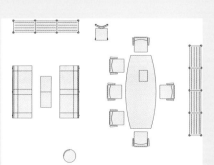

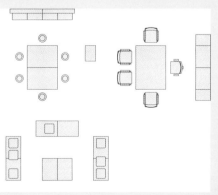

Team leadership – from formal to informal

▸ The miniaturization of computer technology and software programs that are increasingly easier to operate open up many possibilities for projecting the communicative focus of an office in a convincing way. If the office desk becomes a secondary working location too, this will serve to place the main focus of office planning on cooperation. The generation change in leading positions also encourages this development.

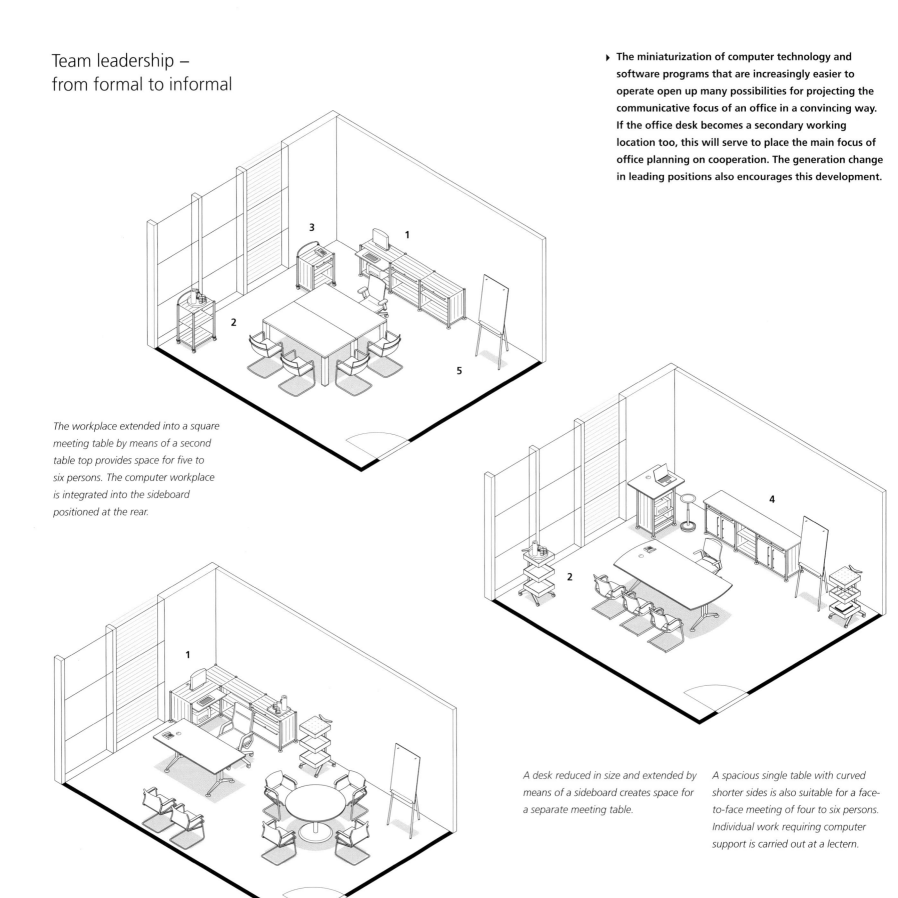

The workplace extended into a square meeting table by means of a second table top provides space for five to six persons. The computer workplace is integrated into the sideboard positioned at the rear.

A desk reduced in size and extended by means of a sideboard creates space for a separate meeting table.

A spacious single table with curved shorter sides is also suitable for a face-to-face meeting of four to six persons. Individual work requiring computer support is carried out at a lectern.

Scale 1:100 / dimensions in cm

(1 cm = 0.39 inches)

Area 30 sqm

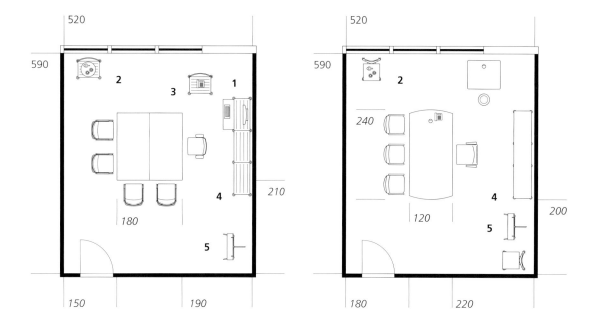

1   PC cabinet with pull-out keyboard
2   Catering server for providing snacks
    and refreshments for participants
3   Server for telephone and incidentals
4   Sideboard for files and documents
5   Flipchart for preparation
    or documentation of discussions

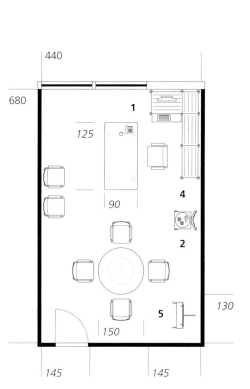

A modern leadership approach logically results in a meeting at the workplace becoming a workplace for meetings. Not only for space economy reasons is it useful to carry out a new arrangement and weighting of "workplaces" in offices in which meetings are the order of the day.

Work processes and forms are also changing with computers becoming an integral part of executives' offices. While concentrated and personal work used to take place at a traditional writing desk, using corresponding paper documents, "desktop" and documents are now available on the computer screen in digital form. If the computer that tends to disturb personal dialogue is placed on a side table, a lectern or a sideboard with an integrated pull-out keyboard, this will create space for a generous meeting table to promote human interplay among subordinates and colleagues.

At such a place that is defined for mutual dialogue, visitors do not feel like an intruder into the personal sphere of the host, so that potential obstacles to open dialogue may be reduced by selecting appropriate furniture. The office swivel chair and cantilever chairs should therefore be specified from one product family so as not to emphasize differences in status where they are after all only counterproductive.

Sitting opposite one another at a rectangular table serves to underline the formal character and position of a superior, whereas a square table reduces this effect considerably. At a round table, this impression is not created at all if one type of chairs and equal seating positions are provided.

Coherent concept –
a host of variations

▶ **One particular challenge for specifiers is the question as to how solutions may be developed using one coherent range that considers both individual preferences and different space geometries. Reduction to archetypal basic elements can maximize the degree of flexible utilization.**

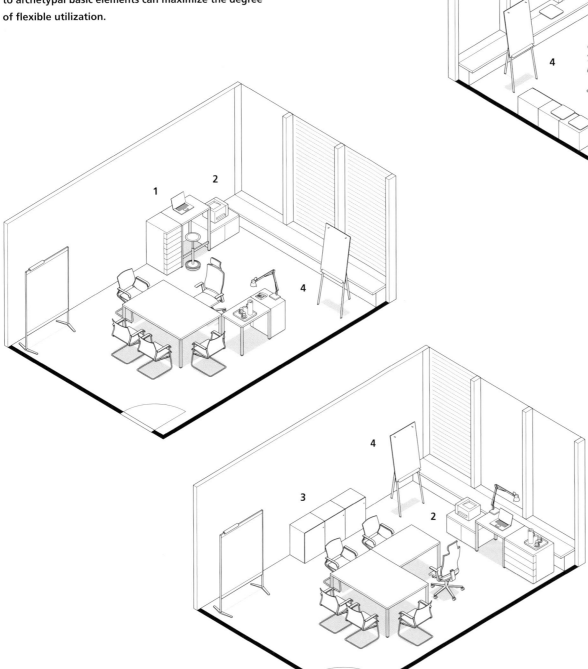

Inversion of standard ratios: the small table of the arrangement positioned orthogonally across the corner uses the adjoining storage unit to create a computer work surface; the main table, exactly twice the size, forms the meeting table, …

… or the computer workplace is provided separately in standing height, extended by a storage unit in the same height. The adjoining table, half the size, functions as a sideboard for conference snacks and refreshments.

In an L-shaped configuration, the large table combined with the next smaller format provides a conference solution for up to six persons. The smallest table at the rear is arranged as a computer workplace with corresponding side elements.

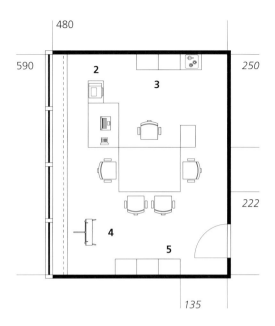

480

590   2   3   250

222

4

5   135

1   Lectern with side storage unit
2   Low storage unit with workplace printer
3   Storage unit in table height as sideboard
4   Flipchart for preparation or documentation of discussions
5   Low height storage unit with cushion on top

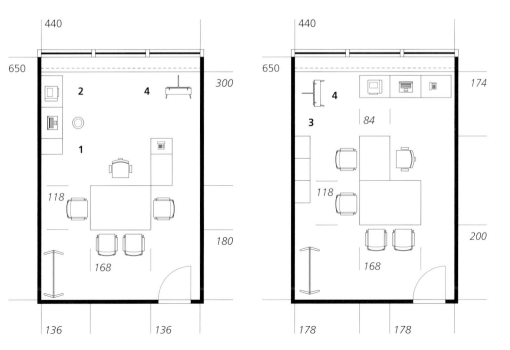

440

650   2   4   300

1

118

180

168

136   136

440

650   4   174

3   84

118

200

168

178   178

Executives, in particular, can benefit considerably from the potential offered by miniaturized and portable computer technology. On the one hand, they rarely work on the computer for longer, uninterrupted periods and therefore do not need a large-format display and corresponding, ergonomically defined minimum viewing distance in comparison to staff who work at displays with a strained posture for hours on end. On the other hand, executives frequently have their "virtual" workplace outside the office – for example, in conferences, at customer's premises or also at home.

A "computer workplace" may be kept extremely flexible as the only prerequisites are power supply and access to the network. In the specifiers' options, the interior comprises universal single tables and matching storage units for office materials, suspension files or binders. The arrangement of such modules may be flexible and reconfigurable depending on organizational and design requirements as the formats of the tables and storage units are based on the principle of DIN A paper sizes. That means the next largest format of the tables provides a double surface area, while the side lengths remain in constant proportions. All dimensions are therefore related due to their harmonious proportions, regardless of their specific combination. Tables and storage units may be grouped and combined entirely as required without creating a chaotic impression. In combination with the three functional heights – low, sitting and standing – such proportioned modules may be used to develop highly individual, functionally flexible solutions with a coherent design language, particularly for creating various types of "communication workplaces".

From a manager's office
to a meeting room

▸ **When the work of a manager involves primarily leadership tasks, the office becomes a meeting room. Depending on whether the number of participants remains unchanged or changes, various furnishing concepts are possible in line with those used for specifying conference and meeting interiors: ranging from static to flexible. In both environments, the integration of media technology is becoming increasingly important for shared visual presentation and editing of digital information.**

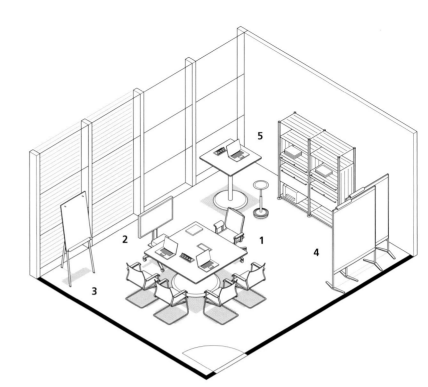

A table with a central pedestal ensures ample legroom on all sides – and with integrated connectivity it serves as both a meeting table and a workplace. An additional table in standing height as a separate individual workplace combines the advantages of affording a degree of privacy for documents with the possibility of changing posture.

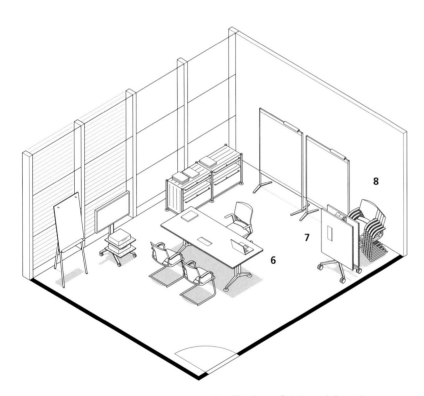

Combinations of static and dynamic: the spacious meeting place for a maximum of eight persons comprises a permanently positioned single table and a mobile, folding table that may be added as required. Both tables have integrated connectivity and may be networked by means of easy-to-handle plug-in cables.

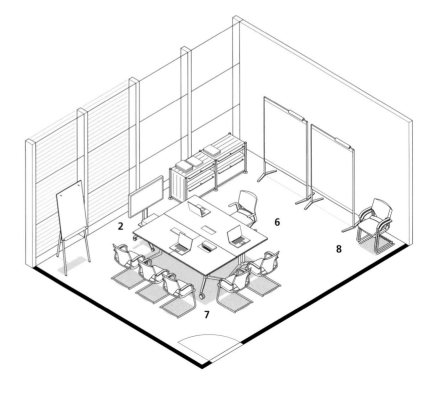

Scale 1: 100 / dimensions in cm

(1 cm = 0.39 inches)

Area 28 sqm

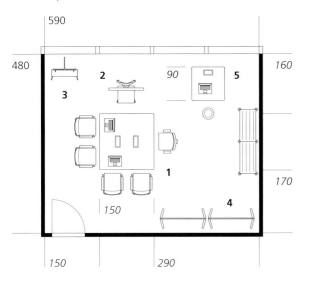

1 Table with central pedestal for meetings and as a workplace
2 Display server for use in meetings, operable via
   table-integrated connections
3 Flipchart for preparation of discussions
4 Pinboard for "analogue" visual presentation and
   documen-tation of discussions and as a "vertical" storage space
5 Table with central pedestal as a "lectern" with connectivity
6 Work and meeting table …
7 … extendable by means of a folding table for a group
   of up to eight persons. Both tables with network-capable
   computer connections
8 Stackable cantilever models as visitor chairs

Although the much praised idea of a paperless office is still not reality, the need for storage space for files has declined as an increasing number of documents are scanned or filed digitally in a network from the beginning. And paperless meetings where participants have their own laptops with them are becoming more and more the order of the day.

As already described, modern media technology is finding its way into conference rooms. A conference office should also be equipped in such a way as to allow every participant to "make public" the contents of his or her individual computer screen via a shared display to support cooperation with media technology.

Such a meeting environment requires a suitable table with integrated connectivity modules for several computers and a show-me function. The connectivity modules, connected in series, are in turn networked with a shared display. That allows participants to present the contents of their individual computer on a display for everyone to see well at the push of a button. As a large-format flat display, this may, for example, be moved up to the meeting table on a server structure.

Once participants' computers are connected in the shared network, data recorded or annotated during the meeting may be transferred to individual computers and later retrieved from the network. For meetings with varying number of participants, a static single table may be extended by a folding table if required – providing the latter matches in terms of design and may be "linked" technically with the single table.

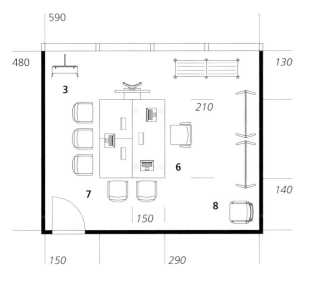

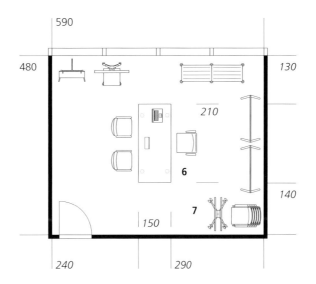

A manager's office
as a communication centre

▸ A change in leadership approach should be visible on all management levels in order to make it credible both internally and externally. Spacious executives' offices provide a host of potential – in terms of space – for promoting discussion processes in differentiated ways while retaining a feeling of prestige.

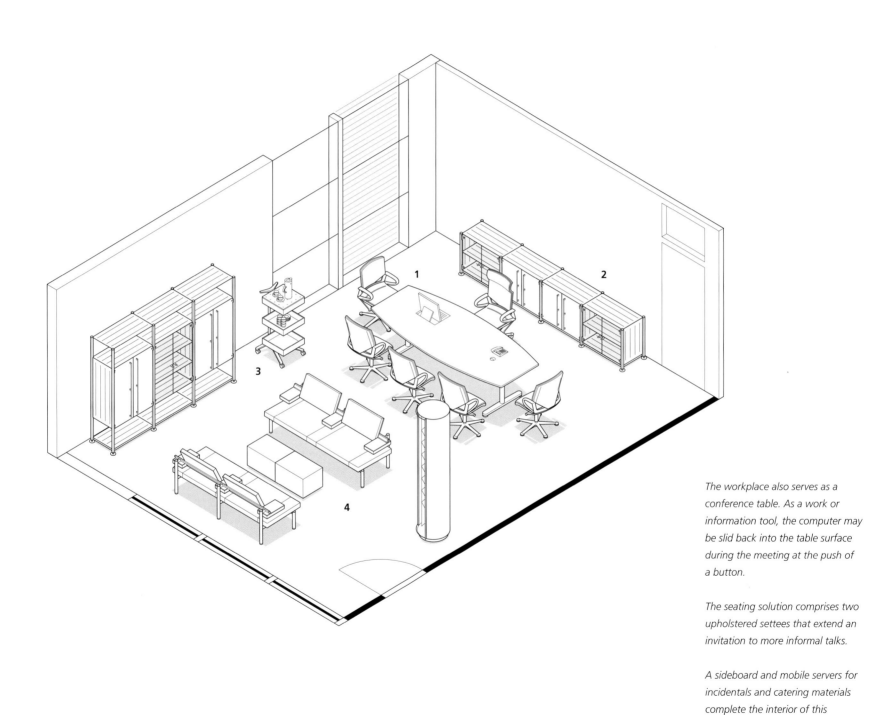

The workplace also serves as a conference table. As a work or information tool, the computer may be slid back into the table surface during the meeting at the push of a button.

The seating solution comprises two upholstered settees that extend an invitation to more informal talks.

A sideboard and mobile servers for incidentals and catering materials complete the interior of this communication office.

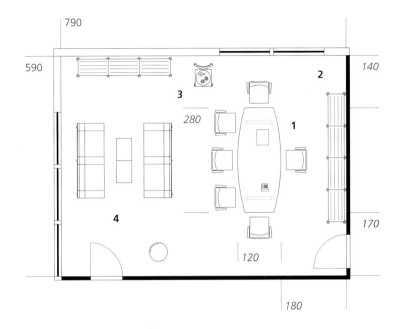

1 Table for meetings and as a workplace with
   integrated computer display
2 Sideboard with doors and glazed display elements
3 Server for catering materials
4 Seating units for informal talks

Literature on business developments describes two key factors that are responsible for changes in the function and activities of management: on the one hand, the acceleration and changes in information channels due to technical media, and on the other hand, a rapidly changing market that forces companies to depart from obsolete forms of organization in order to achieve shorter decision and development cycles.

Both factors have a direct influence on the extent and type of necessary communication within top management areas. As specialization in individual fields is rising and market developments are becoming increasing complex, a manager's competence can no longer be defined by his or her omniscience in the respective area of responsibility. What is much more important and decisive for a company is the manager's ability to coordinate, to promote the smooth interplay of many people and tasks, to motivate and to focus different departments on a common goal.

On the other hand, the traditional idea of how a manager's office is furnished still has some justification: particularly in times of dynamic change, space organization patterns are gaining in importance that demonstrate a clear leadership structure and continuity as they communicate predictability and orientation both internally and externally. Such concepts may also be implemented using corresponding, communication focused design. The generous dimensions of the classic "boss' desk" allow it to function as a spacious meeting table in the specifiers' option if table legs are positioned sufficiently far apart to provide ample legroom. The boat-shaped geometry of the table top looks less formal and promotes dialogue. The swivel chairs, with the exception of the shoulder supports on the host's chair, have the same degree of comfort and quality. Last but not least, a table with an integrated computer with a display that discretely recedes into the table surface together with the keyboard and mouse for promoting a barrier-free dialogue promoting atmosphere.

The communication environment is complemented by two settees positioned face-to-face, thus encouraging more informal talks. If the seat area of the settee can be pulled out, the result is an office couch for a power nap – highly recommendable in view of long working hours in top management.

Designing leadership culture

▶ **In addition to revamping traditional executives' office to make them more communication-oriented, there may be an opportunity for using new design solutions to set clear points of reference for a modern culture of leadership and communication. An additional high table for meetings has a dynamic quality, increases the degree of human interplay and may even shorten the length of the meeting quite substantially – and people can talk about the future more openly and creatively sitting on benches than on opulent soft furniture.**

Manager's office with various groups of furniture units comprising single tables and storage modules, coordinated in terms of form and proportions.

The result is a new interpretation of classic furnishing scenarios: by integrating a table element, the "sideboard" becomes a separate, personal computer workplace; two high tables with media connectivity become a dynamic place for meetings and presentations and last but not least, side tables with a cushion on top create an informal corner seating solution.

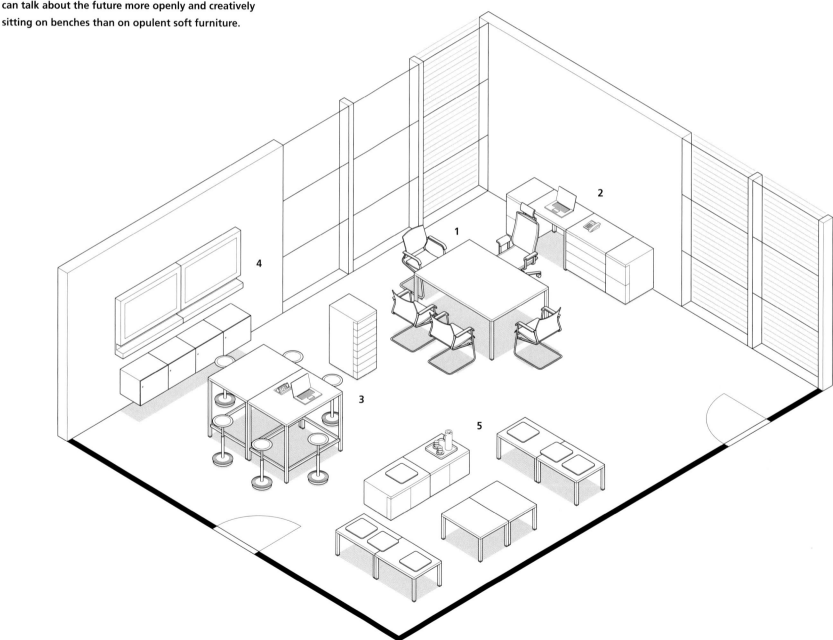

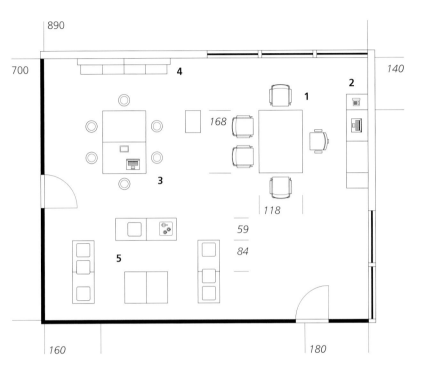

1 Table in sitting height for meetings and as a workplace
2 Sideboard with individual elements with a personal work
  surface for a notebook
3 High table as a conference area, with integrated connection
  point for laptops, for six to eight persons
4 Two large wall-mounted displays,
  operable via the connections of the specific high table
5 Small tables and storage units in low height with
  additional cushions, teamed with other furniture elements,
  providing perches for informal talks

The interior of a manager's office that should represent a modern leadership culture has to abandon awe-inspiring ostentation of power and status. Instead of using demarcation lines and intimidation, the goal is to communicate openness, transparency and team orientation. For it is this very image that is at the centre of in-company public attention that examines any discrepancies between the theory and reality of such new positioning. Unconventional ideas should therefore also reflect innovative furnishing concepts.

In the specifiers' option, the entire office is furnished with a coherently designed concept comprising single tables and storage units that add new highlights in terms of form and function. The three functional heights of "low", "sitting" and "standing" provide specifiers' options for supporting different dialogue scenarios: for a meeting at a large table, for demanding presentation requiring interaction, for a meeting standing up and for informal talks in a corner with the bench layout.

The PC workplace is directly allocated to the meeting table and is integrated into a variably configured "sideboard" comprising individual modules.

The dynamic meeting layout, which also allows the use of digital media for visual presentation purposes, comprises two high tables with integrated connection points for laptops and it is networked with two wall displays for interactive presentations.

An unconventional interpretation of a casual corner seating unit invites participants to more informal discussions: cushions have been placed on low tables and storage units to transform them into pausal perches.

Coherent design creates equal status for all scenarios; typical, traditional preferences have been intentionally avoided. These alternatives give the host the opportunity of differentiating the communication atmosphere to suit the function, occasion and the desired proximity to one's dialogue partners or of changing one's stance and posture during a discussion in order to get things going again should there be a deadlock.

Work, meeting and side tables for communicative workplaces

Single tables and table systems

Ideally, dialogue partners (whether colleagues or executives and subordinates) should sit at a table that creates a feeling of equal status. For this purpose, it is advisable to specify multi-directional tables or table systems that resemble conference tables more than writing desks. Modesty panels, even if recessed, tend to convey a counterproductive impression and recall consultation places in a customer service hall. The appearance of a private "neutral meeting area" is underlined if the table is not dominated by technical equipment – such as computers and displays – that set up barriers. If a display is required for individual work, as no separate space is available for this purpose, it should be possible to slide it into the table surface whenever the desk is required for meetings.

In general, all high-quality table solutions are suitable as combined work and meeting tables. Pedestal table ranges or similar constructions with a recessed table leg have the advantage of providing generous legroom all-round, also across the corner. It is important to specify tables with sufficiently large spans between table legs. Oval, boat-shaped or barrel-shaped table tops promote a communicative focus. Although round tables offer the most direct scope for interaction and totally equal sitting positions, they are less suited as a workplace.

System table solutions with extension elements, ideally in the same form and size, may be used as an alternative to large single tables for creating a meeting table configuration. The advantage of such a solution is that the same standardized tables can be incorporated as are used in conference rooms – and that tables remain variable, i.e. they can be scaled down or extended by adding a further table top. Legroom on the shorter sides is however more restricted, and places are clearly defined due to the modular principle and non-recessed table support frames.

In principle, it should be possible to equip tables for applications involving modern work and presentation media. The more effective and natural the integration of media connectivity into table tops, the less it interferes with interaction. It should ideally be possible for surplus cables, power adapters and battery chargers to "disappear" underneath the surface of the table (see also page 192).

Materials and surface finishes

The emphasized significance of a manager's office requires materials with first-class workmanship that meet the desired level of prestige and merge with the interior design theme. Fine particle board or MDF panel are suitable for table tops; for system tables, bending resistant materials are recommended, such as laminboard, so that additional bracing by means of underframes is not necessary, which in

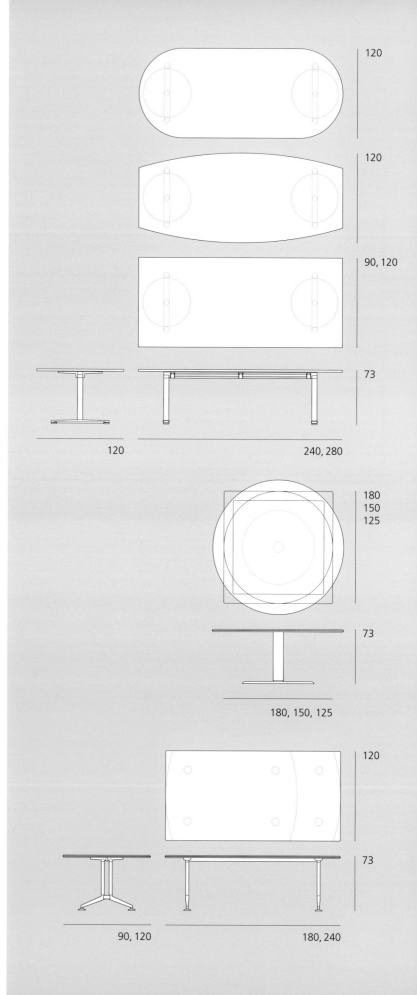

Specifiers' option:
table from the Palette conference
table range and Sito cantilever chair

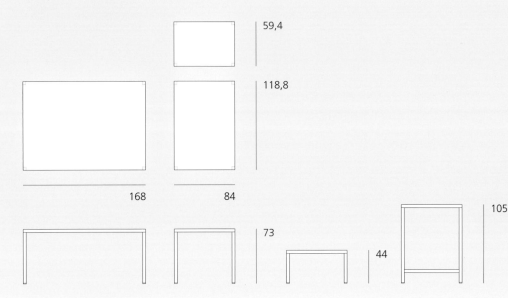

59,4

118,8

168

84

73

44

105

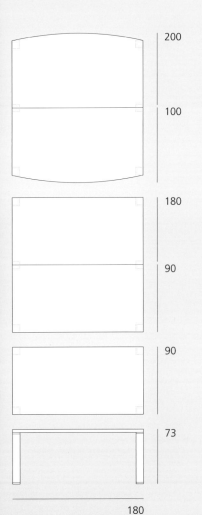

200

100

180

90

90

73

180

turn does not restrict legroom. Various types of table edging provide ample scope for customization. As surface finishes, various veneers and staining in a choice of colours to match the interior or also linoleum should be available. Solid wood lipping, optionally with integral impact-resilient profile, is recommended as edging to meet higher demands on wear and tear.

The same high standard of workmanship also applies to table frames which should be specified with adjustable glides to level out any floor irregularities. For frame structures subject to high wear and tear, it is advisable to use either steel or aluminium as these materials combine precise dimensional stability and a high-quality finish. Polished or chromium-plated surfaces on foot sections, anodized or matching colour-coated frame components on less exposed parts of the frame guarantee aesthetically pleasing and enduring quality.

Universally configurable single tables

are an unconventional alternative to traditional furnishing options for executives' offices. Such tables are archetypal solutions with four table legs positioned flush with the corners.

The balanced width-depth ratio of 1:√2 and table sizes with a ratio of 1:2 permit just one set of surface proportions to be used. In any configuration, the result is a harmonious overall appearance – while allowing full scope to change the layout spontaneously and adapt it professionally to current requirements. Maximum standardization and a high degree of individuality can thus be combined with perfection. If such a table range covers three functional heights, table functions may not only be structured horizontally, but also vertically: in low height for storage and sitting, in conference table height for working and conferencing, in standing height for discussions and presentations.

Materials and surface finishes
In line with archetypically reduced form, universal usability requires materials with a multi-directional character, allowing full scope for combination. Black-grey through-dyed tops in timber substitute, for example MDF, which are only treated with a durable, polyurethane-based lacquer, are a high quality alternative to coated table tops. Such table surfaces with natural inclusions and lively irregularities look like stone but have a pleasant, warm tactile quality. Frames should reflect the purism of the form and material of the table tops, for example, with square table legs in shot-blast stainless steel, combined with a concealed underframe.

Media technology in a conference office

A personal computer workplace

A computer workplace may be separated from the main workplace in executives' offices if a computer is only used occasionally – for email correspondence, internet and database research or project preparation. The large work and meeting table may then be completely devoted to analogue activities and face-to-face communication – with the possibility of connecting digital equipment there too if required. Dividing up work surfaces has three advantages: the meeting table is not dominated by technology but promotes human interaction. Secondly, the "private sphere" is quite consciously not part of the communication scenario, and thirdly, if a changeover between analogue and digital work requires a change in location, dividing up work surfaces allows movement and change in posture – which is highly advisable for heavily stressed managers with long working days.

Flat screens and computers, which are becoming smaller but with increasing performance, allow such a computer workplace to be designed compactly. Depending on specific space geometry, available space and preferences, it may be integrated to the rear of the meeting table, for example, into a sideboard from the same furniture range, or it may be a small table with casually positioned single storage units in matching material and dimensions.

The furniture system solution is more static but it can be extremely compact if the surface for keyboard and mouse are extended by means of a pull-out shelf. Additional devices such as a computer

unit and printer can be accommodated in the sideboard, provided that outlets for connecting cables and perforated rear panel elements are specified to prevent the accumulation of heat when sideboard doors are closed.

Configurations that form a PC workplace using additive elements are easy to change and can be combined with great versatility. Low height tables or storage units can accommodate technical equipment; the work table in sitting height or also in standing height is extended by means of the surfaces of the side storage units also available with specifiable drawers. Slot-on cable clips supply vertical cable management on table legs; flexible nets underneath table tops can be used to store power adaptors, socket strips and surplus cables.

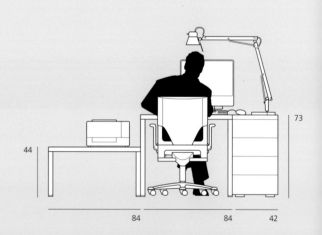

Materials and surface finishes

Whether a sideboard solution from one furniture system is specified or casually grouped single elements – the materials and surface finishes of the computer workplace should be coordinated with the "main table" to create a coherent appearance, for example, by adding a horizontal decor top with the same surface finish and edging, as well as similar vertical structures. For example, table frames comprising anodized aluminium profile and polished foot sections correspond with the double bullnose vertical profiles, also clear anodized, of the furniture system. If table frames are bright chromium-plated, this finish should also be reflected in the structure of the sideboard. Modular table systems are generally in steel or aluminium to create units that are durable and also have precise joints.

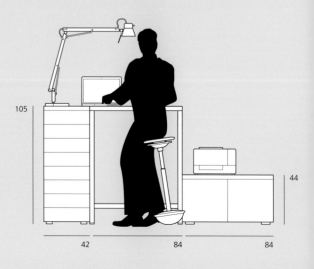

If additive, freely configurable solutions are selected, table tops and storage units should comprise identical materials and finishes. Surface finishes and workmanship should have a common appearance and quality standard from all sides so that they may be used as stand-alone units. Panel material such as MDF is very suitable and should be multidirectional as on universal single tables.

Media for visual presentation at the work/meeting table

In line with the development in conference rooms, digital media for visual presentation are increasingly required in addition to analogue media that are generally an integral part of a conference office, such as a pinboard or a flipchart. Notebooks brought along to a meeting or the screen of a PC are highly unsuitable due to their small size. A portable digital projector, placed on a table and projected onto a wall, requires facilities for darkening the room. Another disadvantage is the noise development and cable clutter

on the table surface. It is much more professional to use large-format screens which may be moved up to the table or permanently mounted on the wall. In both cases, the display should be operable via a notebook on the table – either a meeting table or a high table. For this purpose, the table should be equipped with corresponding connection points and networked with the large display. It is ideal to choose a solution that permits any participant to connect his or her notebook and present contents on the large display at the push of a button. If the large display has interactive functionality it

can be operated by a finger or a pen. In this way, presentations may be annotated and operated on the display itself, which in turn greatly improves direct interaction among participants

For visualization media, see also page 200–205.

Specifiers' option, on the left: Solis swivel chair and single table from the DinA table and storage unit range

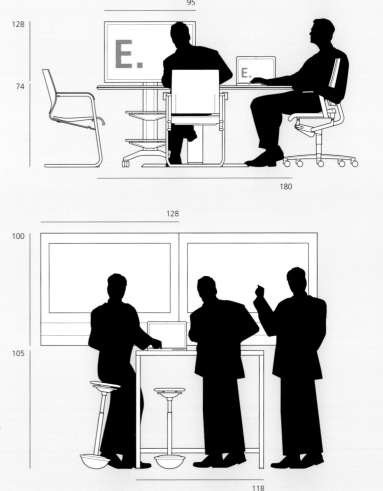

235

Sitting in a conference office

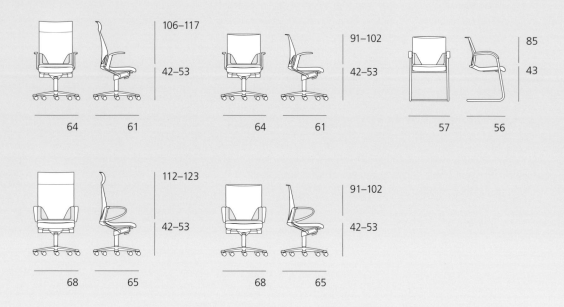

Task chairs and conference chairs
In a communication-focused managers' office, such chairs for tasks and conferences should, on the one hand, demonstrate the significance of the office occupier within the corporate structure; on the other hand they should reflect the corporate design of the whole company. It is therefore advisable not to use a separate range of executives' chairs, but models from product families with specific versions for combining both aspects.

Another point to be considered is ergonomic quality: bulky upholstery and elegant covers alone do not guarantee relaxed sitting – it is often the case that superficial, status-oriented thinking results in unhealthy sitting qualities. It is important to specify ergonomically shaped backrests that adjust efficiently and automatically to varying body sizes and dimensions and provide support for any posture. Automatic synchro-adjustment, affording a correctly coordinated seat/backrest ratio, thus promotes essential changes in sitting positions.

Specifiers' option:
Logon single table and cantilever
chair from the Sito range

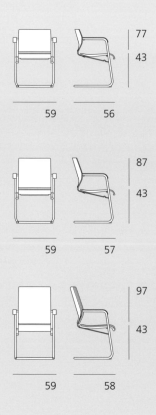

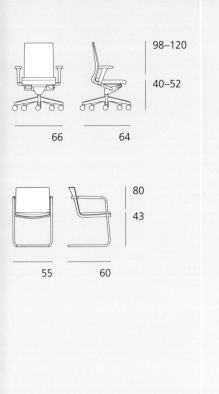

98–120

40–52

66 64

80

43

55 60

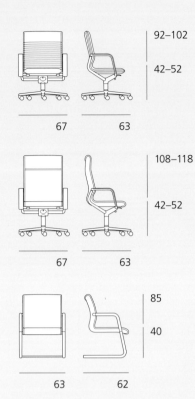

92–102

42–52

67 63

108–118

42–52

67 63

85

40

63 62

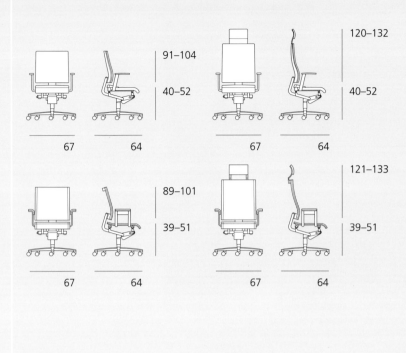

91–104

40–52

67 64

120–132

40–52

67 64

89–101

39–51

67 64

121–133

39–51

67 64

As visitor and conference chairs, models from the same range or coordinated ranges should be used: the usual length of meetings determines whether swivel chairs on castors, swivel chairs on glides or cantilever models are the right solution. The longer meetings take, the more important promotion of movement and ergonomic qualities are.

For further information on swivel chairs, see also page 62–65.

Materials and surface finishes
To achieve a coherent design language and multifunctionality of the office as a work and conference room, it is advisable to select the same covers for task chairs and conference chairs. The traditional choice is generally leather, a material that continues to convey a high level of prestige and one that will develop a characteristic patina if it is high quality. Alternatively, there are also high-quality covers in textiles or micro-fibres now available that often provide a better sitting experience and look just as prestigious.

Frames should be teamed with the materials and surface finishes of the table frames. Polished aluminium or matt chromium plating harmonize well with anodized, brushed or coated surfaces with a silver matt finish; bright chromium plating also works well with black coated structures.

Zones for teamwork

▸ New, process-oriented forms of work such as group work and project work are invariably replacing strict departmental division of office staff for the sake of accelerating workflows. Modern office building concepts therefore focus on the versatility of space layout and partitioning to meet the need to work individually, in small or larger groups. Rooms ideally with large empty spaces are best suited to this purpose so that partitioning is not determined by the constructional layout elements of a building, but can be carried out freely and flexibly.

We need more freedom as in a state of turbulence we can no longer plan and regulate everything from the top. The greater the turbulence, the more strategy and responsibility for goals and objectives have to be delegated to lower levels. This should take place where signals indicating turbulence can be seen soonest.

Günter A. Luedecke

From conferencing to group work

The rapid changes taking place in the working environment make new demands on the entire organization of a company. The sooner information is selected and evaluated by individual departments and the sooner all those involved in the process can network their knowledge, the faster and more efficiently developments and improvement processes can take place. This may not mean that costly dead ends can be completely avoided, but it can have the lasting effect of reducing time wasted in this way. The more conscious all employees are of situations depending on and resulting from their individual behaviour, the sooner shortcomings can be recognized and frictional losses avoided – and the faster individuals can really assume their responsibility too.

This does, however, also mean that decision-making and areas of competence will be shifted more and more to lower levels within the company and, in terms of time, can be brought forward. Organizational structures therefore also change virtually automatically in line with communication structures. New process-oriented forms of work, such as group and project work, inevitably replace traditional, rigid departmental division of work in order to optimize the whole workflow process. Such intensive networking does, however, require much more info-exchange than before. Fine-tuning, consulting colleagues, joint organization, as well as definition, sub-division and revision of goals and objectives are key parts of the daily workflow and must be reflected in interior planning.

In recent decades, experiments have been carried out with various office forms. Open-plan offices have emerged which, in turn, have been replaced by cellular office structures and offices with workplaces for two persons. However, conventional cellular office structures are the worst possible environment for dynamic, cross-functionally networked projects. How can spontaneous consensus be achieved if corresponding space for a meeting first has to be organized via email or a telephone and if the scheduled date does not only depend on those concerned being reached but also on the availability of suitable meeting facilities? Long distances between offices and a shortage of meeting rooms hamper personal contact that is so important for team processes as this requires more commitment.

Today, "combined forms of office environments" are now regarded as established mixed forms between traditional cellular offices and communicative networking that link the needs for privacy and concentration with the aspects of community and communication. Depending on the structural grid of the building, extremely compact individual offices and also multiple offices can be grouped around an inner communal area from which they are screened off acoustically by means of partially glazed, room-high walls. Transparent glazing combines offices with the communal area and allows eye contact between offices for the purpose of facilitating interaction. The communal zone itself provides areas for breaks and meetings, as well as service functions such as a copying machine, a tea kitchen, fax machine, etc. This serves to promote informal communication in particular.

With the right choice of furniture and equipment, work can also be partly carried out in small groups. Besides, temporary workplaces can be kept on standby for hot desking, for example, for members of the field force who do not have a permanent workplace in the building and, in between fine-tuning discussions, would like to deal with their email correspondence or compare their mobile stock of data with the intranet.

The communal zone of a combi-office is not a suitable option for medium-term project work or for long-term group work as propagated in "new forms of work". Everyone has a fixed workplace in such an office and the layout is often based on conventional departmental thinking. In practice, glazed areas are often covered in posters and calendars or blocked by coat-stands. The feeling that is conveyed is that such a space structure serves to strengthen the private office sphere rather than openness for group interaction. But project work requires the individual to merge with the work of the team. The structure of work groups may be very different in character and generally stable for a certain period of time. Any process optimization and every new project changes the size and constellation of the team and thus the layout of workplaces.

Modern office building concepts are therefore inspired by the idea of a flexible office: the focus is on the locational flexibility of workplaces within an office building, the versatility of space layout and partitioning, and organizational and technical flexibility. Such an approach allows work to be carried in small groups or larger teams as required. Rooms with large empty spaces are best suited to this purpose so that partitioning is not determined by the constructional layout elements of a building, but can be carried out freely and flexibly. Leaving status symbols or architectural trends aside, the overriding planning principle should be to promote the interplay of work groups.

It is no coincidence that teamwork is rooted in creative professions. Eighty per cent of our ideas grow out of personal communication. Architects, designers, advertising and PR agencies were the first to make use of this simple realization: two people are always more creative than one, three know more than two, four more than three, and so on. There has not been any conclusive research on the critical size of work groups. It can be assumed that similar limits in terms of numbers apply as to conferences that use moderation techniques: the ideal size of a group is between six and twelve.

Organizational forms and methods:
partly autonomous and process-oriented

In the meantime, group organization is also being implemented in "quite normal" companies to an ever increasing degree – not only in production areas but also in administration. In the traditional staff and line organization, operative processes pass through individual departments with many handover points and potential loss of information.

If procedures deviate from the norm, additional detours are required via several management levels to obtain necessary decisions and amended instructions. This entails long flow times and increases costs. As the main focus today has to be on customer orientation, and markets are subject to heavy fluctuations, the number of such deviations has risen so drastically that competitiveness is at risk if there is strict adherence to traditional, statically focused organizational structures.

In group work however, employees organize themselves. They plan staff capacity, lay down working hours, assign tasks and coordinate matters. For this purpose, each group has a spokesperson as a contact person to the group coordinator. He or she is responsible for ensuring the smooth interplay of various groups, and for coordinating goals and objectives – with both the group coordinator and management.

The decisive advantage is that those employees who are involved in the real work and value-added process can directly contribute and implement their ideas and skills. This results in highly practice-oriented procedures. This work model is particularly suited to regularly-recurring, operative processes to optimize the workflow, increase productivity and to achieve better customer orientation by means of greater flexibility.

Project work is an extremely efficient organizational form for all corporate areas which deal with the development of innovative ideas, for example, in marketing, strategic corporate development and product development.

In contrast to group work, where fixed teams constantly work together, a project work-group is newly formed for a specific task which is clearly defined in terms of contents and time. On completion of the task in hand, the team is dissolved. Projects are no longer processed by one department after another, but representatives of all those departments involved in the process chain work together synchronously in the project group as required.

Cross-functional teamwork has other advantages for a company apart from the obvious time-saving and cost-saving aspect and the motivating sense of achievement for employees: experiencing the challenges faced by co-workers serves to further develop skills, thus giving people a keener appetite for networking – furthermore a change in team members for every new project promotes social skills and prevents rigid group structures.

Even operative processes are more and more frequently being regarded as projects today. Processing a large order for example requires as much creativity, imagination, talent for improvization and ongoing fine-tuning as a development project.

Due to growing customer orientation and the dynamics of competitive conditions, it may be assumed that project work and corresponding interior concepts will have an even greater influence on future office environments than they do today. If the consumer also functions as a producer – the concept of a "prosumer" increasingly figures in marketing theories – as he or she has to define products and services individually by means of requirements and specific wishes, a company must therefore be in position to combine all necessary special areas of competence in a flexible, project-oriented organization. The miniaturization of IT and roaming possibilities, with access to shared and personal knowledge databases, liberates individuals from workplaces with a fixed location. Other groundbreaking organizational forms may also be easily integrated into these concepts, such as desk sharing, non-territorial office work or temporarily used workplaces. Last but not least, such teamwork environments with integration of large-format, interactive displays ensure efficient, synchronous cooperation of locationally distributed project work groups too.

Reshape the environment,
don't try to reshape men.
Buckminster Fuller

Furniture and equipment:
for mobile or variable combination

In a combi-office, individual offices are configured statically by means of wall-connected storage units and compact desks, while a combi-zone should be furnished with variable and mobile table ranges for a high degree of flexibility so that discussion layouts may be organized, spontaneously extended or downsized again as required. Only in such a way can a layout adapt to varying forms of work, such as discussion, a presentation or individual work. Due to specific cable installations, free spaces for variable group communication are defined by service units that are generally permanently positioned, for example, for a tea kitchen.

Communication zones in group and project offices are directly integrated into the workspace area. In a group office, employees from various departments cooperate on a particular work process. For this purpose, individual areas of work within a room are reflected in clear sub-groups, for example, in "work bubbles". Although the number of employees in a group and the special layout of these working areas are stable in the medium term, it is advisable to use tables and storage units allowing flexible combination as the dynamics of general conditions require repeated fine-tuning and constant adaptation. The concept of "just-in-time manufacturing", that is able to adjust to fluctuating order books with necessary capacities and skills, finds its counterpart in a "JIT Office" which can react to necessary changes with flexibility – without any complicated reconfiguration measures.

In contrast, a project office requires a very high degree of flexibility. Team members only work together temporarily, and they come from quite different fields of work. The team is extended in some work phases whilst others are carried out with the core team. Spontaneous, self-organized changes in the constellation and size of a project group are as much the order of the day as changes in forms of work: individual project stages are worked on by specialists, and interim results and further procedures are presented and agreed upon within the team. This dynamic changeover is best reflected by using mobile, multifunctional tables which are also complemented by mobile displays for visual presentations.

As dynamic conference forms make a conference room a conference workshop, communication-focused and process-oriented group or project work transforms a conventional office with its fixed, hierarchically oriented workplace layout into an office workshop allowing variable and versatile applications.

Communication zones
in a combi-office

▶ A combi-office is regarded as a compromise solution designating a change from a traditional departmental structure in the direction of modern, flexible forms of office work. While individual cellular offices and offices for two to a maximum of four employees have a static layout and continue to underline the privacy of a personal workplace, a communal zone provides space for informal communication and temporary, dynamic forms of group work. Mobile, multifunctional table ranges and seating allowing variable handling, support a self-organized changeover of work forms and make it easier to "learn" new forms of cooperation. The same applies to the interior of a separate conference room which should primarily support dynamic teamwork.

The question as to how quickly a company should and can develop from a statically oriented departmental and line organization to dynamic and project-oriented forms of work depends to a large extent on the business segments of the company and its culture – which has frequently evolved over decades. In spite of the general trend towards speed, adaptability and customer orientation there are still quite a few industries in which traditional preservation of the status quo, scarcity of goods and "deceleration" account for the decisive competitive edge. Take, for example, goods from the luxury industry, such as exclusive single malt whiskies or cognacs whose value is determined by conservative processing methods and the duration of storage. The same applies to the multi-facetted nature of processes: increasing specialization and standardization require nothing less than principles based on the division of work, while the individualization of customer wishes makes cooperative project orientation the focal point of organization. If one is aware of the degree to which tradition, experience, knowledge and habit also influence human behaviour, it will become completely clear that there are no patent solutions for reflecting future-proof office structures in terms of organization and space. On the contrary, it is necessary to analyze industry-specific, economic conditions in a holistic perspective and to describe corporate goals in order to draw up and pass specifically useful measures using a variance analysis based on business processes. Yet, in spite of so much differentiation there are still some common denominators that

should be considered: the networking and expansion of employees' knowledge, strengthening of community-building processes and competence by means of participation in the development and contents of business processes, as well as the promotion of mental agility and creativity are key factors for maintaining and increasing competitive performance. This, in turn, requires communication and cooperation to be promoted by spatial structures.

Combi-offices are therefore an efficient solution if the focus continues to be on department-oriented, concentrated individual work and human interplay is limited to informal community-building and sporadic fine-tuning or group work. Combi-offices should also be preferred if the step from a culture shaped by cellular offices and division of work to flexible forms of organization and work seems too large, and therefore a more "evolutionary" than "revolutionary" change is advisable so as not to cause any serious internal frictional losses and resistance during the changeover. As "offices" within the combi-system are formed by reversible system walls, subsequent modifications in spatial structure are possible, even extending to complete removal of individual room structures, which does, however, involve considerable time and effort.

Contrary to commonly held prejudices, integrating communal zones does not necessarily require more space compared to the classic standard layout of an office building as a dual structure with two opposite offices connected via a central corridor.

Compact space utilization system with wall-connected storage units and reduction in storage space due to digitalization of documents lead to smaller, personal office space, and separate spaces for meetings and breaks are no longer needed as they can be included in the open area of the combi-zone.

Fully glazed wall and door elements facing the communal zone support transparency and spontaneous interaction. The same applies to partial glazing between offices that also allows people to look in and out of adjacent offices. A short glance is enough to see whether a phone call can be passed on to colleagues or whether they are available for a personal face-to-face conversation. As usual, such concepts that mark a change compared to the previous space layout and usual behavioural patterns can only "function" if individuals are aware of the advantages – and if clear rules of the game ensure that this new openness is not thwarted by unreflected leanings towards the old sense of space: little is gained if objects are placed in front of glass elements or the latter lose their transparency as posters or calendars have been stuck onto them …

The concept and furnishing of a communal zone in particular provide scope for focused promotion of both social interaction and new forms of work. It is however not a satisfactory solution simply to move technical equipment such as a copier, a printer or a fax machine to a combi-zone with a view to linking necessary work processes with personal interface. If such service functions are required less and less as rapid technological change in computer technology and ongoing digitalization are transforming work procedures, walking to a fax or copier is simply superfluous. In the long run it is more advantageous to support needs that will not change in the foreseeable future: a small kitchen for warm and cold refreshments and snacks for breaks is just as much one of those basic needs as "public" information channels, for example, a small library or a bulletin board. If inviting seats and tables are planned for such areas, both mental and physical nourishment are more likely to take place on the spot, thus creating opportunities for human interplay and info-exchange.

If the open combi-zone is consciously designed as a "semi-public conference environment" too, informal communication will combine with focused promotion of communal development processes. Who can resist the engaging effect of such a community that is reflected in spatial terms for everyone to see? If mobile, universally usable and flexibly combinable single tables are used instead of a static table configuration, this will not only facilitate functional adjustment to groups of varying size and requirements in terms of methods: easy variability allows versatile applications and increases space utilization efficiency; it does not require the room to be prepared by maintenance crews, it activates joint participation and thus strengthens the degree of identification the process, it allows spontaneity in group dynamics and last but not least, "proves" subliminally that changes within a company are not only permitted by means of personal participation, but are even desired. High-quality, freely positionable displays for interactive visual presentation, such as pinboards or flipcharts, are a helpful addition to conference work.

Besides an open conference area, an additional, separate room is required for scheduled and confidential meetings, conferences or workshops. On the one hand, two groups may conference in parallel; on the other hand, this is a room for longer conferences which would tend to impair concentration on the part of staff in the "offices" if the open space were used for this purpose. A dynamic furnishing concept should be used here too for the sake of multifunctional utility and as a welcome training effect for participation-oriented forms of cooperation and communication. If a coherently designed range is specified for both areas, which includes all necessary conference tools, advantages in terms of facility management may be combined with maximum variability. In addition to mobile tables, small mobile desks, pinboards and flipcharts already mentioned, as well as mobile servers for refreshments, writing utensils and incidentals should be kept on standby. To allow unused furniture units to be kept on standby in a compact store room, tables and desks should have pivotable or foldable tops and chairs should be stackable for compact storage.

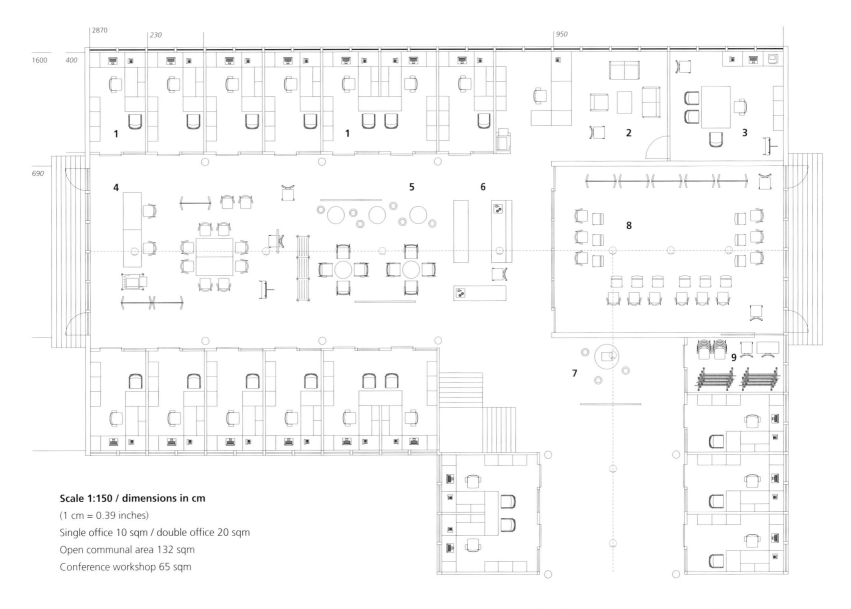

Scale 1:150 / dimensions in cm

(1 cm = 0.39 inches)

Single office 10 sqm / double office 20 sqm

Open communal area 132 sqm

Conference workshop 65 sqm

In principle, the same table and chair models can also be used for furnishing a zone for breaks and relaxation, providing they meet requirements in terms of durability, easy care, seated comfort and easy handling. Standardization benefits must however be seen in the perspective that no differentiation of core functions is possible by means of design. Small circular tables and a number of sitting and standing places promote the desired degree of informal communication in this case much more efficiently than rectangular conference and seminar tables. Chairs should also convey a feeling of casual lightness and relaxation and not the impression of aesthetically designed, yet work-oriented tool quality. And last but not least, communal areas in particular should provide both orientation and variety by means of correspondingly differentiated design.

1 Offices for one person and two persons which may be closed off to the communal area using sliding glass elements

2 Secretary's office with reception area

3 Meeting office for management or departmental heads

4 Area for group work with mobile, single tables, pinboards for visual presentation and vertical display, flipchart for preparation of discussions, as well as a mobile screen for media support in the group

5 Area for breaks and informal communication at bistro tables and high tables

6 Central, open small kitchen for the communal zone, the reception area, as well as the conference workshop

7 Info-point with high tables with touch-sensitive display, intranet and internet access

8 Conference workshop with dynamic interior

9 Store room for mobile conference tools

Communication zones
in a combi-office

Single office 10 sqm / double office 20 sqm
Open communal area 132 sqm
Conference workshop 65 sqm

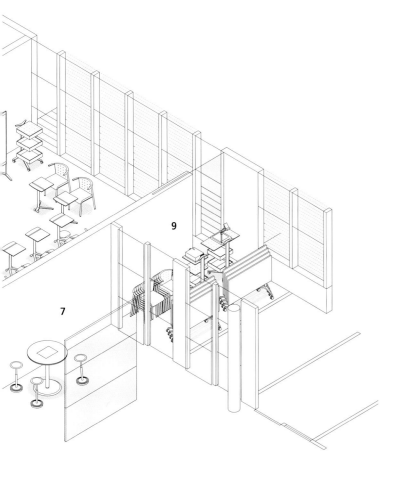

1 Offices for one person and two persons which may be
   closed off to the communal area using sliding glass elements
2 Secretary's office with reception area
3 Meeting office for management or departmental heads
4 Area for group work with mobile, single tables,
   pinboards for visual presentation and vertical display,
   flipchart for preparation of discussions, as well as
   a mobile screen for media support in the group
5 Area for breaks and informal communication
   at bistro tables and high tables
6 Central, open small kitchen for the communal zone,
   the reception area, as well as the conference workshop
7 Info-point with high tables with touch-sensitive display,
   intranet and internet access
8 Conference workshop with dynamic interior
9 Store room for mobile conference tools

The concept of the combi-office in the specifiers' option contains further aspects that provide ideas and perspectives for future-oriented solutions which are hardly ever considered today: tables in an open, variably furnished conference zone may also be used for temporary individual work without special hot desking places being kept on standby. The miniaturization of computer technology has long since brought about the following situation: employees who frequently work out of the office, for example, in the field force or as consultants at customers' always have their "workplace" with them. This group does not need a workplace of its own at the company but should, however, have the possibility of dealing with email correspondence in the office between appointments and fine-tuning discussions, of preparing material for discussions, of informing themselves about the status of a project or compiling presentations. All that is needed for such tasks is a table surface, a chair, power supply and access to a digital network.

To allow digital documents to be presented or information to be accessed spontaneously from the internet or from the in-company network during a dialogue process in the conference zone too, it is advisable to specify a mobile, large-format and ideally inter-actively operable screen. Such a screen can be easily allocated to a specific conference setting if necessary connection points are available.

Screened off in front of the store room, a high table with a horizontally integrated touch–sensitive display and mobile leaning aids are positioned as a place for confidential, informal communi-cation. Such a layout allows intensive discussion and shared processing of digital data in a small group.

The integration of such intuitively operable and communication-oriented Roomware® elements with corresponding access to a digital information room promotes info-exchange, increases efficiency and facilitates the acceptance of this increasingly important virtual dimension of a company. A combi-zone should therefore as a matter of course include intelligently configured floor ports for connecting power, network and multi-media cables.

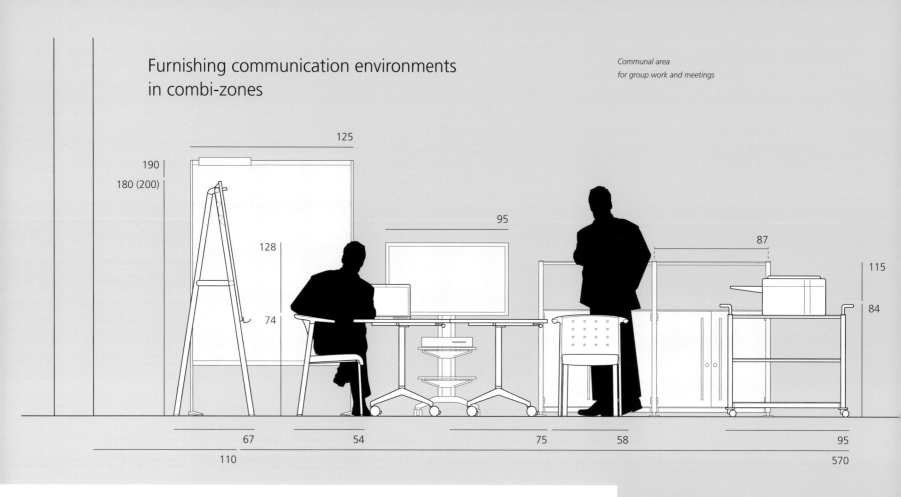

Furnishing communication environments in combi-zones

Diagram dimensions: 190, 180 (200), 125, 128, 95, 87, 74, 115, 84, 67, 54, 75, 58, 95, 110, 570

Multifunctional, flexibly configurable task and conference tables

The task and conference tables are designed as mobile units with lockable swivel castors for the purpose of simple, self-organized handling. They should have a cable channel with an integrated socket strip to allow electronic devices such as a laptop, a PDA or a mobile telephone to be used (and recharged) for both individual work and also for conference applications. If the table is to be moved to a new location, the unplugged input cable is parked within the channel in the table frame. A table depth of 75 cm is sufficient for work and meeting applications; the width should be 150 cm to allow plenty of scope for combination.

If the table top articulates pivotally around a central beam, such a table may be easily moved through doorways and round corners, and compacted neatly in the store room.

Materials and surface finishes
For mobile use, it is advisable to select frame combinations of steel and aluminium that combine mechanical precision and high stability with high-quality workmanship and appearance. Bright chromium-plated or polished finishes for foot sections show hardly any signs of use even if subjected to high wear and tear. When selecting table surfaces, emphasis should be placed on durability for utilization in a semi-public environment. Laminates or sealed surfaces supply a suitable surface finish for such needs.

Seating, storage space and mobile shelf/storage units

For the purpose of conveying a coherent and professional overall impression, it is useful if the design of stackable chairs, shelf units and mobile storage units corresponds with tables. Frames and structures in aluminium profile, coordinated with table frames, and surface finishes that are both high-quality and hardwearing combine functional quality with aesthetic excellence.

See also planning guide for a conference workshop, page 136–141.

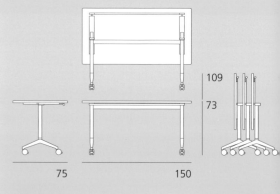

Dimensions: 109, 73, 75, 150

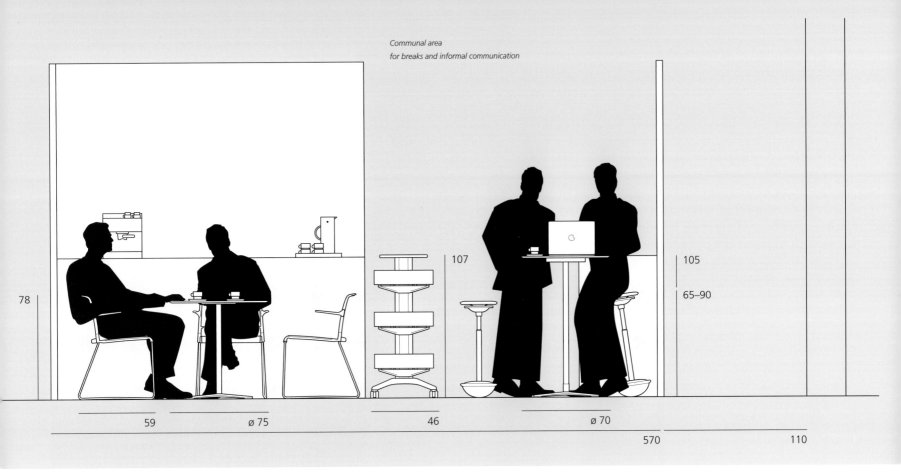

Communal area
for breaks and informal communication

78   59   ø 75   107   46   105   65–90   570   110

Visualization displays

Irrespective of whether they are analogue or digital, visualization displays should be easy to allocate to workplaces and allow intuitive operation.

Flipcharts with a foldable frame and a removable board that allows variable height-positioning, easily compactable pinboards with flat, curved foot sections and frames of mobile screens should preferably be in the same coherent design and quality to avoid the impression of an arbitrary conglomerate of units.

For further details on media support, see page 200–205.

Cafeteria chairs and tables

They are designed in a way so as to create a casual, informal appearance. It is ideal to specify easy-care, compactly stackable skid-base chairs, which have flexible membrane seat and back frames in plastic, combine a high degree of seated comfort with optical transparency and easy handling. The constructional principle of using round steel rod, which supports the front seat frame and integrates with the back rest frame at the rear to form a stable structure, makes such chairs very light. The form and materials should allow casual posture and changes in sitting positions that are typically required in informal meetings. To match the chairs, tables in sitting and standing height (if necessary in a low version too), with circular or square tops should be specified. Through-dyed table top materials such as HPL are extremely hardwearing and can also be manufactured with

slender dimensions and correspondingly graceful aesthetics, which can be further enhanced by including chamfered edging. Circular tops with a diameter of 60 or 75 cm support a communicative setting and allow a variable numbers of seats, while square tables can be easily grouped to a form a larger, communal table surface.

Tables with integrated, interactive displays

They are not only suitable for showrooms or conference rooms with sophisticated technical equipment, but also for informal meeting environments. After all, it is much easier to discuss a presentation in a casual atmosphere and to process it accordingly than at a workplace. Information may be accessed from the network and discussed, or computer games such as digital chess can be played jointly on the screen. What is decisive for pro-

moting communication is horizontal integration of a display and intuitive operation which any dialogue partner can learn by seeing and doing.

For further details on integrating media into tables, see page 195.

Materials and surface finishes
The table frame and top should not look like a foreign body in a communication setting, but merge with the overall ambience in terms of form, material and surface finish. With table tops coordinated with the finish of the other tables, pedestal tables with a black, textured base plate and a column in chromium-plated or anodized aluminium team perfectly with other tools in the conference workshop.

Group office and project office with dynamically configurable workplaces

▸ **A project office incorporates various functional zones for work, informal communication and different methods of interface within a team. Furnishing elements that structure the room and are either static or freely position-able are used for quick and simple reconfiguration of workplaces to support both scheduled work phases and spontaneous improvization, the latter being an integral part of project work.**

1 Medium-height shelf units as the focal point of the layout, providing connection points for network and power supply, and storage space for workplace printers
2 Mobile table with integrated techni-stations
3 Mobile, open shelf units as personal storage space
4 Area for informal communication – high table and library
5 Shelf unit with open and closed compartments as a permanently installed partition
6 Info-exchange table – with mobile tables, materials servers, flipchart, pinboards, server for fax and copier
7 Mobile tables with pivotable top and stackable chairs as spares for temporary workplaces

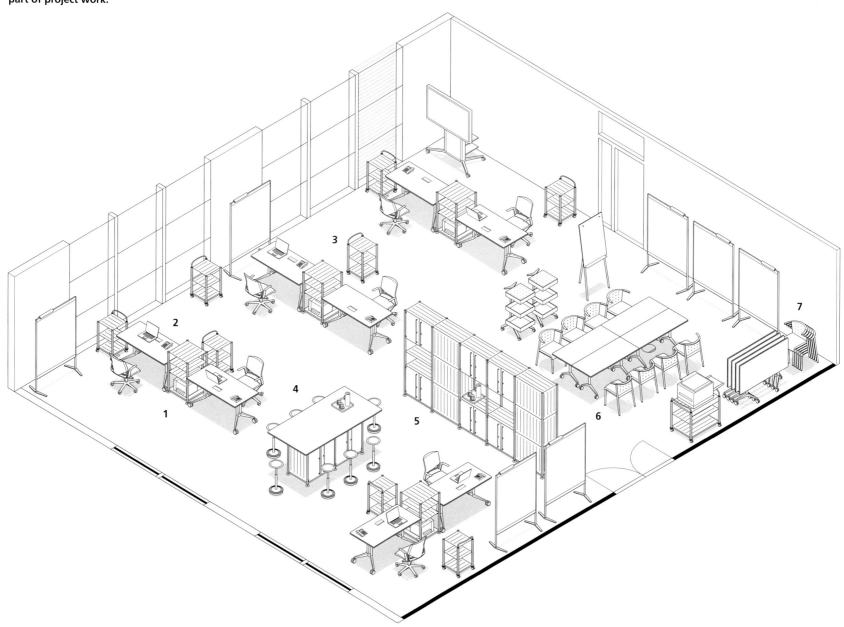

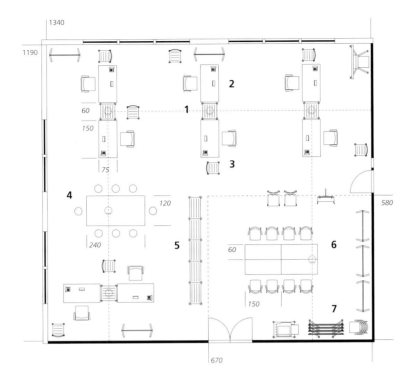

Self-organized adjustment of furniture and equipment to varying forms of individual and group work provide essential support for process orientation of the project group. If group members configure the work environment they need at a particular time themselves this will serve to bond teams, increase identification with the project task and reduce facility management costs as no additional maintenance crews are needed for reconfiguration. However, it is of paramount importance to specify variable electrical installations and data networking facilities for various furnishing scenarios during the room planning stage – and that means integrated into the floor, as organizational and space flexibility simply becomes superfluous if the furnishing layout and thus the form of work are, in the final analysis, determined by perimeter channels …

The basic concept for specifying a project office includes static furnishing elements which divide the room into the three core function zones of working, informal communication and teamwork using different methods as well as mobile tables, chairs and visualization displays which are freely configurable and may be allocated as required. Static elements serve functions which should ideally be permanently installed for reasons of weight or due to the position of power and data connections; however, they are also important orientation and structuring elements.

The shelf structure thus divides the room into an informal communication area and a zone for method-based teamwork. The shelf compartments serve as storage space for tableware, snacks and refreshments but also for any technical literature required. If a modular multi-directional furniture system is used, the side of access may be allocated to one area or the other, or also shared, depending on the contents of the compartments, for example, for open compartments as a pass-through or with doors on both sides. The "place" for informal communication is clearly defined as a meeting point by means of a high table which, in the specifiers' option, comprises the same system structure and also serves as storage space.

In the zone for workplaces, there are medium-height, square shelf units, positioned according to the grid of the floor ports, with a lower shelf that is removable to provide easy access to the floor port. Cable outlets or permanently installed power and data network connections ensure that up to four mobile workplaces may dock onto each of these "towers" in variable configurations. Compartments that open multi-directionally accommodate not only technical equipment but also any analogue documents which must be immediately available at the workplace.

The task tables are equipped with lockable castors to allow easy repositioning. The number of tables is determined by the number of participants, in this case eight, who have their fixed workplaces in the project office. To avoid having cables channelled on the table surface and to store surplus cables, network adaptors and battery chargers, each table has a spacious cable channel with an integrated connectivity box for a computer and a telephone which can be connected to the socket strips in the shelf unit by means of short plug-in cables. And last but not least, mobile storage units for incidentals, specified either as open or closed structures, are allocated to personal work tables.

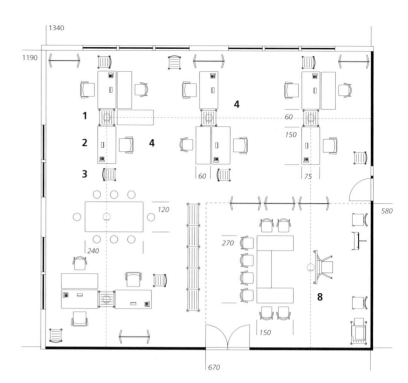

Scale 1:150 / dimensions in cm
(1 cm = 0.39 inches)
Area 160 sqm
Info-exchange area 40 sqm

As employees are generally involved in several projects with varying team constellations, frequently requiring spontaneous fine-tuning and discussion, mobile single tables, coordinated with work tables in terms of dimension and design, are kept in the corner on standby for dynamic group work,. These tables may be used not only for conference layouts, group work or introductory presentations but also to extend work surfaces. In contrast to work tables, they have a table top which pivots vertically along the longitudinal axis so that they may be moved away and stored compactly when not in use.

Zone for group discussions should ideally take place in a screened off corner of the room so that concentrated individual work and group discussions do not disturb each other. This is where ideas are developed and discussed, and further processing and implementation are organized and delegated. The same tools should be used as already specified for a conference workshop: light and easily positionable pinboards as shared work surfaces, which may also be used as double-sided vertical displays and screens at work places, a flipchart for preparation of discussions and documentation of action plans and the above-mentioned mobile tables with pivotable table tops which may be configured as required, depending on the specific form of work and number of participants. Graceful, slender and mobile frames with cantilever

shelves, boxes and drawers accommodate writing materials, while a heavy copier is positioned on the mobile server which is from the same furniture system as the workplace servers, the equipment towers, the high table and the shelf structure (that functions as a partition).

As virtually every process step today is carried out by means individual work at the computer, presentation and shared processing of digital documents should also be possible. Media disconnects lead to loss of time and transmission errors during the changeover from individual work to team work, particularly in project work. Lighting conditions have to be adapted to different forms of data projection – this would create permanent annoyance in a room in which people are also working. For this purpose, it is therefore advisable to select a mobile large-format screen. This may be allocated to both workplaces and group work areas. If the display

is also interactive and can be operated on the screen direct by means of a pen, a pure presentation surface is transformed into a digital work surface which should have an electro-mechanically adjustable tilt function.

A project office is marked by a combination of permanently installed workplaces with a personal touch and temporary, neutral workplaces; static and mobile furnishing elements, office and conference equipment, as well as special modular units and standardized elements – the latter not permanently configured, but in continuously changing constellations. Attention should therefore be paid to specifying hardwearing quality and allowing scope for versatile combinations, while preserving coherently recognizable design. Otherwise, the impression of an improvized arrangement and an arbitrary conglomerate of elements may soon replace that of a professional work environment.

1 Medium-height shelf units as the focal point of the layout, providing connection points for network and power supply, and storage space for workplace printers
2 Mobile table with integrated techni-stations
3 Mobile, open shelf units as personal storage space
4 Dynamic team-building around the static shelf unit, comprising work tables and mobile side tables
5 Area for informal communication – high table and library
6 Shelf unit with open and closed compartments as a permanently installed partition
7 Info-exchange table – with mobile tables, materials servers, flipchart, pinboards, server for fax and copier
8 Mobile large-format screen for media support in the info-exchange area

Project office for 8 to 12 persons
The static, medium-height shelf units accommodate power and network connections, as well as a workplace printer. The mobile task tables and the mobile tables with pivotable tops may be quickly configured into various formations – depending on the stage of the project and work.

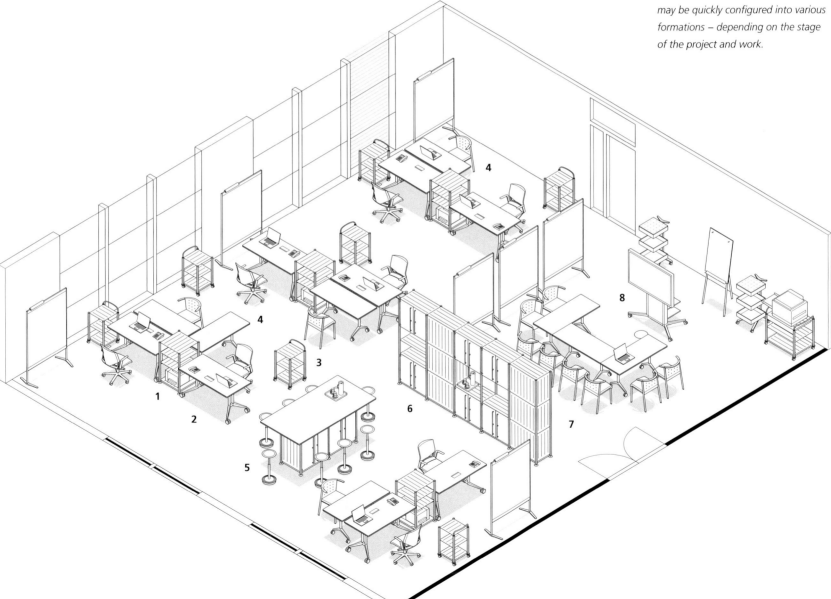

Group office with variable work "bubbles"

▸ A group office combines workplaces at which various sub-stages of more complex tasks and processes are organized, worked on and continuously coordinated within the group, partly autonomously and by group members themselves. In order to adapt skills and capacities to a dynamic framework without any time delays, a furnishing layout must be capable of reflecting variable changes in team structures.

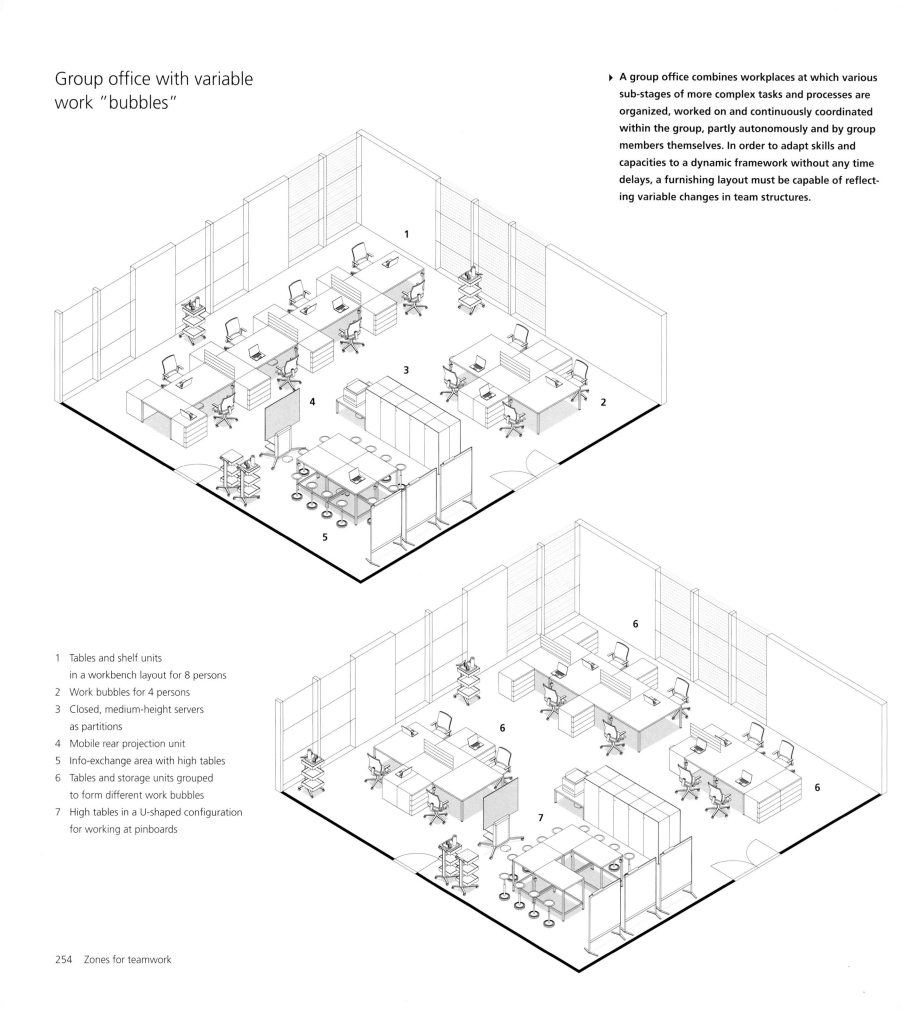

1 Tables and shelf units
   in a workbench layout for 8 persons
2 Work bubbles for 4 persons
3 Closed, medium-height servers
   as partitions
4 Mobile rear projection unit
5 Info-exchange area with high tables
6 Tables and storage units grouped
   to form different work bubbles
7 High tables in a U-shaped configuration
   for working at pinboards

Scale 1:150 / dimensions in cm
(1 cm = 0.39 inches)
Area 142 sqm
Info-exchange area

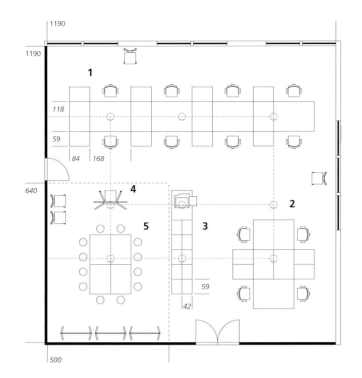

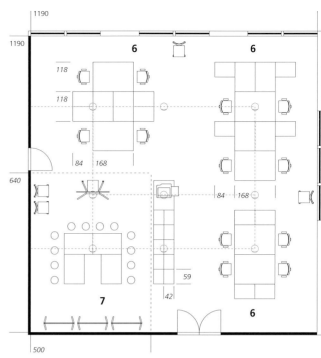

A dense arrangement of workplaces at shared table surfaces ensures close cooperation among group members. Such small, compact areas combine a high degree of interaction with the desired degree of personal privacy, the latter created by using vertical partitioning elements that can be arranged on the table top as required.

An excellent alternative to static workbench arrangements can be achieved by using large-format single tables, which can be placed side by side to create a row where the short sides only are used for seating. Work bubbles may be extended, downsized, reconfigured or even divided up at any time to reflect changes in workflows and team structures. In order to achieve minimum space requirements per workplace (applicable in some European countries, including Germany), table-height storage units, coordinated with tables in terms of materials

and dimensions, are added, which in turn serve to define individual workplaces within the work bubbles and provide storage space for personal belongings and work-related incidentals.

Similar to work bubbles, a communication area for joint fine-tuning processes is integrated, which also comprises standing height tables which may be added to. These tables may also be easily reconfigured, for example, for presentations. Info-exchange in a standing position is one of the most efficient forms of dialogue with respect to both duration and participation. In the specifiers' option, mobile, height-adjustable leaning aids have been included to provide necessary partial relief of physical pressure. The analogue and digital visualization displays, described in the section on a project office, and mobile storage units for materials should also be available in a group office to make work schedules and measures more transparent.

In the specifiers' option, filing cabinets in a block configuration are used to partition and screen off work bubbles; due to their modularity, such cabinets also permit variable and free-standing arrangement, provided that rear and side views have the same common quality of materials and surface finish as fronts and upper sides.

An extremely calm and harmonious overall appearance is created if all furniture elements, whether they are tables in sitting, standing and low height or various storage units, have the same rectangular proportions and a corresponding ratio of 1:2, which is in strong contrast to conventional office furniture dimensions. This maximizes combination versatility and also reduces visual complexity in any conceivable constellation.

Mobile furniture
in group and project offices

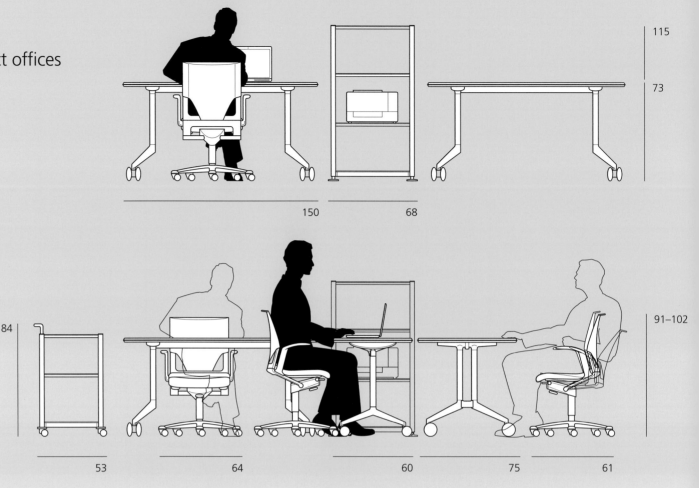

Office swivel chairs

Chairs should not only meet the ergonomic requirements of worldwide standards and directives on VDU workplaces, which include infinitely variable height adjustability, as well as a minimum backrest height of 450 mm. It may generally be said that sitting still is per se an unnatural, forced position, the negative consequences of which for body (and spirit) are best countered by means of so-called dynamic sitting. In order to promote intuitive changes in posture, the tilt of the seat platform and the backrest should ideally change with increasing resistance synchronously in relation to body movement. Resilient materials should also provide support when the user bends to the side. Much-praised

individual adjustability and lockability of the seat/backrest ratio, seat depth, backrest height and three-dimensionally adjustable armrests may have a counterproductive effect in this case: any adjustment effort increases the probability of wrong adjustment and impairs desired changes in posture, not to mention the chaotic appearance of chairs with a design-crisis of differently adjusted functions. There is always an aesthetic dimension to ergonomics too. It is therefore useful to select office chair concepts that adjust automatically to varying body dimensions and sizes and sitting positions. Special attention should be paid to specifying a backrest that is specially designed to support the whole lumbar region of the spine. Providing office chairs have

correspondingly high-quality and time-stable design, it is useful choose covers, upholstery and seat shells that may be exchanged, and mechanical elements that allow easy maintenance and repair. Such an approach allows almost unlimited re-use or recycling of components that are material-stream intensive and highly energy-consuming during the production stage. At the same time, the appearance of an office chair can be adapted to new requirements again and again by using a new colour scheme and upholstery materials. Such a combination of longevity and human desire for change is probably the most effective contribution to economically and ecologically sustainable office design, which focuses on optimally high and lasting utility quality.

Materials and surface finishes

Seat shells in polypropylene or frame constructions in break-proof polyamide or aluminium with stretch material are ideal materials for the seat and backrest as they are both resilient and hardwearing. For effective body temperature stabilization and to avoid electrostatic charge, upholstery material for the seat and backrest comprising pure wool or a blend of wool and cotton is highly suitable. Materials such as die-cast aluminium for star bases and mechanical parts, CFC-free foamed polyurethane for cushions, polypropylene for seat and back shells or polyamide for frame constructions and armrests meet requirements in terms of longevity, environmentally compatible production and recyclability.

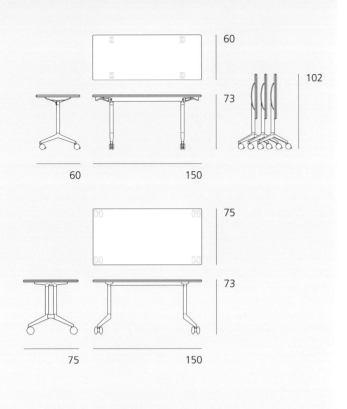

60 73 102 60 150 75 73 75 150

Mobile task tables

The concept for designing workplaces in group or project offices is based on maximum, self-organized flexibility and can therefore be achieved by using mobile tables. The integration of connection points for technical equipment and cable channels, which can be easily connected to floor ports via corresponding cables, may also be simply repositioned and reconfigured for tables fitted with modern information and communication technologies. Instead of having to channel cables to the table surface individually, the supply of all necessary connections is permanently integrated into the table, including storage space for network adapters, surplus cables and battery chargers,

e.g. for telephones. Table portals in the table surface, with a hinged 180° opening mechanism, provide convenient and fast access.

For detailed information, see also integration of media technology into tables on page 192.

To facilitate easy, mobile handling, tables must have lockable "wheels" with a diameter that allows them to overcome small barriers such as low thresholds of doors. Frames with a central supporting beam, uprights and T-shaped foot sections provide maximum legroom. The table height corresponds to usual standards for office and conference workplaces of 73 cm. Due to frequent changes in forms of work, it is neither necessary nor useful to specify

the function of height adjustability in this case as flexible configurability requires corresponding table heights. Hardwearing table surface finishes and edging with integrated impact-resilient profile are recommended for mobile and flexible applications.

The mobile conference and seminar tables to match such work tables have a pivoting mechanism which allows the table top to be rotated around the underframe. If this automatically activates the rotational movement of the mobile foot sections, such tables cannot only be moved easily through doorways and around corners, but can also be compacted extremely neatly. As is the case with all functional furniture units, it is optimally intuitive and easily comprehensible handling that determines whether functions are used efficiently.

For detailed information on mobile conference and seminar tables, see also page 108.

Storage units, cabinets and shelf units

The array of necessary furnishing elements for organizational, storage and technical functions can easily convey the impression of randomly selected elements. In the concept stage it is therefore advisable to specify system furniture units which may be configured modularly to meet individual requirements, which allow subsequent adjustments and are coherently designed in spite of great functional diversity. Every furniture unit is individually specified for the required function using industrially manufactured modules such as profiles of various height, adjustable glides or swivel castors, shelves, cladding elements, doors, pull-out accessories and drawers, and such modules are pre-assembled or finally assembled in transportable units.

Materials and surface finishes
Materials for modular system furniture units must combine precision and secure and integrated joints with high stability. Supporting structures therefore match table frames in aluminium profile, optionally with a bright chromium-plated or clear anodized finish to guarantee both durability and recyclability. To match table surfaces, extremely robust materials such as laminate or linoleum in light colours are recommended for decor tops, which may also be used as work surfaces. Shelves, allowing variable height positioning, comprise stable, one-piece sheet steel with a textured, scratch-resistant surface. Side and rear panels are also in angled sheet steel with profile strips for additional stability and texture. Colours should be subdued and material-compatible, for example, in silver. The same applies to door fronts and drawer fronts which should also comprise highly dimensionally stable materials, for example, aluminium sandwich panel. In project offices with a prestigious interior, fronts and decor tops should be finished in matching veneer.

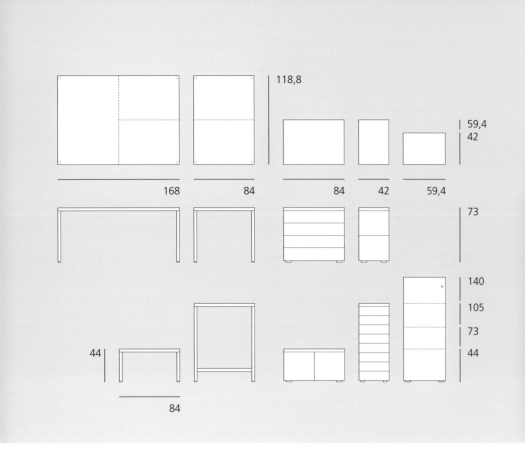

118,8

168   84   84   42   59,4

59,4
42

73

140
105
73
44

44   84

Variable furnishing options
in group and project offices

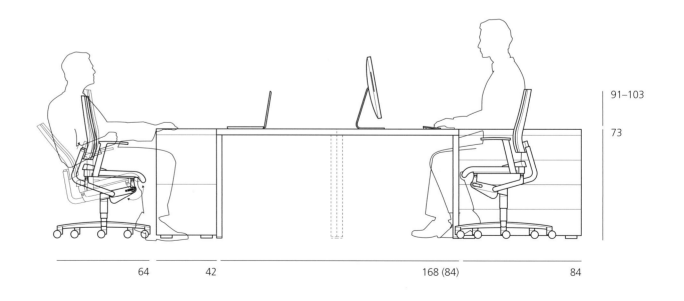

91–103

73

64   42   168 (84)   84

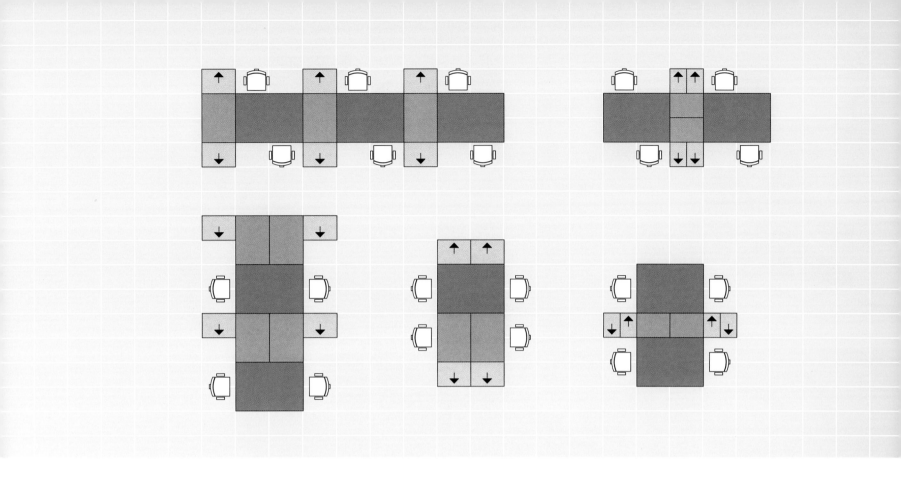

Variable, single table and storage units

Single tables that may be added to as required, and matching, free-standing storage units, which also provide a high degree of flexibility for changing teams structures, are an interesting alternative to mobile tables and individually configurable system tables as they do not emphasize the temporary character of a specific combination used.

The tables comprise classic, four-legged frame structures with flush edging and neutral table tops, with design and materials that are matched with the surface finishes of the storage units. The combination of tables and storage units thus defines homogeneous work surfaces. It is particularly important to consider proportions and the coordination of dimensions of such elements.

The functional heights of low, sitting and standing should therefore be used for both tables and storage units.

As conventional office furniture dimensions, depending on how they are combined, invariably produce a complex array of different forms, it is advisable to reduce proportions to a single width/depth ratio. This ensures a coherent appearance in any constellation and permits virtually limitless scope for combination and application.

By reduction to archetypal core functions in terms of design and function, every furniture unit can assume new tasks. Current requirements only determine whether a large table serves as part of a workbench, a double workplace or a spacious manager's table or is used for meetings and conferences.

That is why easily mountable and removable accessories are used as an exclusive solution for specific storage and technical functions such as table-to-table connectors, cable channels and cable management nets or organizer inserts for drawers and other pull-out elements.

For detailed information on basic concept, materials and accessories, see page 114.

Consultation and sales

▸ The change from a seller's market to a buyer's market has direct implications on the design of customer service areas and showrooms. If goods and services are becoming increasingly transparent and comparable due to worldwide standardization the internet and virtually limitless availability, the main differentiation potential lies in the quality of dialogue and relationships between a salesperson and a customer. A showroom for "goods" becomes a space for adventure and communication which is finely tuned to promoting dialogue and customer relations.

**Whoever wishes to sell something has to master the language.
But whoever wants to buy something is understood by everybody.**
Gabriel Garcia Márquez

Informing and consulting or from a salesperson to a customer-oriented dialogue partner

Globalization, comparability, transparency

Dynamic globalization, IT-supported standardization of business processes and the rapid spread of the internet have also clearly changed the relationships between producer and retailer, as well as retailer and customer. Scope for global mass production, the development of expanded economic zones without any trade barriers and virtually limitless availability result in an oversupply of goods and services in almost all sectors. In developed economies, demand markets in which sellers could allocate goods to customers as if they were supplicants is a thing of the past. At the same time, companies – whether industry or trade – have heavily invested in digitizing their business processes to achieve sufficient profit margins in spite of increasing price pressure. The automation of business processes with the standardization it entails has long since embraced customer relations too: the internet has become established as a "virtual marketplace" in conjunction with sophisticated logistic systems in many areas in addition to conventional trade structures and often enough to the detriment of the same. It has however often been the case that automation and digitization of customer relations, which were intended to contribute to reducing costs, soon increase price pressure. If the internet offers a high degree of price and performance transparency and a competitor is only a mouseclick away, the customer's inhibition threshold to change suppliers is considerably lower. And: the more standardized the processes, the easier it is to "imitate" them. If more and more do the same, the competitive edge will disappear – and price pressure will rise again.

Automation in the banking sector is a good example for such unwanted consequences: the system that was initiated for withdrawal, paying in and money exchange processes did in fact benefit the customer who is no longer tied to bank opening times to carry out these processes. The downside is that those business and private customers who are interesting for the bank just use self-service areas and do not enter the cashier's hall where selling really takes place. Conceptual names such as "self-service with service" which aim to link the self-service area more closely to the selling area again and involve considerable investment in space conversion, and show what efforts are needed if customer loyalty is at risk of disappearing as a result of automation.

Multi-channel customer relations

Markets have split up. On the one hand, there are companies that aim at mass markets and pursue a consistent cost strategy for their products and services in order to offer them as cheaply as possible. On the other hand, there are companies that distinguish themselves by offering added benefits and thus position themselves in the upper price segment. Especially with high-quality services and products, it is being increasingly recognized that the greatest differentiation potential versus competitors and in turn the greatest loyalty potential towards customers may be found in personal customer relations. Such companies therefore differentiate their business processes as well: in addition to automation and digitization of operative processes, the way in which customer relations are organized at the real point of sale is becoming more and more important.

How else can suppliers of comparable and "immaterial" products, such as insurance companies, banks or travel agencies, distinguish themselves if not by means of the quality of the interiors in which customer relations develop? It is necessary to combine media and virtual "meetings" between customer and supplier with human interface in real space, whether through television, cinema and printed advertising, PR measures or online presence.

While hardly any value is assigned to personal consultation on the part of customers either in salesrooms for low-complex and cheap products, for example, in supermarkets – after all the risk of taking a wrong decision and its consequences are generally predictable – the customer's fear of making a poor buying decision increases in line with the price and the stake. Fear invariably triggers the need for security and trust. This emotional feedback is deeply rooted in the human psyche and in instinctive behaviour, and is a key reason for the establishment of social communities. Fear secures the survival of the individual as it involves a feeling of being safe and protected within a community; feelings such as security and trust are after all based on human social relationships. Fear of a making a wrong decision can, as a result of this emotional bond, only be overcome by means of building up trust. This does, by the way, explain an apparent paradox: the more expensive a purchase is in comparison with one's personal income, and the longer term the consequences of such a purchase are, the more emotionally and thus tendentially irrationally such decisions are made. No one would buy a house from an estate agent whom they found unpleasant. One would find many rational reasons why this or that house was not the right one. In reality it is "gut instinct" that makes the decision, and rationalizing the pro's and cons of the buying decision. From the point of view of the seller and advertising this means appealing to the mind but touching the heart in order to be successful.

Business processes: from a noncommittal encounter via informal creation of trust to a formal conclusion of a transaction

Sales talks may be both planned or also commence spontaneously and incidentally. Planned consultation with a fixed appointment is generally based on mutual prior knowledge, that means on a degree of advance trust that was earned before whether as a result of existing customer relations, a brand promise or recommendations, or also of focused "pre-selection" on the part of the customer. Depending on the intensity of prior knowledge, prior experience or personal contact, any dialogue starts off with strengthening positive social interaction which is also accompanied by rituals entrenched in instinctive behaviour and socialization: shaking hands to show that one is not armed, an invitation to take a seat as a sign of trust on the part of the host, taking a seat and thus forfeiting the possibility of attack or escape, offering refreshments as a form of sharing and emphasizing a sense of community – all this is deeply rooted in our subconscious and serves to strengthen trust.

The situation between customers and sellers is however more complex, open and noncommittal in the case of unplanned encounters. Curiosity and the need for information have to be aroused in order to overcome threshold fear. Positive stimuli that draw people's attention are as much involved as the smooth transition from a public to a more engaging, private space. If the customer's body language signalizes interest in doing business, talks are generally initiated during a stage of movement. If a relationship is created after the first few sentences, the conversation and thus the relationship is deepened – frequently while still standing as this gives the customer the feeling of still being able to "escape". Sitting down on a comfortable upholstered seat on the other hand already shows a high degree of trust. Accepting an offer generally takes place in such informal contacts. By the way, this explains why politicians like to have their photos taken sitting on a settee together if they wish to demonstrate a very close and warm relationship. Body language shows whether outward appearances correspond to one's real feelings. In contrast, concluding the transaction is again formal – by going to the cash desk together or by signing the contract at the consultation desk.

Interior design: between openness and privacy

As is the case with any kind of human interplay, differentiated interior design can provide focused support for different psychological processes and dialogue phases in a selling scenario. Knowledge of interconnections of which one is frequently not conscious is as old as trading itself. On the one hand, there are the spatial factors of "public", semi-public" and "confidential" and on the other hand, the corresponding furnishing parameters of "moving", "standing" and "sitting" can be found quite early on such as in very old concepts of marketplaces: for example, the spatial structure of a bazaar where the way in which goods are displayed encourages people to buy. A bazaar sends out visual stimuli and acoustic methods of address within an open space, right at the interface to the real selling area, a method that is intended to overcome threshold fear. Adjoining there is the open-access, semi-public customer area in which people move around and stop to have a closer look when interested, and finally there are rooms that are hidden from sight or even locked in which the formal transaction is carried out, generally when seated. The degree of privacy required actually depends on the value of the specific nature of the business or on social conformity on the part of both seller and customer.

Modern shopping centres work on the same principles today: large glazed panels, which can often be opened up completely, are used to link selling premises optically and even in real terms with public walkways and areas that widen into inside squares. The smoother the transition, the lower the inhibition threshold is to entering the selling area. Lighting is also decisive: the lighter and more clearly structured, the more inviting such an area is.

Internal space division in a modern showroom should also follow marketplace principles: the hub is the "stage" for customers. Seeing and being seen combines the interests of customers with those of sellers. Towards the periphery it is advisable to use screens to partition off the space loosely into semi-public areas which provide the opportunity for informal talks, ideally at high tables. These should be interspersed with comfortable seating that extends an invitation to linger and browse through detailed information. Finally, peripheral areas are reserved for consultation workplaces whereby extra attention should be paid to screening such areas off from busy, public zones. The benefit for the quality of dialogue and relations derived from communal eating and drinking has now also become firmly established in high-quality showrooms. An espresso bar with small snacks not only serves to help bridge waiting time – it also makes it easier to approach customers and build up a social relationship.

A new challenge: combination of a virtual and a real selling scenario

An issue that has not been given due consideration so far is how multi-channel customer relations are reflected in interior design and functionality. If a customer becomes acquainted with a seller via the internet and has pre-selected or even designed his or her own product using a product configurator, it would be useful for him for the benefit of consistent communication to recognize this design and his preliminary work at the real point of sale. The opposite is often the case: the way in which a computer is used in consultations is detrimental to building up a relationship and interaction with the customer. Surveys show that consultants spend between 40 and 60 per cent of their consultation time on the computer instead of with the customer, who is doomed to being passive while this happening – generally without being able to see the computer screen. There are, however, already solutions for communication-promoting integration of computer technology where both consultant and customer speak about digitally displayed documents and can edit them together interactively on the display direct, for example, using a pen. Such active participation on the part of the customer in drawing up a solution serves to increase identification considerably and thus facilitates the transaction.

A customer service area as a marketplace for information, encounter and communication

▸ **In most service businesses, the foyer is not only the visiting card and reception area of a company, but as a customer service area it is the real fulcrum of customer relations. Whether they are located in public authority offices, banks, insurance companies or travel agents and even at airport and railway station counters, such areas constitute the physical and spatial point of interface between sellers and the market. Orientation, structuring and steering of lengths of stay and smooth running are the functional goals of interior design, while interface, the quality of relationships and concluding a business transaction are the communicative goals.**

Planning and specifying such areas requires particular sensitivity if the aim is to combine differing and sometimes apparently contradictory requirements in the field of tension and interest between customer needs, organizational and security requirements and technological scope within a coherent space and furnishing concept:

- On the one hand, a self-service zone with 24-hour service should be as open to the customer service area itself as possible; it should however be possible to close it off easily from the customer service area outside opening hours.
- Counters for dealing with routine daily business should offer speedy service to save time and cost for personnel. At the same time, customers should be encouraged to spend more time there so that they can be won over for interesting and lucrative offers.
- Obtaining general information or even dealing with individual stages of transactions should be delegated to customers themselves via self-service functions provided by interactive media, to relieve the workload on counter service staff. But this should not be at the expense of personal contact.
- On the one hand, interior design should provide a feeling of openness, clear arrangement and transparency to reassure within unfamiliar spaces and, on the other hand, a degree of privacy in a screened off area for intensive consultation.
- Last but not least, waiting periods should not be regarded as an imposition, although they are unavoidable and, in some cases, even necessary to ensure optimal utilization of staff capacity.

In view of such complex requirements, it is highly advisable to carry out the planning of interiors and workflow on the basis of a communications analysis.

It is no coincidence that traditional service counter areas are being transformed more and more into customer-oriented meeting places as centres of communication similar to the ancient principle of a marketplace.

Customer-led processing steps, general information provided by the service provider in question, active means of approach and random meetings, as well as customer consultation, including providing specific factual information, are key issues by means of which the length of a consultation and how it progresses are defined by and can be steered by considered arrangement and design of furnishing elements: the central point should run from the self-service area towards the inside and allow visible access. As an area for interface and browsing, it should arouse interest and be correspondingly attractively designed to make waiting periods as interesting and informative as possible. There are also integrated electronic displays, in addition to seats and side tables. The vertical displays function as public animation and provide information; customers can familiarize themselves with current offers interactively at the horizontal displays. The partially transparent heart of the zone comprises a bistro table with an espresso bar and high tables for informal conversation and to bridge longer waiting periods.

As the area is clearly structured with defined walkways and pre-oriented vistas, customers can always be seen by service staff, consultants and salespersons whose "stands" are located in peripheral areas – for example, a quick-service counter, a place for consultation while standing, work and consultation places with self-service for longer talks or meeting rooms at the rear to meet maximum requirements in terms of competence and privacy.

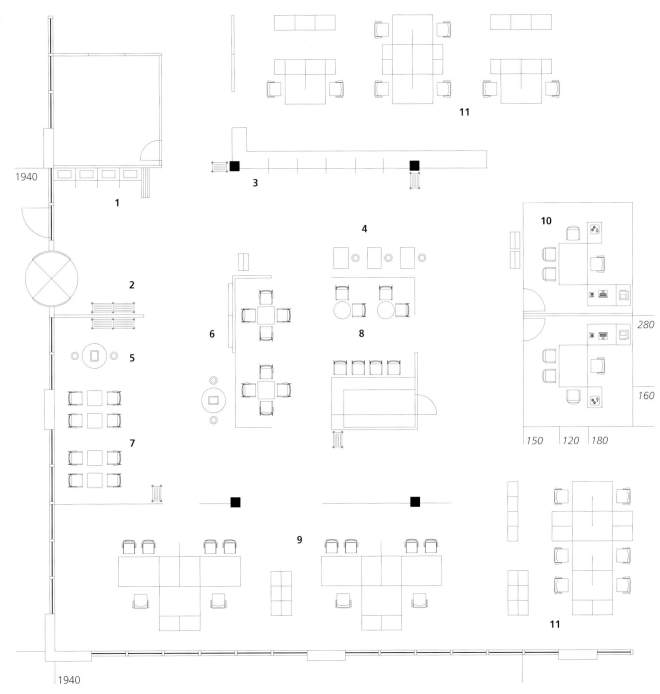

Scale 1:125 / dimensions in cm
(1 cm = 0.39 inches)
Public area 293 sqm
Consultation rooms 20 sqm each

1940

1

11

3

4

10

2

6

8

280

5

160

7

150 120 180

9

11

1940

1 Self-service area

2 Display shelves with information brochures

3 Counters for quick service

4 High tables for completing forms

5 High tables with interactive info-terminals

6 Wall displays as a "news ticker"

7 Waiting area with chairs and low tables

8 Espresso bar and info-café

9 Open-plan consultation places with screens

10 Closed off consultation places

11 Back office

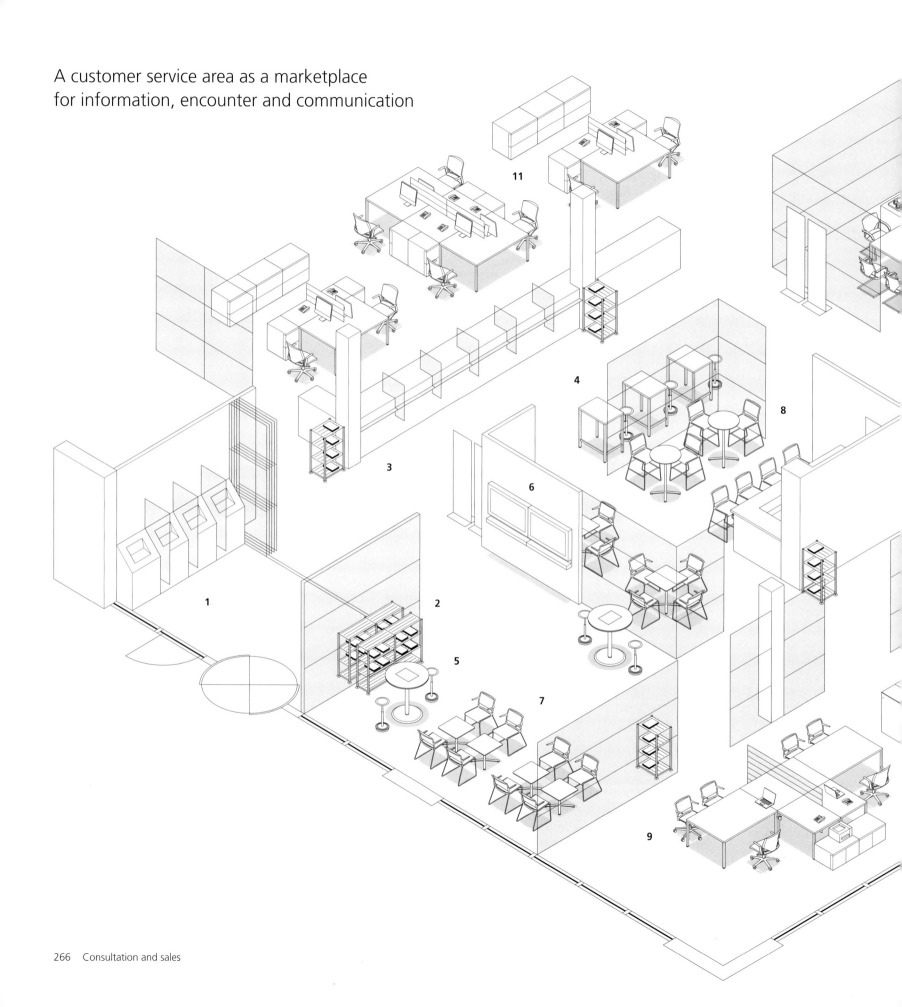

A customer service area as a marketplace
for information, encounter and communication

The main area of the room develops along the central axis leading from the self-service area out to the customer service zone: an open-plan area for sitting and standing provides space for informal communication and has both analogue and digital information on standby. The latter is shown publicly in animated form via wall displays, while specific information can be called up interactively at the table-integrated displays. Horizontal integration automatically ensures the right degree of privacy required by customers.

A bistro area with an espresso bar is located in the centre of the room for the purpose of bridging longer waiting times and promoting more intensive dialogues by means of a semi-public character. Non-transparent wall panels and glazed elements are attractive features that are alternated in such a way as to allow people to have unobstructed views to various service areas.

The quick-service counter is located adjacent to the entrance; it includes a high table which serves as an area for promoting special offers and for approaching customers direct. The open-plan consultation places can be found in the quiet, peripheral areas on the opposite side. One can see into them but they are partially screened off to provide a psychologically necessary minimum degree of privacy.

The access to the two separate meeting rooms is screened off by an office. Glazed elements have been used to partition these rooms in order to retain the feeling of spaciousness in the back room and an overall impression of space, in spite of the need for some visual and acoustic privacy.

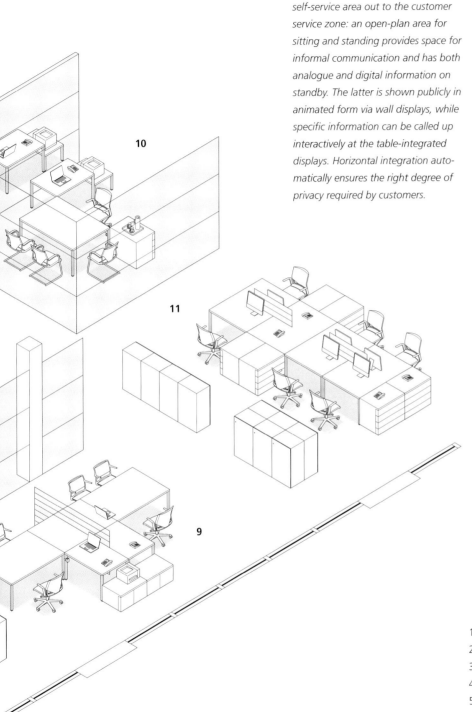

1   Self-service area
2   Display shelves with information brochures
3   Counters for quick service
4   High tables for completing forms
5   High tables with interactive info-terminals
6   Wall displays as a "news ticker"
7   Waiting area with chairs and low tables
8   Espresso bar and info-café
9   Open-plan consultation places with screens
10 Closed off consultation places
11 Back office

Consultation workplaces

▸ The quality of relations and consultation is the key to success for companies in the service sector. A consultant's workplace should therefore primarily aim to: base talks with the customer on the right degree of trust and competence to ensure that they result in a transaction being concluded. A consultation workplace is no longer a place of refuge for the consultant but should provide space for the customer. Integrating computer technology into such a discussion process should also follow these principles. The focus should be on providing information for the customer and not on information for the consultant.

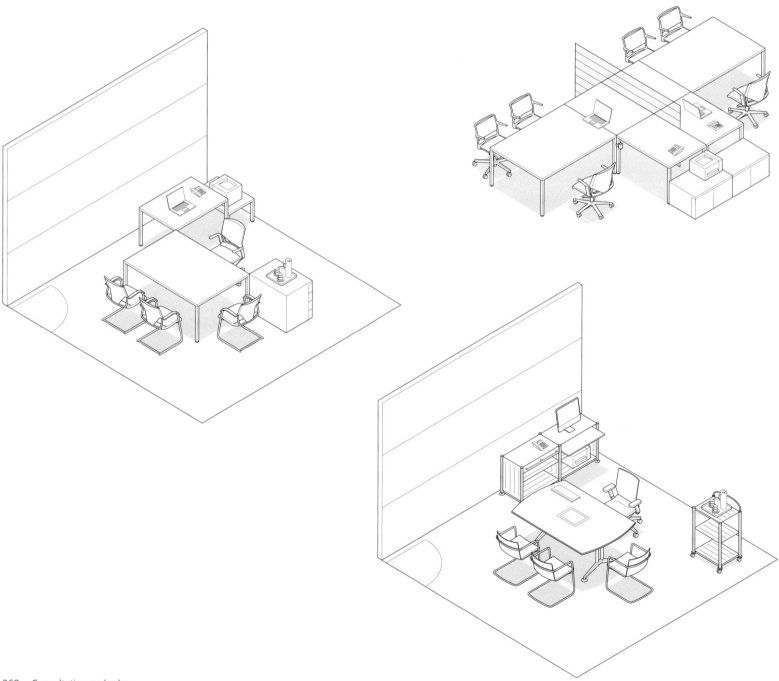

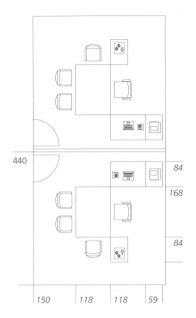

440

84

168

84

150 118 118 59

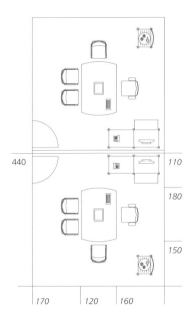

440

110

180

150

170 120 160

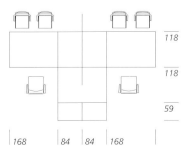

118

118

59

168 84 84 168

Modern organizations use concepts which no longer envisage consultation taking place at a personal desk, but in separate consultation rooms which may be occupied as the need arises. This has many benefits: space utilization planning is more economical in total as a room may be used by several consultants, the neutral character of the interior reduces inhibitions, and it also serves data protection as no customer documents are left lying around on the table.

The key factor for positive formation of customer contact is the question as to whether the chemistry is right between customer and consultant, whether dialogue is shaped by competence, openness and trust or by uncertainty, aloofness and dominance. As human subconscious activates all our senses, a specific environment can help to strengthen both the consultant's personality and the customer's self-esteem positively.

What is psychologically important is that the consultation place is visually and acoustically shielded from disturbances and people being able to see in from the outside: for this purpose, door and wall elements in translucent materials are ideal. In addition, the transparency of the room can be controlled variably by means of special glass technologies: if a room is free, the glass panelling can be set on "transparent"; if the room is occupied, the glass can be set on "private" and automatically becomes opaque. Furniture should therefore be more understated than intrusive to place the focus on the customer. It should, however, not appear austere and forbidding. Hanging up pictures or posters creates a more private, and confidence-building atmosphere.

Ideally, the customer and consultant should sit at a table at eye height. For this purpose multi-directional tables are therefore suitable which have a conference character rather than a resemblance to writing desks. The choice of tables – whether straight, orthogonal or rounded table forms with a recessed frame – depends on the specific design and utilization concept. The former provide a high degree of flexibility and may be easily reconfigured for scheduled appointments with a larger number of participants, while the latter are more static but can promote interaction more efficiently.

The integration of a computer into a consultation place requires special care and consideration. If a consultant spends too much time on the computer and if the display is not visible for the customer, this will serve to impair the creation of trust and a good relationship rather than promote it. The miniaturization of computer technology allows portable equipment, like a laptop, to be used. Fitted with correspondingly long and channelled cables, a laptop may be simply placed on the main table after the consultant has discreetly used it to check in databases while it was on the adjacent table. The display can be positioned so that it can be seen by both consultant and customer for the purpose of discussing contents displayed. A second display that is horizontally integrated directly into the meeting table and can be accessed as required marks a more satisfactory solution. The consultant is then able to show the proposed products and discuss them with the customer. If the display has interactive functionality, the contents may be rotated towards the customer like a piece of paper and worked on jointly using, for example, a pen. However, the general principle applies: the more actively involved the customer is in finding a solution, the more willing he or she is to conclude a transaction.

An atmosphere of partnership is also strengthened by specifying seating from one product family.

Info-café

▸ **Due to its specific informal character and the type of catering it offers, a café has always been regarded as an ideal place to bide time, gather information and make contacts. It is important to be able to see both out and in, and to provide focused support for varying needs by mean of corresponding furnishing and equipment solutions. Depending on the application profile, such an info-café may additionally be used as a small presentation and lecture room for special occasions.**

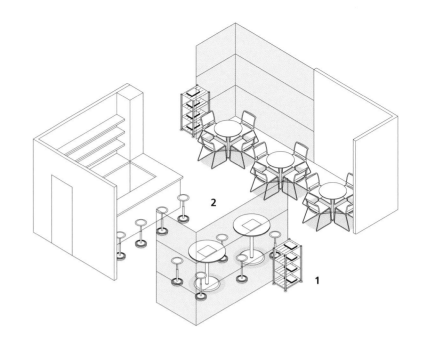

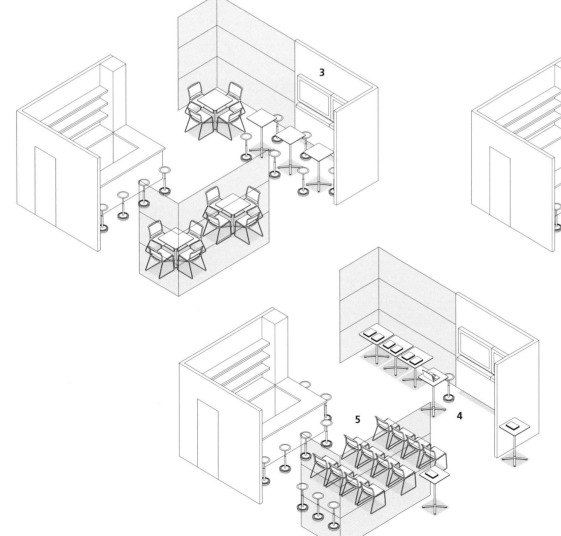

1   Shelves for magazines or brochures
2   High tables with integrated interactive displays
3   Wall-mounted flat screens
4   A high table functions as a lectern
5   Concourse seating for a lecture

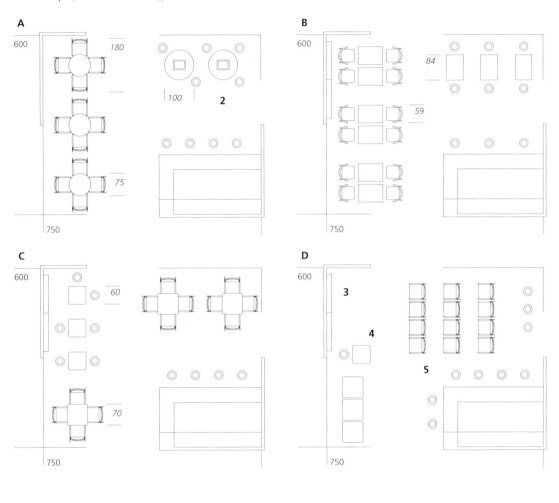

A | 600 | 180 | 100 | 2 | 75 | 750

B | 600 | 84 | 59 | 750

C | 600 | 60 | 70 | 750

D | 600 | 3 | 4 | 5 | 750

(A) Circular tables in sitting and standing height promote interaction and allow variable choice of seating. Equipped with integrated interactive displays, high tables may be used by customers as sources of information and by sales staff for presentations during informal sales talks. Gracefully designed chairs and tables, for example, with membrane seat and backrests and with slender table tops allow high-density arrangements without creating the impression of overcrowding.

(B) Modular, rectangular tables in sitting and standing height offer much more variability for combining tables. Such tables may be grouped together spontaneously by guests to form table surfaces of varying size. An info-café can then also be used as a conference and meeting room – outside normal opening hours. Seating with a corresponding size should be selected to match a more compact table form.

(C, D) If multifunctional applications are intended from the beginning, an info-café is equipped with extremely light, compactly stackable chairs that are linkable in rows. The same applies to tables which may be moved aside and stored compactly to allow the room to be used for presentations and lectures. The high-resolution and interactive wall displays, used as a media information display in the daily running of the café, can be used for AV support of topics in such a scenario.

A café is a neutral public place and serves as a meeting place that combines information with hospitality. The spatial concept considers both seeing and being seen, as well as providing information, personal interface and info-exchange; a place at the counter, a high table and corner seats for undisturbed reading, seats for private chats and social group events.

Small info-cafés can also be striking places if they have an interesting selection of food and refreshments on offer and are attractively equipped and furnished. Depending on the specific design and utilization concept, various furnishing solutions are possible:

Customer service halls and high-quality showrooms can be used for special events outside normal opening times in order to target new customer groups: an info-café that has become established as a place that promotes communication and business through meetings and info-exchange is a perfect solution for this task.

Communication zones in a showroom

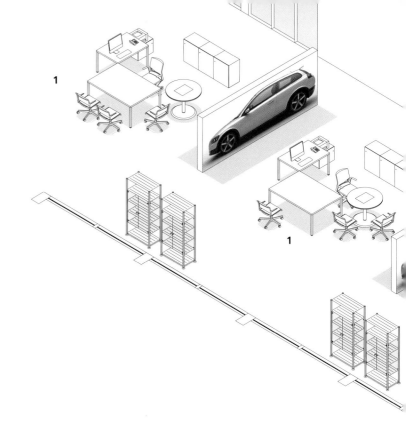

1

1

▶ **In high-quality showrooms it is not only the real presentation of goods that plays a decisive role for the quality of relationships and conclusion of a business transaction, but also the way in which various processes for approaching customers and conversing with them are reflected. The way in which noncommittal addressing of customers can progress via informal build-up of trust, factual analysis and consultation to a formal conclusion of a transaction is reflected in the parameters of human activities of movement, standing and sitting for which corresponding furnishing specifications are available.**

Similar to a customer service area, in a showroom it is also important to achieve a synthesis of various organizational sequences and customer needs and the psychological aspects of the selling processes.

Times where there is not much customer traffic should be used for dealing with administrative tasks at the desk or for optimizing the display of goods. There is a psychological aspect in addition to the economic one of using personnel capacity: hardly anything serves to raise the inhibition threshold to entering a showroom more than an empty shop with sales staff who are merely standing around, either concerned with themselves or waiting for signals from whoever is looking out for approaching customers. It is therefore advisable to integrate mini-workplaces into the peripheral areas of a showroom that should not resemble office tables and chairs but rather convey high design quality that reflects the specific character of the showroom.

After a customer has entered the showroom, has found his or her bearings and has been approached by sales staff, it is useful to move over to a high table for more in-depth talks. This is where real customer analysis starts with the question and answer process. A high table not only creates an informal, on par atmosphere but also becomes an anchoring place for presenting and explaining information, products and goods to the customer. This is where the customer generally decides whether or not to buy a product or service. Additional leaning aids will provide comfortable support to allow a conversation involving elderly people to take place while standing too.

If drawing up a contract requires a longer time or if any other waiting time has to be bridged for customers or accompanying persons, lounge-type seating will provide an appropriate setting. The right sitting height and the more private character of such seating underlines personal ties. Depending on the specific space and organization concept, such areas may be positioned in the showroom as "hubs", or semi-public niches

should be available that convey greater privacy. It is in any case advisable to arrange processes in such a way that the customer is not left alone until a formal transaction has been completed or he or she should at least be given additional information that serves to corroborate a buying decision.

However, the formal conclusion of the transaction with signing of the contract or payment takes place at the cash desk, a consultation place or mini-workplace. The latter has the advantage that tedious queuing up at the cash desk can be avoided – and that the salesperson can take leave of the customer personally. Although unconscious rituals are of paramount importance for approaching and greeting a customer, saying goodbye to demonstrate to customers that they have taken the right decision and to leave them with a good feeling is equally essential. Such after-sales support is especially important if a customer has committed himself or herself through the contract, but the sales agreement cannot be fulfilled due to delays in delivery.

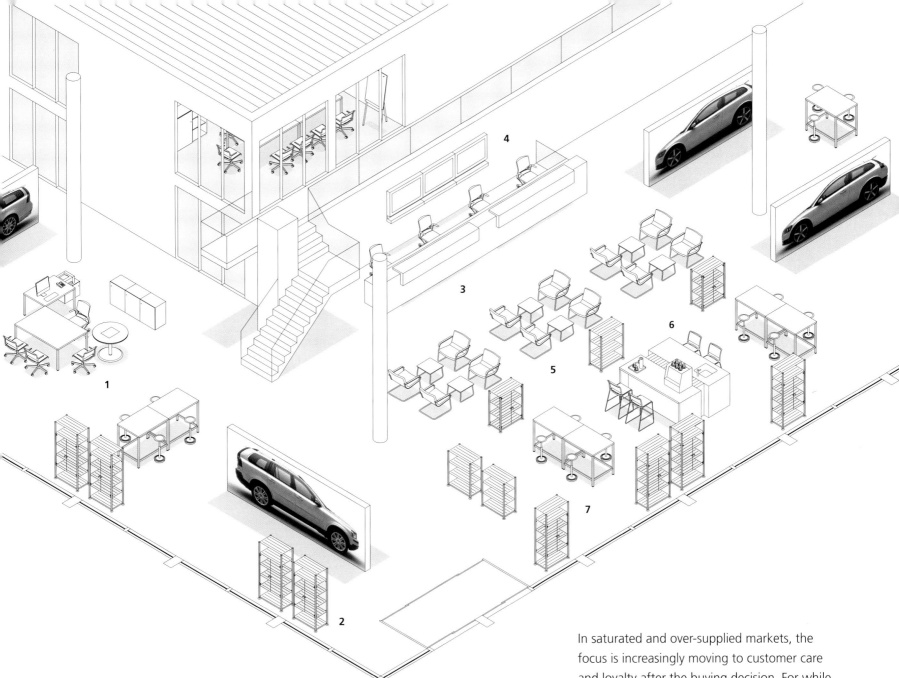

1 Consultation place with additional info-exchange table
   equipped with an integrated display for joint product configuration
2 Glass displays for presenting accessories
3 Reception counter
4 Wall-mounted flat screens for information videos
5 Lounge with cantilever chairs and low tables
6 Self-service coffee bar
7 High tables with leaning aids for consultation while standing

In saturated and over-supplied markets, the focus is increasingly moving to customer care and loyalty after the buying decision. For while the selling process ends for the salesperson upon conclusion of the transaction, the actual utilization phase determines customer loyalty. What the customer experiences during this period and the question as to whether he or she receives after-sales service are decisive for customer loyalty. Besides multimedia customer loyalty programmes, an attractively designed showroom combined with a warm, personal interface play a key role in determining whether a customer will remain one or not.

Furnishing places for consultation and information

Mini-office

A mini-office in a showroom should convey professionalism and an ambience that is not related to that of a conventional office environment. The tables and storage units are in a format that may be used multifunctionally and combined freely. By using new technologies (flat screens, laptops or table-integrated displays), the table becomes a shared work and communication surface.

For such multifunctional applications, it is advisable to select either tables with recessed frame structures providing maximum legroom all round, or models with table legs positioned flush with the table edge and concealed underframes. A table depth of approximately 120 cm provides sufficient space for looking at catalogues and documents without creating too much distance to the person sitting opposite. A table width of 170 to 180 cm allows seating along both the shorter sides and the long sides if necessary. Tables should be fitted with adjustable glides to level out floor irregularities. Two different types of storage units are suitable: either elements from the same modular furniture system as is used in the showroom for shelves for sales literature and the reception counter, or the coherent language of the consultation place is emphasized by using compact single elements that match the table range perfectly in terms of material and form.

Materials and surface finishes
The recessed table frames with cantilevered foot sections are in aluminium, a material that combines high dimensional stability and precision with robustness and high design quality. Polished or bright chromium-plated surfaces on foot sections as well as clear anodized or coated uprights and underframes are suitable finishes that may be teamed with an overall design theme. Table tops comprise grade E 1 particle board with hardwearing, solid wood lipping. Depending on the character of the showroom and goods to be presented, there should be a wide choice of technically-industrial surface finishes such as laminate or linoleum, as well as high-quality real wood veneers. Impact-resilient profile integrated into the table edge gives table tops a slender appearance and protects them against damage when chairs are drawn up to the table.

The modular furniture system consists of vertical aluminium profile, optionally bright chromium-plated or clear anodized. Shelves, allowing variable height positioning, comprise stable, one-piece sheet steel with a textured, scratch-resistant surface. Side and rear panels are also in sheet steel coated to match the supporting structures in the colour silver; fronts of doors and drawers should match the table top surfaces.

On four-leg table models, the frame comprises brushed stainless steel legs and a concealed, screw-fitted steel underframe. Table top materials such as through-dyed, MDF panel can be used for both table tops and storage units. Such materials combine the natural lightness of the raw material of wood with an industrially finished appearance, and are especially suitable for showrooms with a high-quality design. Attention should be paid to specifying finishes with protecting lacquer that is preferably resistant to impact, scratching and liquids.

Swivel chairs and visitor chairs

Swivel chairs and visitor chairs should convey an ambience that does not recall conventional office furniture. With a view to supporting both corporate design and creating equal furnishing status for both the consultant's and the customer's seat, chairs should be selected from one product family and be coordinated in terms of form. If compactness is a criterion, it is advisable to select models with a coherent shell construction which combine ergonomic quality with a low-complex appearance. However, if lightness is important, models with a semi-transparent membrane back frame and seat platforms are ideal. When specifying the consultant's chair, which must provide comfort for longer periods of sitting, it is best to choose models with automatic synchro-adjustment that consider current ergonomic requirements of dynamic sitting, while for visitor chairs, a level of comfort and ergonomics is sufficient to accommodate a maximum sitting period of 60 minutes.

For typology of swivel chairs and visitor chairs as well as materials and surface finishes, see also page 62 to 65.

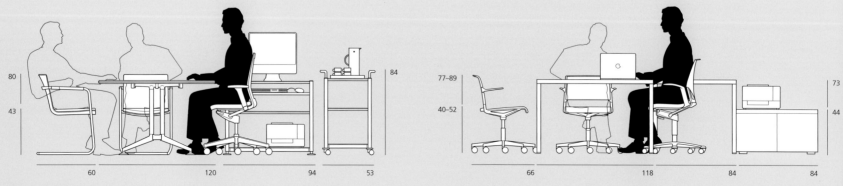

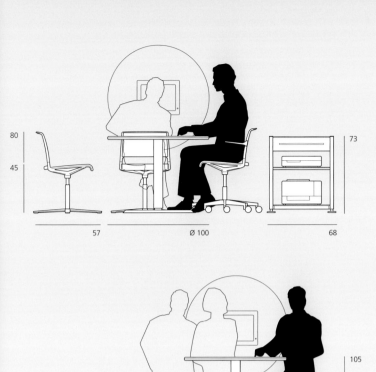

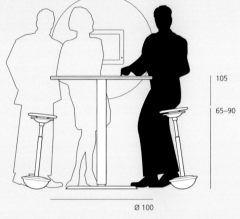

Specifiers' option:
ConsulTable in high table height

Interactive meeting tables

Integration of media information into the real showroom and a face-to-face consultation process is a key aspect for retaining a high degree of consistency in customer communication. Meeting tables with horizontally integrated displays that can be operated interactively by means of a finger or a pen are a convincing solution for showroom scenarios. Using this equipment, a user interface can be called up from the internet with which the customer is familiar, and this is then edited by means of a shared dialogue process. Small, additional programming features such as being able to rotate the contents of the screen towards one's dialogue partner serve to increase active customer involvement and thus identification with a specific solution. Material samples or high-quality printed literature can also provide additional, focused support of virtual imaging.

In the conceptual stage of preparing such a solution, it is absolutely necessary to consult the IT department. For, if the digitally supported consultation process is incorporated into ordering processing or even the manufacturing process, this will reduce the cost of follow-up processes considerably, in addition to optimizing the selling process. When specifying a showroom, the position of tables and corresponding floor connections should be determined in advance. Whether tables are to be used as an autonomous solution or with network connections should also be discussed with the IT department.

When choosing suitable tables, manufacturers should be preferred who combine a high degree of competence in integrating media technology with time-stable design quality and a wide range of various surface finishes. It is advisable to select a circular table with a height of 73 cm, optionally also in a high table version with a height of 105 cm that emphasizes equality and provides optimal support for human interplay. The diameter should be at least 75 cm, maximum 90 cm, to leave sufficient space for additional literature. It is ideal to specify versions with a pedestal column allowing concealed cable management and which have a base plate for guaranteed stability.

Materials and surface finishes
The table frame should combine high precision with stability. It is therefore advisable to specify constructions with a steel, levelling base plate with a hardwearing and scratch-resistant coating. The pedestal column, also in steel, is finished to match the frame of the consultation tables, optionally bright chromium-plated or with matching coating. The steel tray underneath the table top should ideally be low-profile and matt black for reducing the optical volume of the structure. The material of the table top should be sufficiently stable to accept a cut-out for the display. Depending on the size of the top, MDF panel or solid laminboard are suitable materials. Table lipping and table top finish should be coordinated with the specific consultation places to support a coherent overall appearance.

Bar and lounge furniture in showrooms

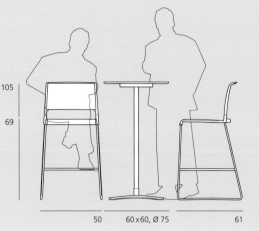
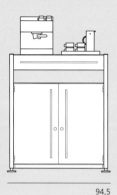
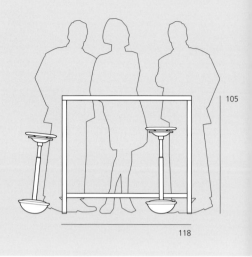

105 69 50 60 x 60, Ø 75 61 94,5 105 118

High tables

High tables should match the furniture used in work and consultation places, and be rectangular with corner-flush table legs and a footrail, the latter combining high stability with ergonomic benefit. Using the same harmonious surface proportions as for task tables, they may be freely arranged in the room and regrouped or combined as required. This allows easy adaptation to changing sales promotion activities without requiring any extensive reconfiguration or without creating the impression of disorder.

Alternatively, circular bistro tables with a central pedestal column may also be used as high tables. A circular form increases participation but does not allow several tables to be grouped together to form larger surfaces. The right choice therefore depends primarily on the envisaged utilization concept.

Materials and surface finishes
The rectangular high tables with table legs positioned flush with the table edge should be from the same range as the task and info-exchange tables used at consultation places. Frames and surface finishes are also coordinated. The footrail has a hardwearing, black plastic sheath as anti-scratch protection.

Circular high tables with a pedestal column have a levelling base plate in steel with a textured coating. If the position of tables is frequently changed it is advisable to specify a low-profile star base in die-cast aluminium which is significantly lighter. The diameter of the table is then limited to 60 cm in order to guarantee necessary stability. In both cases, the pedestal column is in round steel tube and bright chromium-plated or coated to match the other furniture units. However, the diameter of pedestal columns is larger on models with a base plate.

On more spacious models with a table top diameter of up to 75 cm, the top may be specified in terms of material, lipping and surface finish to match the task and info-exchange tables with a recessed table leg. On the other hand, for graceful models with a star base, stable, scratch-resistant and impact-resistant, through-dyed materials such as HPL may be selected as an alternative. These allow slender table top dimensions which appear even more graceful if chamfered edging is used.

Leaning aids that tilt in any direction and are height-adjustable are a useful addition to high tables. They relieve strain on legs for both customers and sales staff during longer discussions. Alternatively, bar-height stools may also be used, specifiable with bright chromium-plated steel rod and seat and back frames in flexible, semi-transparent material to match the graceful visitor chairs.

Lounge chairs and tables

Comfortable cantilever chairs are an interesting alternative to conventional seating with soft upholstery in waiting and lounge environments. They combine an elegant appearance with a high degree of seated comfort and easy handling. That is equally important for re-arranging a showroom and also for spontaneous adaptation of seating units to currently required numbers of seats. Matching low tables complement the chairs by forming inviting communication hubs.

Materials and surface finishes
The frames of the cantilever chairs comprise resilient, round steel tube. Bright chromium-plating combines elegance with high scratch-resistance and aesthetic longevity. Shells in upholstered plywood or plastic generally have either textile or leather covers. If the upholstery platform comprises a steel frame with tension springs embedded in polyurethane foam, the same degree of seated comfort may be achieved as for voluminous armchairs but using considerably more slender dimensions. The armrest pads should have a pleasant tactile quality, for example, using veneered plywood pads which may optionally also be padded and covered. High-quality textiles or selected leathers are recommended as covers. Exchangeable covers prolong service life and also ensure a favourable environmental balance.

The table frames are finished to match the cantilever chairs. When using wooden table tops, the same surface finishes and veneer variations should be available as for the armrest pads.

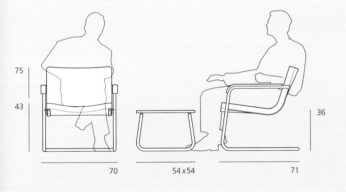

Specifiers' option:
Bar-height chairs and high tables from the Aline range

Presentation and storage facilities in showrooms

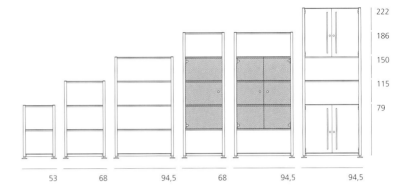

Presentation and storage furniture units

The challenge for furnishing showrooms is to achieve a coherently designed and high-quality appearance for various presentation and storage furniture units. Modular furniture systems are an excellent solution: if every furniture unit is specified and assembled individually from industrially prefabricated components there are hardly any limits in terms of dimensions storage facilities and design. Moreover, every model may be extended, downsized or re-arranged as required. Such systems comprise supporting structures, horizontal shelves, vertical cladding and storage elements such as doors, drawers and file drawers. If a variety of surface finishes is available for doors and fronts of pull-out accessories, furniture units may be precisely coordinated with a specific interior design theme. Adjustable glides on supporting profiles are necessary to level out floor irregularities.

Materials and surface finishes
As individual elements are generally assembled on site, it is necessary to use materials that are high-quality, robust and particularly dimensionally stable: supporting profiles in aluminium, optionally bright chromium-plated or clear anodized, adjustable glides in die-cast zinc with an anti-slip undersurface. Single, quad-profile structures should be specifiable to function as mobile service or equipment trolleys with double swivel castors in high-performance, break-proof plastic. For shelves, rear and side panels it is advisable to use coated, pre-stressed sheet steel. Drawers and file drawers are designed to accept high load capacity and are therefore in coated steel too. Aluminium sandwich panel is suitable for drawer fronts and doors. This material combines low weight with a host of possible surface finishes, ranging from coating in different colours to real wood veneers.

Alternatively, cladding elements and doors should also be available in toughened safety glass to allow integration of glazed displays into structures. Concealed power supply fittings in the profiles allow low-voltage display lights to be integrated without having to channel any additional cables.

Transit areas, foyers and lounges

▶ Informal communication has, on the one hand, always been regarded as the most effective and energetic way of strengthening the social community and, on the other hand, of initiating change processes and developing new ideas. The increasing complexity of entrepreneurial interconnections, by means of which the possible implications of decisions can no longer be monitored and formally considered in advance, requires places for informal encounters to be located in the centre of communication-oriented buildings and interiors.

Spontaneous and informal
– communication in passing

If one doesn't talk about a thing, it has never happened.
It is simply expression … that gives reality to things.
Oscar Wilde

Informal encounters as the basis of building up
social trust, networking knowledge and innovation

The power of informal communication over and above regular communication channels is becoming apparent in the communicative analysis of key change processes, for it was always informal encounters which have, on the basis of great personal trust, broken up and changed seemingly entrenched structural systems. Keynote decisions on German reunification were, for example, prepared while then incumbent Soviet President Michail Gorbachev and German Chancellor Helmut Kohl were out walking. In the aftermath of this development it was not only the political divide of East and West that crumbled, but also when a basic prerequisite for economic globalization was created.

This aspect of informal communication is presumably a special reason why static political structures that are based exclusively on maintaining power and preserving the status quo aim to prevent informal encounters between lower ranking people. Terms such as the "grapevine" or "subversive behaviour" are, after all, an expression of fear of change. There is indeed hardly any more effective method of disseminating information and sowing the seeds of doubt than doing so by spreading them in informal conversations with the seal of strict confidence. Whenever superiors eye break-time conversations with suspicion and disqualify them as wasting paid working time, this is equally inadequate as the similarly narrow-minded opinion that breaks are primarily for the purpose of physical regeneration.

In such situations it is often overlooked that informal communication has always been the prerequisite for any form of social community. Chatting over the garden fence, brief info-exchange when bumping into a friend in the street, and gossiping to colleagues in the company car park are inherent, quite normal facets of social behaviour in both private and work-life. On the one hand, they serve to foster human relations, and on the other hand, new interfaces and ideas often evolve in the course of personal communication. And this naturally always entails questioning the status quo and thus frequently functions as a psycho-hygienic vent to reduce stress too.

What used to be undesirable and even appeared suspicious is today acquiring key significance in the communicative network of a company due to processes of permanent adaptation and dynamic change: informal communication is a constituent part of team building, identification and togetherness, as well as for knowledge sharing and creativity. How often does it occur that when seeing one's dialogue partner one thinks of an important topic that needs to be finely tuned in any case, that necessary links and complex interfaces are discovered in the course of the conversation, that new ideas arise during info-exchange or that the effects of a measure on other areas suddenly become transparent. Although one might try very hard to make the consequences of armchair decisions completely predictable and transparent, with an increasing degree of complexity there is less probability of having considered everything in advance and having initiated all necessary measures. Yet another aspect favours focused promotion of informal communication: unlike planned meetings, which are often fraught with tedious coordination of dates, getting past the secretary to speak to the boss or official administrative channels, such unplanned and spontaneous meetings can soon have direct effects within the company.

Types of dialogue: coincidental, unplanned, from non-committal to confidential

Analyses of coincidental, informal dialogues within organizations go to show company concerns are almost always discussed in addition to private topics. An encounter that starts with a non-committal greeting and commonplace phrases can soon develop into an intensive exchange with binding or even confidential arrangements. The same applies to the number of participants: as varied the subject of conversations and the dynamics of social interactions are, the less constant the number of those involved in the conversation. A conversation may start involving just two people, but the number involved can soon increase spontaneously if somebody picks up an interesting buzzword in passing. The group can, in turn, shrink in size again if individual participants move away to continue a conversation confidentially, or if interest in continuing disappears or current tasks and appointments require a person to leave.

Space functions and arrangements: joint utilization interest and hubs

If informal encounters are to be promoted in a focused manner, the spatial prerequisites have to be created for such "opportunistic" communication. While walkways and transit areas used to be planned as a necessary evil so that the distances from the entrance to the office were as rational as possible, it is today just these in-between areas that bring people together and encourage them to linger. Narrow and monotonously designed "civil servant corridors" prevent spontaneous stops and info-exchange instead of promoting them.

Usual places for informal communication include entrance areas, lounge zones, for example, in front of a lift or at the copying machine, the post room, the tea kitchen, the staircase, lavatories, in-between zones, foyers and areas for breaks. As semi-public areas, they lend themselves to ad hoc conversations, providing there is a common reason for going there as is the case for service areas and communally used functional areas. Such places of encounter are quite consciously planned and designed to take the varying requirements of informal conversations into consideration. Modern, communication-oriented architectural planning therefore

goes beyond the concept of service and functional zones being generally allocated to different departments. By means of intelligent planning and careful design of transit zones it focuses on allowing staff from as many different areas as possible to meet. This has the advantage that hubs are created between different departments without disrupting effective units and centres. A simple basic rule applies: the more frequently paths converge and cross, the greater is the probability of meeting and exchanging information. Informal communication will profit even more if these points of convergence encourage people to linger, for example, if throughways widen out into a square, and monitors, newspaper racks, a bulletin board or a beverage vending machine are provided. A certain amount of "congestion" to trigger interaction is quite desirable, although everything is done to avoid this on the road to keep traffic moving.

Demands on interior design: animation, diversity and a quality of well-being

How important it is for modern organizations to create inspiringly designed zones for informal communication can be seen in the history of so-called break-out areas in the USA: with a view to increasing the corporate loyalty of highly qualified employees and or creating privileges that went beyond monetary remuneration, such people were also given the opportunity of carrying out their tasks and duties outside the office building as they pleased – to no small extent because the uniform dreariness of such office work environments was anything but conducive to creativity. After quite a short time, the consequences of isolating work from communal spaces and working hours became noticeable: both common bonds, social group feeling and important informal networking of key areas of competence decreased substantially. The logical consequence was that new office building concepts are designed to reflect the multi-faceted character of opportunities for informal meetings in public and semi-public environments within architectural structures by integrating such break-out spaces: terraces, bistro areas, lawns, benches, lounges and corners for being alone, as well as for confidential conversations or casual contact reflect the translation of a busy village concept to an office building. Connecting people has thus become one of the key objectives of building and space planning. To ensure that such conversation hubs are really used, instinctive behaviour should be considered in the planning and specifying stage: instinctive inter-action between people and interiors is simply negated by means of rooms with a wrongly scaled height that make individuals look small, corners that do not provide sufficient privacy vis-à-vis the flow of traffic and people listening in, or with seats arranged directly underneath stairs that do not provide any protection against physical danger or eavesdroppers. No one will be encour-aged to linger if there is a draught, or a high level of noise or echoing that make it difficult to hold a conversation. Such a place also requires adequate, ideally accentuated lighting that is coor-dinated with varying needs for a public or a private atmosphere. Using a different type of flooring for walkways and areas for breaks and relaxation can be as useful for unconscious orientation as including coloured coding of walls. Plants, daylight, elements with running water or ambient fragrancing may be used to enhance the atmosphere and create a quality of well-being.

With regard to furniture, quite pragmatic aspects should be considered and included: storage surface for a briefcase, writing surfaces for a diary and note-taking, as well as leaning aids, tables and seats that support different dialogue scenarios – both larger ad hoc groups of varying size and a confidential tête-à-tête. A minimum degree of relief from physical strain should not be forgotten either. Why should the potential of the digital world not be used in such a setting too? Interactive, electronic bulletin boards or advertising pillars can obviously provide greater scope for animation, catching people's attention and communicating up-to-date news than conventional visualization methods. And why is there no access to the digital network at these locations? How simple it would be if many topics could be dealt with together on the spot during a chance encounter instead of having to arrange a further meeting at the workplace.

Outlook: to combine real and virtual communication spaces

While new media have now moved into conference and seminar environments, equally important informal communication areas have so far been largely ignored. Yet, combining real information spaces with virtual ones holds great potential for building up a lively and efficient communication network. So-called internet cafés show that this does, of course, inevitably require a com-pletely different type of computer technology to be integrated compared to just plugging in a laptop. Instead of promoting mutual communication as an internet café should do, users interact there individually and solely with a computer. However, displays horizontally integrated into table tops, which can be easily operated with a finger or a pen, give people the possibility of discussing contents and editing them together today. The trailblazing concept of a cooperative building that supports human communication and interaction processes has many other new possibilities and perspectives in store that just have to be used …

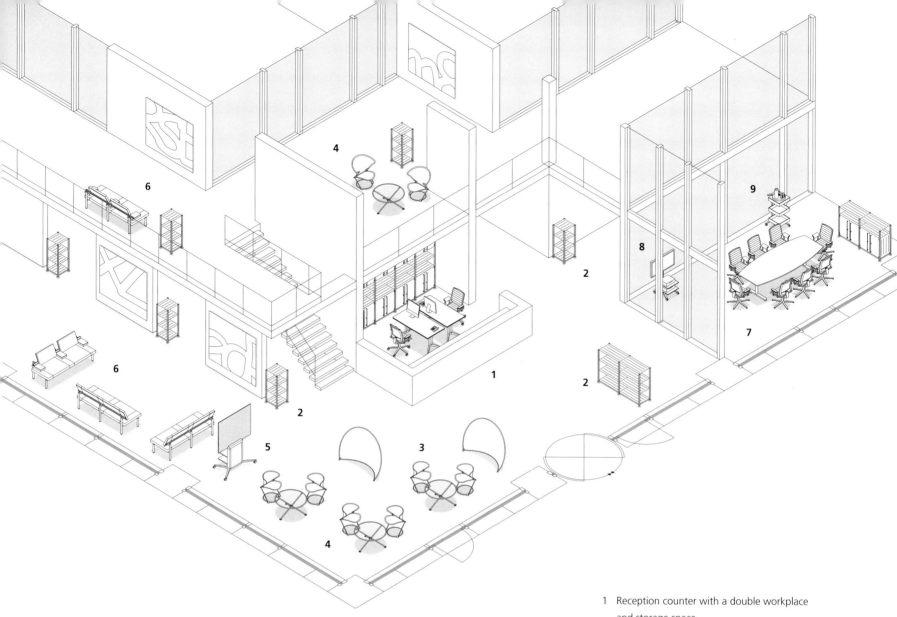

Reception foyer

▶ **A reception area is the central hub in the meeting network of a company. It is therefore an ideal place for promoting different kinds of communicative activities: formalized processes such as welcoming, registration and checking out, as well as informal info-exchange, focused orientation and obtaining information or arranged appointments. Space planning and specifying should consider such a spectrum of applications and create correspondingly conducive environments.**

1 Reception counter with a double workplace and storage space
2 Open shelf unit for newspapers or brochures
3 Spacious lounge area, partitioned off by screens with flexible netting
4 Chairs with semi-transparent membrane covering, and glass tables
5 Mobile display – optionally with interactive screen
6 Settee with armrests and side tables that fold down from backrest
7 Separate conference room
8 Mobile flat screen for presentations
9 Server for incidentals and refreshments

The communication culture of a company starts in the entrance area: like a visiting card, it shapes the first impression that visitors gain. Many companies have understood this and assign particular value to communicating a corporate image that is high-quality and often striking. Corporate design conveys something about the company's attitude, both externally and internally; it is part of corporate communication. Reception areas can be designed to appear dull and uninviting and make a visitor feel "small", or they can extend a very warm welcome to linger a while.

Yet, that is not everything: a foyer is also a place for welcome and farewell rituals, chance encounters and scheduled meetings, for informal info-exchange and focused information. The interior should therefore be designed to link various communication scenarios: registration and orientation at the reception counter, addressing guests, visitors and staff by means of exhibitions and interactive media; if several visitors or employees arrive or depart simultaneously, and last but not least, confidential conversations in peripheral areas which are screened off to provide varying degrees of privacy.

The variety of communication levels in combination with different lengths of time spent in the foyer requires corresponding spatial arrangements and coordinated furnishing solutions. The reception desk should ideally be clearly recognizable and centrally located. As waiting periods are generally brief it is neither necessary nor desirable to provide seating. However, should a longer waiting period be involved, it may be bridged by moving to peripheral zones with plenty of information available. Seats with small side tables with an unobstructed view to the reception desk should certainly be available to make visitors feel comfortable. As this is generally an environment with which visitors are not completely familiar and they therefore need some instinctive rear protection, light, mobile, semi-transparent screens are ideal for providing just the right degree of psychological privacy. Electronic, ideally interactive boards, inform and animate both visitors and employees, and extend an invitation to spontaneous info-exchange. Last but not least, a separate meeting room with transparent glass panelling and professionally equipped with media technology allows discussions and negotiations to be conducted on the spot without giving visitors and guests the feeling of being dealt with "on the doorstep".

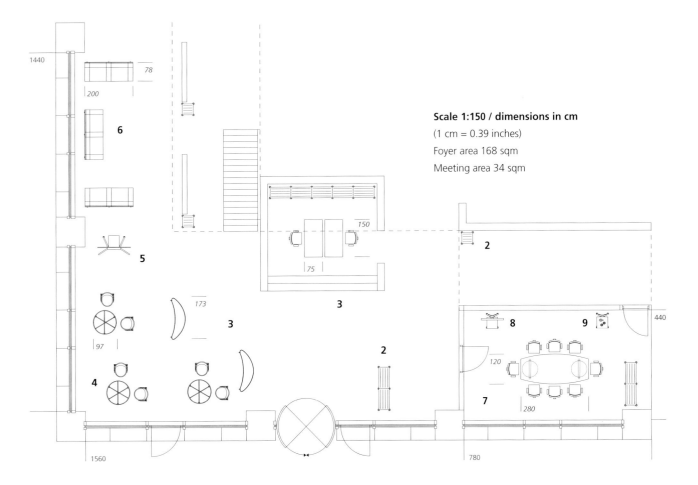

Scale 1:150 / dimensions in cm
(1 cm = 0.39 inches)
Foyer area 168 sqm
Meeting area 34 sqm

Lounge and foyer
in a seminar area

▸ Breaks are not only intended for physical and mental regeneration but are also an inherent part of the learning process itself and thus the fostering of social relations. Planning and specifying space and furniture should therefore include both screened off, corner seating arrangements as well as open-plan areas, and allow access to an ideally attractively designed outside zone.

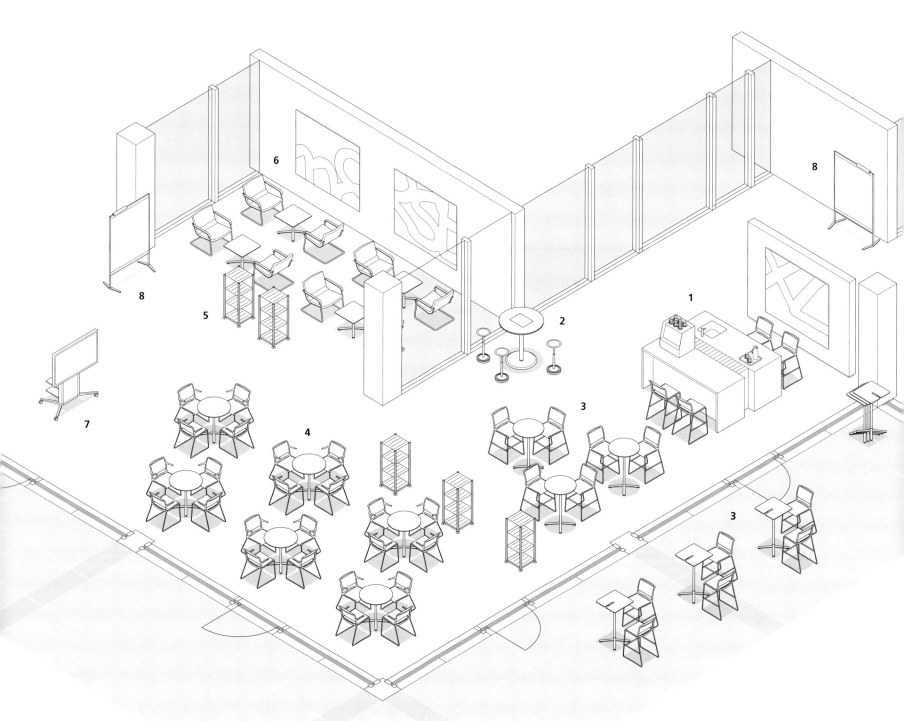

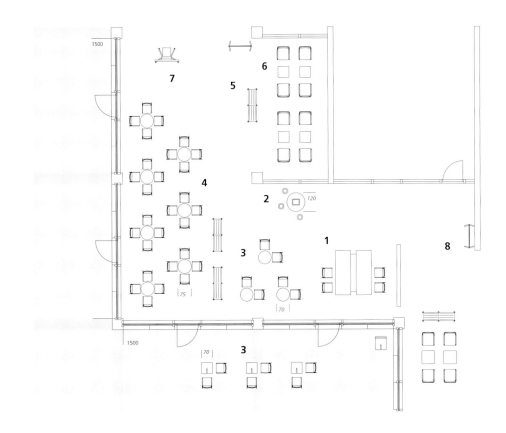

Scale 1:200 / dimensions in cm
(1 cm = 0.39 inches)
Area 225 sqm

1 Cafeteria
2 High table with integrated, interactive display
3 High tables with bar-height stools
  (stackable high tables too in the outside zone)
4 Bistro tables with stackable chairs
5 Newspaper rack
6 Lounge with cantilever chairs and low tables
7 Mobile flat screen for event information
  or transmitting lectures
8 Display for event information

The areas immediately outside seminar and training rooms are just as important for the learning process as for cultivating social relations. Informal conversations which take place during breaks, when people comment on, discuss, compare notes on or even criticize what they have just experienced, are decisive steps for digesting and reflecting on the contents of seminars. The real test of the usefulness in daily business practice takes place during subsequent info-exchange between participants.

Apart from talking about the seminar, such a situation may result in some new personal contacts, and may even lead to the start of new business relations if seminar participants are from different companies. Communicative, mental processing of what has been experienced, providing a networking service for business contacts and regeneration – these are the goals on which architecture and the furnishing concept should focus. Natural light and the opportunity to enjoy some fresh air, either in a garden or on a terrace, are key factors for relaxation and regeneration.

Space division and furniture should provide individual facilities to meet varying requirements during breaks and for communication by using defined zones and small groups of various types of seating – ranging from armchairs in a screened off lounge, bistro chairs and tables to stools and high tables in an open-plan area. Catering units, providing refreshments and snacks for hard-working conference participants, should not be forgotten either. Espresso machines for self-service should at least be provided in addition to traditional coffee and tea pots. Last but not least, there should also be racks or shelf units to hold conference literature and incidentals.

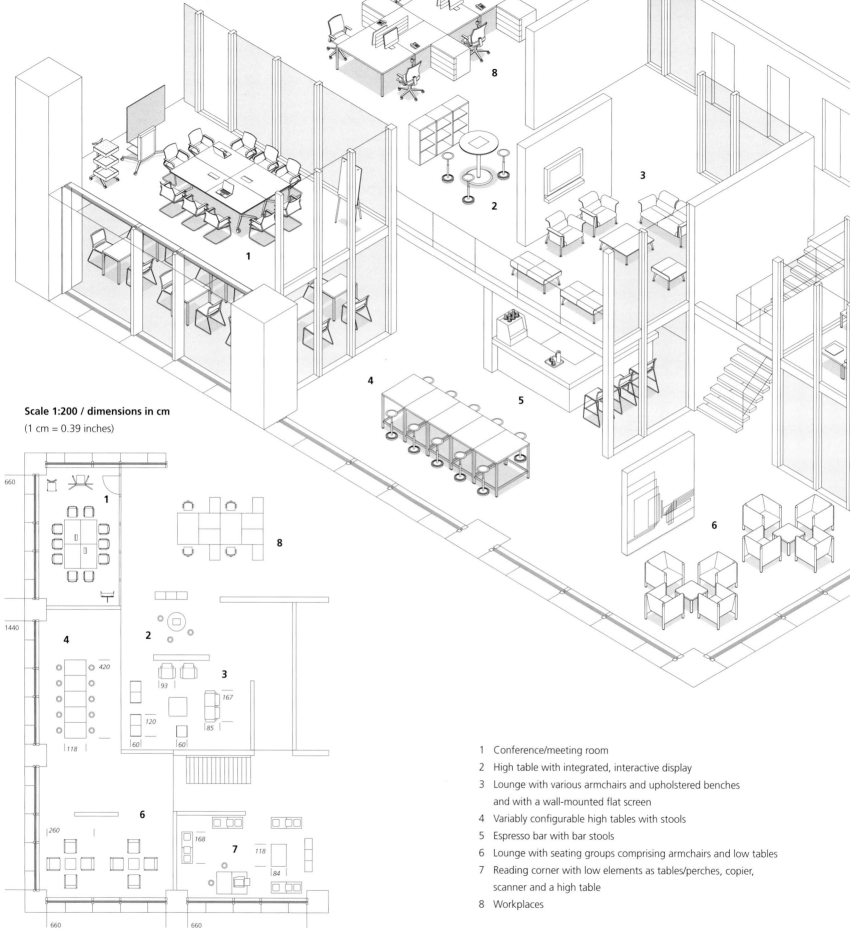

Scale 1:200 / dimensions in cm
(1 cm = 0.39 inches)

660

1440

420

93

167

120

85

60

60

118

260

168

118

84

660

660

1   Conference/meeting room
2   High table with integrated, interactive display
3   Lounge with various armchairs and upholstered benches
    and with a wall-mounted flat screen
4   Variably configurable high tables with stools
5   Espresso bar with bar stools
6   Lounge with seating groups comprising armchairs and low tables
7   Reading corner with low elements as tables/perches, copier,
    scanner and a high table
8   Workplaces

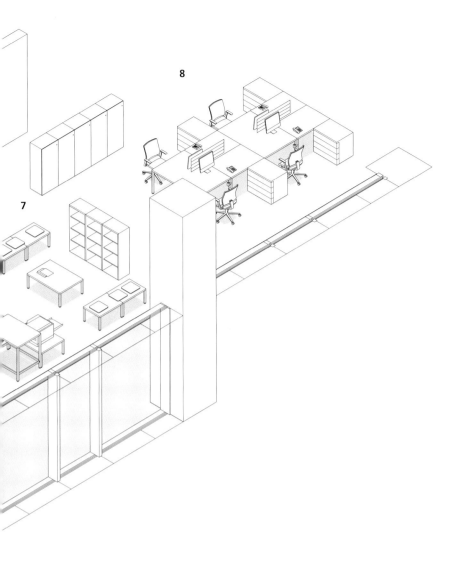

8

7

Between office work and a living environment: neighbourly activity

Life is the art of encounter.
Vinícius de Moraes

▸ **The integration of break-out areas into office buildings is regarded as a key factor for fostering meetings and info-exchange among employees from different areas of a company. Such a concept is generally neutral in terms of space required as immediately adjacent zones are included and few separate meeting rooms are necessary.**

Creativity and capability for change are key factors for facing global competition. The former requires the environment to be designed inspiringly while the latter should serve to strengthen the build-up of togetherness and factual networking within the organization. In both cases, the prerequisite is the promotion of identification, encounter and info-exchange. Planning and specifying such environments should be oriented towards the public space of a village with a specific layout of paths, squares and corresponding facilities such as cafés, a library and information displays. In addition to recreation areas, they sometimes also include leisure and wellness facilities. A key criterion for space planning is to combine well-structured openness with semi-public niches that convey a degree of privacy.

If they provide differentiation in terms of design and have animating facilities, such hubs will not only support unplanned encounters, but will also become significant places where people arrange to meet to converse there in a correspondingly informal atmosphere. Such an approach results in fewer separate meeting rooms having to be specified which are in turn only required for more formal meetings with a high degree of privacy or longer sessions and meetings that need professional media technology. As the floor space per person for conventional offices is also declining due to digitization of documents and the use of flat screens, such a concept can be realized from liberated space if planned intelligently.

Encounter and relaxation

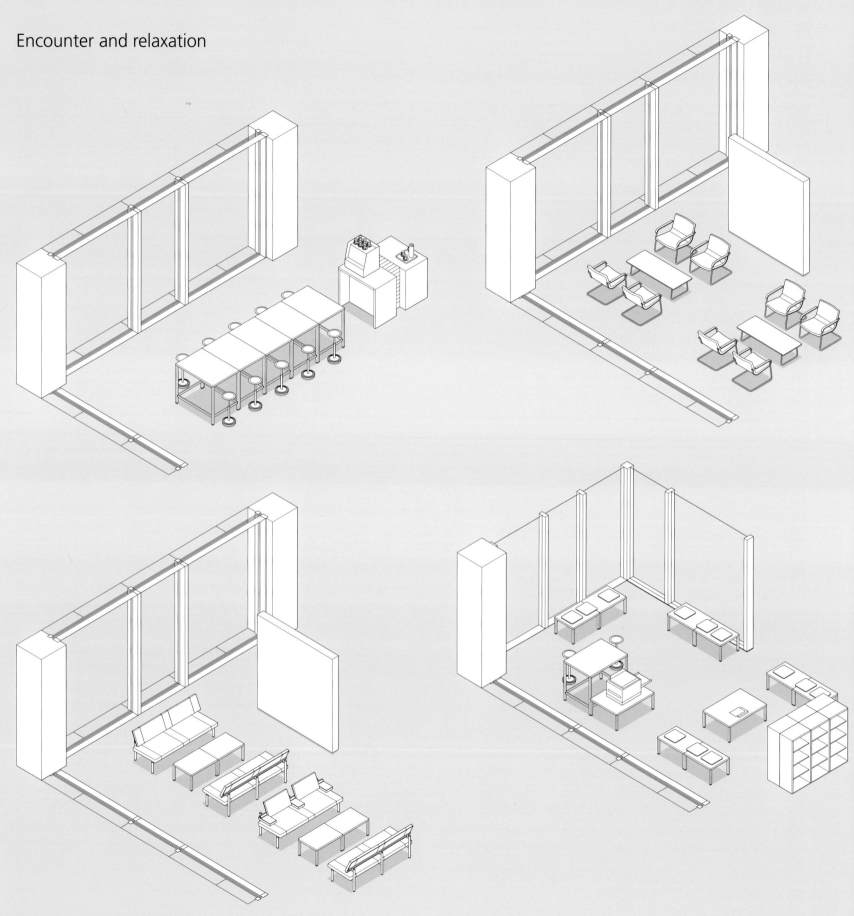

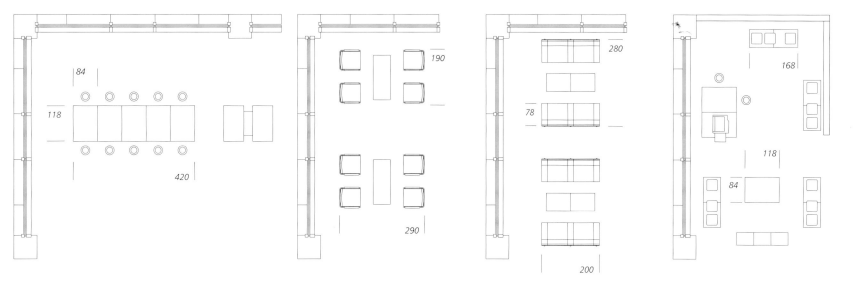

The high table configuration allowing multidirectional use is an effective addition to conventional furnishing solutions for bistro and café applications. It sets the scene as people can have a quick cup of coffee or tea while having sufficient space for temporary storage of documents or for reading a newspaper. If the configuration comprises freely combinable single tables it may, for example, be divided up to accommodate team meetings with a few swift movements and re-arranged in separate hubs.

In addition to the bistro area, it is becoming increasingly important to integrate different types of lounges. The more private atmosphere of a group of seating units with soft upholstery conveys a feeling of comfort, relaxation and well-being. They extend an invitation to phases of regeneration and promote familiar, informal info-exchange. Lounges should differ in terms of space planning, colour scheme and the character of the furniture to facilitate orientation and, at the same time, to provide significant differentiation to suit various kinds of appointments and encounters.

Light and graceful individual chairs may be easily repositioned to accommodate more people spontaneously joining the circle. Multi-seat settees, however, emphasize structure and order, yet they create greater proximity if dialogue partners sit next to each other. Models with armrests that fold down out of the backrest, which also serve as small table surfaces, may optionally be used as two single seats or as a communal settee.

If a particularly casual atmosphere is desired in reading corners, while also ensuring that places are not occupied too long, stable side tables are an excellent solution that is both variable and original. Such tables additionally serve as a shelf for technical equipment or may also be used as a perch if a seat cushion is added. The high table should in this case be matching to create a coherent overall appearance.

Groups of seats in reception areas and foyers

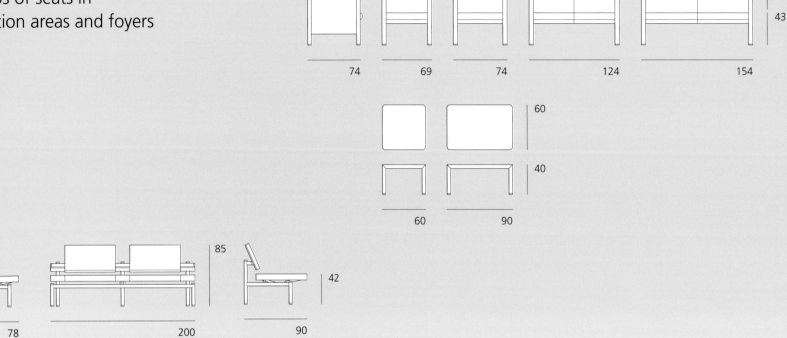

The choice of the right range depends on application options, positioning within the space or room and on the overall design concept. A host of different ranges are available for this purpose.

Variably usable settees
Beam seating units, two metres in length, are a real alternative to conventional lounge ranges in terms of both form and function if they can be optionally converted from a three-seater to a two-seater with defined single seats by folding down sections of the backrest. When folded down, armrests can serve as small side tables. If the seat depth can be enlarged by means of a swivel mechanism, a fully-fledged couch will be available for power napping. Open frame structures create a more graceful appearance and facilitate floor cleaning.

Materials and surface finishes
For the purpose of specifying greater spans between foot sections it is advisable to use colour-matched steel frames. The seat and reclining surfaces should also comprise stable and hard-wearing materials such as solid wood frames. If the support brackets of the back cushions that are visible to the rear are in veneered plywood, folding them down will produce small veneered side tables. As the positions of the settees are generally not changed and they are correspondingly heavy, renewable raw materials such as rubber coconut matting may be used as upholstery. High-quality textiles and leather should be available for covers.

Chair, settee/bench and table ranges for open-plan areas
Lounge ranges used in open-plan areas should meet human requirements for a degree of protection. For such an environment it is an excellent solution to choose cube-shaped units with high side panels that convey a feeling of warmth and safety and which merge perfectly with any interior design theme. With a view to allowing a wide range of layout alternatives, such a range should include individual chairs, and settees or benches to accommodate two to three persons. If the side panels are framed by the legs this will produce a distinctive appearance and edges additionally protected against impact. It is advisable to select a sitting height that makes it easy for users to stand up. Matching small side tables in coordinated formats replicate the frame structure of the seating units.

Materials and surface finishes
Frames should be specified using high-quality materials such as aluminium tube, coated, clear anodized or bright chromium-plated to match other units. The adjustable glides should be suitable for both soft and hard floors. Side panels and back should be stable and hardwearing, for example, comprising a solid wood frame with comfortable upholstery, and covered with flexible material. Air-permeable foam with high density cushioning provides a pleasant sitting climate and firm support. A wide range of high quality textiles and leather should be available as upholstery material. Table tops may be in birch plywood with various, coordinated veneers.

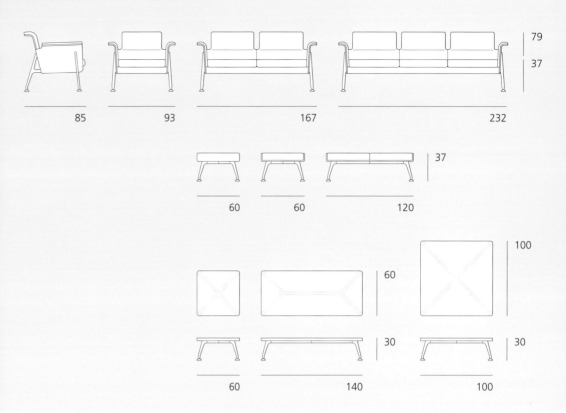

| | | | | 79 |
| 85 | 93 | 167 | 232 | 37 |

| | | | 37 |
| 60 | 60 | 120 | |

| | | 100 |
| | 60 | |

| 60 | 140 | 100 |
| 30 | 30 | 30 |

Specifiers' option:
armchairs from the Avera range (1);
settee, armchair and side table
from the Cubis range (2)

2

Armchair, settee and table ranges for screened off areas

If the lounge is a niche formed by architectural features of the building, the focus should be on the open and inviting character of the soft furnishing range. Casual forms with cantilevered armrests and backrests allowing different sitting positions are suitable for such environments. The upper section of the backrest can then also serve as a support for conversations held in a standing position. It is a particularly attractive solution if side and back panels comprise moulded plywood shells with aluminium foot sections so that models have a light appearance in spite of their volume. Firm, ergonomic seated comfort is important in this case too.

With regard to materials, surface finishes and covers, the same applies as for the other types of lounge furniture already described. Table tops in glass or granite may also be used for side tables in addition to wood if the frame is designed as a neutral support. The table frame should be in the same material as the legs of the armchairs and settees, for example, in die-cast aluminium, optionally polished or bright chromium-plated.

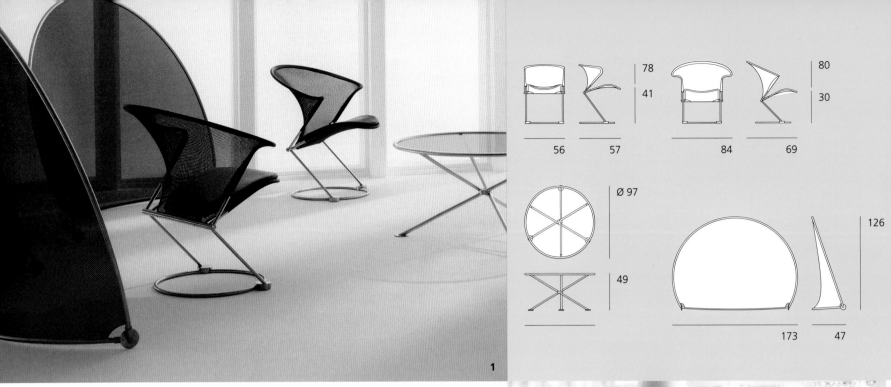

1

2

Furniture for informal lounges
in office buildings and seminar environments

Chairs with netting, and screens in open foyers

Chairs with netting are an excellent choice for underlining lightness and transparency. Low weight allows variable furniture units that may be regrouped easily and in a host of different ways due to their organic form. Slender material cross-sections combined with transparent netting create a light and airy atmosphere, even in high-density arrangements. If the chairs are also stackable, spares may be kept compactly on standby. Automatic adjustment of the fabric to varying body dimensions and sizes and optimal rear ventilation ensure a high degree of seated comfort; in combination with such a resilient frame, even dynamic sitting is possible.

If a degree of privacy is required more for psychological reasons than out of visual or acoustic necessity, the room may be divided into zones by using spherical, easily compactable screens with elasticated netting. Circular glass tables, with a matching frame complement the chairs and the screens to create a functionally and aesthetically coordinated range.

Materials and surface finishes
The high stress on resilient frame structures requires durable and elastic materials such as sprung stainless steel and curved stainless steel rods. High-performance polyester is a suitable material for the netting. A leather-covered cushion may be added for additional comfort.

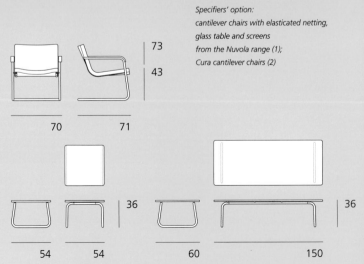

Specifiers' option:
cantilever chairs with elasticated netting,
glass table and screens
from the Nuvola range (1);
Cura cantilever chairs (2)

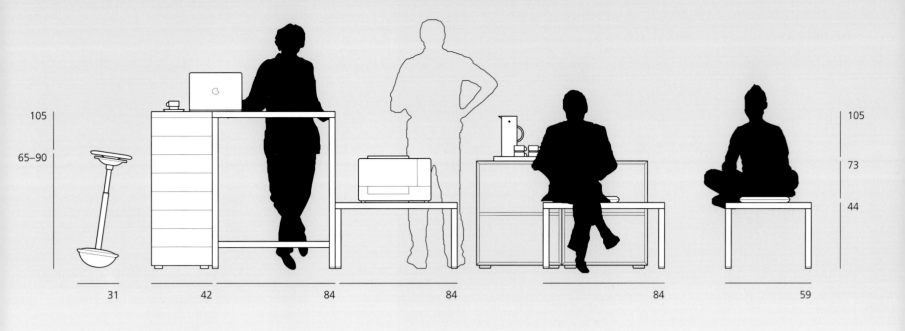

**Cantilever chairs
and matching tables**

The appearance and sitting experience
derived from cantilever chairs convey
a cross between a spacious upholstered
chair and a graceful chair with netting.
They combine a slightly resilient frame
structure in round steel tube with
a slender upholstery base. A frame
construction with tension springs
embedded in polyurethane foam can
provide a similar degree of comfort
to traditional furniture with soft
upholstery. However, the cantilevered
frame appears much lighter in this case.
Coordinated side tables have the same
frame structure in round steel tube.
Table tops should be finished to match
the armrest pads of the chairs.

Materials, surface finishes and covers
Bright chromium-plated round steel
tube for frames and exchangeable,
upholstered sections with high-
quality textile or leather covers ensure
longevity and sustainable value.
As for table tops, a choice of veneers
should be available for the optionally
upholstered and covered armrest pads
in timber substitute.

**Universal tables and storage units
for break-out areas**

Tables and storage units, with neutral
and high-quality design, open up versatile and creative furnishing options.
If they are available in the functional
heights of low, sitting and standing,
virtually all requirements can be met
using coherent, recognizable design.
Reduction in terms of form and
material to one basic type of four-leg
table widens application scope: such
a table in low height can function
equally well as a couch table, as shelf
space or with an added cushion, it even
becomes a perch. Specified in sitting
height, it serves as a bistro table or a
desk and even as part of a meeting
table configuration if dimensions are
coordinated accordingly and there is a
flush-fit of table edges when tables are
grouped.

Combined as a group in standing
height, tables form a counter or
a presentation surface; if single tables
are used only they can function as
mobile desks. The same applies to
storage units, which may be used
free-standing or combined with tables,
providing dimensions and materials
match table surfaces.

Materials and surface finishes
Table legs in shot-blasted stainless
steel and mounted flush with corners
and edges, and a concealed steel
underframe ensure stability and an
elegant appearance. Table tops and
storage units may comprise through-
dyed MDF panel that shows the lively
pattern of this material. The seamless
body structure is mitre jointed which
gives the units a monolithic character.
Surfaces should be protected with
a lacquer that is ideally resistant to
scratches and liquids.

Appendix

Bibliography

Ahrens, R., Scherer, H., Zerfass, A.:
Integriertes Kommunikations-
management, Frankfurt 1995

Aicher, O.: Die Küche zum Kochen,
München 1987

Allen, T.: Managing the flow of
Technology, Cambridge 1977

Alexander, C.: A Pattern Language,
New York 1977

Ammelburg, G.: Konferenztechnik,
Düsseldorf 1991

Branzi, A., De Lucchi, M., Sottsass, E.:
Citizen Office, Weil am Rhein 1994

Binnig, G.: Aus dem Nichts,
München, Zürich 1989

Birkenbihl, V.: Kommunikation für
Könner, Landsberg am Lech 1988

Birkenbihl, V.: Stroh im Kopf?,
Landsberg am Lech 1996

Bolz, N.: Die Sinngesellschaft,
Düsseldorf 1997

Bourdieu, P.: Zur Soziologie der
symbolischen Formen, Frankfurt 1974

Büchergilde Gutenberg (Hg.):
Chancengleichheit, Sozialpartnerschaft,
Gerechtigkeit – Werte mit Zukunft?,
Frankfurt, Wien, Zürich 2001

BUND und UnternehmensGrün (Hg.):
Zukunftsfähige Unternehmen,
München 2002

Bund Deutscher Innenarchitekten (Hg.):
Innenarchitektur in Deutschland,
Stuttgart 2002

Burkart, R., Hömberg, W.:
Kommunikationstheorien, Wien 1995

Claus, S.: Kommunikationsorientierte
Gebäudegestaltung, Erlangen 2003

Conen, H.: Die Kunst mit Menschen
umzugehen, Köln 1991

Czpiin & Proudfood Consulting (HG.):
Unausgeschöpftes Potential – Globale
Produktivitätsstudie 2003, o. O.

Darnstädt, C.: Cyberspace-Shopping –
Entwicklungstrends im Erlebnishandel,
6. Band der Reihe muk premium,
Hannover 1995

Datz, F.: Management von
Kundenartikulationen im Internet,
11. Band der Reihe muk premium,
Hannover 2002

Schneider F., Struhk H.:
Das Kombi-Büro: Büroraumkonzepte
mit Zukunft / Akzente-Studien-
gemeinschaft, Murnau 1990

DEGI Deutsche Gesellschaft für
Immobilienfonds mbH (Hg.):
Zukunftsorientierte Bürokonzepte
– eine Betrachtung aus Sicht der
Immobilienwirtschaft, Frankfurt 2003

Deutscher Werkbund NRW (Hg.):
Produkte und Gestaltungsmaßnahmen
für die Einheit von Arbeit und Ökologie,
Düsseldorf 1995

Diller, H.: Vahlens großes Marketing
Lexikon, München 1994

Döring, N.: Sozialpsychologie des
Internet. Die Bedeutung des Internet
für Kommunikationsprozesse,
Identitäten, soziale Beziehungen und
Gruppen, Göttingen 1999

Eickhoff, H.: Himmelsthron und
Schaukelstuhl, München, Wien 1993

Englich, G., Remmers, B.: Interior
and specifiers' handbook for
communication areas, Bad Münder
1997

Forgas, J. P.: Soziale Interaktion und
Kommunikation – eine Einführung in
die Sozialpsychologie, Weinheim 1999

Fox, M.: Revolution der Arbeit,
München 1996

Frey, R.L., Staehelin-Witt, E.,
Blöchliger, H.: Mit Ökonomie zur
Ökologie, Stuttgart 1993

Ganslandt, R., Hofmann, H.:
Handbuch der Lichtplanung,
Erco Edition. Braunschweig 1992

Geberzahn, W.O. (Hg.): Arbeiten
in der Gruppe. Braunschweig,
Wiesbaden 1995

Geffroy, E.K.: Das einzige was stört
ist der Kunde – Clienting ersetzt
Marketing und revolutioniert Verkauf,
Landsberg/Lech 1994

Gerken, G., Luedecke, G.A.:
Die unsichtbare Kraft des Managers,
Düsseldorf 1988

Godau, M., Remmers, B.: Design
entdecken – der Werkbund macht
Schule, München 2007

Görg, B.: Zukunft des Managers,
Manager der Zukunft, Wien 1989

Goleman, D.: Emotionale Intelligenz,
München 1995

Gottschalk, O., Segelken, S., Wohlleber, J.:
Büros planen und nutzen,
Eschborn 1996

Guntern, G.: Im Zeichen des Schmetter-
lings, Bern, München, Wien 1992

Hahne, A.: Kommunikation in der Organisation: Grundlagen und Analyse – ein kritischer Überblick, Obladen 1998

Haken, H., Wagner, M.: Cooperative Phenomena, Berlin, Heidelberg, New York 1973

Hall, E.T.: The hidden Dimension, New York 1966

Henn, G.: Technische Universität München, Fakultät für Maschinenwesen Garching, München 1998

Hertzberger, H.: Lessons for students in Architecture, Rotterdam 1991

Hertzberger, H.: De ruimte van de architect. Lessen in architectuur 2, Rotterdam 1999

Herzog, T. (Hg.): Europäische Charta für Solarenergie in Architektur und Stadtplanung, München, Berlin, London, New York 2007

Hormann, J., Harman, W.: Future Works: Trends für das Leben von morgen, Stuttgart, München 1991

Horx, M.: Trendbuch. Der erste große Deutsche Trendreport, Düsseldorf, Wien, New York und Moskau 1993

Kirkpatrick, D. L.: Konferenz mit Effizienz, München 1994

Klauder, W.: Trends, die die Arbeitswelt revolutionieren. Alex/Stooß (Hg.) Berufsreport. Der Arbeitsmarkt in Deutschland – das aktuelle Handbuch, Berlin 1996

Koberg, D., Bagnall, J.: Der Universal-Reiseführer, Gütersloh 1976

Kohlhammer, U.: Produktmarketing, Stuttgart, Berlin, Köln 1989

Kull, S.: Ökologisches Verantwortungsbewusstsein, 3. Band der Reihe muk premium, Hannover 1992

Koselleck, R.: Vergangene Zukunft. Zur Semantik vergangener Zeiten, Frankfurt 1979

Kulich, C.: Erfolgreich präsentieren, Stuttgart 1990

Lay, R.: Weisheit für Unweise, Düsseldorf, München 1998

Leeds, D.: Die Kunst der Kommunikation, Zürich und Wiesbaden 1988

Luhmann, N.: Organisation und Entscheidung, Wiesbaden 2000

Mann, R.: Das ganzheitliche Unternehmen, Stuttgart 1995

Mann, R.: Das visionäre Unternehmen, Wiesbaden 1990

Mann, R.: Die fünfte Dimension der Führung, Düsseldorf, Wien, New York, Moskau 1993

Malik, F., Stelter, D.: Krisengefahren in der Weltwirtschaft, Zürich 1990

McDonough, W., Braungart, M.: Cradle to Cradle, New York 2002

Merton, R. K.: The self-fulfilling prophecy. Social theory and social structure, New York 1957

Morgan, P.S., Little, A.D.: Die heimlichen Spielregeln, Frankfurt, New York 1994

Morris, D.: Der Mensch, mit dem wir leben, München 1982

Müller, U.: Umwelt und Verkehr, Göppingen 2000

Naisbitt, J., Aburdene, P.: Megatrends Arbeitsplatz, Bayreuth 1986

Nefiodow, L.: Der sechste Kondratieff: Wege zur Produktivität und Vollbeschäftigung im Zeitalter der Information, Sankt Augustin 2000

Norman, D.A.: The Invisible Computer, Cambridge, London, 1998

Nozik, R.: Philosophical Explanations, Oxford 1981

Ogger, G.: König Kunde – angeschmiert und abserviert, München 1996

Office Systems: Design for the contemporary workspace. New York 1986

Peters, T.: Der Innovationskreis, Düsseldorf, München 1998

Pietschmann, H.: Die Wahrheit liegt nicht in der Mitte, Stuttgart, Wien 1990

Popcorn, F.: Der Popcorn Report – Trends für die Zukunft. München 1992

Postman, N.: Wir amüsieren uns zu Tode, Frankfurt am Main 1985

Rezabakhsh, B.: Die Marktmacht von Konsumenten im Zeitalter des Internet, 12. Band der Reihe muk premium, Hannover 2003

Rechswald, R., Schlichter, J.: Verteiltes Arbeiten – Arbeit der Zukunft, Berichte des German Chapters of the ACM, 54, Stuttgart 2000

Riesenbeck, H., Perrey, J.: Mega-Macht Marke - Erfolg messen, machen, managen, Frankfurt, Wien 2004

Riffkin, J.: The Age of Access, New York 2000

Rust, H.: Die sanften Managementrebellen, Wiesbaden 2003

Sassen, S.: Metropolen des Weltmarkts. Die neue Rolle der Global Cities, Frankfurt 1997

Schönert, W.: Werbung, die ankommt – 199 Beispiele. Erfolgsregeln. Praktische Folgerungen, Landsberg/Lech 1992

Schnabel, U., Sentker, A.: Wie kommt die Welt in den Kopf? Reise durch die Werkstätten der Bewusstseinsforscher, Reinbek bei Hamburg 1997

Schwarb, T.M. et al.: Mobile Arbeitsformen: Verbreitung und Potenzial von Telearbeit und Desksharing, Bern 2000

Segelken, S.: Kommunikative Räume, Baden-Baden 1994

Siemens Kultur Programm: Arbeitsräume heute und morgen, Berlin, München 1991

Sprenger, R.K.: Aufstand des Individuums, Frankfurt, New York 2000

Stein, Peer Holger: MarkenMonopole – Konzept & Analyse, Nürnberg 1997

Streitz, N., Konomi, S., Burkhardt, H.-J. (Hg.): Cooperative Buildings – Integrating Information, Organization and Architecture, CoBuild'98, Berlin, Heidelberg, New York 1998

Streitz, N., Siegel, J., Hartkopf, V., Konomi, S.: Cooperative Buildings – Integrating Information, Organizations and Architecture, CoBuild 99, Berlin, Heidelberg, New York 1999

Streitz, N., Remmers, B., Pietzcker, M., Grundmann, R. (Hg.): Arbeitswelten im Wandel – fit für die Zukunft?, Stuttgart 1999

Sturm, G.: Wege zum Raum. Methodologische Annäherungen an ein Baiskonzept raumbezogener Wissenschaften, Opladen 2000

Terlaga, K. L.: Training Room Solutions, Trumbull 1990

Thiele, A.: Mit neuen Medien wirkungsvoll präsentieren, Landsberg/Lech 1991

Toffler, A.: Machtbeben. Düsseldorf, Wien, New York 1990

Ulrich, E.: Arbeitspsychologie, Zürich 2001

Velthoen, E., Piepers, B.: Kantoren bestaan niet meer. The demis of the office, Rotterdam 1995

Vester, F.: Neuland des Denkens, Stuttgart 1983

Watzlawick, P., Beavin, J., Jackson, D.: Menschliche Kommunikation, Bern 1969

Watzlawick, P.: Wie wirklich ist die Wirklichkeit?, München 1976

Weiß, C.: Verdammt zur Spitzenleistung, Bonn 2005

Weyh, H./Krause, P.: Kreativität. Ein Spielbuch für Manager, Düsseldorf, Wien, New York 1992

Wurman, R. S.: Information Anxiety, London 1991

Zinser, S. (Hg.): Flexible Arbeitswelten, Zürich 2004

Articles in collected works
an magazines

Absatzwirtschaft: Computergestützt Tagen, Absatzwirtschaft 12/1990

AIT-Forumdiskussion: Das Büro – die Einfahrt in den Daten-Highway?, AIT 10/1996

Alt, F.: Von wegen Einsamkeit! Schmetterlinge statt Dinosaurier, Mensch & Büro 5/1996

Der heiße Ort Büro, Bauwelt 13/1989

Balck, H.: Office Performance – Komlexe Erfolgsmessung für Nutzer, Betreiber und Dienstleister, In Das moderne Büro, Management Circle und iafob (Hg.), Tagungsband zur gleichnamigen Konferenz am 21./22.3.2002

Bamesberger, A.: The Dot.Com Work Place – Space, Technology, Culture and Work: Network of Places, in: Bullinger, H.-J. (Hg.): Arbeiten in der dot.community, Office-21-Zukunftsforum 2000, Stuttgart 2000

Positionen – Artikel: Liegen, Sitzen, Stehen, Bauwelt 13/1992

Benitz, G.: Das Büro von übermorgen, in: konradin, Ausgabe 5, Leinfelden-Echterdingen 2007

Bohlender, S.: Die Arbeit kommt zum Mitarbeiter, Mensch & Büro 3/1996

Bolz, N.: Produktivkraft Kommunikation, in: Streitz, N., Remmers, B., Pietzcker, M., Grundmann, R. (Hg.): Arbeitswelten im Wandel – fit für die Zukunft?, Stuttgart 1999

Kommunikation ist Trumpf, Chefbüro 3/1993

Danner, D.: Undogmatic, Training and technology centre Alsecco in Gerstungen, in: ABIT International Office Environment, Stuttgart 1997

Davenport, T.: What are High-End-Knowledge Workers, and why study them, Art of Work, Research Note, Issue 14. Accenture Institute for Strategic Change, 2001

Dworschak, M.: Geistesblitze auf dem Flur, in: Der Spiegel 13/2002

Eickhoff, H.: Der Tisch, Bauwelt 17/1993

Englich, G., Wagner, A., Müller, K.: Info-Pool, Studie 400, Versuchslabor für neue Arbeitskulturen (Wilkhahn), Englich+Wagner, Berlin 1992

Englisch, M.: Human Interfaces – Design für multimediale Arbeitsumgebungen, in: Streitz, N., Remmers, B., Pietzcker, M., Grundmann, R. (Hg.): Arbeitswelten im Wandel – fit für die Zukunft?, Stuttgart 1999

Strafford (Hg.): Espace de travail, travail de l'espace, Édition 2006

Freimuth, Dr. J.: Kommunikative Architektur im Unternehmen, Harvard Manager 2/89

Froitzheim, U.: Nur noch Container, Wirtschaftswoche 24/1996

Fuchs, W./ Puell, R.: Bürokratie & Avantgarde, Bauwelt 39/1994

Glaser, W.R.: Telearbeit – große Prognosen und kleine Veränderungen, in: Streitz, N., Remmers, B., Pietzcker, M., Grundmann, R. (Hg.): Arbeitswelten im Wandel – fit für die Zukunft?, Stuttgart 1999

Geo Wissen: Chaos und Kreativität, Gruner + Jahr AG & Co, Hamburg, 2/1990

Geo Wissen: Verkehr und Mobilität, Gruner + Jahr AG & Co, Hamburg, 2/1991

Geo Wissen: Kommunikation, Gruner + Jahr AG & Co, Hamburg, 2/1989

Gerken, Gerd: Radar für Trends – Zukunftsletter, Trend News, 2/1991

Glaser, H.: Von der Zukunft der Arbeitsgesellschaft, IHK Berlin (Hrsg.), Büroarbeit von morgen in den Büros von heute?, Berlin 1997

Gottschalk, O.: Bürokonzeptionen und ihre kommunikative Eignung, IHK Berlin, (Hrsg.), Büroarbeit von morgen in den Büros von heute?, Berlin 1997

Gröschl, J.: Auf der Datenautobahn zum Arbeitsplatz, in: F.A.Z. vom 10.01.2004

Hamilton, u.a.: The New Workplace. Business Week, 29. April 1996

Hartkopf, V. et al.: The use of enabling matrix to capture evolutionary best practices: The case of the Intelligent Workplace at CMU, in: Streitz, N., Remmers, B., Pietzcker, M., Grundmann, R. (Hg.): Arbeitswelten im Wandel – fit für die Zukunft?, Stuttgart 1999

Heringer, H.-J.: De Saussure und die unsichtbare Hand. Cahiers Ferdinand de Saussure 39, 1985

IHK Berlin (Hg.): Büroarbeit von morgen in den Büros von heute?, Berlin 1997

Kadritzke, U.: Leben im Büro, IHK Berlin (Hg.), Büroarbeit von morgen in den Büros von heute?, Berlin 1997

Krause, J. R.: Schöne Schulzeit, AIT 5/1997

Lainer, R., Wagner, I.: Connecting Qualities of Social Use with Spatial Qualities, in: Streitz, N. et al., Cooperative Buildings – Integrating Information, Organization and Architecture, Heidelberg 1999

Lentz, B.: Macht hat, wer macht, Capital 3/1995

Luhmann, N.: Evolution und Geschichte, Zeitschrift für historische Sozialwissenschaften, 2. Jahrg. Heft 3, 1976

Maatz, B.: Unternehmenserfolg und Büroraum, Office Design, April 1993

Moltke, I., Andersen, H.H.K.: Cooperative Buildings – The Case of Office VISION, in: Streitz, N. et al., Cooperative Buildings – Integrating Information, Organization and Architecture, Heidelberg 1999

Moran, T.P.: Walls at Work – Physical and Electronic Walls in the Workplace, in: Streitz, N., Remmers, B., Pietzcker, M., Grundmann, R. (Hg.): Arbeitswelten im Wandel – fit für die Zukunft?, Stuttgart 1999

Nitschke, A.: Fragestellungen der Historischen Anthropologie, Süssmuth, H., Historische Anthropologie, Göttingen 1984

Ottomann, H.: Soho ist überall, Mensch & Büro 2/1996

Ottomann, H.: Der Tod der Distanz und das Büro, Mensch & Büro 3/1996

Penn, A., Desyllas, L., Vaughan, L.: The space of innovation: interaction and communikcation in the work environment, in: Environment and Planning B: Planning and Design, Vol. 26/1999

ProduktEntwicklung Roericht: Studie 300/9.88 Konferieren, Roericht, N., Schmitz, B., Englich, G., u.a., Ulm 1988

Plateau, M.: Informationsgesellschaft, Kommunikationsweise und sozialer Raum, Forum Wissenschaft 1/1996

Remmers, B.: The existential factor, change and identity in architecture for the working world, ABIT International Office Design, Stuttgart 1997

Remmers, B.: Gesprächsbereit, Konferenzkultur im Wandel, md 5/1996

Remmers, B.: Zukunft der Büroarbeit – Zukunft der Kommunikation, IHK Berlin (Hg.), Büroarbeit von morgen in den Büros von heute?, Berlin 1997

Remmers, B.: Vom steinzeitlichen Palaver zur modernen Kommunikationsförderung, in: Streitz, N., Remmers, B., Pietzcker, M., Grundmann, R. (Hg.): Arbeitswelten im Wandel – fit für die Zukunft?, Stuttgart 1999

Remmers, B.: Spezialisierung versus Integration – von der Information zur Kommunikation, in: GMD-Spiegel 1/2, 1999

Remmers, B.: Wandel und Identität, in: Komar, R. (Hg.) für Institut für Designforschung Stuttgart, Design Bericht, Stuttgart 1997

Remmers, B.: Ganzheitliche Unternehmenskultur als Synthese von Design, Sozialorientierung, Ökologie und Ökonomie, in: Sturm, H. (Hg.), Geste & Gewissen im Design, Köln 1998

Remmers, B.: Räume zum Arbeiten, in: Schricker, R. (Hg.), Innenarchitektur in Deutschland – zwischen Tradition und Vision, Stuttgart 2002

Remmers, B.: Design und Nachhaltigkeit im Unternehmen, in: Internationales Forum für Gestaltung (Hg.), Design und Architektur: Studium und Beruf, Fakten, Positionen, Perspektiven, Basel, Boston, Berlin 2004

Remmers, B.: Ergonomie und Design im Büro: Gestaltungsaspekte einer integrierten Systemergonomie, in: Ralph Bruder (Hg.) Ergonomie und Design, Stuttgart 2004

Remmers, B.: CSR – ein Mehrwert in China? Chancen und Risiken eines mittelständischen Engagements auf dem chinesischen Markt, in: Schoenheit, I., Iwand, W., Kopp, R., (Hg.), Corporate Social Responsibility, Verantwortung für nachhaltiges Wirtschaften in China, Berlin, Wien, Zürich 2006

Remmers, B.: Second Life der anderen Art, Ökologische Produktpolitik, In: politische ökologie 105, München 2007

Riewoldt, O.: Innenarchitektur der Gegenwart, Office Design, München 1994

Quickborner Team: Wir brauchen eine neue Konferenzsituation, Harvard Manager 2/89

Sandten, D.: Zwischenspiel, IHK Berlin (Hg.), Büroarbeit von morgen in den Büros von heute?, Berlin 1997

Schlesinger, C.: Platz da!, in: Wirtschaftswoche, Nr. 34, 2007

Schwarb, T.M., Vollmer, A.: Desksharing – neues Element flexibler Büroorganisation, in: Rey, L. (Hg.) Mobile Arbeit in der Schweiz, Zürich 2002

Streich, B.: Form follows digital function, Bauwelt 16/1995

Streitz, N., Geißler, J., Holmer, T.: Roomware for Cooperative Buildings: Integrated Design of Architectural Spaces and Information Spaces, in: Streitz, N. et al., Cooperative Buildings – Integrating Information, Organization and Architecture, Heidelberg 1999

Streitz, N. et al.: Kooperative Gebäude und Roomware für die Arbeitswelten der Zukunft, in: Streitz, N., Remmers, B., Pietzcker, M., Grundmann, R. (Hg.): Arbeitswelten im Wandel – fit für die Zukunft?, Stuttgart 1999

Striffler, H.: Das Gruppenbüro am Beispiel ÖVA-Haus, Mannheim, IHK Berlin (Hg.), Büroarbeit von morgen in den Büros von heute?, Berlin 1997

Thomas-Woyton, S.: Deutsches Architektur Zentrum, DAZ Berlin, IHK Berlin (Hg.), Büroarbeit von morgen in den Büros von heute?, Berlin 1997

Ullmann-Margalit, E.: Invisible Hand Explanations, Synthese 29, Dordrecht 1978

Zinser, S.: Change-Management im Büro – Neue Anforderungen an Bürogestaltung und –arbeitsplätze, in: Wirtschaftspsychologie 19, 2002

Zinser, S.: Immobilien- und Bürokonzepte zur Performance-Steigerung, in: Facility Management 2002, Tagungsband, Merching 2002

Index

Authors

Guido Englich, born in 1961, German and theatre studies at the Freie Universität Berlin, then industrial design at the Hochschule für Künste, Berlin. Publications such as the "MacReiseführer" for the rororo Taschenbuch Verlag evolved out of the design workshop MacLab founded together with Anna Wagner in 1988. Since 1990 he has been doing free-lance work at Design Office Englich+Wagner in Berlin and since 1998 at Englich+Partner. Projects focus on the fields of product development, communication and media design. In 2004 he was appointed Professor of "Strategic Product and Concept Design" for the industrial design course at the Burg Giebichenstein University of Art and Design Halle. He has been Dean of the Faculty of Design there since 2006.

Burkhard Remmers, born in 1960, studied German and history at the Universität Augsburg. After graduating, he left academia to work in the office furniture industry. In 1995 he became Head of Marketing and Public Relations at office furniture manufacturers' Wilkhahn where he has been responsible for International Communications since 2006. The focus of his work is on developing holistic concepts involving communication, space, design and sustainability. He has written numerous international special publications, contributed articles to many books and has also initiated many exhibitions, amongst others for the Deutscher Werkbund Nord.

Photographic credits

Title, P. 63, 76, 77, 85, 101, 121, 137, 233, 236, 291, 292 Axel Bleyer, Ohlsbach

P. 4, 26, 122, 278 Martin Schlüter, Hamburg

P. 12 from: Spiro Kostof, History of architecture

P. 12 from: Annali di architettura 1994/6

P. 12 from: Weber-Kellermann, Landleben

P. 13, 14, 16, 17, 18, 86, 164, 303 Guido Englich, Berlin

P. 22, 24, 216, 238 Wilkhahn, Spain

P. 28 Tim M. Hoesmann, Berlin

P. 38, 40, 41, 58, 61, 63, 65, 83, 109, 114, 115, 119, 121, 137, 163, 235, 248, 258, 277, 292 Vojislav Nikolic Frankfurt/Main

P. 39 Arnoud Verhey, Rotterdam

P. 64 Poul Ib Hendriksen, Århus

P. 65, 71 Andreas J. Focke, Munich

P. 85 Wolfgang Pulver, Munich

P. 109 Jochen Stüber, Hamburg

P. 118, 119, 275 Jürgen Holzenleuchter, Berlin

P. 139, 140 Armin Kammer, Löhne

P. 144 Peter Teschner, Hamelin

P. 145 Mareike Sonnenschein, Hanover

P. 149 Corinne Rusch, Zurich and Vienna

P. 173 Klemens Ortmeyer, Brunswick

P. 176 Thomas Mayfried, Munich

P. 189 Wilkhahn Germany

P. 198/199, 294 Yoshiyuki Hosaka/SS Kikaku Co., Ltd./Tokyo "by courtesy of Tama Art University"

P. 260 Vitus Lau – M Moser Associates, Design M Moser Associates, Hong Kong

P. 291 M Moser Associates, Shanghai (PRC)

P. 298 Karin Vonow, La Punt-Chaumes, Switzerland

P. 303 Regine Rabanus, Hanover